£30.50
D
KD

THE POWER OF
FILM PROPAGANDA

THE POWER OF FILM PROPAGANDA

MYTH OR REALITY?

Nicholas Reeves

continuum
LONDON • NEW YORK

Continuum
The Tower Building
11 York Road
London SE1 7NX

15 East 26th Street
New York
NY 10010

First published 1999
Reprinted 2003
© Nicholas Reeves 1999

British Library Cataloguing in Publication Data
A catalogue record for this book is available from the British Library.

ISBN 0 82647 390 3 (paperback)

Library of Congress Cataloging-in-Publication Data
Reeves, Nicholas, 1946–
  The power of film propaganda: myth or reality? / Nicholas Reeves.
    p. cm.
  Includes bibliographical references and index.
    ISBN 0-304-33871-0 (hardcover). — ISBN 0-304-33872-9 (paperback)
    1. Motion pictures in propaganda—Europe—History. I. Title.
PN1993.5.E8R43   1999
302.23´43´0940904—dc21

                                                    99-10122
                                                    CIP

Typeset by BookEns Ltd, Royston, Herts.
Printed and bound in Great Britain by
Biddles Ltd, King's Lynn, Norfolk

Contents

Acknowledgements

This book originated in an undergraduate course in the history of film propaganda that I began to teach in 1989, and my students will recognize that the five examples of European film propaganda at the heart of that course are also central here. More importantly, as I began to work on that course, my own views about the history of propaganda began to change, not least because the very process of formulating the questions that I put to my students stimulated me to rethink my own approach to my work. Thus, out of these day-to-day exchanges with my students, a variety of issues began to acquire an entirely new importance and, over time, it became clear that many of these questions revolved around the single, deceptively simple, central issue: did the propaganda work? Did the propaganda films reach their target audiences and did those audiences take from the films the messages which the propagandists had intended?

The first result of my new preoccupation with these issues was a re-evaluation of my own earlier work on official British film propaganda during the First World War, in which I argued that, notwithstanding the enormous success of *Battle of the Somme* and a handful of other films, the official films as a whole made only a small impact on wartime public opinion. But as I continued to discuss a variety of other examples of European film propaganda with my students, I became increasingly interested in trying to develop a comparative approach out of which more general conclusions might be formulated, and it is precisely that comparative approach that has resulted in this book. Thus I owe a very special debt to my many students on that course in the history of film propaganda. Not only did they strengthen and reinvigorate my interest in the issues that are at the heart of this book but, in the process of discussing these issues with them, I was able to clarify and refine my own thinking. The screening of appropriate propaganda films was always an important part of the course, and it was perhaps most particularly in the ensuing discussion of those films that I learned the importance of taking proper account of the way in which particular audiences 'read' the films that they see, not least because the films invariably provoked such disparate responses from these late-twentieth-century student audiences.

If I owe a special debt of gratitude to my students, however, the nature of this book is such that it builds directly on the painstaking and rigorous research of a group of scholars who have, over the last twenty years, carefully investigated the history of film propaganda. The endnotes provide some indication of my indebtedness to their work and, while any misapprehensions or weaknesses in my ensuing analysis are, of course, entirely my own responsibility, their work represents the indispensable foundation on which my discussion of these particular examples of film propaganda has been built. In addition to that general debt, a number of people agreed to read all or part of this book in draft. I am always surprised at just how generous very busy scholars are with their time, and I therefore wish to express especially warm thanks to Barry Davis, Phil Taylor, Richard Taylor, Susan Tegel, David Welch and Philip Woods for the care with which they read my drafts and for the thoughtful and constructive character of their comments.

Having said all that, this book would never have been written without the unfailing support and encouragement of my wife Denise and my daughter Becky. There have been many times during the writing when I lost faith in my ability to see it through to a successful conclusion, but their confidence in me never wavered and, whenever it mattered most, they always gave me the reassurance and encouragement that enabled me to carry on. Scholars invariably acknowledge their debt to other scholars but, important as that is, it is the debt that I owe to the two most important people in my life that matters most to me. Quite simply, without them this book would never have been completed.

For Becky

Introduction

One of the most striking characteristics of the early history of the cinema is the startling speed at which the new medium reached audiences all over Europe. The first demonstration of the Lumière brothers' *cinématographe* to a paying audience took place in Paris on 28 December 1895; within a few short months it had been seen all over Europe and beyond. Thus, less than two months later it was in London; in April 1896, Vienna and Geneva; in June, Madrid, Belgrade and New York; in July, St Petersburg and Bucharest. Indeed, by the end of the year it had reached even more exotic locations, with screenings taking place as far afield as Egypt, India, Japan and Australia. Nor was there anything accidental about this for, while the Lumières could not have anticipated the extraordinary scale of the new technology's popularity, they were well prepared to exploit it once it did happen. Drawing on the resources of their Lyons photographic factory, they had used the months between the first private demonstration of the equipment (in March 1895) and that first public exhibition to build up a stock of equipment and to train a team of operators capable of exploiting the *cinématographe*'s unique capabilities. For, unlike its rivals, their equipment served as both camera and projector and thus, wherever the Lumière operators went, they not only showed the films that they had brought with them, they also shot new footage which would in turn be used in future Lumière presentations.

Indeed, it was this particular characteristic of their equipment that explains an especially interesting example of the way in which the technology was first exploited – in Russia, Lumière cameramen were shooting footage even before the first public film show was held. The place was Moscow; the date, 14 May 1896; the event, the crowning of Nicholas II, the new Russian Tsar. The cameramen filmed the royal procession in the Kremlin courtyard; two days later they filmed the presentation of the Tsar to his people, and it was only on the following day that the first film show took place in St Petersburg, over 400 miles away.[1] Thereafter, Russian audiences took to the new medium with as much enthusiasm as everyone else, and by September the Lumières had established a permanent presence in Moscow.

Moreover, that initial link with the Tsar was never lost. The Lumière programme was shown to the royal family in July 1896 and, after a further screening the following autumn, the extent of the Tsar's curiosity became clear – as the Lumière operator recalled: 'The Tsar professed great interest and asked many questions concerning the mechanism ... and wished me success with the Lumière invention in Russia.'[2]

In the years that followed, Nicholas II's fascination with cinema intensified. Surviving footage of the Tsar and his family provides one kind of evidence of that fascination, but the Tsar also became an avid member of the film audience, ultimately building his own private cinema at the royal palace at Tsarskoe Selo, outside St Petersburg. Moreover, that enthusiasm for cinema persisted to the very end of his reign. In August 1915, in the wake of the major setbacks suffered by the Russian armies earlier that summer, he took the extremely controversial decision to assume personal control of the armed forces, and thus left Petrograd (the renamed St Petersburg) for Mogilev (120 miles east of Minsk), where he was to remain at General Headquarters until the end of 1916. But none of this was allowed to disrupt his access to the cinema – he installed his own private cinema, and his regular letters to his wife record both the frequency of the screenings and his undiminished passion for the films that he saw, notably the thriller serial *The Exploits of Elaine*, which he watched in regular weekly parts throughout the second half of 1916.[3]

For all his personal enthusiasm for cinema, however, the Tsar apparently had a rather jaundiced view of its importance. In 1913, three years earlier, he had written:

> I consider that the cinema is an empty, totally useless, and even harmful form of entertainment. Only an abnormal person could place this farcical business on a par with art. It is complete rubbish and no importance whatsoever should be attached to such stupidities.[4]

While there is, at the very least, a tension between this observation and the abundant evidence of the Tsar's own passion for the cinema, his words certainly articulated one widely held attitude towards the new medium. Cinema was an enormously successful form of commercial entertainment, but the very basis of that success was its ability to attract unprecedented audiences from the millions of working-class men, women and children who made up the rapidly growing urban populations of the early twentieth century. It was, in other words, an essentially working-class medium of commercial entertainment and, for many contemporaries that in itself meant that it could not have any aesthetic value; by definition, art and popular culture were mutually exclusive. Moreover, the nature of the films that those countless millions watched was such that it was perhaps easy to categorize them as trivial and unimportant. For, while very early audiences had been enthralled by a wide variety of factual footage, long before 1913 those factual films had been displaced by narrative films of fiction, in which melodrama and comedy, spectacle and romance were pre-eminent. Moreover, in stark contrast to the anonymity that had concealed the identity of the first actors in the earliest fiction films, a newly emerging star system was reinforcing and intensifying the pleasures which the new medium offered its mass audience. Thus, not least because the cinema had now taken this particular form, it was seen as an 'empty, totally useless ... form of entertainment', quite unworthy of any serious attention.

But if many dismissed the cinema in this way, not everyone took the same view. Anxieties about the dangers of the new medium were one of the ways in which a sense of its importance was articulated, and they were expressed wherever the cinema won large audiences – even the Tsar had pointed out that the cinema might be 'harmful'. In part, such anxieties focused on the physical dangers of the environment in which the films were seen, but invariably the darkened world of the cinema was seen to present moral dangers as well, especially to young and unsupervised members of the audience. Moreover, it was argued even more frequently that the films themselves posed a real threat to traditional moral standards, and it was not long before anxieties like these gave rise to film censorship, even if in Russia (as elsewhere) that censorship was as often political as it was moral. What all these views shared, however, was a recognition of the power of the new medium, and while that was a source of disquiet to many, there were others in Russia who saw it much more positively. One of the very early Lumière screenings had been watched by the writer Maxim Gorky, and he was deeply impressed by what he saw, commenting that he was sure that there would be 'a wide use' for such a medium – 'the thirst for such strange, fantastic sensations as it gives will grow ever greater...'.[5] In 1911, the writer Leonid Andreyev was even more enthusiastic in his assessment of the potential of cinema:

> The miraculous Cinema! ... Having no language, being equally intelligible to the savages of St Petersburg and the savages of Calcutta, it truly becomes the genius of international contact, brings the ends of the earth and the spheres of souls nearer and gathers the whole of quivering humanity into a single stream. The great Cinema! ... It copes with everything, conquers everything, conveys everything.[6]

The Tsar might dismiss cinema as 'complete rubbish' – others took a very different view, and it was those other views that would soon prevail.

Within a year of the Tsar's comments Russia was at war; within four years the old regime was at an end and the Bolsheviks had taken power. Propaganda was of central importance to the new regime and, within that context, the argument about the power of film as a medium appeared to be won. For the Bolsheviks were convinced that cinema was singularly well-placed to translate their message into a form that would make a decisive impact on the vast, largely illiterate, population of the new Soviet Union. Their faith in film as a medium of mass propaganda was clearly articulated by Anatoli Lunacharsky, the first head of the People's Commissariat of Enlightenment (the Bolshevik ministry charged with responsibility for propaganda):

> Cinema's strength lies in the fact that, like any art, it imbues an idea with feeling and with captivating form but, unlike the other arts, cinema is actually cheap, portable and unusually graphic. Its effects reach where even the book cannot reach and it is, of course, more powerful than any kind of narrow propaganda.[7]

The old-fashioned Tsarist regime had been overthrown by the essentially modern force of Bolshevism; in his failure to understand the real potential of the modern medium of cinema, Nicholas II had demonstrated once again just how outmoded he was. The new realities of the early-twentieth-century industrial world were quite different from those which had held sway a hundred, or fifty, or even twenty years earlier. Mass societies, with increasingly urbanized populations, demanded new forms of mass entertainment; in its very ability to play that role, cinema might also be used as a new and potent weapon of propaganda. In recognizing these realities, the Bolsheviks showed just why they had been victorious over the old regime. They understood the nature of the twentieth-century world; they understood the power of propaganda; they understood the particular potential of the new mass medium of the cinema to deliver just that transformation in the hearts and minds of ordinary Soviet citizens that was at the very centre of their revolutionary project.

Yet it is the purpose of this book to seek to re-examine precisely these assumptions. Perhaps Lunacharsky's view of the potential power of film as a medium of propaganda was misplaced? Perhaps the Tsar was not quite so naive and ill-informed as his remarks seem to indicate? Perhaps 'the masses' are not so easily manipulated as the enthusiastic proponents of film propaganda like to assume? Not that any of these doubts were heard during the years when cinema was the dominant mass medium, for from the end of the First World War to the coming of television in the 1950s, almost everyone shared the same view of the immense power of the medium of film. Increasingly rigorous censorship was the negative expression of this consensus; an increasing commitment to film propaganda its positive equivalent. Thus it was not simply revolutionary regimes which attempted to use this new medium of mass persuasion. The First World War, with its unprecedented need to enlist the active support of the whole of society in the prosecution of the war, confronted every belligerent government with immense problems of managing and manipulating public opinion and, by the end of the war, they had all made some attempt to take advantage of cinema's apparently unique access to those very millions whose attitudes they sought to influence. By the time Lunacharsky was putting the case for the importance of cinema as a medium of propaganda, the experience of war had created a consensus across the industrialized world about the power of the new medium. In a world of mass politics, politicians of every political colour recognized the need to manage and manipulate the attitudes and aspirations, the hopes and the fears, the beliefs and the ideologies of the masses they sought to govern. And while regimes like those led by Lenin and the Bolsheviks in the Soviet Union, or Hitler and the National Socialists in Germany, gave propaganda in general, and film propaganda in particular, a very high priority, almost the same assumptions about the potential power of film propaganda were made in democratic political cultures as well.

Inter-war Britain provides a remarkably clear illustration of this fact. During the First World War, the British government had, for the first time, engaged in a systematic and sustained campaign of official film propaganda, even if within days of the war's end, the new Ministry of Information was closed down and all the new mechanisms for official film propaganda were abandoned. That might suggest that it was seen as an exceptional activity, in which British governments would only engage in time of war and yet, just six years later, mounting concerns were being expressed about the extent to which Hollywood penetration of British markets was so weakening the domestic film production industry as to imperil Britain's ability to hold its own in this most important arena. Those concerns were articulated by no less a figure than the Prime Minister himself, who, speaking in a 1925 House of Commons debate on unemployment, drew attention to 'the enormous power which the film is developing for propaganda purposes, and the dangers to which we in this country and our Empire subject ourselves if we allow that method of propaganda to be entirely in the hands of foreign countries.'[8] Three years later, in 1928, that same Conservative Government legislated to protect the industry from ever-more serious Hollywood competition, and while some of the motivation for that legislation was economic, politics was in fact at the heart of the matter. Indeed, six years earlier, the Conservative Party had become the first of the British political parties to experiment with using film as a medium for domestic, party propaganda, a lead quickly followed by all the other parties.

Precisely the same consensus about the power of film as a medium of propaganda can be identified in the work of those inter-war commentators and academics who examined the role of cinema. The specific nature of their particular theories varied – the central thrust was almost always the same. Thus two of the more colourful explanations characterized the mass media as either a 'magic bullet', capable of inflicting propaganda wounds on the mass audience that was powerless to resist, or as an 'hypodermic needle' in which, once again, the masses could not resist the messages which were being injected into its body politic.[9] Such views were grounded in a wider social analysis which emphasized the way in which industrialization destroyed the defences of traditional societies, leaving the new mass societies uniquely vulnerable to the power of the new mass media. Technology was at the heart of it, both effecting the transformation of industrialization and giving birth to the mass media which provided the new means of controlling those transformed societies. From the totalitarian right to the revolutionary left, and including most moderate political opinion in between, the mass media in general, and film in particular, were seen to be well-placed to deliver unprecedented opportunities for the management and manipulation of mass public opinion.

Given this inter-war consensus, the Second World War saw an even greater commitment to film as a medium of propaganda. Where the First World War had seen governments taking their first, tentative initiatives in this field, the Second World War saw the resources of entire film industries made available to wartime governments as the struggle for the hearts and minds of the belligerent societies intensified. Thus the quantity and the form of film propaganda changed out of all recognition and, even if many governments worked hard to conceal their role in wartime propaganda, pre-war notions of the power of film remained largely intact at the end of the war. Indeed, in the context of growing post-war Western hysteria about Communism, Senator McCarthy's determination to purge Hollywood of any vestige of Communist influence demonstrates that these assumptions were still as potent as ever. And, at just the same time, on the other side of the Iron Curtain, there was no diminution in the state's commitment to the use of film. The Soviet Union continued to see film as a key medium through which to construct its propaganda and, with its new power in Central and Eastern Europe, a number of other film industries followed the Soviet model.

With the coming of television in the 1950s, the focus shifted and governments and politicians increasingly concentrated their attention on the new, domestic screens which proliferated so quickly. To a remarkable extent, the assumptions that had been made earlier about the power of film were transferred to television; television was seen as being endowed with just the same attributes that had been associated with film. In the Western democracies, politicians subject television programmes to the closest possible scrutiny and demand access to the networks to enable them to make use of this new weapon of propaganda; the moral panics which periodically grip these same societies invariably identify in television a key source of perceived threats to their traditional ethical and cultural standards. In the world of the Soviet Union and its client states, the argument was a little more complex. For many years it was assumed that television provided a key weapon in the hands of the party with which to indoctrinate its population with the virtues of communism; when those regimes finally fell, access to Western television was seen as an important source of the dissatisfaction which ultimately brought those regimes down. But notwithstanding these differences, the nature and intensity of current debates about the role of television provide the clearest evidence of the extent to which, nearly a hundred years later, those early-twentieth-century assumptions about the power of the mass media continue to dominate. Thus whether it be in anxieties about the relationship between television and violence, or in concerns about the special impact of television on children, or in fears about the concentration of ownership in the hands of a small number of individuals, the common assumption remains that the mass media occupy a uniquely powerful position at the very heart of our global culture.

On the other hand, the inter-war consensus between politicians and academics about the power of the mass media has not persisted through the post-war years. During the Second World War, detailed studies of the extent to which the American *Why We Fight?* films had been able to modify the attitudes of newly enlisted servicemen provided the first empirical data of the limited power of film propaganda. They revealed that the films had been significant in conveying factual information, but had had no effect 'on men's motivation to serve as soldiers, which was considered the ultimate objective of the orientation programme.'[10] Indeed, those studies constituted a turning point in academic approaches to the role of the media; over the next decade the inter-war consensus about the unlimited power of the media was abandoned as a series of empirical studies gave rise to a new orthodoxy, which stressed, in contrast, the limits of the power of the media. Thus, for example, a new emphasis on the audience suggested that it was not in reality the blank slate upon which the propagandist could write at will; it could in fact exercise considerable discrimination in the consumption of those propaganda messages. Moreover, while propaganda might be good at reinforcing existing attitudes, it was largely ineffective in changing values that were determined to a far greater extent by family, peers and other important social influences.[11]

The new consensus that emerged in the 1950s and early 1960s did not last long, and from the late 1960s onwards views about the role of the media have been much more contested. On the one hand there have been attempts to reconstruct the notion of their power, both in empirical studies, which claim to demonstrate the persuasive power of the media in particular situations, and also in a variety of theoretical approaches which have sought to formulate new, more complex models of society, in which the role of the media, is once again, seen as fundamental. On the other hand, the earlier emphasis on the ability of the audience to mitigate the power of the media has not gone away, arguably reaching its most extreme formulation in the post-modernist notion of the 'reader as writer'. Thus there is now no clear consensus about the power of the media, and as Curran, Smith and Wingate quite properly observed, the situation is characterized by 'divergent and indeed totally contradictory views about the place of the media in society, and the degree of influence it radiates'.[12] But, as they also point out, all scholars now recognize that the media are not autonomous institutions. Any effective analysis of their power must locate their role in the context of a wide variety of competing social forces, and historical analysis is singularly well suited to such an approach.

Historical enquiry enjoys one crucial advantage over the analysis of the role of the media within contemporary society, namely the opportunity to develop that analysis with the benefit of the knowledge of the wider and subsequent history of the societies in which those media functioned. Thus, this particular book explores the history of film propaganda in Europe from the First World War to the 1950s (the years when cinema was the dominant medium of popular entertainment), and the analysis is developed within the wider context of both an understanding of the societies within which that propaganda was constructed, and the direction those societies took after the propaganda campaigns had ended. The films of the First World War, for example, will be examined in the light of knowledge about changing public opinion in the war as a whole; the Soviet films of the 1920s will be discussed within the context of an understanding of the nature of Soviet society in the 1920s, and the radical transformation of that society which followed in the years after 1928; the power of National Socialist film propaganda will be analysed by reference to the political culture of the Third Reich and the extent to which it was able to effect that radical transformation that was at the heart of the Nazi project. In other words, in an analysis of these historical case studies it is possible to judge whether the propagandists achieved their objectives – whether the power of film propaganda really was as large as so many at the time assumed.

There is a further reason for embarking on such an analysis at the present time, however, for the last 30 years have seen a dramatic increase in the quantity and range of historians' interest in the field of propaganda in general, and the history of film propaganda in particular. The launch of the *Historical Journal of Film, Radio and Television* in 1981 was both an indication of the extent to which rigorous historical investigation of the field was already becoming established, and served also as an important stimulus to future work in this field. The end result is that we now have a good understanding of the history of film propaganda across a wide variety of examples, and the attempt to try to reach some general conclusions about its efficacy is possible in a way that simply could not have been attempted even 10 years ago. That said, a remarkable attempt to do just that was made in 1968 by two Swedish scholars, Leif Furhammar and Folke Isaksson.[13] In the course of one lavishly illustrated text, they ranged over the whole history of film propaganda, from its beginnings in the First World War, through to American propaganda about the Vietnam War in the 1960s.

Their book was written at a time when the scholarly investigation of the history of film propaganda was in its infancy; all the detailed work that has been completed since then offers the prospect of developing conclusions that are more securely founded, and the five case studies of European film propaganda that are at the heart of this book draw extensively on that research. Restricting the discussion to five significant examples creates the opportunity to explore each in sufficient depth to enable consideration of three central, recurring areas. First, what led a party, or a government, or a group of individuals to embark on propaganda in the first place? Why was propaganda so important? What was it envisaged that the propaganda would be able to achieve? Why, in particular, was film seen as an especially appropriate medium in which to bring that propaganda to life? Secondly, each case study will examine the ways in which those objectives were translated into practice, which in turn raises questions of production, distribution and exhibition. Thus, what were the institutions and practices which were developed to lead to the production of the films? Did those who formulated the need for the propaganda seek to make the films themselves and, if not, precisely how did they ensure that others made the films on their behalf? Once the films were made, what steps were taken to ensure that the films reached their target audiences? Thirdly, each case study will explore the impact that the films made on their target audiences. Clearly, this third area goes to the heart of the problem of the power of film as a medium of propaganda, although it is equally clear that it is in this area that the questions are most difficult to answer. Thus, did the films reach their target audiences? If they did, what meanings did those audiences construct in the films that they saw? And once they left the cinema, did they carry those meanings with them? Did those meanings endure in the days, and weeks and months that followed? In short, did the propaganda work?

The choice of the five case studies was not easy, although it was informed by a variety of different factors of which three were perhaps especially important, namely the depth and extent of scholarly analysis of a particular topic, the availability of the films, and the importance of examining the role of film propaganda within a variety of different political cultures. This last is perhaps the most important criterion of all, and it explains, for example, the inclusion of two British case studies – for a variety of constitutional, economic, ideological and social reasons, British political culture during the First World War was profoundly different from what it was to become just 20 years later in the Second World War, while those elements of continuity which also bound the two societies provide an interesting additional frame of reference. Finally, while four of the five are examples of state-sponsored film propaganda, Italian neo-realist cinema provides an example of a group of film-makers working within a commercial film industry, who took advantage of the special opportunities available to them to put together a concerted and determined campaign of film propaganda.

The first case study, official British film propaganda targeted at the domestic population during the First World War, provides an early example of a government attempting to use the new medium of cinema with no previous experience of this kind of activity. Britain in 1914 was still very much a democracy in the making, with all adult women and a substantial minority of adult men still denied the vote and, in the very special circumstances of war, the opportunities for effective participation in decision-making were severely circumscribed. Thus this first example provides the opportunity to assess the power of film propaganda in a political culture still in transition towards 20th-century Western democracy. The second case study – Soviet film propaganda in the 1920s – provides another example of a political culture in transition, albeit in this case a society in transition towards the full-blooded totalitarian regime which

Stalin was to construct in the 1930s. For a variety of reasons, the Bolshevik Party lacked both the means and the will to exercise that close, detailed supervision of the new Soviet film industry which was to be achieved a decade later, and Soviet film-makers in the years up to 1928 enjoyed a considerable degree of freedom as they experimented, across a wide variety of forms, in an attempt to construct the first proletarian films to meet the needs of the first proletarian society. Moreover, in responding to that challenge, they engaged in an enormously wide-ranging debate about almost every aspect of the new medium and its role in society. Thus, in all these ways, an assessment of the role of film propaganda in the Soviet Union of the 1920s raises issues of rather wider relevance than would be derived from an examination of film propaganda in the Soviet Union of the 1930s, where the propaganda existed side by side with the most ruthless and extensive state terror, and where the work of the film-makers was so closely supervised by the party.

On the other hand, just such supervision was exercised in National Socialist Germany, and this forms the third case study. Goebbels certainly envisaged that film would be able to deliver that radical transformation in ideas, attitudes and beliefs for which the Bolsheviks had been striving in the Soviet Union, and he was able to exercise a formidable level of influence over the German film industry to ensure that only those films that he deemed appropriate were produced. Yet, Nazi Germany was not in reality the monolithic, totalitarian society described in the propaganda of its enemies, and the regime always sought to maximize public support for its policies, while diligently monitoring each and every shift in public opinion. Equally, at least throughout the years of peace, it did rather less to disturb the established German economic and social structure than its more radical rhetoric might have suggested, and the precise way in which Goebbels set about ensuring that the German film industry produced just the kind of films that he required is entirely consistent with that essentially cautious approach.

By the time of the Second World War, Britain had at last achieved complete adult suffrage and, to a much greater extent than in the First World War 20 years earlier, film propaganda was conducted within an incomparably more pluralistic, inclusive and tolerant political culture. Nevertheless the scale and extent of influence which the Ministry of Information Films Division ultimately exerted over the British film industry reveals some striking parallels with the National Socialists' grip on the German film industry, and it was certainly the case that, by the middle years of the war, few if any films reached British cinemas of which the MoI did not approve. Equally, many of the most important wartime propaganda films were seen by huge audiences, and thus this particular case study raises especially interesting questions about both the extent and the limits of the power of film propaganda. The final case study examines the Italian neo-realist cinema in the years immediately after the war. The films made by this small group of film-makers represented a determined attempt to break away from the constraints of the culture of Italian Fascism, and the radical innovations of their films made an immense impact on world cinema. But their purpose was also political. The film-makers wanted to confront the ideological legacy of Fascism by radically changing the attitudes of the mass of the Italian population, and it is in the extent to which they were able to achieve these political objectives that this case study is ultimately focused.

There remains one final, introductory matter, namely the problem of definition. The word 'propaganda' presents innumerable difficulties, not least because over the centuries its meaning has developed in ways that have become less and less precise. Its origins are clear enough, deriving from a decision by Pope Gregory XV, who in 1622 issued the Papal Bull *Inscrutabili Divinae* establishing the *Sacra Congregatio de Propaganda Fide* (the Sacred Congregation for the Propagation of the Faith), with a mission of winning back those who had been lost to the Church in the Reformation.[14] Very soon the new Congregation became known colloquially as 'the propaganda' and for the next two centuries the term was used to describe evangelizing activities of this kind. In the first half of the nineteenth century, however, this exclusively religious connotation was dropped, and the word (in this broader sense) came into regular usage during and after the First World War. Once it had lost its religious connotation, however, the meaning became incomparably less clear, and the problem of definition was compounded by the fact that, in this wider usage, it was almost always used pejoratively. Many historians attribute this to the prominence of atrocity propaganda during the First World War, although in fact it occurred much earlier. Thus the *Oxford English Dictionary* cites Brande's *Dictionary of Science* of 1842, defining the word as 'a term of reproach to secret associations for the spread of opinions and principles which are viewed by most governments with horror and aversion'.[15]

However, although the word has so often been used as a term of abuse, it does not take much imagination to understand the logical difficulties with such a definition – one person's 'truth' is all too often another's 'propaganda'. Thus whether or not that which is being presented is true or false, it is the way in which it is used (and not its 'truthfulness') that determines whether or not it is in fact propaganda. Almost every social scientist, and many of the historians who have written about propaganda, have made their own attempts at definition; perhaps the most perceptive recent definition is offered by Terence Qualter:

> Any act of promotion can be propaganda only if and when it becomes part of a deliberate campaign to induce action through influencing attitudes. Once it is established that any statement, book, poster or rumour, any parade or exhibition, any statue or historic monument, any scientific achievement or abstract of statistics, whether true or false, rational or irrational in appeal or presentation, originates as the deliberate policy of someone trying to control or alter attitudes, then that thing or activity becomes part of a propaganda process.

Or as he himself puts it more succinctly: propaganda is 'the deliberate attempt by the few to influence the attitudes and behaviour of the many by the manipulation of symbolic communication'.[16] Thus Qualter understands that propaganda cannot be defined by reference to its form; its essence lies in the use that is made of the book, the parade, the scientific achievement, or the film. Propaganda takes place whenever an individual or a small group attempts to influence the attitudes and behaviour of the many, and it is not therefore an activity which can occur without intention. Moreover, those who engage in propaganda will always understand that this is indeed the project on which they have embarked, and to that extent precise definitions must always be made by reference to the particular set of circumstances within which the propaganda is conducted. Certainly it is with this particular meaning that the term will be used in the remainder of this book, and it is not least for that reason that the precise objectives of the film propaganda (and in that sense its precise meaning) will be established in each of the five case studies that follow – it is only by reference to those objectives that an appropriate assessment of the power of film propaganda can, in fact, be made.

NOTE

Throughout this book the titles of films are given in English – this convention is a commonplace in English-language discussions of Russian films, and it has been followed throughout.

NOTES

1. Jay Leyda, *Kino: A History of the Russian and Soviet Film*, London, 1973, pp. 17–20.

2. Quoted in Leyda, *op. cit.*, p. 22.

3. *Ibid.*, pp. 90–1.

4. Quoted in Richard Taylor, *Film Propaganda: Soviet Russia and Nazi Germany*, London, 1979, p. 35. A revised edition was published in 1998 by I. B. Tauris.

5. Quoted in Leyda, *op. cit.*, p. 20.

6. Leonid Andreyev, 'First letter on theatre', 10 November 1911, quoted in Richard Taylor and Ian Christie (eds), *The Film Factory: Russian and Soviet Cinema in Documents 1896–1939*, London, 1988, pp. 30–1.

7. Anatoli Lunacharsky, 'Revolutionary ideology and cinema – Theses', 9–31 March 1924, in Taylor and Christie (eds), *op. cit.*, p. 109.

8. Baldwin speaking on 29 June 1925, quoted in Margaret Dickinson and Sarah Street, *Cinema and State: The Film Industry and the British Government 1927–84*, London, 1985, p. 19.

9. The history of research into the power of the media has been summarized by many writers – see, for example: Sandra J. Ball-Rokeach and Muriel G. Cantor, *Media, Audience and Social Structure*, Beverley Hills, 1986; Denise McQuail, *Mass Communication Theory: An Introduction* (2nd edn), London, 1987; Ken Ward, *Mass Communications and the Modern World*, Basingstoke, 1989.

10. Carl Hovland *et al.*, *Experiments on Mass Communication*, 1949, quoted in Terence H. Qualter, *Opinion Control in the Democracies*, London, 1985, p. 133.

11. The new orthodoxy was summed up by Joseph T. Klapper, *The Effects of Mass Communication*, New York, 1960.

12. James Curran, Anthony Smith and Pauline Wingate (eds), *Impacts and Influences: Essays on Media Power in the Twentieth Century*, London, 1987, p. 2.

13. Leif Furhammar and Folke Isaksson, *Politik och film*, Stockholm, 1968. The book was translated into English by Kersti French and published in London in 1971 under the title *Politics and Film*.

14. For a detailed discussion of this see Peter Guilday, 'The Sacred Congregation de Propaganda Fide', *Catholic Historical Review*, Vol. 6, No. 4, January 1921, p. 480.

15. *The Compact Edition of the Oxford English Dictionary*, Vol. 2, Oxford, 1979, p. 2326.

16. Qualter, *Opinion Control in the Democracies*, London, 1985, pp. 122, 124.

CHAPTER 1 Official Film Propaganda in Britain during the First World War

The British government's decision to declare war on Germany on 4 August 1914 came at a singularly uncertain moment in British politics for, while the later nineteenth century had seen a number of important constitutional reforms, the process of constructing an effective and inclusive parliamentary democracy was still far from complete. Thus, while there had been a fundamental move away from an essentially local politics, in which the exercise of various kinds of 'influence' over a comparatively small electorate had largely determined the outcome of elections, towards a more national politics in which political parties, clearly identified with recognizable programmes, campaigned for the support of a much larger electorate, a number of important elements of the old politics still remained. So, for example, while there had been considerable progress towards a more equitable definition of constituencies, they still varied considerably in size; plural voting had been reduced but not eliminated; and, most spectacular of all, only a minority of the adult population was enfranchised – four men in ten were still denied the vote, while no women at all were allowed to vote.

Moreover, while the nineteenth-century reforms had been accomplished without substantial party conflict, Lloyd George's 'People's Budget' of 1909 (which represented a modest attempt to apply a more democratic approach to fiscal policy by starting to relate taxation to the ability to pay), precipitated a major constitutional crisis in which the Conservative Party backed the House of Lords' rejection of the budget. In the bitter political conflict that ensued, the Liberal government eventually had its way, but only after two general elections had been held and its parliamentary majority had been substantially reduced. Indeed, in these radically changed circumstances, the government had to rely on the support of the Irish Nationalists to sustain its parliamentary majority, and it was only a matter of months before that led to another attempt to introduce Home Rule for Ireland. Once again the

House of Lords opposed the government, and while the 1911 Parliament Act limited its powers to those of delaying legislation to which it was opposed, that delay enabled both Conservatives and Unionists to foment opposition to the Bill. In a rapidly worsening situation, an Ulster Volunteer Force was established, which led the Nationalists to respond by organizing the Dublin Volunteers. The emergence of these private armies threatened to destabilize Irish politics completely, and it was far from clear what impact any future Irish civil war might have on politics on the mainland.

Nor was Ireland the only crisis confronting British society on the eve of the First World War. The government's continuing resistance to votes for women had led to the radicalization of parts of the suffrage movement, and a minority of suffragists now resorted to increasingly violent forms of direct action to further their cause. Moreover, the immediate pre-war period also saw important qualitative changes in the character of industrial relations. Moves were made to try to develop new levels of solidarity between different groups of workers traditionally divided by skill or occupation, culminating in 1914 in the formation of the so-called Triple Alliance of miners, transport workers and railwaymen. At much the same time, a number of violent clashes between striking workers, the police and troops appeared to indicate that British industrial relations were entering a new and much more dangerous period. In all, this potent combination of constitutional crisis, a deeply contested party politics, a continuing failure to respond successfully to the demands of both Irish nationalists and women suffragists, coupled with the emergence of an apparently radicalized working class, appeared to signal that Britain in 1914 was on the brink of a political crisis of potentially revolutionary proportions.[1] Even if that expectation was misplaced, the deep cleavages which characterized British politics on the eve of the war did not augur well for a conflict which would, in the end, require support from the population as a whole on a scale quite unprecedented in the British experience.

In the event, the situation could not have been more different. The German invasion of Belgium and Britain's subsequent declaration of war on Germany on 4 August totally and immediately transformed the mood of the population. The British people rallied to the patriotic cause in a frenzy of jingoistic enthusiasm and, almost overnight, divisions which had seemed so unbridgeable only days before were apparently forgotten in the first heady days of war. Thus, for example, both the Labour Party and the trade unions committed themselves to the war – battalions were soon to be formed consisting almost entirely of miners or railwaymen. Militant and moderate suffragists ended their pre-war campaigns and devoted their energies instead to supporting the recruitment drive. The Ulster Volunteer Force was transformed into the 36th (Ulster) Division, and implementation of Home Rule was delayed until the end of the war. Perhaps most striking of all, the bitter conflicts of pre-war party politics were set aside, and the Conservative leader, Bonar Law, committed his party to 'patriotic opposition'. An electoral truce meant that by-elections would no longer be contested: Liberal and Unionist MPs appeared side-by-side on recruiting platforms and party politics in the constituencies was, in effect, suspended. As the businessman F.S. Oliver wrote to his brother in Canada as early as 12 August: 'England is already a different place than it has been for years past.'[2]

It was indeed a remarkable transformation and, from the point of view of a government anxiously contemplating the state of public opinion, a singularly welcome one. In the light of the myriad divisions and conflicts which had so threatened pre-war Britain, the opening weeks of the war revealed a quite extraordinary level of patriotic unity. Nor did this new-found unity prove short-lived. The conviction that the war had been caused by German aggression that had to be stopped proved immensely durable for, as John Bourne has argued, Germany proved to be the 'perfect enemy', and whenever enthusiasm for the war began to flag:

> ... there was always another German 'atrocity' waiting round the corner ready to refresh the national resolve – the policy of 'frightfulness' towards the civilian populations of France and Belgium, the bombardment of Hartlepool, Scarborough and Whitby, the sinking of the *Lusitania*, the use of poison gas, the execution of Nurse Edith Cavell, the Zeppelin – and, later, the Gotha – bombing raids on civilian targets, unrestricted submarine warfare, the imposition of a punitive peace on Russia and Romania.[3]

Thus, from the outbreak of the war to its conclusion four-and-a-half years later, all the evidence suggests that the majority of the civilian population believed in the morality of Britain's cause. Germany was perceived to be the barbaric aggressor, and the way in which Germany fought the war sustained this initial view that such 'frightfulness' had to be resisted.

The power and persistence of this particular image of the enemy did not, of course, derive simply from the nature of German policy and German actions. As soon as the war began, an intensely jingoistic press embarked on unofficial propaganda with unrestrained enthusiasm, and throughout the war it never missed an opportunity to lecture its readers about the moral turpitude of the enemy. Indeed, that 'propaganda of hate' which was such a constant ingredient in the ideological climate of the war on the home front, probably represented Fleet Street's most important contribution to the war effort.[4] And if the press took up this role with enthusiasm, it was equally willing to co-operate in the suppression of news which might in any way endanger the war effort.

In the early months of the war, the service departments' intense anxiety about the management of news led to the total exclusion of journalists from the front, and it was not until May 1915 that this prohibition was lifted. But it very quickly became clear that these official anxieties were groundless for, almost without exception, the journalists who were now allowed access to the front presented their readers with just that highly selective and optimistic view of the war which the intelligence officers of GHQ, who supervised their work, were so eager to construct. Indeed, so well did the journalists understand their role that Douglas Haig (commander-in-chief in France from 1915 until the end of the war), commented: 'I must say that the correspondents have played up splendidly'.[5]

Thus a lack of accurate, detailed information about the way in which the war was being fought was just as important an ingredient in the domestic situation as the presence of partial, prejudiced propaganda, not least because the reality of war on the Western Front was so profoundly different both from anything which had been anticipated before the war, and from the images of war which continued to survive at home. For serving soldiers, of course, these myths were all too quickly dispelled by the actual experience of war and one might have expected men home on leave to have shared their experiences with their friends and relatives. In practice it seems that few did. Instead they shared (with combatants in all wars) a profound reluctance to communicate the reality of a war which was so far outside the experience of those who stayed at home. Philip Gibbs wrote of the soldiers living 'in a world which is as different from this known world of ours as though they belonged to another race of men inhabiting another planet';[6] an anonymous letter in the *Nation* in October 1916 spoke for thousands of soldiers in expressing a profound sense of alienation from everyday life in England:

> It is very nice to be home again. Yet am I at home? One sometimes doubts it. There are occasions when I feel like a visitor amongst strangers whose intentions are kindly, but whose modes of thought I neither altogether understand nor altogether approve...[7]

Hardly surprising then that so many soldiers decided to remain silent.

OFFICIAL PROPAGANDA AND WARTIME PUBLIC OPINION

In all these circumstances there was apparently little need for official propaganda. Pre-war conflicts and divisions were set aside as outrage at German aggression forged a new wartime unity; wartime British governments prosecuted the war secure in the knowledge that the domestic population was persuaded that their cause was just. In reality the situation was rather more complex than this. A conviction that the war was just did not in itself lead to the conclusion that the *way* in which it was being fought was equally just. Indeed, it was precisely in relation to popular perceptions of the domestic conduct of the war that the initial unanimous enthusiasm of wartime society began to break down. Thus, while the majority of the population remained convinced of the essential justice of the British cause, a growing minority increasingly felt frustration, disillusionment, even anger at some aspects of their experience of the war. War may have appeared to resolve many of the conflicts that were so evident in pre-war British society, but the inequalities that had given rise to some of those conflicts had not been resolved and, in appropriate circumstances, they would re-emerge. Moreover, in the context of a war in which it became increasingly necessary for the government to mobilize all the human resources of the nation in support of the war effort, it became as important to dispel disillusionment as it was to sustain the conviction that the war was just.

Not that any of this was clear in the early weeks or even months of the war. The government found itself in the happy position in which the de-claration of war was greeted with an unprecedented outpouring of patriotic enthusiasm, and the three-quarters of a million men who flocked to enlist in the first two months of the war provide the clearest evidence that this was indeed the case. And while the heightened emotion of those early weeks did not endure, what replaced it was probably just as welcome from the government's point of view: a less emotional, more stable attitude, in which society came to terms with the fact that the war would last far longer than anyone had anticipated. This new acceptance is not difficult to understand because, for the vast majority, the war had not yet made any fundamental change to the quality of their life. Of course the minority who had volunteered had already experienced radical change, but for everyone else 'business as usual' was a largely accurate description of the domestic wartime situation. Pre-war expectations that the war would be fought by a professional army, sustained and supported by the people at home, continued to make sense throughout the first 18 months and what changes there were, were neither opposed nor even resented; as Holcombe Ingleby, a Conservative MP, accurately observed at the end of 1915, 'everyone is quietly content to persevere – even unto the end'.[8]

Over the next year or so, however, that quiet perseverance was steadily undermined, and the mood of Britain in the spring of 1917 was profoundly different from that at the end of 1915. Part of the reason lay in the nature of the war itself, for there was little in these months for the British public to celebrate, with the Somme offensive in particular giving many their first real understanding of the nature of the war that was being fought on the Western Front. But the changing domestic experience of war was probably just as important, for it was in these same months that the war began to intrude more and more painfully into people's everyday lives. In 1916 the government belatedly decided to introduce military conscription, and the apparently insatiable manpower needs of the army led to increasing numbers of women moving into new sectors of the workforce. Moreover, the demands of war provoked other important economic changes as well. Full employment gave the most disadvantaged a real improvement in their living standards, but the combination of growing shortages and restrictions on the one hand, and rising taxation and prices on the other, meant that many others saw their real living standards fall. The growing bitterness of those who experienced these changes was profoundly exacerbated by the fact that, in spite of the war, the more privileged classes seemed able to continue to live much the same comfortable lives as they always had done. Indeed, more and more people concluded that an unscrupulous minority was exploiting this situation for their own personal gain and, as Trevor Wilson observes, 'the word "profiteering" entered working-class language as one of the war's most potent terms of abuse'.[9]

Thus by the spring of 1917, in the wake of an especially severe winter, a new situation was developing. Belief in the justice of the war remained, but a growing pessimism about both the military and the domestic position coincided with a mounting sense at home of injustice about the way in which the war was being conducted. German aggression had offended a deeply held British sense of fairness; mounting inflation, growing shortages and, above all else, the unequal way in which the burdens of war at home were being shared, offended that sense of fairness as well. The extent of the change in the public mood is evidenced most clearly by the fact that industrial unrest, which had been such a marked feature of pre-war Britain, reappeared. A first wave of strikes took place in May 1917; it was followed by further strikes in August and November, reaching a climax in January and early February 1918, where short strikes were widespread all over the country. This should not be seen simply as a return to pre-war normalcy. The act of going on strike during war constituted a much more powerful expression of dissatisfaction, and it represented a much more serious challenge to a wartime government where the very ability to sustain the war effort could be undermined by industrial action.

Certainly the government watched these developments with growing anxiety, and from mid-April 1917 regular detailed reports on the labour situation were prepared for the War Cabinet. What these reports revealed, however, was that it was resentment at the worsening food situation which was the primary cause of this mounting popular anger, and that meant that the remedy was largely in the government's own hands.[10] For there was no absolute shortfall of food supplies; the problem lay in the way in which that food was being distributed and a fair and efficient system of rationing would go a long way towards meeting the workers' demands. In the end just such a system of rationing was introduced, with the foundations in place by February 1918, and a uniform, nationwide system completed by mid-summer. It soon became clear that the strike movement had passed its peak. However, the collapse of the strikes was not simply a response to domestic events; it coincided with the capitulation of the Bolsheviks, and the terms which the Germans subsequently exacted at Brest Litovsk in 1918 provided a stark reminder of the extent of German ambitions. Moreover, on 21 March, the long-anticipated German offensive began. The scale of the German advances brought back fearful memories of the opening weeks of the war; the collapse of the Fifth Army constituted the worst British defeat of the war. While it might have been expected that this would intensify anxiety and disillusionment, in practice it had a quite different effect. It was one thing to voice frustration and anger, even to go on strike, when the war seemed to be bogged down in an interminable stalemate; it was quite a different matter when the German armies were once again on the march. Thus, not only did the strikes collapse, the nation united once again in its opposition to the enemy. Indeed this time that opposition was characterized by a passion and a degree of xenophobia which surpassed anything that had gone before; a tide of hatred of the enemy swept all before it, persisting long after the German advance had been halted, and remaining the dominant element in the public mood right to the end of the war. It is an extraordinary fact that the great majority of the British people ended the war much as they had begun it – their determination to defeat Germany perhaps even more passionate, even more implacable than it had been in August 1914.

However, while the changing mood of wartime public opinion is clear enough, what is less clear is whether official propaganda played any role in determining those changes. For it was of course during this war that a British government embarked, for the first time, on a large-scale, sustained campaign of official propaganda and, in spite of the fact that popular opinion at the outset of the war was so passionately committed to the war effort, Prime Minister Asquith's cabinet took the decision to set up an organization 'to inform and influence public opinion abroad and to confute German mis-statements and sophistries'[11] within days of the declaration of war. That organization was duly established within the offices of the National Insurance Commission at Wellington House in London, under the leadership of Charles Masterman, a member of Asquith's cabinet and a former journalist and writer.[12] For while the state of domestic public opinion would not require government intervention for many months, there was an immediate recognition of the need to influence public opinion outside Britain: to counter German propaganda, to seek to retain the support of Britain's existing allies and, above all else, to try to persuade neutral nations in general, and the United States of America in particular, to join the war on the British side. This exclusive preoccupation with influencing public opinion outside Britain may help to explain the speed with which this initiative was launched for, in its initial formulation, such wartime propaganda was in effect an extension of peacetime diplomacy.

That said, it was a politically sensitive decision. The majority of civil servants and politicians probably viewed the prospect of official propaganda with considerable distaste, and it may well have been partly for this reason that the job was not given to the Foreign Office, but rather to a new, wholly secret organization which Masterman established at Wellington House. While the policy of secrecy was clearly justified by his, rather sophisticated, view that official propaganda could only be successful if the recipient was ignorant of its provenance, it also derived from an anxiety about the way in which both public and parliamentary opinion might respond to the decision. That secrecy was largely maintained until Masterman's original organization was replaced by a more public Department of Information (DoI) in February 1917, although public scrutiny was still kept to a minimum, and it was only when the DoI was replaced by the Ministry of Information (MoI) in March

1918, under the flamboyant leadership of the Canadian press baron and proprietor of the *Daily Express*, Lord Beaverbrook, that it achieved a really prominent public profile. Even then the original policy of secrecy was far from dead: writing in September 1918, Beaverbrook asserted that 'the greater part of propaganda must be conducted quietly and unofficially and without advertisement. The Ministry can advertise its wares but it dare not advertise the vendor.'[13]

Throughout the first half of the war, official propaganda remained loyal to its original brief of concentrating exclusively on influencing opinion abroad, but as domestic morale started to decline, the propagandists were not slow to respond. In May 1917, the month in which strikes once again became widespread, John Buchan (the novelist whom Lloyd George had appointed as Director of the DoI at its inception in February 1917), wrote to the Prime Minister pointing out that when his Department had been set up, no provision had been made for domestic propaganda. He was now convinced that such a situation should not continue: 'In the present state of popular feeling I am very strongly of the opinion that it is necessary to do a considerable amount of propaganda in Britain itself', and he suggested a number of initiatives, notably 'a series of lectures and addresses in all the chief centres';[14] four days later his proposal was approved by the War Cabinet. In the event, however, a new organization was established to put this new policy into practice. Following the model of the Parliamentary Recruiting Committee (which had been responsible for organizing the military recruitment drive in the first 18 months of the war), the National War Aims Committee (NWAC) was based on the constituency organizations of the three main political parties and was led by the two Chief Whips; Buchan sat on its executive committee, but it was administered as a wholly separate organization from the DoI, its independence seen as critical to its potential success.

The new organization was launched by Lloyd George at a public meeting on 4 August 1917, and this very public act both separated the NWAC from the more covert style of the mainstream of official propaganda, and put it firmly in the camp of those private organizations which had disseminated propaganda on the home front from the very earliest days of the war, the most important of which was immediately taken over by the NWAC.[15] Its objectives were clearly defined – strengthening national morale, combating pacifism, spelling out the advantages of an Entente peace, explaining the meaning of a German peace, inspiring war workers at home and encouraging unity by stifling party and class dissension. Moreover, while it developed a variety of methods to achieve these objectives (leaflets, articles for the press, films, posters, cartoons, postcards and so on), its major weapon was the most traditional one of all – the public meeting. By the end of the war it had on file almost 4000 reports of meetings held in the constituencies, each report typically listing several meetings.

Thus there is a clear relationship between the chronology of official domestic propaganda and the changing pattern of public opinion, with the NWAC launched in August 1917 to try to combat that growing war-weariness and disaffection which had emerged earlier in the year, and which eventually reached its climax in the first two months of 1918. Yet it could be argued that the government had responded somewhat slowly to the changing situation. Buchan had identified the problem in May, but the NWAC was not launched until three months later, and it was to be a further three months before the War Cabinet agreed to substantial funding for the new organization. Therefore, while the NWAC was campaigning through the crucial winter of 1917/18, these delays meant that it was only after public morale had rallied that it really got into its stride, and it was probably rather too late to play any major role in effecting that change, although it may have helped to establish the new xenophobia which gripped the country in the closing months of the war.

OFFICIAL FILM PROPAGANDA – THE FIRST 18 MONTHS

There is no such problem with the chronology of official film propaganda, however, for unlike every other form of official wartime propaganda, the first film was screened as early as December 1915. Indeed, had the circumstances been different, the official films would have emerged even earlier in the war, for both the cinema trade and those responsible for official propaganda had been putting the case for film propaganda from the very beginning of the war. Nor was there anything surprising in this, for while cinema was a comparatively recent phenomenon in British society, it had quickly established a powerful position in popular culture. With a pricing policy that undercut the theatres and the music halls, at the outbreak of war it was already the dominant form of popular entertainment, with more money being spent on cinema tickets than the combined receipts of all other forms of commercial entertainment put together – indeed, by the summer of 1916 20 million cinema tickets were being sold each week.[16] Moreover, the British experience was in no way exceptional and cinema had established much the same position in every industrial society. Thus, if the ambition was to influence mass public opinion either at home or abroad, the medium of cinema was uniquely placed to reach those huge target audiences.

In effect there are two separate questions that have to be answered – why did official film propaganda predate all other domestic official propaganda by over 18 months? On the other hand, why was it delayed until the very end of 1915? The answer to both questions lies in a combination of the form which the official films took and the means that were used to produce and distribute them. For in making the case for official film propaganda, both Charles Masterman (within government) and the cinema trade (outside it) were determined that official films must be factual films, films which, as one trade paper put it, recorded 'the actual likeness of events'.[17] Ideally such films should be shot at the front line, recording all the drama and excitement of the action; if that was impossible, then other kinds of actuality footage would have to do – troops in training, the logistics of supplying and maintaining a large modern army, the new demands which war was making on British industry and so on. Above all else, the footage must be authentic, 'real British war films, as distinct from faked war dramas' as the British ambassador in Bucharest argued.[18] That remark helps to explain this very particular insistence on the importance of the factual film. Faked war films had been screened before, notably during the Boer War, and the legacy of that experience had created considerable audience scepticism about films that purported to represent the realities of war. If official films were to succeed, they had to be very different from those earlier faked films, and there was a unanimous expectation that the very fact of their official provenance would persuade the audience that the films were, indeed, authentic. Thus in marketing the films, very great emphasis was placed on their official character, an approach which in itself differentiated film propaganda from almost every other form of official propaganda; not only was no attempt made to conceal its origin, the propagandists did everything possible to draw the audience's attention to it.

If, however, the case for factual, official propaganda films was being made from early in the war, why was it not until the end of 1915 that the first film was released? The explanation lies above all else in the prevailing establishment view of the cinema – Masterman's wife Lucy surely understated the situation when she wrote that 'the cinema was still regarded as a kind of music-hall turn, probably vulgar and without serious importance'.[19] Very few of those who worked in Whitehall or Westminster had any first-hand knowledge of the cinema; it had grown up initially in the fairgrounds and music halls and, while it had long since moved into more permanent locations, it still retained an almost exclusively working-class audience. It was regarded as at best a trivial, at worst a pernicious, means of filling the leisure time of those who knew no better, and the idea that it might make some contribution to the serious business of winning the war was both incomprehensible and distasteful. All the more remarkable, therefore, that Masterman should have taken such a different view, although the fact that he was exclusively concerned with trying to influence public opinion abroad may have been important; he was certainly very conscious that German films were increasingly being seen in areas like the Balkans and Asia, with their 'immense illiterate populations for whom no literature was any use.'[20]

But if Masterman and his colleagues at Wellington House were persuaded of the need for official films, those views were not shared elsewhere in Whitehall. In particular, they were not shared in the service departments and yet, if a single foot of authentic factual film was ever to be shot, then it was those departments that would have to be persuaded; and *that* proved enormously difficult. Determined to achieve a rigorous management of wartime news,[21] the services were convinced that if official films were ever made, then – as Lucy Masterman put it – 'every sort of secret would escape'; in any event, it was simply 'infra dig for this country to allow its forces to be portrayed for the delectation of foreigners'.[22] Thus it was only after considerable public pressure and much private negotiation and persuasion, that agreement was eventually secured.[23] What emerged, in fact, was two quite separate agreements. In the first, Wellington House was allowed to shoot footage for a single film,[24] while in the second, the Trade Topical Committee (a committee which represented the major film companies which worked in the field of 'topical' or factual film), secured permission to send cameramen to the front. Not least because this second agreement made provision for sustained front-line film-making, it provided the basis for the vast majority of official films that were to follow, even if the title and form of the Committee was to change on a number of occasions during the war.[25]

This relationship between the service departments and the cinema trade resulted in the films being seen at home more than 18 months before any other official domestic propaganda and yet, while the implications of that decision were considerable, they do not appear to have been discussed explicitly. From the outset, all the relevant parties simply assumed that the films would be distributed at home as well as abroad, and a combination of pragmatic and financial considerations probably led to this view. Certainly no one in government was willing to fund the production of official films and, equally clearly, the cinema trade would only shoulder those financial obligations if it could be sure that it would enjoy a reasonable return on its investment. Thus, while the Topical Committee agreed to provide all the equipment and pay the cameramen's salaries, it was given in return both exclusive access to the front and the exclusive right to exploit the films commercially in Britain and the Empire (with the exception of India and Egypt, where the War Office retained exhibition rights). In a society which had been starved of detailed information about the war for so long, there was good reason to expect that authentic front-line footage would prove good box office, even if a proportion of the profits would be paid to military and naval charities. Moreover, from the propagandists' point of view, the commercial exploitation of the films made good sense, for it was in the cinemas that the mass audience was to be found. In sum, the long months of negotiation had produced an agreement which reconciled the rather different interests of all the three major parties.

Certainly the way in which the films were initially exploited provides ample evidence of the coincidence of commercial and political objectives. The very first official film was the Wellington House production *Britain Prepared*, and every effort was made to ensure both its commercial and its political success. The première on 29 December 1915 was attended by an audience which constituted, in effect, a cross-section of the ruling Establishment, with the First Lord of the Admiralty offering a ringing endorsement of the film in an address during the interval; and it took place in

London's Empire Music Hall, a venue otherwise used to launch the cinema's most prestigious (and most commercial) products.[26] In the event, the expectations of both the propagandists and the trade were amply fulfilled, and both must have been particularly pleased to read a second leader in the *Manchester Guardian* the next day which argued that the exhibition of the film demonstrated that the cinema was much more than 'a mere amusement ... and its importance is destined to increase with time. The moving picture is the new universal language.'[27] Moreover, the film ran in this most prestigious location for a further month and, in addition to screenings in other London cinemas, by May 1916 it had been shown in 61 towns outside London and was booked to be shown in a further 50. While not a runaway success, it was an entirely respectable start, although in all the circumstances a failure to attract audiences would perhaps have been even more remarkable. This was, after all, the very first official film, and while it did no more than offer images of munitions manufacture, and military and naval training, its patriotic audience was still enthusiastically committed to the war, more than willing to be persuaded by the film's (undoubtedly impressive) images of Britain's technological, military and naval power. Indeed, had this not been the case, it would be difficult to explain how such a long, and often repetitive film could have achieved even this modest level of popularity.[28]

On the other hand, while *Britain Prepared* never claimed to do any more than demonstrate Britain's preparedness for war, it was immediately followed by the first films produced under the Topical Committee's agreement with the War Office, which were marketed in a very different way – a full-page advertisement in the trade press, for example, boldly announced 'The British Army in France. The Official Pictures'.[29] Over the next six months, 27 short films were released, and the propagandists must have expected that they would have been received even more enthusiastically. In reality, while one or two reviews were enthusiastic (*The Times* in particular argued that they were 'excellent, both in subject and workmanship'[30]), the overall response was very different – even *The Times* suggested that it was possible to identify the heavy hand of the Censor, and others were even more critical. The *Star* admitted that 'most people were disappointed', arguing that the films might as well have been taken during pre-war manoeuvres,[31] but it was left to the trade paper, *The Cinema*, to voice the toughest criticism of all. In an editorial headlined ' "Done" Again!' it argued that the marketing of the films represented nothing less than 'a fraud on the long-suffering British cinema public'.[32]

The nature of the films makes it easy to understand this acute sense of disappointment. The cinema trade's long-standing desire to film at the front derived from an assumption that it would be possible to achieve close, dramatic footage of the fighting itself, and while the advertising never explicitly promised footage of that kind, this was almost certainly what the paying audiences anticipated. In practice, a combination of the technological limitations of the cameras and the deeply cautious approach of the intelligence officers who supervised the cameramen, meant that none of these films included any such footage, concentrating instead on those rather more mundane, less dramatic activities, which were also a crucial part of life at the front.[33] Thus the Western Front films released in the first half of 1916 demonstrate that, even in a strongly favourable climate, propaganda films can fail.

All that changed, and changed dramatically, with the release of the next film, *Battle of the Somme,* in August 1916. Here at last was a film that caught the popular imagination, and its release inaugurated a period of remarkable success for the official films. *Battle of the Somme* draws on footage shot by two official cameramen, Geoffrey Malins and J.B. McDowell. Malins started filming on 25 June 1916; on 29 June he was joined by McDowell, and they continued to film the preliminaries, including the massive artillery bombardment.[34] On 1 July they were in position at two different locations with Rawlinson's Fourth Army to film the opening day of the offensive. They continued to film on the Somme until 10 July. Two days later, the first rushes of their footage were seen in London by the Trade Topical Committee, whose members were so impressed that it was decided to release it in the form of a single, major film. Just under a month later, on 7 August 1916, the completed film (which ran for an hour and a quarter) had its first trade show, and three days later it was screened to an invited audience. At that screening an enthusiastic message of support for the film from Lloyd George (the recently appointed Secretary of State for War) was read to the audience, and the film was extensively reported in the national press the following day. Three weeks later it received the most prestigious endorsement of all – following a private screening at Windsor, the King (George V) urged people to see it, and this too was widely reported. This initial publicity was complemented by extensive advertising in the trade press and a number of additional trade shows.

All this vigorous promotion clearly paid off, for when *Battle of the Somme* went on public exhibition in London on 21 August, it opened at no less than 34 cinemas simultaneously; a week later it went on national release, 100 prints being distributed nationwide. The film did extraordinarily good business wherever it was shown. The opening week in London proved enormously popular, with numerous cinemas reporting that they were simply unable to cope with the scale of demand, and the London experiment of screening the film simultaneously at a number of different cinemas (an unusual practice at the time) was repeated in most major cities. It was a huge success everywhere, with cinema after cinema playing the film to full houses, often having to turn would-be patrons away and, while no national box-office statistics for the film were collected, Nicholas Hiley has calculated that it probably achieved 20 million attendances in its first six weeks. Moreover, it continued to be shown in British cinemas for many months thereafter, and it is thus very likely that a majority of the domestic population saw the film.[35] It was indeed an extraordinary phenomenon, quite without precedent in the history of the British cinema.

In the best traditions of the mainstream commercial cinema, the propagandists were not slow to repeat their success, and six months later, in January 1917, they released the *Battle of the Ancre and the Advance of the Tanks*. While the approach was broadly similar to *Battle of the Somme*, *Battle of the Ancre* had the considerable additional advantage of including extensive footage of the tank, the British army's new wonder weapon, and it appears to have been quite as popular as its predecessor. Moreover, by the time it was screened, the propagandists had already enjoyed another huge success in the form of *The King Visits His Armies in the Great Advance*, released in October 1916. While the popularity of this latter film could not be explained in the same terms as the battle films, the fact that it offered a remarkably intimate and informal picture of the King provides explanation enough for the enthusiasm with which patriotic audiences responded to the film. In all, the film propagandists could surely regard the first 15 months of their work with some considerable satisfaction. *Britain Prepared* had made a sound, if unspectacular start and, while that initial success was not sustained with the short Western Front films that were released in the first six months of 1916, that was soon forgotten in the face of the spectacular success of the three major films released between August 1916 and January 1917. Moreover, the domestic success of the films was broadly paralleled overseas, and by the end of 1917 official British films had been sent to some 40 foreign countries.[36]

GROWING PROBLEMS IN THE LATER MONTHS OF THE WAR

Yet, within weeks of the release of *Battle of the Ancre* the situation was to change once again. By the time the third battle film, *The German Retreat and the Battle of Arras*, reached the cinemas in June 1917, it was clear that the public appetite for official films of this kind had passed its peak – indeed, three months earlier, at a special lunch for the trade, the propagandists freely admitted that some exhibitors had lost money on the official films; they were urged to continue to book them because they brought a new, more prosperous clientele into the cinemas.[37] In May, Lord Beaverbrook (who had been appointed chairman of the committee which was now responsible for official film-making at the front), argued that a radically new approach was needed – 'the present style of films is played out. The public is jaded and we have to tickle its palate with something a little more dramatic in the future if we are to maintain our sales.'[38] The release of *Battle of Arras* still went ahead, albeit with one important change: footage of the dead and wounded (which had been such a significant feature of both the earlier battle films) was largely removed – images like this would never again be seen by wartime audiences.

Thereafter even more radical changes were introduced. *Battle of Arras* was the last of the feature-length factual war films; in future the battlefront footage was released in a new, official newsreel. The newsreel was an established part of the weekly programme in British cinemas, although by this time it was the two newsreels owned by French companies which dominated the British market, namely *Gaumont Graphic* and *Pathé Gazette*. The one British newsreel, *The Topical Budget*, was very much the poor relation, and yet it was through this vehicle that Beaverbrook planned to re-establish access to the British audience. Accordingly, in May 1917, the *Official War Office Topical Budget* was advertised to the trade, and this relaunched *Topical Budget* was to be the flagship for official film propaganda's attempt to win back the audience which it had lost over the preceding winter.[39] To complete the new approach, the propagandists subsequently added a series of weekly 'magazine' films, designed to complement the 'newspaper' approach of the newsreel. The first series of these films concentrated on colonial or allied troops; it was later supplemented by a second series of regimental films, the primary purpose of which seems to have been to provide positive images of happy, smiling soldiers, in the strongest possible contrast to some of the footage that had been included in the earlier Western Front films. In addition, in these closing months of the war, the Admiralty agreed to the production of a number of films about the navy; further films about the royal family and a variety of films about different aspects of life on the home front were released as well.[40]

All of this constituted a significant change in emphasis from the approach of the earlier official films: the propagandists recognized that they were confronting an entirely new situation in the spring and early summer of 1917, and they reformulated their policy accordingly. Unwilling to abandon their long-standing commitment to the factual film, they nevertheless made crucial alterations in the all-important field of the war films, by managing their content more carefully and by introducing radical changes in the form of their presentation. In short, they made a determined attempt to restore audience interest in a product that had lost its appeal. But none of these initiatives restored official film propaganda to the popularity which it had achieved in 1916 and the early part of 1917. The evidence of that failure is demonstrated in a number of different ways, of which the experience of the new official newsreel is one of the most striking. *The Topical Budget* had always been overshadowed by *Gaumont Graphic* and *Pathé Gazette*, but there was every reason to suppose that its relaunch as the *War Office Topical Budget* in May 1917 would change that position – not only was it to enjoy exclusive access to the footage shot by the official cameramen at the front, but it acquired exclusive rights to the French official newsreel as well. In practice this seems to have made almost no difference at all, with its small sales to 78 cinemas a week rising to just 82 by the end of the year. Perhaps even more significant, sales only finally increased in the early part of 1918 when the newsreel began to move away from a primary emphasis on the war towards an editorial policy that was much closer to the sporting and 'human interest' focus of the other newsreels, a change that was given public recognition at the end of February 1918 by the decision to change its title to *Pictorial News (Official)*.

Thus, not only did the launch of the official newsreel fail to solve the problem identified by Beaverbrook in May 1917, it seemed to demonstrate that in this most critical period of the war there was no longer a significant public audience for factual war footage – certainly none of the other official films proved any more popular. Confirmation of the extent to which the situation had changed is provided by the way in which the press reported the official films, for whereas they had attracted a great deal of attention up to and including the release of the *Battle of the Ancre*, thereafter press coverage fell away almost entirely.[41] But it is financial data that perhaps reveals the extent of the propagandists' failure most clearly. In the first three months of their exhibition, *Battle of the Somme* and *Battle of the Ancre* grossed £65,000; in the 18 months from January 1917 to June 1918, the total income achieved by *all* official films amounted to the princely sum of just £70,023.[42] That figure looks small enough in itself, but given that it *includes* the £35,000 earned by *Battle of the Ancre*, the extent of the failure of the later official films becomes all too clear. In other words, a film propaganda strategy that had won audiences so successfully earlier in the war simply failed to achieve its objectives in the last 18 months of the war. All the changes initiated in the summer and autumn of 1917 did nothing to remedy the situation: the films simply did not have the power to attract a paying audience, commercial exhibition no longer reached the target audience.

Indeed, by February 1918 the propagandists themselves recognized the new realities, and decided for the first time to try to reach the target audience *outside* the cinemas, by launching the first of the so-called 'cinemotor' tours. The idea was simple enough: the cinemotor (a lorry, equipped with generator and projector), would set up in a town or village; the 25-foot screen would be erected, and a free film show would be presented to anyone who chose to come. If the people would not come to the official films, then the official films would be taken to the people. It was undoubtedly a novel idea, and an experimental cinemotor tour in Wales in February 1918 was successful enough to convince the propagandists that they should take the idea further. Two major tours took place, the first in April and May, with ten cinemotors visiting 68 parliamentary constituencies, and a second tour in September and October, when 20 cinemotors visited a further 72 constituencies. Individual attendances ranged from 350 to 15,000, and an analysis of attendance reports suggests that an average of 163,000 people attended the cinemotor shows for each week of the tours.[43] These figures look impressive enough, until it is remembered that the original strategy of commercial exhibition had enabled the official films to reach the millions who went to the cinema every week.

If the cinemotor tours represented one last attempt to find an audience for the factual films, the last months of the war saw the beginnings of an altogether more radical approach to official film propaganda. In the autumn and early winter of 1917 the trade press became increasingly critical of the films themselves, arguing that they lacked 'human interest' and 'cohesion' and that they were capable only of securing 'fleeting attention'; what was needed was films 'with the attractiveness and power of a war-story picture with human interest running through'.[44] While appeals like this made little immediate impact on those responsible for the existing production of official films, a brand new propaganda agency proved much more receptive to just such ideas. The National War Aims Committee (NWAC) had been launched in August, and by October 1917 it had decided to break entirely with the established traditions of official film-making: it would produce a mainstream feature film, with high production values and major stars, taking full advantage of cinema's special ability to construct a believable fictional narrative. The National Film took as its starting point a successful German invasion of England, examining in lurid detail what this would mean for the occupants of Chester. Moreover, the film placed considerable emphasis on the wartime strikes, in order to demonstrate just how unpatriotic and destructive they had been.[45] Thus, alone among official film propaganda, The National Film set out both to reinforce hatred of the enemy and to attack head-on the new public mood which found its most potent expression in the strike movement. In the event, however, all the considerable energies invested in its production proved to be of no consequence and the film served only to provide a peculiarly vivid demonstration of the practical difficulties of working in the very different form of the feature-length fiction film. For, while the decision to embark on such a film was made in October 1917, the lavish scale of the production meant that it was only nearing completion in June 1918, by which time the public mood had changed dramatically, with the strikes largely over and Britain united again in an even greater determination to defeat Germany. Ironically, even that was not the end of it for, just before the production was finished, a fire at the premises of the London Film Company destroyed much of the film, and it was only finally completed after the war was over. At that time, the content of the film was deemed wholly unsuitable for post-war audiences, and the film was never shown.[46]

On the other hand, at just the same time as the NWAC was pioneering this new approach, those responsible for the majority of official propaganda began to re-examine their attitude towards the cinema of fiction. When the Ministry of Information was formed in February 1918, it volunteered to help in the production of The National Film, and when much of the film had to be re-shot later in the year, it was the MoI Cinematograph Department which took responsibility for the film.[47] While this took up almost all of the Department's existing film production resources, it spent much of its short life exploring ways of expanding that film production capacity. Indeed, as the war ended, it was considering an even more radical change in policy, namely abandoning the practice of releasing official films altogether and putting in its place a new, 'discreet' approach in which the provenance of the films would be concealed from the audience. The paper which advocated this new strategy argued that not only would such a policy by-pass that hostility to official films which had always been displayed by the cinema trade and the audience, it would also give the MoI much greater flexibility, enabling it to produce films with little overt propaganda content.[48] Although the war ended before any of these new policies could be implemented, the fact that the propagandists were rethinking their strategy in these more radical terms provides yet more evidence of the extent of the continuing failure of film propaganda policy.

THE FILMS AND THEIR AUDIENCE

What then does all this reveal about the power of film as a medium of propaganda? How effective were Britain's official films during the First World War in influencing wartime public opinion? First, and most obvious, there is a clear relationship between the chronology of changing audience attitudes towards the official films and the chronology of changing wartime public opinion. No official films were released in the early months of the war when domestic enthusiasm for the war effort was at its height and, when the first film was released at the very end of 1915, domestic attitudes towards the war were still largely positive. In such circumstances, where audiences had been starved of actuality footage of the war for so long, it would have been quite extraordinary if those first films had not been able to find an audience. In fact, while *Britain Prepared* did achieve some success, the short films from the Western Front that were released over the first six months of 1916 did not sustain that initial popularity, and thus demonstrate all too clearly that, even in favourable circumstances, propaganda films are no more guaranteed an audience than any other kind of film. The situation changed, of course, with the release of *Battle of the Somme*, which initiated a brief period of very considerable success for official film propaganda, but once again the particular chronology of that success is important. The three films that were so popular at that time were released between August 1916 and January 1917, *before* the first clear signs of changing attitudes to the war became evident in the strikes of March 1917. In other words, while they achieved their success in the face of a more sceptical public opinion than had existed earlier in the war, they were nevertheless seen at a time when popular support for the war was still secure, and the popularity of these films offers no evidence of their ability to change public opinion. Indeed, given the remarkable and unprecedented character of these particular films, it would have been extraordinary if they had not achieved that success.

That this analysis is well-founded is demonstrated even more clearly by the way in which the situation changed thereafter. The dramatic shift in public opinion that took place over the winter of 1916/1917 revealed itself most clearly in the outbreak of strikes in March 1917 and, from then until February the following year, the situation (from the government's point of view) only deteriorated. In these very different circumstances, the official films were increasingly powerless. The first signs of this change appeared as early as February 1917, when *Bioscope* reported a sharp decline in audience interest in *Battle of the Ancre* in some Scottish cinemas.[49] By the time the third battle film, *Battle of Arras*, was released in June 1917 the scale of the transformation was clear; the film was as spectacular a failure as the two earlier battle films had been successes. Working on the assumption that audiences had become bored with the battle films, the propagandists replaced them with the official newsreel and a new series of short, factual films. But when these initiatives also failed to win back the audience, it became clear that the problem went much deeper than this. No matter how ingenious the propagandists were in reshaping the form of their factual films, they were never again able to reach that mass cinema audience which had made the medium so attractive to them in the first place. In the new climate, there was simply no longer an audience for the official films, and so desperate did the propagandists become in their search for that lost audience, that they eventually resorted to the free film shows of the cinemotor tours. Indeed, as the war ended, they were even giving serious consideration to abandoning the factual film altogether. In short, the domestic reception of the official films demonstrates above all else the inability of film propaganda to alter attitudes towards the war: while the war was popular, audience appetite for the official films was almost insatiable; once attitudes to the war changed, that huge interest disappeared, almost overnight.

There is perhaps one small qualification to add to that rather stark conclusion. The official newsreel did do rather better business in the last year of the war, perhaps reaching as many as 3 million of the 20 million who were, by that time, attending the cinema each week,[50] and to that extent it does perhaps suggest that the new strategy was not a complete failure. On the other hand, the scale of that success was limited, for even at the height of its wartime popularity the distribution of the official newsreel still lagged far behind its main competitors, *Pathé* and *Gaumont Graphic*, giving the propagandists only partial access to the mass audience. Moreover, by the time the newsreel had achieved this greater success, the climate of opinion had changed again, with Britain gripped once more by that anti-German jingoism that had been there at the outset. To that extent, even the greater popularity of the official newsreel in the closing months of the war demonstrates that film propaganda was the servant, not the master of the audience it sought to control.

Having said all that, during a comparatively short period of the war the official films did achieve huge popularity, and the surviving evidence gives us a remarkably clear insight into the way in which contemporary audiences responded to the most popular film of that period, *Battle of the Somme*.[51] At a time when film reviews had not yet become established as a regular feature of the national or local press, the film attracted unparalleled attention and, almost without exception, the comment was enormously enthusiastic. Thus, whether it was the *Manchester Guardian* or the *Daily Mirror* or the *Birmingham Gazette* or the *Kinematograph and Lantern Weekly* (one of the leading trade papers of the day), the view was invariably the same – *Battle of the Somme*, they claimed, gave its audiences a unique insight into the realities of war on the Western Front. It had achieved an unprecedented degree of realism: as the *Yorkshire Evening Press* put it, 'never before has such a production been screened ... it is all so real'.[52] And these claims about the film's unprecedented ability to construct an accurate view of the nature of the war were endorsed even in journals written for a service audience. Thus, for example, the *Regiment*, which often criticised civilians' woeful ignorance of the war, argued that the film might at last shake those civilians out of their complacency and teach them 'the true meaning of war'. [53] There is a certain irony in this, for what was arguably the film's most famous sequence may well have been faked. Part III of the film opens with a 21-second sequence which apparently shows men going 'over the top', into battle. While the evidence is not absolutely conclusive, the very strong probability is that this sequence was shot in a trench mortar school well behind the lines.[54] Even if we assume that this is indeed the case, the contemporary audience was unaware of this possibility – this was, as the *Manchester Guardian* put it, 'the real thing at last'.[55]

It is equally clear that audiences were deeply moved by the film, to the extent that from the outset some argued that the film was 'so gruesome ... as to be hardly bearable'.[56] Such objections reached their climax in a letter written by the Dean of Durham to the editor of *The Times*, protesting that:

> ... crowds of Londoners feel no scruple at feasting their eyes on pictures which present the passion and death of British soldiers in the *Battle of the Somme* ... a 'film' of war's hideous tragedy is welcomed. I beg leave respectfully to enter a protest against an entertainment which wounds the heart and violates the very sanctities of bereavement.[57]

The precise nature of the Dean's objection to the film is important, for it prompted many of those who came to the film's defence to draw particular attention to the manner in which the film had been received by the audience with whom they had seen it. Almost without exception, they pointed out the intensely emotional response of the audience, placing particular emphasis on the reverent, almost religious mood of people deeply moved by the images of war which *Battle of the Somme* presented to them. James Cooper spoke for many when he argued that Dean Henson's claims were both untrue and uncharitable: in reality 'the tears in many people's eyes and the silence which prevailed ... showed that every heart was full of love and sympathy for our soldiers'.[58] Moreover, this evidence is all the more striking because, unlike today, people did not watch films in respectful silence, but rather responded actively and noisily to what they saw on the screen. In stark contrast, the highly charged atmosphere in which *Battle of the Somme* was received bears eloquent testimony to the power of the film to involve and move its contemporary audience.

Nor is this in any sense surprising. At the end of the twentieth century, *Battle of the Somme* retains its ability to move its audience profoundly, notwithstanding the enormous changes that have taken place since, both in the form of the factual film and in attitudes towards the representation of violence on the screen.[59] The combination of the technological limitations of the equipment with which the official cameramen worked, and the intensely suspicious approach of the intelligence officers who supervised their work, meant that there was far less footage of the dramatic realities of front-line action than many had anticipated,[60] but *Battle of the Somme* nevertheless gave its audiences (now as then) an unprecedented insight into the nature of the war on the Western Front. Many patriotic contemporaries were impressed by the dramatic footage of the artillery bombardment which preceded the attack on 1 July 1916, but it is the human dimension of the film that is even more remarkable. Above all else, this is a film about the hundreds of thousands of ordinary soldiers (German as much as British) who saw action on this particular part of the front – the generals are (with one exception) conspicuous by their absence. And while the early part of the film presents a number of sequences of apparently happy soldiers, who smile and wave to the cameraman as they march by, it is the images of men about to go into action, or of men returning from action, that prove the most enduring. Thus, for example, in a famous sequence in Part III, soldiers about to go into action wait in a sunken road in No Man's Land; they stare unseeing at the camera, the anxiety, the tension on their faces almost palpable.

After the brief moment of the men going 'over the top' into action, the remainder of the film includes many sequences in which the pain and trauma of the fighting can be read all too clearly on the soldiers' faces; invariably they too fail to respond to the camera, too exhausted or too distraught to care.[61] Moreover, it is not always easy to distinguish German prisoners from British soldiers (although the former can be recognized by the absence of their helmets), and the audience is left with an overwhelming sense of the *common* experience which all have endured. The most harrowing moments in the film come in a two-minute sequence at the end of Part IV which presents explicit and detailed images of the dead. A slow pan across a heap of bodies at the bottom of a crater is followed by a succession of shots of individual dead soldiers, and the sequence ends with footage of the unceremonious manner in which the German dead are buried on the battlefield – the British soldiers, smoking as they work, stack the bodies side by side, awaiting burial in common graves. But none of this makes a chauvinistic point; once again it is the horror of war, regardless of the nationality of its victims, that makes such a powerful impact on the audience. The contemporary audience was deeply moved by these sequences; 80 years later, in spite of everything that has happened since, these sequences retain their power to move and disturb.

On the other hand, the meaning that they held for contemporary audiences was clearly quite different from the meaning constructed by late-twentieth-century audiences. Today, *Battle of the Somme* fits very easily into a perception of the First World War as the war, above all others, in which millions of human lives were needlessly sacrificed; in 1916 it made a very different statement. In endorsing the film at its first screening, Lloyd George had argued that it would reinforce popular commitment to the war, encouraging munitions workers, in particular, to work even harder, and part of the audience clearly responded to the film in just these terms. Thus the *Army and Navy Gazette* suggested that, in enabling civilians better to understand the nature of the war, it would make them even more determined 'that the nation must be utterly crushed that has brought so dreadful a war upon mankind',[62] and this notion of shaking complacent civilians into a proper recognition of the sacrifices that were being made on their behalf is echoed in a number of other reviews. James Douglas in the *Star* went so far as to assert that the film was 'the only substitute for invasion', demonstrating 'the power of the moving picture to carry the war to British soil'.[63] But perhaps the most direct expression of a powerful patriotic response to the film came from those whose viewing of the film prompted them to write to the press. One correspondent argued that the film would take audiences out of their 'smug security' and give them 'an insight into the horrors and discomforts our troops are suffering', and thereby stimulate 'a sense of admiration for their bravery'.[64] Another suggested that he came away from the film 'feeling humiliated and ashamed, for at last I was able to realise what Britain's soldiers were doing for her',[65] while yet another, who had three sons serving in the army, argued that the film 'if possible, increased my admiration and sympathy for them and their fellows and their cause'.[66] The views of all those who wrote in this way were perhaps encapsulated in the words of yet another correspondent, who wrote:

> I have lost a son in battle, and I have seen the Somme films twice. I am going to see them again. I want to know what was the life, and the life-in-death, that our dear ones endured, and to be with them again in their great adventure ... If the Dean had lost what I have lost, he would know that his objections are squeamish and sentimental.[67]

Even more remarkable, given her peculiarly privileged access to information about the war, was the response of Frances Stevenson (Lloyd George's secretary and mistress) for, after a private viewing of the film, she wrote in her diary in much the same terms about the film's ability to enable her to understand her brother's death: 'I have often tried to imagine myself what he went through, but now I *know*: and I shall never forget.'[68]

Thus, for very many the film clearly succeeded in fulfilling its patriotic propaganda objectives. Yet this was not the only conclusion which audiences drew from the film. In reporting on audience responses in Leeds, *Bioscope*'s correspondent argued that, while the film did 'teach what war really means', it would in consequence 'do more to preserve the peace of the world than a hundred peace societies and thousands of sermons',[69] a view echoed by James Cooper in *The Times* who suggested that 'no better means could be found of making English men and women determined to stop the repetition of such a war as the present one'.[70] An editorial in the *Manchester Guardian* went even further:

> ... no good can come of gilding war into a romance. The more of its trappings that are stripped from it, the more will men see its waste, its madness and its cruelty, as well as its glory, and the more earnestly will they cleave to peace.[71]

Moreover, while none of this discussion went the further step of arguing that, on the evidence of the film, the war was so terrible that it should be brought to an immediate end, the more cautious conclusion – that the film demonstrated the need to avoid any repetition of the war – could perhaps be seen as a step in that direction. Thus it is possible that the film may have played some part in contributing to that change in attitudes which took place over the winter of 1916/1917. The surviving evidence makes it clear that some audiences *outside* Britain drew more radical conclusions from the exhibition of the film,[72] and it may be that the propagandists did have evidence to suggest that some in the domestic audience responded in the same way – certainly, after the summer of 1917, no official British film included detailed footage of the dead and wounded.

However, set against speculation of that kind, there is overwhelming evidence testifying to the way in which, for all its impact, contemporary audiences incorporated *Battle of the Somme* into their own existing ideology. Images which, at another time or in another place might have served to convince audiences of the inhumanity and barbarity of war, served in Britain in the summer and autumn of 1916 to reconfirm existing convictions that Britain's cause was just. Nowhere is this more clearly demonstrated than in James Douglas' lengthy and strongly felt review, for while he shared with so many others an acute sense of the pain and horror of the war revealed by the film, he integrated that response into his own clear conviction of the essential justice of Britain's cause. His review concluded with these words:

> The bravery of our boys is past our imagining. 'Every one of them,' said a wounded officer to me who fought on the First of July, 'every one of them is a hero.' His eyes filled with tears as he spoke. I thought of his words as I saw our soldiers bringing in a dying comrade under shell-fire. He died half-an-hour after he passed on the back of a soldier. I shall not soon forget his good English face. Nor shall I soon forget the face of the dead German soldier who is lying there waiting to be buried by the British soldiers who are digging the graves on the battlefield. These are dreadful sights, but their dreadfulness is as wholesome as Tolstoy's 'War and Peace'. It shakes the kaleidoscope of war into human reality.

Now I know why soldiers are nobler than civilians in their tenderness and their chivalry and their charity. They have seen war, and they hate it as we can never hate it.

Therefore I say that these pictures are good for us. The dead on the battlefield, the drivers of the gun-teams steering the wheels clear of the corpse, the demented German prisoners, the kindly British soldiers showering cigarettes upon their captives, the mangled heap of anguish on the stretcher, the half-naked wounded men in the dressing-station – let our men and women see it all and vow that earth shall be delivered from it all. Dying men, dead horses, the dead dog lying beside his dead master – these vilenesses are war. War is the enemy, and Germany is its patentee, its idolater, its worshipper. It is our task to beat the German sword into a ploughshare so that the nations may learn war no more.[73]

Up to the penultimate sentence, Douglas' words make us much sense now as they did then, but it is those last two sentences that are all important. Notwithstanding the power of the film, notwithstanding its ability to move and affect an audience, its *meaning* is constructed by the audience, not by the film. The audience, like any cinema audience, brings to the film its own ideology, its own preconceptions, its own prejudices and assumptions, and it is only out of the interaction between the images on the screen and the ideology of the audience that the meaning of the film is constructed.

Further evidence of this is provided by data about the way in which young people responded to *Battle of the Somme* and *Battle of the Ancre*. As part of its enquiry into the role of the cinema in the life of the nation, the National Council of Public Morals commissioned an investigation into the wartime film preferences of children at a number of London schools, which revealed that the 'battle' films were remarkably popular. In a large study of nearly 7000 children, they were ranked fourth in a hierarchy of the eight most popular film categories (more popular, therefore, than 'crook films', serials, 'love films' or education films). Even more revealing, when asked to write about their favourite films, one schoolboy described a sequence in *Battle of the Ancre* in these words:

Now the whistle shrills, and they leap over the parapet, rat, tap, tap, go the German machine guns, but nothing daunts our soldiers. Crack! And their gallant captain falls. This enrages the men to fury. At last they reach the German lines. Most of the Germans flee for their lives shouting 'Kamerad! Kamerad!' etc. Now the British and German wounded are brought in, some seriously, some slightly. Soon after follow the German prisoners, some vicious looking scoundrels that I should not like to meet on a dark night, others young boys, about sixteen years of age.[74]

There is almost no relationship between the film itself and this account; the boy has described a film which only he saw, a 'film' that was constructed rather more by popular fictional accounts of the war, than by anything which he had seen in *Battle of the Ancre*. Once again, meaning in the film is built out of the interaction between the film and its audience, even if, in this extreme case, the relationship between the film and this particular member of the audience is decidedly unequal!

CONCLUSION

This sense of the power of the audience to construct its own meaning in the propaganda films that it sees, provides an appropriate point at which to draw this discussion of official British film propaganda during the First World War to a conclusion. For different reasons, the films only reached their target audience for a little over a quarter of the war's duration – not, in itself, the most compelling demonstration of the power of film as a medium of propaganda. Moreover, the huge popularity which they achieved during those 18 months was a product both of the novelty and emotional intensity of the films, and of the fact that they were screened at a time when public opinion was still broadly committed to the war. Once the public mood changed, the propagandists could no longer persuade their audiences to go to see the official films. Official film propaganda proved all but impotent in the face of the challenge posed by the disillusionment and war-weariness that became more and more evident in the 12 months that ended in February 1918.

Thus, whatever the propagandists may have thought at the time, whatever the commentators and academics were to write in the inter-war years, public opinion in Britain during the First World War was more influenced by the changing nature of the war and by people's own direct, personal experience of the war, than it was by the official films, or indeed any other form of wartime propaganda. Growing weariness, frustration and anger were the products both of a changing war situation that was increasingly characterized by higher casualties and apparent stalemate, and of a changing domestic situation in which ever heavier burdens were imposed in ways that were increasingly seen to be unfair. Set alongside these important developments, the official films played an increasingly minor role. Equally, in the final months of the war, dramatic changes at the front (with Germany apparently poised to defeat Britain), and important changes at home (with new government policies to remedy the unfairness of the domestic burdens of the war), were able to achieve what the films never could – they dissipated the weariness and redirected the anger, and the nation united once more in its hatred of the enemy and its determination to see the war through to a victorious conclusion. In all of this, the official films played very little, if any, part. For while the propagandists believed that film propaganda played a key part in its battle to win and retain the hearts and minds of the people, this does not in itself mean that it did. In fact, while the nature of the history of propaganda is such that we can never be entirely sure, in this particular case the power of film propaganda does seem to have been more mythical than real.

NOTES

1. The classic exposition of such a view is to be found in George Dangerfield, *The Strange Death of Liberal England*, London, 1936.

2. Quoted in Arthur Marwick, *The Deluge*, Harmondsworth, 1967, p. 33.

3. J.M. Bourne, *Britain and the Great War 1914–1918*, London, 1989, p. 210.

4. The phrase is Cate Haste's and her study remains the most detailed analysis of unofficial wartime propaganda (Cate Haste, *Keep the Home Fires Burning: Propaganda in the First World War*, London, 1977).

5. Quoted in Bourne, *op. cit.*, p. 208.

6. Quoted in John Ellis, *Eye-Deep in Hell: Life in the Trenches 1914–1918*, London, 1976, p. 189.

7. *Ibid.*, p. 195.

8. In a letter to his son written on Christmas Day 1915 – quoted in Trevor Wilson, *The Myriad Faces of War: Britain and the Great War 1914–1918*, Cambridge, 1988, p. 169.

9. *Ibid.*, p. 529.

10. Wilson draws extensively on these reports in his analysis of industrial conflict in this period (Wilson, *op. cit.*, pp. 519–30).

11. Public Record Office (PRO), CAB 41/35/48, Prime Minister to the King, 31 August 1914.

12. For a full discussion of the history of Britain's official wartime propaganda see M.L. Sanders and Philip M. Taylor, *British Propaganda during the First World War*, London, 1982; a brief summary is offered in Nicholas Reeves, *Official British Film Propaganda during the First World War*, London, 1986, pp. 8–43. The remainder of this account of the organization of official propaganda is based on these two sources.

13. PRO, INF4/5, *The Organisation and Functions of the Ministry of Information*, September 1918, p. 79.

14. PRO, CAB 24/13/GT774, *Propaganda at Home – Memorandum by Director, Department of Information, to the Prime Minister*, 18 May 1917.

15. The Central Committee for National Patriotic Organizations.

16. Nicholas Hiley, 'The British cinema auditorium', in Karel Dibbets and Bert Hogenkamp (eds), *Film and the First World War*, Amsterdam, 1995, p. 162.

17. *Bioscope*, 3 September 1914, p. 859.

18. PRO, FO371/2573/127947/127947, Sir George Barclay to the Foreign Office, 24 August 1915.

19. Lucy Masterman, *C.F.G. Masterman: A Biography*, London, 1939, p. 282.

20. *Ibid.*, pp. 282–3.

21. This was in fact a comparatively recent preoccupation, deriving in part from the success achieved by the Japanese in managing news during the Russo-Japanese War; see Philip Towle, 'The debate on wartime censorship in Britain 1902–1914', in Brian Bond and Ian Roy (eds), *War and Society: A Yearbook of Military History*, London, 1975, pp. 103–16.

22. Masterman, *op. cit.*, pp. 282–3.

23. For a more detailed discussion of these negotiations see Reeves, *op. cit.* (1986),

pp. 45–56. The account of the organization of official film propaganda which follows is largely based on the same source, pp. 56–88.

24. The film was *Britain Prepared,* which was premièred in London at the end of December 1915.

25. Thus the Committee was renamed the British Topical Committee for War Films in May 1916; its role was subsequently transferred to the new War Office Cinematograph Committee in October 1916; responsibility for official films finally passed to the Ministry of Information Cinematograph Department in June 1918.

26. Like *Quo Vadis?* and *Birth of a Nation.*

27. *Manchester Guardian,* 30 December 1915, p. 4.

28. The film ran for three hours and forty minutes, and even making allowance for the different conventions of factual film-making at the time, it is difficult to imagine it being well-received in other circumstances.

29. *Bioscope,* 13 January 1916, p. 190

30. *The Times,* 5 January 1916, p. 11.

31. *Star,* 5 January 1916, p. 3.

32. *The Cinema,* 17 January 1916, p. 2.

33. For further discussion of the circumstances in which these films were made see Reeves, *op. cit.* (1986), pp. 94–113 and pp. 145–57 for their content.

34. For a more detailed discussion of the circumstances in which the cameramen worked and the production of the film see Reeves, *op. cit.* (1986), pp. 94–113; S.D. Badsey, 'Battle of the Somme: British war-propaganda', *Historical Journal of Film, Radio and Television,* Vol. 3, No. 2, 1983, pp. 99–115; Nicholas Hiley's introduction to Geoffrey H. Malins (ed. by Low Warren), *How I Filmed the War,* London, 1920, reprinted by the Imperial War Museum in 1993.

35. Hiley argued this estimate in 'The Battle of the Somme and the British news media', a paper he presented at a conference held at the Centre de Recherche de l'Historial de la Grande Guerre, in Péronne on 21 July 1992.

36. For further discussion of the overseas distribution of the films see Nicholas Reeves, 'Film propaganda and its audience: the example of Britain's official films during the First World War', *Journal of Contemporary History,* Vol. 18, 1983, pp. 463–94.

37. For further discussion of the declining popularity of the films see Reeves, *op. cit.* (1986), pp. 223–7.

38. House of Lords Record Office (HLRO), Beaverbrook Papers, Series E, Vol. 14, File 'Cinema General May 1917 3-2', Beaverbrook to Hutton Wilson, 8 May 1917.

39. For more detailed discussion of the nature and role of the wartime official newsreel see Luke McKernan, *Topical Budget: The Great British News Film,* London, 1992, pp. 19–63. The further discussion of the official newsreel below derives from the same source.

40. For further discussion of these films see Reeves, *op. cit.* (1986), pp. 169–97.

41. See Reeves, *JCH* (1983), pp. 480–90.

42. PRO, INF4/1B First Report of the War Office Cinematograph Committee, September 1918.

43. Reeves, *JCH* (1983), p. 474.

44. 'Where is the British patriotic film?' *Kinematograph Weekly*, 27 September 1917, p. 107.

45. British Film Institute (BFI), William Jury Papers, Envelope 7, Arnold Bennett to Jury, 7 November 1918.

46. Indeed, so unacceptable was its style and ideology that it was decided to destroy the film – see Reeves, *op. cit.* (1986), pp. 125–30 and pp. 215–16.

47. BFI, William Jury Papers, Envelope 2, unsigned *Memo*, 24 October 1918.

48. HLRO Beaverbrook Papers Series 11, File 'Cinema Schemes', MoI *The Cinema*.

49. *Bioscope*, 15 February 1917, p. 737.

50. The estimate is Luke McKernan's in McKernan, *op. cit.*, pp. 46–7.

51. For a more detailed discussion of the reception of the film see Nicholas Reeves, 'Cinema, spectatorship and propaganda: *Battle of the Somme* (1916) and its contemporary audience', *Historical Journal of Film, Radio and Television*, Vol. 17, No. 1, 1997.

52. 'Amusements in York. The picture house', *Yorkshire Evening Press*, 29 August 1916, p. 3.

53. 'Quite between ourselves', *Regiment*, 2 September 1916, p. 219.

54. For a detailed discussion of the extent of faking in the film see Roger Smither, ' "A Wonderful Idea of the Fighting": the question of fakes in "The Battle of the Somme" ', *Historical Journal of Film, Radio and Television*, Vol. 13, No. 2, 1993, pp. 149–69.

55. 'Film pictures from the Somme', *Manchester Guardian*, 11 August 1916, p. 4.

56. J. A. Farrar to the editor, *Manchester Guardian*, 15 August 1916, p. 10.

57. H. Hensley Henson to the editor, *The Times*, 1 September 1916, p. 7.

58. James Cooper to the editor, *The Times*, 2 September 1916, p. 3.

59. In the years before the Imperial War Museum issued a video of the film with a piano accompaniment, I showed the film to undergraduate audiences in its entirety, in silence. Even in these enormously artificial circumstances the film held the audience's attention – indeed, a significant minority of those audiences were deeply moved by what they saw.

60. For further discussion of the practical difficulties under which the cameramen worked see Reeves, *op. cit.* (1986), pp. 94–113.

61. The film's ability to convey much of its meaning through the expressions on the soldiers' faces is lost almost entirely in the video print – it is only when the film is seen on the screen that the image achieves the level of definition in which this becomes clear.

62. 'Army notes: the Somme films', *Army and Navy Gazette*, 9 September 1916, p. 582.

63. James Douglas, 'The Somme pictures. Are they too painful for public exhibition?', *Star*, 25 August 1916, p. 2.

64. Robert Heatley to the editor, *Manchester Guardian*, 2 September 1916, p. 4.

65. 'Forty-six' to the editor, *The Times*, 2 September 1916, p. 3.

66. Jas Walmsley to the editor, *The Times*, 4 September 1916, p. 11.

67. 'Orbatus' to the editor, *The Times*, 2 September 1916, p. 3.

68. A.J.P. Taylor (ed.), *Lloyd George: A Diary by Frances Stevenson*, London, 1971, p. 112.

69. *Bioscope*, 7 September 1916, p. 957.

70. James A. Cooper to the editor, *The Times*, 2 September 1916.

71. 'The pictures on the Somme', *Manchester Guardian*, 21 August 1916, p. 4.

72. In both The Hague and the United States (Reeves, *op. cit.* (1986), pp. 245–6).

73. Douglas, *op. cit.*

74. *The Cinema: Its Present Position and Future Possibilities. Being the Report and Chief Evidence of an Enquiry Instituted by the National Council of Public Morals*, London, 1917, p. 280.

CHAPTER 2 Film Propaganda in the Soviet
Union, 1917–1928

For much of the First World War, the British government had attempted to
keep its propaganda activities secret and, for many years after the war the true
extent of the British government's role in the first half of the war remained
hidden.[1] In total contrast, the new Bolshevik regime, established in Russia
after the successful coup of October 1917, made absolutely no attempt to
conceal its propaganda; its People's Commissariat of Enlightenment was
established at the outset, responsible not just for education but for propaganda
as well. Indeed, education and propaganda were indivisible for the Bolsheviks,
both different facets of the same primary task of 'enlightenment' which was
central to their revolutionary project. This notion of propaganda as a tool of
'enlightenment' derives first and foremost from the ideology to which the
Bolsheviks were committed, for at the heart of Marxism was the proposition
that the revolutionary transformation of capitalism into socialism would
create a society in which, for the first time, human beings would break free
from alienation and thus achieve their true humanity. Socialism was envisaged
as a society in which human beings would become free, autonomous
individuals, able at last to realize their full human potential, and it followed,
therefore, that the Bolsheviks had no reason to conceal what they were doing –
indeed there was every reason to be as open and as straightforward about it as
possible. Moreover, Lenin and the Bolsheviks believed that their ideology was
grounded in hard, empirical data; Marx had identified the fundamental
scientific laws which govern human existence and any attempt to conceal this
'truth' from the people they served would be absurd. Therefore the position of
the revolutionary Bolshevik regime was precisely analogous to that of the
seventeenth-century Sacred Congregation for the Propagation of the Faith.
For, just like the Catholic Church, the Bolsheviks believed that they had to
take the 'gospel' of revolutionary socialism to all the people. Propaganda was
the central tool of enlightenment – indeed, propaganda to teach the people the
'truths' of Marxism–Leninism would in itself constitute one of the central
means whereby that enlightenment would be achieved.

LENIN AND PROPAGANDA

Yet if the Bolsheviks' singular approach to propaganda can be traced back to basic Marxist principles, Lenin's revisionism gave it an even greater importance. He argued that Marx's claim, that it was through the class struggles of capitalism that the working class would develop its revolutionary consciousness, was misplaced. Revolutionary consciousness 'could only be brought to them from the outside'; left to themselves they would develop only 'trade-union consciousness', pursuing the 'bourgeois' goals of better working conditions, higher pay and the like.[2] They would achieve revolutionary consciousness only if they were given appropriate leadership by a revolutionary intelligentsia that had developed an accurate analysis of the true nature of capitalism. That rigorous, complex analysis would then be translated into simple ideas, and it was these ideas that would be presented to the working classes through propaganda. Thus, it was this propaganda that would arouse the workers' revolutionary consciousness, and it therefore acquired an importance in the Leninist analysis that has no precedent in Marxism.

Lenin set out this strategy in his 1902 essay *What Is To Be Done?* and, in the years that followed, his small group of revolutionary socialists attempted to put it into practice in the very hostile world of late tsarist Russian politics. Until the outbreak of the First World War their progress was limited, but the war effected radical change in Russian society, and in these transformed circumstances the Bolsheviks were at last able to make substantial and rapid progress. Thus, while party membership was less than 10,000 before 1914, it exceeded 20,000 when Nicholas II abdicated in February 1917 and, just six months later, it was more than a quarter of a million.[3] By November, the Bolsheviks were able to mobilize almost ten million votes in the elections for the Constituent Assembly, held just weeks after they had seized power in their comparatively bloodless October coup. Propaganda played an important role in this spectacular transformation, and 1917 provides innumerable examples of the extent to which the strategy outlined 15 years earlier had been faithfully followed. Time and again the Bolsheviks transformed Lenin's complex analysis of why the time was ripe to make an immediate bid for power into hugely popular and simple slogans, slogans which struck home powerfully with their target audience – the disaffected soldiers and workers on the streets of the Russian cities. 'All power to the Soviets', or the even more breathtaking, 'Bread, Peace, Freedom', encapsulated the aspirations of an ever-larger proportion of the population, more and more of whom were (in their growing desperation) willing to lend their support to Lenin and the Bolsheviks.[4]

Important as propaganda had been in the years up to 1917, it became even more important once the Bolsheviks took power, not least because of the particular circumstances in which that happened. For the Bolshevik victory in October 1917 was premature. Most obviously, notwithstanding their recent progress, the Bolsheviks still did not command the active support of the majority of the population and, when it became clear that they would not accept the results of the November Constituent Assembly elections and hand over power to the Socialist Revolutionaries,[5] it was only a matter of time before a further struggle for power would begin. October 1917 was therefore the opening skirmish in the real battle for power; the war was not won until the Bolsheviks had defeated their enemies on the battlefields of the Civil War, three years later. The experience of the First World War had taught all the belligerents the importance of winning the battle for the hearts and minds of the people, and throughout the Civil War the Bolsheviks always committed desperately scarce resources to propaganda. Moreover, while military victory ensured that the Bolshevik position was incomparably more secure after 1920 than it had been before, the Civil War years left a terrible legacy of bitterness and resentment, and no one could argue that the Bolsheviks enjoyed the wholehearted support of all the people they now ruled. Finally, Lenin's death in 1924 once again raised doubts about the survival of Bolshevism and, while in the event it did not lead to a challenge to the Bolsheviks' power, no one knew this at the time. Thus, the changing political imperatives of the first seven years in power drove the Bolsheviks to continue to give propaganda a very high priority.

But there was another, less obvious, more important way in which the Bolshevik seizure of power in 1917 was premature for, while Lenin may have rejected Marx's expectation that the class struggle alone would raise the workers' revolutionary consciousness, he shared Marx's recognition that such a transformation in consciousness would be slow and difficult. The cultural baggage which had accumulated over centuries of pre-revolutionary history could not be swept aside in a moment and, just like Marx, Lenin assumed that it was only the long, bitter struggle to overthrow capitalism that would effect that transformation in the ideology of the mass of ordinary people out of which, and *only* out of which, a truly socialist society could be constructed. Socialism could not be built in a society that was still committed to bourgeois, capitalist ideology; it required the active, enthusiastic participation of the mass of the people whose ideology had been transformed through the furnace of the class struggle. The Bolsheviks had taken power at a very early stage in this historical process. The decision to embark on the final dismantling of Russian serfdom had only been taken in 1861: by the time the Bolsheviks took power in 1917, the attempt to replace Russian feudalism with a capitalistic Russian economy was far from complete and, while an industrial sector had been constructed, it was little more than an important island in a sea of rural backwardness. Thus, against everyone's expectations, the first socialist revolution had come, not in the advanced, industrialized West, but in a Russia that was still a world away from the modern, industrial society in which Marxists everywhere assumed the socialist revolution would be made. The Bolshevik victory was therefore, in this most fundamental sense, wholly premature.

The dilemma which therefore faced Lenin and the Bolsheviks in the early months after the October coup was a formidable one indeed. Economic modernization was clearly the overriding priority, but what about the transformation of attitudes and ideology which was just as much a precondition for the successful construction of a truly socialist society? Was there any way in which they could take steps to remedy that ideological 'backwardness' which was, in itself, one of the most striking characteristics of the situation in which they now found themselves? One answer would have been to concentrate entirely on the economy, secure in the knowledge that the forces of economic modernization would, in the end, deliver the necessary ideological transformation. But the problem with such an approach was its time scale – however dynamic Bolshevik economic policy, it would be two, probably three generations before the economic modernization of this vast, sprawling, backward economy would be complete. Surely there must be a quicker way? Surely it was possible to embark on the task of ideological transformation at once, ensuring at the very least that this aspect of the revolution would be achieved alongside the programme of economic modernization?

The Bolsheviks concluded that there was and, in a word, it was propaganda that would provide it. For while propaganda appeared to be simply one of the tasks entrusted to the new Commissariat of Enlightenment which was apparently primarily responsible for education, in reality Bolshevik education always served a political purpose. Thus, for example, while Lenin attached great importance to the need to achieve universal literacy, he was quite clear about why it was so important:

> As long as there is such a thing in the country as illiteracy, it is rather hard to talk about political education ... The illiterate person stands outside of politics. First it is necessary to teach him the alphabet. Without it there are only rumours, fairy tales, prejudices, but not politics.[6]

Education was thus both the precondition for politics, but also in itself a key weapon in the war for the transformation of the beliefs and ideology of the citizens of the new society. Education, in other words, was another form of propaganda. And propaganda was at the heart of the Bolshevik project for, in effecting radical change in attitudes and ideology, it would 'create' the new men, women and children who would be able to build socialism. In short, propaganda was at least as important to the Bolsheviks in power as it had been in the struggle for power – not without reason has Peter Kenez defined the Soviet Union in the first decade of its existence as the 'Propaganda State'.[7]

EXPECTATIONS FOR FILM PROPAGANDA

If propaganda in general was so important, what particular role did the Bolsheviks envisage for film as a medium for propaganda? In spite of

Russia's comparative economic backwardness, cinema had become established by 1914 as the dominant form of urban, working-class entertainment, outselling all other forms of commercial entertainment put together, although attempts to take cinema to the rural population had not proved successful. At first, this urban market was built almost entirely with imported films, but from 1908 onwards domestic film production began in earnest, and Russian film-makers quickly demonstrated that they were at least as imaginative and inventive as film-makers elsewhere. Certainly the traditional view that little work of interest was done in Russia in the years before the Revolution has been comprehensively destroyed by recent scholarship which has demonstrated just how wide-ranging, sophisticated and distinctive Russian film production of this period was.[8] Moreover, when the war deprived Russian exhibitors of most of their normal sources of supply, Russian film producers quickly responded to the new situation and, by 1916, imported films accounted for just 20 per cent of the films showing in Russian cinemas.[9]

The experience of war also provoked an entirely new understanding of the political potential of cinema, and early in the war the tsarist regime took the decision to allow only its own official cameramen access to the front. While this was broadly similar to the decision taken rather later in Britain, it did not lead to the production of successful propaganda films like *Battle of the Somme*. The Skobelev Committee, a charitable body set up to provide help to veterans of the Russo-Japanese War, was the unlikely institution charged with supervising official film-making, a task for which it appears to have been wholly unsuited. Certainly few official films reached Russian cinemas and the way in which film propaganda was handled illustrates the regime's failure to understand the importance of public opinion. That said, others showed a sharper grasp of the new realities. At the beginning of the war, the Duma Deputy Purishkevich argued for a government monopoly in the film industry, and in the following year another politician, V.M. Dementev, proposed that a nationalized cinema should become a monopolistic instrument of tsarist propaganda. None of these ideas were taken further but, at the end of 1916, the Minister of the Interior, Protopopov, set up an interdepartmental commission to develop legislation to supervise the making and importation of films. This initiative provoked the Minister of Education to prepare a counter-proposal for the establishment of a Special Cinema Committee within his Ministry.[10] In the event, with Nicholas's abdication the following February, all of this was too little, too late; it does nevertheless provide an indication of the way in which, even in tsarist Russia, the radicalizing impact of the war prompted even the most conservative politicians to formulate ways in which cinema might play a more important role in the manipulation of public opinion.

The February Revolution made little impact on the Russian film production industry, and in the months between February and October 1917 no less than 245 (largely short) feature films were produced. While some of these made a half-hearted attempt to capitalize on the anti-monarchist sentiments of the period, by and large the studios continued to make the kind of films that had proved popular in the past, with melodramas and crime stories proving especially common. On the other hand, it was in these months that one of the leading directors of the period, Yakov Protazanov, completed *Father Sergius*, in Kenez' judgement 'the crowning achievement of Russian pre-revolutionary cinema and one of the finest silent films ever made anywhere',[11] and the timing of this film's release provides a salutary reminder of the extent of the achievements of the pre-revolutionary cinema. Certainly it was in the knowledge of the substantial commercial and creative achievements of this Russian film industry that the new regime began to formulate its own view of the role which cinema might play in the revolutionary task ahead.

Almost everything that has ever been written about Soviet cinema includes a reference to the account given by Anatoli Lunacharsky (head of the People's Commissariat of Enlightenment) of his conversation with Lenin in February 1922, which apparently ended with a smiling Lenin saying to Lunacharsky: 'Among our people you are reported to be a patron of art so you must remember that of all the arts for us the most important is cinema.'[12] As several historians have pointed out, Lunacharsky is not always the most reliable witness, and Lenin's emphasis on art is potentially misleading – his essentially conservative aesthetics make it very unlikely that he saw cinema as superior to other arts like theatre or literature. On the other hand, the words probably deserve repeated quotation, for they articulate an enthusiasm for cinema which was shared by most other senior Bolsheviks. It was demonstrated even more clearly by Trotsky in July 1923, in a lengthy article in *Pravda* which bemoaned the Bolsheviks' lack of progress in using cinema:

> This weapon which cries out to be used, is the best instrument for propaganda, technical, educational and industrial propaganda, propaganda against alcohol, propaganda for sanitation, political propaganda, any kind of propaganda you please, a propaganda which is accessible to everyone, which is attractive, cuts into the memory and may be a possible source of revenue.

Moreover, the cinema could compete successfully with the 'beer-shop and the public house' – it could even lead people away from the Church. The Church had traditionally appealed to the people through the use of 'theatrical methods', offering 'a range of social-aesthetic attractions not provided by the factory, the family or the workaday street'. To counter this, the Bolsheviks must turn to the cinema, 'the most powerful – because it is the most democratic instrument of the theatre'. It could provide:

> ... images of greater grip than are provided by the richest Church, grown wise in the experience of a thousand years ... The cinema amuses, educates, strikes the imagination by images, and liberates you from the need of crossing the Church

door. The cinema is a great competitor not only of the public-house, but of the Church. Here is an instrument which we must secure at all costs![13]

It was cinema's ability to entertain *and* educate that made it, in Trotsky's view, such a potent weapon. Its huge popular appeal had already attracted people away from the churches, and the manner in which it could present ideas to those mass audiences would enable it to outdo the churches in making its messages memorable and persuasive. It was a powerful case, persuasively argued.

Nor is it difficult to understand why the Bolsheviks were so enthusiastic about the cinema, for Trotsky had not in fact exhausted the list of attributes which made it so attractive to them. Six years before they took power, the writer Leonid Andreyev had drawn attention to some of these other qualities:

> The miraculous Cinema! ... What is there to compare with it: aerial flight, the telegraph and the telephone, even the press itself? It is portable and can be packed in a box: it is sent all over the world through the post like an ordinary newspaper. Having no language, being equally intelligible to the people of St Petersburg and the savages of Calcutta, it truly becomes the genius of international contact.[14]

In essence, Andreyev identified three key ideas. First, cinema was a technological medium, and this in itself made it hugely attractive. The Bolsheviks understood that the socialist utopia of which they dreamed could only be built with the most modern, the most advanced, industrial technology – what then could be more appropriate than a medium like cinema to carry its messages to the people, for cinema was *in itself* a manifestation of such advanced technology. The very act of taking cinema to those rural areas which had never had access to the new technology was an act of propaganda in itself, the projector and its large projected images evidence of the modern, progressive character of the new regime. Secondly, cinema was portable – films could be dispatched all over the world, not least because they could be so easily duplicated. This was equally important to the Bolsheviks, both because of the vast population they needed to reach (over 140 million at the end of the civil war), and the immense geographical area in which that population lived (a total land area of over 22 million square kilometres). Moreover, although late tsarist industrialization had generated some significant urbanization, in 1920 85 per cent of the total population was still to be found living in the rural areas. Thus, while the existing institutions of cinema could reach the urban population, it was the technology's mobility and reproducibility that promised the possibility of taking the films to the vast mass of the rural population.

But perhaps the most important of Andreyev's claims was the notion that cinema was 'equally intelligible' to all for, of the many problems which stood in the way of effective Bolshevik propaganda, the linguistic and cultural diversity of the population was perhaps the most formidable. Over 100 different languages were spoken in the Soviet Union and this, coupled with the fact that three out of every five adults were illiterate,[15] reveals the scale of the problem they faced. Even if the majority of the population had been literate, the need to make literary propaganda available in so many different languages would have been a formidable task, but the extent of adult illiteracy made it essential that the Bolsheviks found other ways of communicating with that population. Cinema seemed to offer the perfect solution – as a 1924 Soviet newspaper put it, 'the cinema is the only book that even the illiterate can read'.[16] For while it is now understood that the 'language' of cinema is not in fact universal, with the construction of meaning being an activity in which the audience actively participates, this was not how anyone saw it at the time. They looked at the world-wide growth of the cinema, in which the same films enjoyed success wherever they were shown, and concluded that film was indeed a 'universal language', capable of communicating the same meaning to different audiences all around the world. Moreover, as cinema moved away from the simplicity of the early factual films into the more complex narratives of fiction films, its ability to communicate to the same world-wide audiences was in no way impaired. The stars who were increasingly used to market these films proved just as attractive in St Petersburg or Moscow as they had been in their native Paris or New York.

Thus, cinema appeared to provide the Bolsheviks with the ideal medium in which to construct their propaganda – modern, practical, uniquely equipped to break through the barriers of language, culture and tradition which so divided their target audience. But while it was one thing to envisage such a role for cinema in the new society, it was quite another to translate such aspirations into practice and, in assessing the extent of Bolshevik success, it makes sense to separate discussion of the Civil War period from the years that followed, when, from every point of view, the circumstances were so profoundly different.

THE ACHIEVEMENTS OF THE CIVIL WAR YEARS

By the time the Bolsheviks took power in October 1917, the war had already had a devastating impact on the Russian economy. Prices had risen by over 700 per cent since 1914, and wages had long since lost the ability to keep pace. Foreign trade had all but collapsed and industrial output declined sharply in 1917, a decline that was intensified by the increasing collapse of the railway network, which in turn made it increasingly difficult to sustain food supplies both to the armies at the front and to the urban populations at home. And yet, bad as all this was, it pales into insignificance in comparison with the catastrophic economic collapse which was to come in the years that followed. By the end of the Civil War in 1921, industrial production was 70 per cent lower than it had been in 1913, a collapse so devastating that many people simply fled the towns in an increasingly desperate search for the necessities of life – the populations of Moscow and Petrograd fell by over half between 1917 and 1920. Even food production, which had been sustained at pre-war levels until 1917, declined by over 25 per cent.[17] Such widespread economic dislocation was made even worse, first by the regime's policy of requisitioning the food needed by the Red Armies, and also by the severe drought in the Volga basin in 1920 and 1921: the results were desperate indeed, and in the ensuing famine some five million people died, even though the regime allowed Western aid into the country.[18]

Desperate as the economic and social conditions were, political realities were almost as harsh. On the one hand, the Bolsheviks recognized the importance of maximizing popular support for their cause, and propaganda was always given a very high priority. Trotsky insisted, for example, that one compartment on all troop trains would be reserved for the propagandists, in spite of the fact that the need to move troops quickly to where they were most needed was a critical aspect of Red Army strategy. On the other hand, the Bolsheviks never had any qualms about riding roughshod over opposition, if (in their judgement) circumstances demanded it. Thus, in the field of economic policy, for example, they were determined to assume direct control of the economy, and the nationalization of the state bank and the formation of the Supreme Economic Council constituted early indications of that determination. In the growing crisis of the Civil War, nationalization was extended to all industrial enterprises, trade was outlawed, workers' control abolished. Most urgent of all, however, was the securing of sufficient food supplies for both the towns and the army and, while an initial attempt was made to purchase grain through a state grain monopoly, as the situation deteriorated, the Bolsheviks simply requisitioned the food they needed, crushing any resistance by force. Both the Red Army and, more importantly, the Cheka (the Bolsheviks' internal security force), used any methods, however brutal, to acquire the resources on which the regime's very survival depended. Indeed it was probably the actions of the Cheka that gave the population its clearest indication of just how 'resolute' the Bolsheviks really were. As early as December 1917 Lenin had called for 'a purge of the Russian land from all vermin', which he defined in part as the 'idle rich', 'priests', 'bureaucrats' and 'slovenly and hysterical intellectuals'; eight months later *Pravda* demanded: 'The towns must be cleansed of this bourgeois putrefaction ... All who are dangerous to the cause of the revolution must be exterminated.'[19] Precisely how many people were killed by the Cheka in these years as it implemented this purge will probably never be known – estimates range from as few as 50,000 to as many as 300,000 and, while such figures may look small in relation to the Stalinist purges of the 1930s, they nevertheless demonstrate the willingness of the new regime to use state terror as one of the ways of sustaining its position.

Thus, in addition to the successes on the battlefield, the Bolshevik victory at the end of the Civil War was the product of two quite different strategies:

propaganda to maximize support for their cause, coupled with brute force to maintain and defend their position. In the course of all of this, the people of the Soviet Union had endured devastation of truly biblical proportions. They had suffered more as a consequence of the First World War than any other belligerent society, and yet Russia's withdrawal from that war served only to impose even greater suffering – economic disintegration, bitter and bloody civil war, the brutal exercise of state terror (on all sides), famine and disease. And while there is therefore a critical sense in which the Bolshevik victory was hollow indeed, it may be that the mass of the people now saw the Bolsheviks as the lesser of the various evils that confronted them. If this was in fact true, then Bolshevik propaganda had clearly served them well. In all the circumstances, a grudging acceptance of their rule was surely the very most that could have been achieved.

It is within this context, therefore, that we have to examine the way in which the Bolsheviks used film as one important medium of propaganda during the Civil War. The mounting economic crisis made it increasingly difficult for the film industry to function: the collapse of international trade cut off access to Western film stock and equipment and made it more and more difficult for the studios to remain in production; interruptions in the electricity supply made it difficult to heat the cinemas; and the mounting crisis in transportation made it more and more difficult to distribute the films. But, most important of all, an essentially capitalistic film industry concluded that it had no future in the brave new world of the Soviet Union, and film-makers began to leave Moscow, first for the sunnier climate of the Odessa studios and ultimately, when the White Armies of the anti-Bolsheviks were defeated, for Berlin or Paris. While this loss of personnel was devastating enough, the film-makers often took equipment with them as well, including (most precious of all), raw film stock and cameras.[20] It is difficult to envisage a more difficult set of circumstances for a regime that had such high hopes of using the cinema as a medium of propaganda. Hardly surprising then, that the Bolsheviks' initial approaches towards the film industry were both tentative and cautious.

Moreover, the Bolsheviks had taken power with no clear strategy for the film industry, and in consequence the early months saw a number of different, uncoordinated initiatives. In January 1918, the Division of Photography and Cinema was established within the Extramural Education Department of the Commissariat of Enlightenment, a department run by no less a figure than Lenin's wife, N.K. Krupskaya. Krupskaya's department was responsible for propaganda among adults, and she was presumably given this new responsibility on the assumption that film would prove especially useful for such a target audience, although the resources at her disposal were extremely limited – one projector, a few newsreels and some educational films.[21] The position improved slightly when the Division subsequently expropriated the assets of the Skobelev Committee, thereby acquiring resources which enabled it to make a few short newsreels. At the same time as these initiatives were taken at the centre, a number of local Soviets took matters into their own hands, including (on occasion) confiscating cinemas for their own use; the Moscow and Petrograd Soviets embarked on even more ambitious measures. Thus, the Moscow Soviet encouraged film workers to monitor the activities of their bosses to try to prevent the movement of film assets out of the city, while the Petrograd Soviet established its own Photo-Cinema Committee, using such funds as it had at its disposal to make short newsreels and maintain some exhibition facilities in the city.[22]

None of this, however, amounted to much more than tinkering, and it soon became clear that the film industry was facing a major crisis. An audit carried out by the Commissariat of Enlightenment found that film production was on the brink of collapse: starved of its normal Western sources of supply since 1914, it was fast approaching the point where there would be no resources left with which to make new films. As for film exhibition, those cinemas that were still in business screened old, scratched prints of films made before the Revolution. In mounting desperation, the Commissariat embarked on a number of abortive attempts to try to remedy these difficulties, culminating in the notorious affair in which the Italian film agent Cibrario was entrusted with no less than one million dollars of precious foreign currency with which to purchase supplies and equipment in the West. He left Moscow at the end of 1918, never to return: none of the equipment was ever purchased, the money was lost. The whole episode marked a startling encounter between Bolshevik naiveté and unscrupulous business practice.[23]

In all these circumstances, the decision on 27 August 1919 to nationalize the film industry must have looked like the decisive strategic intervention which had been so lacking until then. A brand-new organization, the All-Russian Photographic and Cinematographic Section of the Commissariat of Enlightenment (VFKO) would co-ordinate all existing cinema activities and assume responsibility for the future nationalization of individual film institutions. But, in practice, there was a huge gulf between the formulation of policy and its implementation. Companies were nationalized, but in almost every case this happened *after* they had ceased to trade; far from preventing the hoarding or transfer of equipment and supplies (the avowed intention of the measure) it served, once again, to persuade any private companies still operating in areas controlled by the Bolsheviks to leave. Thus, while the Bolsheviks may have had high hopes for the medium of film, in practice, almost every policy initiative which they pursued during the Civil War years proved counter-productive. By the end of the Civil War, film-making had almost ground to a halt and the number of operating cinemas had declined dramatically – of Moscow's pre-war 143 cinemas, for example, not one was still in operation in the autumn of 1921.[24]

On the other hand, such a negative assessment of the Civil War years is misleading, for remarkable progress was made in three areas, namely the training of new film-makers, the production of short agitational films and a number of innovative attempts to ensure that those films reached their target audiences. The first, and in many ways the most important, tackled the acute shortage of trained personnel that had resulted from the recent exodus of Russian film-makers. Not that there was any lack of volunteers: a widespread enthusiasm for cinema, especially in revolutionary circles, meant that there was never any shortage of young people eager to work with film; the problem was how to give them the training which would enable them to translate that enthusiasm into effective film-making. The form of training that had been adopted in film industries around the world was one of apprenticeship: a would-be film-maker would join a studio and working, for example, alongside the cameraman or editor would, by an informal process of assistance and imitation, acquire the relevant skills. But such an apprenticeship model would not work in revolutionary Russia – so many film-makers had left and so many companies had closed down. In addition, there was the further problem of ideology: young film-maker apprentices did not simply learn technical skills, they also assimilated the 'bourgeois' ideology which was at the heart of the commercial preoccupations of these capitalistic organizations.

The Bolshevik solution to this problem was truly revolutionary, even though the idea of a film school had been canvassed before the Revolution.[25] Vladimir Gardin, an established pre-war director and actor, was appointed head of the fiction film section of VFKO in 1918, and he proposed the establishment of 10 new State Schools of Cinema Art, each with a thousand students, to create a new 'army' of film-makers – in the event, VFKO agreed to set up one such school in Moscow, with Gardin as its first director.[26] The purpose of the new initiative was set out by Lunacharsky:

> We need cadres of workers who are free from the habits and strivings of the old bourgeois entrepreneurial hacks and are able to elevate the cinema to the heights of the artistic and socio-political tasks facing the proletariat, especially in the current period of intensified struggle.[27]

Thus, for the first time anywhere in the world, film-makers would be trained in a film school. Established in September 1919, it provided its students with the opportunity to learn their craft in an environment where, alongside the acquisition of technical skills, there was abundant opportunity both for the exposition of revolutionary ideology and for intense debate as to how such ideology might best be translated into film-making practice. Gardin may have been trained in the ways of the tsarist film industry, but he was passionately committed to the rigorous theoretical investigation of the nature of film and, from the outset, his Film School gave the highest possible priority to just such issues. Thus, it was not the celebrated experiments conducted by Lev Kuleshov after he joined the School in 1920 that gave such an impetus to experiment and innovation.[28] Gardin had already put such preoccupations at the very heart of its work, and recent scholarship properly emphasizes his contribution, demonstrating the extent to which Kuleshov's work was, at least in part, a response to Gardin's earlier work, both in his assessment of the role of the actor and in his developing notion of montage.[29] In short, the foundation of the State Film School was much more than a strategy to make good the desperate lack of personnel that had so weakened the industry after the Revolution; the particular form of this initiative put experiment, innovation and theoretical debate right at the heart of its work.

At much the same time, the new regime was taking its first tentative steps towards the production of propaganda films. These first films took the form of simple newsreels, using the very limited resources that had been inherited from the Skobelev Committee. A combination of an acute lack of film stock and the almost total absence of experienced film-makers meant that the results were not especially impressive, and so few prints could be made that they were seen by only a tiny fraction of the potential audience. On the other hand, there were times when even the most simple newsreel could be used to good effect. Following an attempt on his life in 1918, for example, Lenin was filmed walking in the Kremlin, and this footage was used to counter rumours that he was dead. Moreover, the very act of showing footage of the Bolshevik leaders to people who had no previous experience of the cinema may well have forged a new link with the people – it almost certainly constructed a more powerful and enduring image than the static and stylized icons of the tsars. At the very least, it gave those outside the urban areas their first clear image of the Bolshevik leaders, an important achievement in itself in a society in which they were still comparatively unknown.

The short propaganda films that were made soon after were even more interesting. Described by the term *agitka* (literally 'a little agitational piece'), these short films (between 5 and 30 minutes in length) presented simple propaganda messages. Between the summer of 1918 and the end of the Civil War, 60 such *agitki* were made, and while this may not seem an especially large number, given the desperate and mounting shortages of the period it was, in reality, a remarkable achievement. The very first *agitki* were little more than animated posters – a film exhorting the audience to give clothes to the soldiers of the Red Army, for example, consisted of nothing more than footage of the suffering soldiers of the Red Army.[30] But, not least because the early films were commissioned from established studios, it was not long before the Bolsheviks began to take advantage of their expertise in the narrative fiction film. Thus *For the Red Flag* and *Father and Son*, both released in 1919, explore the contrasting ideologies of fathers and sons, although in the former it is the father who joins the Red Army first, while in the latter it is the son who is committed to the cause. In *Peace to the Shacks and War to the Palaces* (1919), a poor peasant boy comes to understand the strength of the Bolshevik position by contrasting his own situation with that of a rich landlord – he too joins the Red Army. The Film School also made a contribution to work of this kind, with *In the Days of Battle* and *Hammer and Sickle* in 1919 and *At the Red Front* in 1920, although its ability to produce more *agitki* was severely constrained by its very limited resources.[31] Indeed, this lack of resources was one of the key factors determining the form of the emerging Soviet film culture, for the absence of film stock forced film-makers back to footage that already existed, and they soon understood that the way in which that footage was edited could determine the way meaning was constructed in the film. Thus, footage of the tsar would have made one kind of statement before the Revolution; precisely the same footage could be used to very different effect in a Bolshevik film, where the juxtaposition of one shot with another, underlined by the explicit ideology of the inter-titles, would create a very different meaning.[32]

The importance of these films becomes even clearer in the third area of achievement in this period, for it was in the field of exhibition that the Bolsheviks made perhaps their most spectacular innovations. Early in the century some entrepreneurs had toured rural areas armed with a projector and a supply of films, and there had even been attempts to establish mobile cinemas on barges. But as the cinema became established in permanent locations in urban areas, it became obvious that this was a more profitable business, and mobile rural exhibition was abandoned.[33] The rapidly deteriorating economic circumstances of the Civil War, however, changed all that. The urban market started to collapse, and in any event the key battles of the war were not being fought in the major urban centres of population. It was, therefore, increasingly important to take propaganda to the people outside the towns, and the Bolsheviks set about establishing a network of *agitpunkty* (agitational centres) at strategic locations, like railway junctions or large settlements. While the facilities had much in common with contemporary community centres (usually including a library, a schoolroom, a canteen, a stage and a cinema), their purpose was political, to make and distribute propaganda in the local area; 140 such *agitpunkty* were established in 1919, and a further 220 the following year.[34]

In the short term, however, the Bolsheviks achieved rather more spectacular success by using trains and other forms of transport as a way of taking propaganda to the people. One compartment in troop trains had always been reserved for the propaganda section of the Red Army, but the range of activities that could be mounted from a single compartment was strictly limited; how much more could be achieved by equipping a whole train for propaganda? The first experimental train, the *V.I. Lenin*, was hurriedly prepared and left Moscow for a trial run on 13 August 1918, its nine coaches equipped with a bookshop, a library, an office and living quarters. The train and its crew spent two weeks distributing pamphlets and newspapers to Red Army units, and the trip was so successful that Trotsky ordered five similar trains, the last of which was finally delivered in 1920. Even more important, a Commission (controlled directly by the Party's Central Executive Committee) was established to develop the initiative further, by constructing a fleet of trains and steamers to establish, in the words of a 1919 resolution, 'ties between the localities and the centre, to agitate, to carry out propaganda, to bring information, and to supply literature'.[35]

The trains equipped by the Commission were certainly better resourced than the *Lenin*. Made up of 16 or 18 coaches, the outside of the rolling stock was lavishly decorated and, while some early examples were rather too sophisticated for the target audience, more realistic imagery was soon employed. Each train had a staff of over a hundred, of whom fewer than 20 were political workers – the majority provided the technical services to support the train's work. For, in addition to propaganda through speeches and lectures, the trains produced their own newspapers, leaflets and posters. The great advantage of the trains was their flexibility – they could be deployed where they were most needed. The *Lenin*, for example, was used in the early weeks of 1919 in areas recently occupied by German troops; later in the year, it was sent to the Ukrainian Front, where battle was now joined with the White Armies whose advance to Tula threatened precious food supplies.

Each section of the train produced propaganda as well as distributing it, and the film section was no exception – whenever supplies of film stock permitted, new footage was shot which would then be returned to the centre and used in future *agitki*. That said, the primary purpose was to take films from the centre to the people and, of all the media employed by the agit-trains, cinema invariably made the greatest impact, not least because so many members of the rural population were encountering it for the first time. Invariably it was the film shows that attracted an audience in the first place and, once people had come to see the films, they would be exposed to other forms of propaganda as well. Film proved especially popular with children, and the trains were careful to cater for their needs separately, with special daytime screenings; evening screenings were targeted at an adult audience. What data there are suggest that the film shows attracted large audiences: in 12 journeys between April 1919 and December 1920 the *October Revolution* held over 430 film shows, attended by over 630,000 people; a three-month trip by the agit-steamer, the *Red Star*, arranged 196 film shows, attended by 225,000 people. In all, film propaganda made an impressive debut on the trains and steamers, and the proposition that cinema was especially well-equipped to reach the disparate populations of the Soviet Union was powerfully endorsed by Nariman Narimanov, an Azerbaijani writer and Party activist:

> In the East, where people have grown accustomed to thinking primarily in images, the cinema is the sole possible means of propaganda because it does not require the preliminary, gradual preparation of the masses. The Eastern peasant accepts everything that he sees on the screen as the most fundamental and genuine reality.[36]

The Party was so impressed with their success that the trains continued to make their propaganda forays into the countryside throughout the 1920s;

they were used in the 1930s as well, although they were eventually displaced by the growth of the cinema network and the growing popularity of radio as an alternative propaganda medium. The agit-trains reappeared, however, during the Second World War.

Thus, the Civil War years were of major importance in the longer-term history of Soviet cinema. A combination of harsh economic realities and the unco-ordinated and apparently threatening policy objectives of the Bolshevik Party drove most existing film companies either out of business or out of the country, and the Bolsheviks were forced to rebuild the film industry almost from scratch. Moreover they were set this task in the most difficult of circumstances, when every conceivable resource was in desperately short supply, and this in itself imposed constraints which no amount of revolutionary enthusiasm could overcome. Notwithstanding these circumstances, however, important foundations were laid, notably the State Film School and the production of the first distinctively Bolshevik propaganda films. Moreover, in using trains and steamers to try to ensure that their propaganda messages reached their intended target audiences, the Bolsheviks took the technology of cinema to hundreds of thousands of people who had never encountered the medium before, and not only did its novelty serve to attract people who might otherwise have stayed away, the very act of showing films in these circumstances was surely effective propaganda. The flickering images on the screen alongside the agit-train spoke directly and eloquently of the modern, industrial society to which the Bolsheviks were so passionately committed. In the truly devastating circumstances of the Civil War, Soviet film propaganda had made a remarkable beginning.

THE 1920s

Impressive as these achievements were, however, the task which now confronted the Bolsheviks was even more formidable. War, revolution and civil war had largely destroyed the urban, industrial economy and had massively weakened agriculture; there was a real danger that even more complete economic collapse was still to come. More important, this rapidly deteriorating situation brought new and deeply worrying signs of dissent in both town and country, encapsulated most famously in the mutiny of the Kronstadt sailors in March 1921 and, while the Party crushed the revolt by force, at the same time it introduced new economic policies designed precisely to remedy the causes of that dissent. Thus, it turned its back on War Communism, the crude attempt at economic management of the Civil War years, and introduced in its place the New Economic Policy (NEP). Significantly, the starting-point for NEP was the abandonment of the compulsory procurement of foodstuffs and its replacement with a tax in kind, set at a much lower level than the earlier compulsory deliveries. At a stroke, this restored the incentive for peasants to increase food production, in the knowledge that any surpluses could be sold for profit on the market – provided that the opportunity for private trade was restored and that there were products for the peasants to buy. Moreover, it was recognized that the quickest way of restoring the production of such consumer goods would be to allow capitalistic enterprise to re-emerge in many small and medium-sized factories, and in the retail and service sectors that supported them. Not that the regime abandoned its attempt to manage the economy: it retained control of the central bank, large-scale industry and foreign trade, and the Supreme Economic Council continued to attempt to manage the economy as a whole. Indeed, even in those areas of the industrial economy where the market was apparently dominant, the government maintained an important presence in the form of government trusts, large semi-private companies which represented another form of the compromise between public and private commerce that was at the heart of NEP.

But none of this could conceal the extent of the change that had taken place. The Party that had been so wedded to the immediate abolition of capitalism, was now committed to its reintroduction. And, in the main, NEP achieved its objectives. Agriculture recovered quickly, and by 1925 had regained the level of output achieved pre-war. The hunger and the desperate shortages of the Civil War were over, and although many of the fundamental structural problems of agriculture remained to be addressed, many peasants were better off than they had been for years. Industrial recovery was equally clear, with output reaching (and invariably exceeding) pre-war levels of production in all industries by 1928. The expansion and modernization of the industrial economy was under way again, even if a combination of a rapidly rising population, mounting urban unemployment and new market-driven wage policies prevented any substantial improvement in the standard of living of urban workers. The platform on which future Soviet economic development could be built was in place by 1928, and NEP had been largely responsible for its construction.

This, then, was the very different environment within which the Bolsheviks set out to translate their huge ambitions for the film industry into practice for, notwithstanding the remarkable achievements of the Civil War years, a very great deal remained to be done. Every part of the pre-revolutionary film industry was in ruins and it would all have to be reconstructed if the Bolshevik dream of using film as the medium capable of reaching the Soviet Union's vast, disparate population was ever to be achieved. Above all, they had to solve the twin problems of reviving large-scale film production, and ensuring that these new films would in fact be seen by the millions of people at whom the propaganda messages were to be targeted. The agit-trains and agit-steamers represented an ingenious short-term solution to the latter problem – over the longer term, the urban cinemas would have to be reopened and a different, more durable method of taking films to the huge rural population would have to be found. It was, indeed, a formidable challenge.

At the heart of NEP was the assumption that market forces were capable of generating sufficient capital to finance Soviet economic recovery, and the immensely profitable character of both the pre-revolutionary Russian cinema and its even more successful Western counterparts, suggested that the film industry was singularly well-placed to play this role. Indeed, even in the very unfavourable circumstances at the end of the Civil War, cinema demonstrated just how powerful an attraction it was. Huntly Carter, an English journalist who visited the Soviet Union regularly at this time, vividly describes buildings devastated by war and neglect which, in spite of frequent breakdowns (resulting from old prints and poor projection equipment), still did very good business.[37] Audiences starved of access to the cinema for so long had no choice but to endure these conditions if they wanted to see a film, and those few companies that had not left Russia during the Civil War were soon in business again. By early 1922 at least five major firms were re-established in Moscow, although the single most powerful company at this time was Sevzapkino of Petrograd, an organization set up by the Petrograd Soviet's Cinema Committee. With the introduction of NEP, it became a private company and quickly established a dominant position in its local market.[38]

What role then did the central government propose to play in this re-emerging film industry? In particular, where did the revival of a commercial film industry leave VFKO, that section of the Commissariat of Enlightenment which had been given responsibility for supervising the full-scale nationalization of the film industry? For a while the government appears to have been unclear how to tackle the problem and, on no less than three separate occasions in 1921, VFKO was the subject of reorganization until, finally, in December 1921 it was decided that it would have to conform to the imperatives of NEP and generate its own capital without access to state funding. Yet the position may still not have been entirely clear for, on at least two occasions thereafter, VFKO asked for state funds to enable it to purchase films and equipment abroad, requests that were denied. By the end of 1921, Peter Voevodin (head of VFKO) was proposing a more radical approach – VFKO should be reorganized as a trust, with capital of 2000 million gold roubles and an export fund.[39]

The government's only response was to set up a commission, which reported the following spring. It proposed a new, central organization to control all forms of film distribution throughout the Soviet Union, retaining the right to lease or rent equipment, studios and cinemas to others. But nothing happened. For months the government prevaricated and it was not until the end of 1922 that this proposal was finally implemented and VFKO was replaced by the Central State Photographic and Cinematographic Enterprise (Goskino). Moreover, there was still no support for Voevodin's assertion that such an organization could only succeed with substantial capital funding. Goskino inherited VFKO's assets but, over the next two years, every attempt to secure additional government investment was unsuccessful for, in the context of prevailing NEP assumptions, such investment was considered unnecessary. Market forces would drive economic reconstruction forward, and the film industry was seen to be in an especially strong position; the long queues waiting patiently to see old films in dilapidated cinemas providing the most eloquent testimony to cinema's continuing ability to sell its products. Therefore, Trotsky argued, with appropriate management, cinema could yield the same revenues to 'the government of the workers' as the vodka monopoly had generated for the tsarist regime; it was not simply the best medium for propaganda, it held out enormous commercial possibilities as well.[40] What possible justification could there be for devoting scarce public funds to an industry so well-placed to generate the capital for its own reconstruction?

Thus, throughout the first two years of its existence Goskino had to manage without public funding and initially progress was very limited. Attempts to persuade Western film companies to invest directly in the Soviet film industry came to little, and the first important breakthrough came from the quite different source of *Internationale Arbeitershilfe* – Workers' International Relief (WIR) – an organization set up by the German Communist Party in 1921 to provide aid for victims of the Soviet famine.[41] WIR initially used Soviet footage to publicize its cause, and it soon began to sponsor the production of new films. Moreover, once the famine was over, WIR helped Soviet organizations purchase film stock and equipment, making credits available in expectation of future profits from the exhibition of Soviet films in the West. Accordingly, in March 1923, Goskino made an initial purchase of film stock and foreign films; a much larger purchase of films, equipment and raw film stock followed in September.[42] In all, WIR arranged for the supply of some 80 per cent of the films, film stock and equipment that were imported into the Soviet Union in the years 1922 and 1923, and there can be little doubt that this aid came at an especially important moment – Goskino's 1924 production of Kuleshov's remarkable comedy, *The Extraordinary Adventures of Mr West in the Land of the Bolsheviks*, would almost certainly have been impossible without it.

That said, perhaps the most important form of WIR intervention came with its capital investment in an individual Soviet film company. Mezhrabpom-Rus was a joint production and distribution company, formed in 1924 between WIR's subsidiary Aufbau (which initially owned half the company) and Rus, an experimental film collective. The company was immensely successful, concentrating on the production of popular films with ever-larger production values. Indeed, it was Mezhrabpom-Rus that first demonstrated that an indigenous company could produce films that would sell well on the domestic market, an approach that was exemplified most clearly in the enormous success achieved by the horror melodrama *The Bear's Wedding* (1926). The company was so successful that it established an important presence in film exhibition as well, acquiring three of the Soviet Union's largest cinemas – two in Moscow and one in Leningrad.

Important as all this was in enabling parts of the Soviet film industry to take the first crucial steps towards recovery, the really decisive breakthrough came with the decision, early in 1922, to import large numbers of foreign films. Lenin ordered these imports in the expectation that, with appropriate marketing, they would generate the box-office income out of which the Soviet film industry could in future be financed. Thus such films would be exhibited as much 'for their receipts' as for their ability to entertain, and while he was careful to emphasize that no 'obscene or counter-revolutionary' films should be shown, it is clear that it was the most popular (and thus the most commercial) foreign films that would fulfil this role most effectively.[43] Although these films were to be used primarily to raise box-office revenues, each programme would also include a short educational or propaganda film, and Lenin had no doubt which would make the larger impact on the audience. As he said to Lunacharsky: 'If you have a good newsreel, serious and educational pictures, then it doesn't matter if, to attract the public, you have some kind of useless picture of the more or less usual type.'[44] Nothing illustrates more clearly the extent of the Bolsheviks' naïve faith in the strength of their ideology – faced with the essentially trivial content of Hollywood films and the inherently serious and 'truthful' message of the Soviet film, any audience would surely choose the latter. Just how misplaced such an assumption proved to be will become clear below.

While such an approach might have been implemented before 1922, it was only then that the necessary economic preconditions were in place. In particular, the foreign blockade of Russia was only finally lifted in 1921, enabling the Soviet Union to trade freely once more, trading raw materials and grain for products needed in the recovery of Soviet industry. Moreover, as the state had retained its monopoly of foreign trade, this situation could be exploited to the full: no individual Soviet company could negotiate with a foreign company, but rather had to ask the Commissariat of Foreign Trade to acquire those goods on its behalf; the goods were then supplied to the Soviet firm in return for a credit, which the firm paid off over a period of time. Thus, in just this way Goskino was given a 2.3 million rouble credit with which to purchase film imports over the coming years.[45] It was to establish a distribution monopoly for all foreign films in the Russian market, and the receipts thus earned would pay off the credit; beyond that, its earnings would be used to invest in further domestic film production. At first sight this approach worked well – Western film companies were eager to gain access to this new market, which gave a new lease of life to films that had exhausted their potential in their original markets. In 1923, the first full year of the policy, some 278 American, German and French films entered the Soviet market and, by the mid-1920s, no less than 85 per cent of the films showing in Soviet cinemas came from abroad. Thus foreign films and foreign stars proved just as successful at the Soviet box office as they did in every other country in which the films were shown. Charlie Chaplin, Buster Keaton, Douglas Fairbanks, Mary Pickford – all rapidly established large and enthusiastic followings in the Soviet Union, and when Pickford and Fairbanks visited Moscow in 1926 their reception was quite as enthusiastic as in Paris, Berlin or London.

But the policy would only achieve its strategic purpose if Goskino played its full part too, and here the results were much less impressive. For while Goskino, in theory, enjoyed a monopoly in the distribution of films, it proved very difficult to translate the theory into practice. The problem was partly one of competition from other, better established, organizations – Sevzapkino, in particular, extended its distribution activities well beyond the Leningrad region, and all attempts by Goskino to persuade the government to restrain its growing role in film distribution were resisted. But, in addition, Goskino was never given the resources necessary to establish a truly national distribution network; in many areas it had to work through the regional or local film distributors, thereby increasing the price of its films to the exhibitor. This difficult situation was made incomparably worse by an inappropriate and confused fiscal policy, the product of over-optimistic assumptions that demand for cinema was so strong that audiences would pay literally any price to see the films. Thus, all cinemas that showed imported films were subject to a national tax of 25 per cent, and many local authorities imposed additional taxes as well – 30 per cent in the case of the Moscow Soviet, for example. The end result was predictable enough – ticket prices rose so high that audiences declined sharply and cinemas were forced to close. In 1924 there were only half as many cinemas open in Moscow as there had been in 1917 and, in more remote areas, the situation was often even worse. The imaginative strategy which Lenin and Lunacharsky had formulated was in imminent danger of total collapse.

Once again, the regime responded with yet another investigation, and its report made dismal reading. In its first six months, Goskino's receipts barely covered its expenses, with almost nothing left over to finance film production – 'at the present time, Goskino is not a productive unit, but lives off its commercial operations, the income from which is barely sufficient to cover all its expenses'.[46] Yet the only result of this report was yet another commission of enquiry, chaired by V.N. Mantsev, and its first report was referred back by *Sovnarkom* (the Council of People's Commissars); its second report (in December 1923) provoked still more discussion, including an All-Union Conference on Cinema Affairs in Moscow in March 1924. The following month, the Mantsev Commission presented its final report, and two months later, on 13 June 1924, *Sovnarkom* finally accepted its recommendations. It had taken an extraordinarily long time, but at long last a viable strategy for the regeneration of the film industry had finally been agreed.

Goskino was replaced by a new company, Sovkino. Its assets were transferred to the new company, but Sovkino was authorized to raise an additional million roubles from a limited stock issue – stock could not be sold to private companies or individuals, but only to those government agencies that were most involved with the industry.[47] Moreover, all the smaller distribution firms were bought out by Sovkino, thereby establishing a real distribution monopoly for the first time. Well-established organizations like Sevzapkino and Mezhrabpom-Rus could continue to compete in film production, but Sovkino would now distribute their films. Finally, excessive fiscal policies were replaced by a more favourable tax regime. All of this coincided with the reorganization of the Soviet Union into a federal structure of seven separate republics, and thus Sovkino's distribution monopoly was limited to the Russian Republic – each of the other republic's state film companies were given similar distribution monopolies within their own republics. In practice, however, in the film industry as in the Union, Sovkino was the key player in the new situation – the Russian Republic contained no less than 90 per cent of the land area, and 72 per cent of the population, of the Soviet Union.

In the new situation, the full benefits of importing foreign films could at last be realized. Sovkino's new market position enabled it to take proper advantage of its status as sole importer of foreign films, and its marketing and pricing policy generated the revenues out of which large-scale domestic film production could be funded. The key to the new situation was the position of the major urban commercial cinemas,[48] for while they constituted only 17 per cent of the total number of permanent cinemas, they generated 80 per cent of the industry's total revenues, a remarkably similar position to that enjoyed by first-run cinemas in Western markets. And, in a rapidly improving economic situation, in which both inflation was under control and the tax on cinema seat prices was capped at 10 per cent, they recovered quickly. By 1925 the number of commercial cinemas in operation exceeded the pre-war total, and by 1928 it was of the order of 1700.[49]

The extent of Sovkino's success in the period 1925–1928 is clearly demonstrated in the revenues that were generated. Thus, within just a year, total revenues earned by the industry had increased threefold, with revenues from domestic films growing even more rapidly, and while growth thereafter was not quite so spectacular, by 1928, for the first time, revenues from domestic films exceeded revenues from imported films. While part of this success can be explained by some reduction in the number of imports (caused by a shortage of foreign currency), there had been a remarkable growth in domestic film production, and an analysis of Sovkino's own financial position tells much the same story. Its 1924 assets of four-and-a-half million roubles had grown to over 13 million roubles by the end of 1927, and by then it was committing four million roubles a year to new film production, almost exactly equal to its total initial capital in 1924.[50] NEP had finally delivered an economically viable Soviet film industry.

Yet, while the rebuilding of the film industry was, of course, an essential precondition for the achievement of the Bolsheviks' goals for film propaganda, it was never an end in itself. The purpose of establishing the industry was to ensure that the films reached the mass audience, and here the

Bolshevik achievement was more mixed. In urban areas, much was achieved. By 1928 over 1500 commercial cinemas were in operation and, in addition, nearly 4500 workers' clubs provided regular film screenings as well.[51] Like so many other Bolshevik 'innovations', the clubs date from before the Revolution, when a small number had been organized by trade unions to serve their members' needs. But the dramatic expansion in their numbers came after the Revolution, when the clubs were seen as essential for disseminating education and propaganda to the urban workers. Not least because the domestic conditions of most urban workers were still so harsh (especially in their overcrowding and lack of private space), the clubs provided an environment in which activities like reading and playing chess could take place. In addition, they almost always included a public space in which concerts, plays and film shows, as well as lectures and public meetings, could be held, and they often organized field trips and sporting activities as well. By the end of the decade nearly 90 per cent of the clubs were equipped for film projection, and most of the remainder had access to equipment shared with other organizations. Moreover, the film shows (which were normally held two evenings a week) proved to be the most popular of the clubs' various activities, even though they were not allowed to show exactly the same films as the commercial cinemas, and usually devoted only one of the two weekly screenings to a feature film, with the second programme made up of short educational and propaganda films.

Sovkino recognized that the clubs were an important additional way of reaching the audience, and films were made available to them on extremely generous terms.[52] However, it was careful to protect the position of the commercial cinemas: the clubs' film shows were limited to their members, they were only allowed to advertise the films in the club or factory and, most important of all, they could not rent feature films until one month after they had been shown commercially. Moreover, although they were guaranteed access to at least 10 per cent of Sovkino's list of foreign films (again, a month after their commercial exhibition), the lion's share of this most lucrative business was reserved for the commercial cinemas. Thus the clubs' ability to compete directly with the commercial cinemas was severely constrained and, in addition, their facilities were incomparably worse. Very few had dual projection, so that there would be a break between reels, and the quality of the (invariably badly worn) prints that they used was such that there were often additional breaks as well. In contrast to the more comfortable seating of the commercial cinemas, the workers sat on hard chairs or benches, and the clubs could not afford to offer the same quality of musical accompaniment. Indeed, the films were invariably accompanied by additional commentary to point out a particular social or political message and, while this normally preceded or followed the film, occasionally it coexisted with the music, or even replaced it altogether.

All of this might have discouraged a potential audience, but the clubs had one huge advantage over their commercial rivals: they were incomparably cheaper, charging just 12 to 15 kopecks, compared to the 30 kopecks to 1½ roubles charged by the commercial cinemas. What data there are suggest that workers went to see films in commercial cinemas quite as often as they did in the clubs, and they probably saw the most popular films in the commercial cinemas. But they did go to the club film shows as well, and the large number of these clubs made them an important additional element in what was, by the end of the 1920s, a thriving urban cinema culture. Moreover, in addition to this considerable success in reaching urban, working-class audiences, the Bolsheviks were even more successful with the soldiers of the Red Army. For obvious reasons, the regime had always given the political education of the army a high priority, and the films that were shown to the soldiers were more strictly controlled than in the population as a whole – no foreign films after 1928, and even some Soviet films were deemed unsuitable. But, as the soldiers were denied access to most other forms of entertainment, the film shows proved popular enough – indeed, it is estimated that, by the end of the 1920s, the average soldier saw three times as many films as the ordinary citizen.[53]

Impressive as all this was, however, there remained the huge rural audience that made up no less than 80 per cent of the total population. The emergency strategy developed during the Civil War had been to take the films to the people on the agit-trains and agit-steamers and, while that practice survived long into the 1920s, it was essentially a short-term, stop-gap solution to a problem which remained just as intractable after the Civil War as it had always been. The rural population was distributed over a wide geographical area, with population densities too small to support permanent cinemas, and another way had to be found of taking the films to the people. The new approach, which began in earnest in 1924, borrowed a term first coined at the turn of the century – the government would embark on a programme of *kinofikatsiya* or cinefication.[54] Mobilizing all the resources at its disposal, the regime would at last take the cinema to the mass of the peasantry. Various strategies were employed, including persuading village co-operatives to buy their own projectors and setting up a new organization, the Society of Friends of Soviet Cinema (ODSK), to try to mobilize grassroots support for cinefication. But, most important of all, the original idea of mobile projection units was revived: a small team of activists and technicians, armed with a projector and a generator, would tour the countryside, showing films to the people.

The task of putting this strategy into practice was given to Glavpolit-prosvet, that part of the Commissariat of Enlightenment responsible for adult and political education – Sovkino also established a special department to concentrate on the distribution of films in rural areas.[55] An essential precondition for this programme was the production of sufficient numbers of appropriate projectors for, as Western manufacturers had moved over to the production of mobile projectors powered by mains electricity, the supply had to be met from domestic production. It was finally achieved by two factories, one in Leningrad and one in Odessa and whereas, in October 1925, there were fewer than 500 fixed projectors in the villages and a similar number of mobile units, by April 1929 there were a total of 4340 projectors in the rural areas. However, these statistics substantially overstate the scale of the achievement. The projectors themselves were extremely unreliable, with the dynamo proving especially problematic, and this, coupled with chronic shortages of spare parts, meant that as many as half of the available projectors were out of action at any one time. That situation was made worse by shortages of appropriate personnel, for the skills that were required for this work were considerable. Not only did operators need appropriate technical skills to operate and maintain the projector and its generator (and a story of a projector being lubricated with tar suggests that not all the operators had received sufficient training), they needed considerable political and social skills as well. Most members of the audience were illiterate and the inter-titles would have to be read aloud – on occasion, they were in the wrong language and had to be translated. The quality of the equipment and of the film prints was such that there were frequent breakdowns, and it was therefore necessary to appease the audience while, at the same time, making good the necessary repairs. And finally, they required political skills. As we will see below, the meaning of the films was not always clear to the audience, and in trying to make good that deficiency operators needed both an understanding of Bolshevik policy and some understanding of the politics of the locality in which the film was being shown.

In all, there was a substantial gulf between the Bolsheviks' ambition for cinema and their ability to realize that ambition in practice. In 1929, the total number of cinema admissions was 300 million, small enough in a society with a population of 150 million. Moreover, while sufficient progress had been made in the countryside to ensure that by 1929 almost half the film performances took place outside the towns, as the rural target audience constituted 80 per cent of the population, dividing that number by the number of tickets sold to rural audiences results in less than one film per person per year. Such a calculation is, of course, wholly artificial – the extent to which the cinema reached particular rural areas varied considerably, and in all areas a significant part of the population did not attend any film shows. But for all its artificiality, it does provide a crude measure of the limited extent to which the Bolsheviks' huge ambitions for the rural population had been realized.

The situation in the urban areas was much more impressive. A similar calculation suggests approximately seven films per person per year, and given that we know that urban audiences were predominantly young (and thus that a substantial part of the urban population only went to a film show occasionally), it is clear that many films did reach the regular cinema audience. Moreover, with soldiers seeing three times as many films as other Soviet citizens, within the Red Army cinema was indeed the key medium of Bolshevik propaganda. In all, set within any context other than the

Bolsheviks' over-optimistic and unrealistic expectations, these achievements would surely have been recognized. Against formidable odds, large-scale film production had been achieved, urban audiences were once again going to the cinema in large numbers, and a substantial start had been made in overcoming the altogether more difficult challenge of the countryside. In another place, at another time, achievements such as this would surely have been the cause of very considerable celebration.

THE FILMS AND THEIR AUDIENCE

In marked contrast, however, in the Soviet Union of the late 1920s the dominant voice was critical and condemning. As late as September 1927, the cultural journal *The Life of Art* was arguing that cinema was still allowed 'to drift on the Soviet sea "rudderless and without sails" '.[56] Moreover, this was just one of very many, increasingly strident, criticisms which reached their climax in the Party Conference on Cinema held in March 1928. While some of this can be explained by reference to absurdly optimistic expectations, it derived primarily from a growing unease about the films themselves – their ideology, their style, their content – and the way in which Soviet audiences responded to them. For in the end, this was the heart of the matter. No matter how successful or inventive the Bolsheviks may have been in persuading people to come to see their films, if the films that those audiences saw failed to deliver appropriate messages, then the required transformation of ideology would never be achieved.

As ever, the evidence that enables us to grapple with these questions is far from complete, but almost all the evidence there is points in the same direction, and thus enables us to reach reasonably safe conclusions. The historiography of Soviet cinema in the 1920s was clouded for very many years by the fact that almost all the attention was focused on a small number of innovative, experimental, *avant-garde* films, exemplified above all else by Eisenstein's 1926 'masterpiece', *The Battleship Potemkin*.[57] These films, which made a considerable impact on Western audiences (especially, but not exclusively, in Germany), were both taken as typical of Soviet film production of the period, and were assumed to have been as popular in the Soviet Union as they were (with certain audiences) in the West. In reality, both assumptions were profoundly mistaken, and it is only by setting them on one side that it becomes possible to make a proper assessment of the extent to which Soviet cinema of the 1920s realized the Party's propaganda objectives. There are, in effect, two different questions that need to be answered here – what were the films that were most popular with Soviet audiences and how did Soviet audiences, respond to the *avant-garde* propaganda films?

The answer to the first question is clear and is implicit in the NEP strategy for the film industry, for the decision to import foreign films only made sense if those films were able to attract large Soviet audiences. Until 1924 it was German films which dominated the Soviet market, but very soon thereafter Hollywood took over, even though Soviet audiences did not always have the opportunity to see American films until some time after their release in the West – Chaplin's 1921 film *The Kid*, for example, did not reach the Soviet Union until 1929.[58] But this seems to have done nothing to diminish the appeal of American films, which proved just as popular with Soviet audiences as with comparable audiences across the industrialized world. Nor is there anything surprising in this. Hollywood production had achieved unequalled economies of scale and levels of capital investment, and these economic advantages (and the technology and resources which they bought), coupled with the imagination and excellence of its film-makers (who were coming from all around the world by this time), resulted in the early 1920s in films that enthralled audiences wherever they were shown. The range of Hollywood's output is perhaps the aspect of its achievement that is most often forgotten, for while the word 'Hollywood' most readily suggests notions of glamour, adventure and romance, all of which were exemplified in the films of the period, its output was by no means limited to films starring Douglas Fairbanks, Mary Pickford or Rudolph Valentino. Holly-wood was also the industry in which Chaplin, Keaton and Lloyd transformed the nature of film comedy, Ford and Cruze laid down the foundations of the western, and directors like Griffith or Vidor tackled difficult and ambitious subjects in films like *Intolerance* (1916) or *The Big Parade* (1925). Moreover, in such marked contrast to today, the studios were managed by men who had grown up with the cinema, who shared their audiences' passion for the movies, and who were determined to make the films those audiences wanted to see. In short, this was a rich and a vibrant industry, in which abundant resources were at the disposal of singularly talented film-makers – hardly surprising then that it produced films capable of winning and holding audiences in almost every country in which they were seen.

Thus in the emerging film culture of the Soviet Union of the mid-1920s, Hollywood films and Hollywood stars were quite as prominent as they were in any other country in which American films were screened. An American journalist, visiting the Soviet Union in the summer of 1925, could not disguise his surprise:

> American films dominate, inundate, glut, overwhelm the Russian motion picture houses today. Clara Kimball Young has a theatre devoted solely to her in Moscow. In the Arbat, centre of the workers' quarters of the Russian capital, a new building celebrates the glory of Douglas Fairbanks in electric letters three feet high. In the leading workers' club and a dozen other places Mary Pickford holds forth ... It is a bit depressing.[59]

While almost any American film was capable of winning a Soviet audience, two particular genres appear to have held a special fascination. American comedies proved hugely popular and, given the quality of the work done by Chaplin, Keaton and Lloyd at this time, this surely needs little explanation – indeed, their particular, non-verbal, physical form of comedy was especially well-suited to crossing otherwise impenetrable barriers of language, culture and tradition. Slightly less easy to understand, however, was the special appeal of the second group of films, which can perhaps most accurately be described as historical extravaganzas. These films, like *Robin Hood* or *The Thief of Bagdad* or *The Mark of Zorro*, were lavishly resourced, exotic dramas, loosely set in some imagined past, with fast-paced, action-packed narratives in which the hero, often faced with apparently insuperable odds, always triumphed in the end. But hugely popular they were, and when the star of so many of these films, Douglas Fairbanks, visited Moscow (with Mary Pickford) in July 1926, his reception was quite as ecstatic as in any other capital city. Indeed, Fairbanks's *The Thief of Bagdad* was the most successful import of the decade, enjoying a continuous year-long run at one of Moscow's most popular cinemas.[60]

While American films retained their appeal right through to 1931 when imports ceased, it was not long before the revenues generated by these films were used to fund increased domestic film production. At first such films struggled to compete successfully with foreign imports, but by the 1927/28 film season the revenues earned by domestic films exceeded those earned by imports. Moreover, it was not simply a question of the volume of production or the financial success of the films. By that time, a small group of enormously talented, young film-makers had produced a body of work which appeared to fulfil all the Bolsheviks' expectations for cinema as a powerful medium of propaganda. The first confident manifestation of that new cinema came with Lev Kulsehov's *The Extraordinary Adventures of Mr West in the Land of the Bolsheviks* in 1924, and was followed in the next six years by the very different but equally innovative work of five other extraordinary film-makers. Thus, in their own distinctive ways, Sergei Eisenstein, Vsevolod Pudovkin, Dziga Vertov, Esther Shub and Alexander Dovzhenko, all challenged prevailing orthodoxies in both the narrative fiction film and the documentary film, often demonstrating just how artificial the traditionally impenetrable boundaries between these two forms were. Their output was not especially large – between them they completed some 30 films in this period, of which a dozen were perhaps of very special interest[61] – but it was the range and depth of their innovation that made their work so memorable. While all broke with tradition in the content of their films, faithfully translating revolutionary ideology into the medium of film, the form of their films was also profoundly different from the work of both earlier Russian film-makers and from the Hollywood films which were so popular with Soviet audiences of the time.

Eisenstein's *The Battleship Potemkin* of 1926 provides an early and clear example of the way in which these new film-makers sought to realize their revolutionary mission. The film was commissioned for the twentieth anniversary of the (unsuccessful) 1905 Revolution, and the original intention was to reconstruct the revolutionary events of the year through a wide-ranging narrative, to be shot in no less than 30 separate locations.[62] When shooting began in March 1925, bad weather forced Eisenstein and his crew first to Baku and then to Odessa, where a short sequence was to be shot of the mutiny on the battleship *Potemkin* and the resulting massacre of Odessa civilians who supported the mutiny. Once in Odessa, however, Eisenstein reformulated his approach: in place of a comprehensive narrative, the mutiny and the ensuing events on land would serve to encapsulate the essence of the revolutionary events of 1905.

The film opens with an examination of the conditions on board the battleship which eventually lead the men to mutiny. One sailor, Vakulinchuk, plays a key role in the mutiny, but just at the point when the tsarist officers have been overcome, Vakulinchuk is killed. His body is brought to the shore in Odessa, where it lies in a tent at the end of the quay, and the following morning the people of Odessa come to pay their respects to the dead revolutionary hero. As more and more people come out to demonstrate their solidarity with the revolutionary sailors, the Odessa authorities decide to reassert their control – the citizens gathered on the stone steps leading down to the harbour are massacred; the *Potemkin* answers by turning its two huge turret guns on the Odessa Theatre. In the conclusion the battleship sails towards the rest of the squadron and, when eventually they meet, the sailors on all the other ships greet their revolutionary comrades with joyful solidarity and *Potemkin* sails to freedom.

From almost every possible point of view, *The Battleship Potemkin* distanced itself from the form of Hollywood narrative which was already so dominant in world cinema by 1925. The film's revolutionary ideology sets it apart, but it was its form that demonstrated the extent to which the new *avant-garde* Soviet film-makers were breaking away from what they saw as the bourgeois shackles of capitalistic film-making. Most obviously, the film dispensed with the assumption that the heart of a narrative fiction film must always be found in one or more central characters who drive that narrative forward. Thus, where a Hollywood director would have put Vakulinchuk (played of course by a major star) centre-stage, leading the revolutionary sailors to their final victory, it was central to Eisenstein's purpose to kill off this character at just the point where he starts to impress himself on the audience. In the place of the traditional hero stood the revolutionary class, embodied by the mutinous sailors of the *Potemkin*, and Vakulinchuk's death forces the audience away from the heroic individual, back to the revolutionary class of which he is a part. In much the same way, while individual members of the ruling class are strikingly presented, the enduring image of oppressive tsardom is found in the serried ranks of the troops who massacre the civilians on the Odessa steps. They are presented as an anonymous, savage force, robotic almost in its total lack of human emotion, and it is these very qualities which make them so terrifying and so memorable.

Innovative as the narrative was, however, it was the methods that Eisenstein used to realize that narrative that were even more revolutionary. And while performance, cinematography and *mise-en-scéne* are all important in the film, each in its own way challenging established conventions, it is the editing that represents perhaps the most decisive break with convention.[63] Nowhere is this more striking than in the Odessa steps sequence which is both ideologically and dramatically at the heart of the film. The confrontation between the inhuman ranks of soldiers and the human crowd (in which Eisenstein carefully draws our attention to particular people), derives its huge impact from the pace and character of the editing. Many of the individual images are powerful and striking in their own right, but it is the force with which individual shots collide that gives the sequence its ferocious intensity, whether (most obviously) in the juxtaposition of images of oppressors and oppressed, or in the equally startling cross-cutting between different shots of the victims of the massacre. The dramatic intensity of the sequence derives in no small part from the rhythm of the editing, as for example in the rapidly accelerating cutting which drives it through to its conclusion. And yet, notwithstanding the often frantic pace of the editing, the events on screen actually last much longer than they would have done in real life, thereby standing on its head the cinema's normal chronological conventions, enabling Eisenstein accurately to convey a sense of the emotional duration of these horrific events.

Thus, in these and many other ways, Eisenstein broke decisively with the conventions of mainstream, narrative cinema and, in common with the other *avant-garde* film-makers, demonstrated that the Soviet Union was indeed breaking out of its bourgeois past. It was an axiom of Marxism that a truly proletarian society would produce its own new proletarian culture, distinguished as much by the form of its cultural products as by their content and, in the work of these *avant-garde* film-makers, the first unmistakable signs of that new film culture could surely be clearly identified. As Alexei Gvozdev argued in his review of *The Battleship Potemkin*, 'form and content have been fused into a powerful unity and a film with a revolutionary theme has found its proper revolutionary artistic form'.[64] Moreover, this claim that Soviet film-makers had achieved a revolution in the form of cinema was quickly and unexpectedly endorsed on a much wider stage. *Potemkin* was widely shown outside the Soviet Union, notably in Germany where it achieved not just critical acclaim, but also very considerable commercial success. Kristin Thompson concludes that it was the most successful film in Germany in the 1925/26 film season and, in all, it was shown in 38 countries outside the Soviet Union. While the precise level of its earnings is unclear, her estimate is that its total overseas income was 'in the range of hundreds, rather than tens, of thousands of dollars'[65] and, if this is right, then the film clearly made a significant financial contribution to the development of the Soviet film industry. The extent of *Potemkin's* commercial success within the German market was, of course, exceptional; what was not exceptional was the critical acclaim. Wherever the film was shown it enjoyed precisely the same hugely enthusiastic critical reception, with particular emphasis being placed on the innovative, experimental character of the film. This was even the case in Hollywood, where a junior executive at MGM suggested that the studio's film-makers would benefit from studying the film and that it might make sense to employ Eisenstein.[66] Indeed, so consistently enthusiastic was the initial Western reception of the work of these particular Soviet film-makers that, as Ian Christie has so persuasively argued, it determined the shape and form of the historiography of the history of Soviet cinema for more than half a century thereafter.[67]

MOUNTING CRITICISM

But it was at precisely the time that these films were being so praised in the West that criticisms of the industry as a whole, and these film-makers in particular, began to grow, and the basis of this mounting wave of criticism is not difficult to identify. For while the *avant-garde* films may have been the subject of almost universal critical acclaim and some commercial success, the dissenting critical voices were all to be found at home, and almost all the commercial success was achieved abroad – by and large, the films failed at the Soviet box-office, where they were invariably perceived as, at best, too serious and 'worthy', at worst, so difficult and innovative as to be all-but incomprehensible. This was of course the heart of the matter: the films had been made in order to transform the ideology of the millions of Soviet citizens – if the films were not seen by those millions, then no matter what other qualities they may have possessed, they were *ipso facto* a failure. The cinema was so attractive as a medium of propaganda because it held out the promise of access to the mass cinema audience; if most of that audience did not go to a particular film, then its propaganda potential could never be realized.

The nature of the problem is illustrated all too clearly in the history of the Moscow exhibition of *The Battleship Potemkin*. It was premièred on 19 January 1926 at the First Goskino cinema, where it ran for just four weeks and, notwithstanding a claim to the contrary in *Kino-Gazeta*, it is clear that it was much less popular than the earlier American box-office hit, *Robin Hood*; two weeks before the release of *Potemkin*, *Robin Hood* had been showing at no less than 11 of Moscow's 12 first-run cinemas. Moreover when, after its enormous success in Germany, *Potemkin* was re-released at the Second Goskino cinema in June, it lasted just two weeks, before being replaced first by Keaton's *Our Hospitality* and, one week later, by *Robin Hood* – back again 'by public demand'.[68] Not long afterwards, another Fairbanks film, *The Thief of Bagdad* was released in Moscow, where it broke all previous box-office records for an imported film. Thus, faced with a choice between a serious, experimental film which explored the nature of the Bolshevik revolutionary tradition, and the swashbuckling adventures of Robin Hood, Moscow audiences knew precisely which film they wanted to see. Just like audiences all around the world, they went to the cinema for entertainment and escape, for excitement and drama; they did not go for political propaganda, still less for propaganda that made considerable intellectual demands on its audience.

And if the *avant-garde* propaganda films proved too serious and too demanding for urban audiences, they were simply incomprehensible to most peasant audiences. The notion that film is a universal language which anyone can understand is, of course, misplaced – the 'language' of cinema has to be learned just like any other language, and Katsigras, the leading activist in the cinefication campaign, made it quite clear that when peasants first saw films they did not understand them at all; even after repeated exposure to films, they often failed to grasp the meaning.[69] Their very lack of exposure to film meant that they had not yet become fluent in its particular conventions and they found even the most straightforward and conventional films difficult to follow – the *avant-garde* films were simply beyond them. This would have been important in any circumstances, but in a society where the peasants constituted 80 per cent of the population, and represented the very people whose ideology the Bolsheviks most urgently needed to transform, it constituted failure of the most serious kind.

But perhaps the clearest indication of the failure of the propaganda films is provided by the considerable success achieved at the Soviet box office by the very different films that other Soviet film-makers were making at exactly the same time. For the majority of Soviet films of the period remained much closer to the conventions and preoccupations of mainstream narrative cinema which had dominated pre-revolutionary Russian cinema. Although a good many of these films worked within 'politically correct' narratives drawn from both recent Russian history or the contemporary Soviet Union, the propaganda (such as it was) was clearly subservient to the melodrama, the glamour, the excitement or, occasionally, the comedy of the film. The career of Yakov Protazanov, a director who had left Russia in 1920, but who returned to the Soviet Union in 1923, provides an especially clear illustration of the way in which an accomplished film-maker could make films that achieved real success with Soviet audiences. Not only was Protazanov much more prolific than his *avant-garde* contemporaries, completing no less than 10 feature films for Mezhrabpom-Rus in the years between 1924 and 1930, his films were consistently popular at the box office, regardless of the extent to which they conformed to prevailing notions of what constituted appropriate content for Soviet films. Thus, only three of his films – *His Call* (1925), *The Forty-First* (1927) and *Don Diego and Pelageya* (1928) – won unreserved critical approval as constituting 'truly Soviet' films, while many of the others encountered a great deal of criticism. *The Three Millions*

Trial (1926), for example, was singled out by Eisenstein as a particularly clear example of a film that was anathema to a revolutionary cinema, and yet it was just as popular with the audience as any of his other films.[70] Another film of 1926, demonstrates the point even more clearly for, while *The Battleship Potemkin* was consistently outsold by the two Douglas Fairbanks' films, it was also outsold by a Soviet film which attracted twice as large an audience. *The Bear's Wedding*, set in the forests of Lithuania, contained all the stock elements of the horror film and Richard Taylor is surely right when he argues that it attracted its large audiences 'through entertainment and diversion rather than through edification, agitation or propaganda'.[71] In the Soviet Union as much as anywhere else, cinema attracted the millions when it provided entertainment and diversion – when it offered edification or propaganda it was a very different story.

In the light of all this, it is hardly surprising that the criticisms became more and more strident. The targets were various: Sovkino was criticized for importing Hollywood films and for encouraging the production of Soviet imitations; the *avant-garde* film-makers were criticized for making films that were incomprehensible to the millions; all Soviet film-makers were criticized for failing to make films that were appropriate for the peasants; the Party was criticized for failing to make the kind of investment in rural distribution and exhibition which would have enabled Soviet cinema to reach the vast peasant audience. This mounting wave of criticism reached its climax in the First All-Union Party Conference on Cinema held in March 1928, where all these criticisms (and more) were rehearsed once again. The recent release of Eisenstein's latest film, *October*, probably sharpened the focus on the role of the *avant-garde* film-makers for, while critical responses to the film were mixed, the film failed once again to win a mass audience. Indeed, many saw in *October*'s failure the clearest evidence of the failure of a group of films that were increasingly caricatured as obscure and elitist, films made in effect for the pleasure and satisfaction of the film-makers, rather than the needs of the millions they were supposed to serve.

In its conclusions the Conference restated once again the high hopes for cinema that had been expressed by the 12th Party Congress, namely that it 'must be the most powerful medium of Communist enlightenment and agitation', adding, in its own words, that 'in the variety and wealth of its formal and technical methods cinema has no rivals'. Moreover, its diagnosis of the problems which currently gripped Soviet cinema accurately emphasized the tension between 'the requirements of the ideological consistency and artistic quality of films and the requirements of the commercial profitability of cinema'. Its conclusion, however, was to argue yet again that it was possible to make films that would meet these ideological imperatives in forms that were both 'intelligible to the millions' and that 'correspond to the requirements of the broad mass audience'. Moreover, it claimed there was no fundamental conflict between 'commerce' and 'ideology': Soviet cinema can and must be a 'profitable undertaking', although it did have the sense to recommend further reductions in the number of imported films! [72]

While much of this may seem like a restatement of traditional policy, in the context of the debates that were dominating Soviet film culture at the time, the emphasis on films that were 'intelligible to the millions' was especially significant. The Conference had also urged the need for closer links between the film-makers and their audience and, in the months that followed, it was this implicit call for a new 'proletarian hegemony' in Soviet cinema that was to become increasingly dominant, reaching its climax in a famous article by the scriptwriter and director Petrov-Bytov. Charging that the great mass of the population had never 'march[ed] beneath the banner' of the great Soviet *avant-garde* films, he claimed that this was because far too many film-makers had a patronizing, almost contemptuous attitude towards the mass of ordinary people. They simply did not have that understanding of the lives of ordinary people which was a precondition for a successful Soviet film-maker. In place of the high-flown *avant-garde* films of the past, he demanded:

> ... films with a simple story and plot ... We must talk in [the peasant's] own language about the cow that is sick with tuberculosis, about the dirty cowshed that must be transformed into one that is clean and bright, about the child that is stirring in the peasant woman's womb ... *Every film must be useful, intelligible and familiar to the millions.*[73]

In contrast to the more balanced approach of the Conference resolutions, Petrov-Bytov's article was typical of the much more strident demands of the wider cultural revolution which now gripped Soviet society. Sovkino was dissolved in the spring of 1930, and its successor, Soyuzkino, under the leadership of Boris Shumyatsky, was to implement that cultural revolution in the cinema. The new orthodoxy of Socialist Realism was proclaimed in 1934, and film-makers (just like writers, painters and composers) were required to conform to its principles.

For cinema, however, this transformation was complicated by the introduction of the new (and hugely expensive) technology of synchronized sound, and it was these technological and economic imperatives, quite as much as ideology, that led Shumyatsky to introduce much stricter controls. That said, the restructuring of Soviet cinema that followed took place within the very different context of the economic, social and political revolutions that transformed Soviet society in the 1930s, in which state terror invariably drove the changes forward, with propaganda playing an important, but altogether subsidiary role. Moreover, while recent scholarship may be right to challenge the excessively black-and-white contrasts that were traditionally drawn between the freedom of the 1920s and the complete control over film-makers exercised by Shumyatsky in the 1930s,[74] the fact remains that the political culture of the Soviet Union of the 1930s was fundamentally different from that which had existed under NEP. The films changed, but incomparably more important, the social and political environment within which ever larger audiences saw those films was fundamentally different from the environment within which Soviet audiences of the 1920s had seen the very different films (both imported and domestic) of the 1920s.[75]

CONCLUSION

What conclusions then emerge from this analysis of Soviet film propaganda in the 1920s? Given the devastation of a once-thriving tsarist film industry, which was the cumulative result of war, revolutions and civil war, a very great deal was achieved. Against all the odds, a significant start was made during the Civil War years, both in the foundation of the Film School, the limited but imaginative production of the *agitki* and in the even more spectacular tactic of taking these films to the people through the agit-trains and the agit-steamers. NEP created a mixed economy, in which, without making any demands on the public purse, a well-resourced and productive Soviet film industry was built. The strategy of using imported foreign films to regain the audience was successful, and those revenues generated the capital out of which both the cinema network was expanded and a film production industry was built. Moreover, the films that this new industry produced included a small group of *avant-garde* propaganda films that challenged many of the conventions that had come to dominate mainstream commercial film-making in the most provocative and imaginative way; associated with them was an enormously vibrant and deeply contested body of theoretical work. Indeed, the combination of these two achievements made a deep and enduring impact on Western opinion and, while this was only briefly translated into commercial success in Germany, there can be little doubt that the attitude of very many Western intellectuals towards the new culture of the Soviet Union was greatly influenced by the Soviet films which they saw in the 1920s.

Having said all that, however, the construction of the Soviet film industry was never an end in itself, nor were the Bolsheviks committed to film as a medium in order to make effective propaganda for Western intellectuals. They were drawn to cinema for almost exactly the same reasons as Masterman had been in Britain at the beginning of the First World War, namely as a medium uniquely well-placed to reach the illiterate millions. And their success in achieving this objective was very much more limited. In part, the problem remained strategic. Films did reach the Red Army and, through a combination of commercial cinemas and workers' clubs, a large part of the urban population as well. But they did not reach the vast majority of the population, still living in the rural areas, where a combination of logistical, technological and personnel problems conspired to confound unrealistic and over-optimistic expectations. Even if these strategic problems had been solved, Soviet film-makers in the 1920s still failed to resolve the problem which is at the heart of so much film propaganda: how to reconcile the conflicting demands of popular cinema and political propaganda. Thus, while they demonstrated an ability to make both propaganda films and commercially popular films, very few films of the period did both. And in their failure to resolve that problem, the decision to import Hollywood films made a difficult situation incomparably worse. All across Europe, film-makers found it difficult to compete successfully with Hollywood products and, while they were simply competing with Hollywood on its own terms – endeavouring to make films that would excite, entertain and amuse the audience – the Soviet film-makers were required to make films that would satisfy the propaganda imperatives of the regime as well.

On the other hand, the fact that the Soviet propaganda films were so well-received in the West created an enduring myth that served potently to reinforce dominant assumptions about the power of film as a medium of propaganda. Coming so soon after a world war that had led all belligerent governments to the conclusion that cinema was uniquely placed to influence the minds of the masses, Western misconceptions about the nature and effectiveness of the Soviet *avant-garde* propaganda films meant that this myth of the power of film was even more firmly established at the end of the 1920s than it had been at the end of the war. In reality, Soviet film-makers in the 1920s, just like British film-makers during the First World War, had discovered just how elusive the dream of effective film propaganda could be.

NOTES

1. It was not until the publication of J.D. Squires, *British Propaganda at Home and in the United States*, in 1935 that any understanding of its role became clear.

2. V.I. Lenin, *What Is To Be Done?*, first published in Geneva in 1902. This quotation is taken from a translation published by S.V. and Patricia Utechin, Manchester, 1970, p. 80; the remaining ideas summarized in this paragraph derive from the same source. In this essay Lenin (following the earlier Russian socialist Plekhanov) draws a clear distinction between propaganda and agitation, with the term 'propaganda' being reserved for the initial complex analysis, while 'agitation' is used to describe the translation of those complex ideas into simple agitational slogans. As current usage of the word 'propaganda' is much closer to Lenin's notion of agitation, it is used in that way here, notwithstanding the distinctions originally drawn by Lenin.

3. Sheila Fitzpatrick, *The Russian Revolution 1917–1932*, Oxford, 1982, pp. 45–6. While the literature on the rise of the Bolsheviks and their October Revolution is immense, Fitzpatrick's book remains one of the best short introductions.

4. *Ibid.*, pp. 43–6.

5. The Socialist Revolutionaries were heirs to the longer tradition of populism, a uniquely Russian form of socialism that had developed in rural Russia in the last 40 years of the nineteenth century; in the Constituent Assembly elections they had won 40 per cent of the popular vote compared to the Bolsheviks' 25 per cent.

6. Quoted in Peter Kenez, *The Birth of the Propaganda State: Soviet Methods of Mass Mobilisation*, Cambridge, 1985, p. 72. Hereafter referred to as Kenez (1985).

7. *Ibid.*, p. 8. Kenez' book offers a singularly thoughtful analysis of the role of propaganda in the foundation of the Soviet state.

8. See, in particular, Paolo Cherchi Usai, Lorenzo Codelli, Carlo Montanaro and David Robinson, with Yuri Tsivian, *Silent Witnesses: Russian Films, 1908–1919*, Pordenone and London, 1989.

9. Peter Kenez, *Cinema and Soviet Society, 1917–1953*, Cambridge, 1992, pp. 18–19. Hereafter Kenez (1992).

10. *Ibid.*, pp. 22–3, and Richard Taylor, *The Politics of the Soviet Cinema 1917–1929*, London, 1979, p. 13. Hereafter referred to as Taylor (1979).

11. Kenez (1992), p. 24.

12. Anatoli Lunacharsky's account is reproduced in Richard Taylor (editor and translator) and Ian Christie (co-editor), *The Film Factory: Russian and Soviet Cinema in Documents 1896–1939*, London, 1988, p. 57. Hereafter referred to as Taylor and Christie (1988).

13. Lev Trotsky, 'Vodka, the church and the cinema', *Pravda*, 12 July 1923 – quoted in Taylor and Christie (1988), pp. 95–7.

14. Leonid Andreyev, *First Letter on Theatre* – quoted in Taylor and Christie (1988), pp. 30–1.

15. Kenez (1985) provides an especially full discussion of both the extent of the problem of illiteracy and the marked variations in its extent. Thus, the average figures conceal huge variations, with almost two-thirds of urban workers being literate while amongst the Chechens literacy was as low as 1 per cent.

16. *Pskovskii nabat*, 3 July 1924, quoted in Taylor (1979), p. 87.

17. Roger Munting, *The Economic Development of the USSR*, London, 1982, p. 45.

18. Geoffrey Hosking, *A History of the Soviet Union 1917–1991*, final edition, London, 1992, p. 120.

19. *Ibid.*, p. 70.

20. Taylor (1979), pp. 46–8.

21. Kenez (1992), p. 31.

22. Vance Kepley, Jr, 'The origins of Soviet cinema: a study in industry development', in Richard Taylor and Ian Christie (eds), *Inside the Film Factory: New Approaches to Russian and Soviet Cinema*, London, 1991, p. 64. Hereafter Kepley (1991).

23. For a detailed discussion of the incident see Jay Leyda, *Kino: A History of Russian and Soviet Film*, London, 1973, pp. 126–8.

24. Kenez (1992), p. 37.

25. Taylor goes further and claims that Gardin had opened such a school in September 1916, with the assistance of the producer Vladimir Vengerov (Taylor (1979), p. 51); Yampolsky, however, suggests that the state of the war meant that the proposal was never put into practice (Mikhail Yampolsky, 'Kuleshov's experiments and the new anthropology of the actor', in Richard Taylor and Ian Christie (eds), *Inside the Film Factory: New Approaches to Russian and Soviet Cinema*, London, 1991, p. 36.)

26. Yampolsky, *op. cit.*

27. Quoted in Taylor (1979), p. 51.

28. Kuleshov's experimental work appeared to demonstrate that it was editing above all else that determined the construction of meaning in cinema: by juxtaposing the same shot of a face with a variety of other shots, he claimed to show that audiences read different emotions on the unchanging face. For a full discussion of his work see Ronald Levaco, *Kuleshov on Film*, Berkeley, 1974.

29. The Soviet film-makers used the French term for editing – *montage*; in subsequent English usage the term is often synonymous with the theoretical analysis of the role of editing developed by Soviet film-makers in this period. Yampolsky, *op. cit.*, explores the significance of Gardin's work in the development of Kuleshov's ideas.

30. This film and the other *agitki* discussed in this paragraph are described in Kenez (1992), pp. 35–6.

31. Taylor (1979), p. 51.

32. This approach to existing footage reached its culmination in Esther Shub's *The Fall of the Romanov Dynasty* (1927), which drew extensively on tsarist footage in its analysis of events leading up to the Tsar's abdication in February 1917.

33. Taylor (1979), p. 53. The discussion of the agit-trains and agit-steamers that follows derives largely from the same source, pp. 53–63, and from Kenez (1985), pp. 59–62.

34. *Ibid.*, p. 52.

35. Quoted in Kenez (1985), p. 59.

36. Quoted in Taylor (1979), p. 61.

37. Huntly Carter, *The New Theatre and Cinema of Soviet Russia: Being an Analysis and Synthesis of the Unified Theatre Produced in Russia by the 1917 Revolution, and an Account of Its Growth and Development from 1917 to the Present Day*, London, 1924, p. 240.

38. Kepley (1991), p. 68.

39. Taylor (1979), pp. 69–70.

40. Trotsky in *Pravda*, 12 July 1923, in Taylor and Christie (1988), p. 96.

41. WIR was launched in Berlin, but quickly established branches linked to other left-wing organizations in many parts of the world. This and the following discussion of the role played by WIR and other Western organizations in supporting the film industry derives from Kepley (1991), pp. 61–79, and Kristin Thompson, 'Government policies and practical necessities in the Soviet cinema of the 1920s', in Anna Lawton, *The Red Screen: Politics, Society, Art in Soviet Cinema*, London, 1992, pp. 34–5.

42. This consisted of 33 fiction films, 50 scientific films, 20,000 metres of negative film stock, 700,000 metres of positive film stock, a complete electrical outfit for the First State Cinema Factory and 30,000 roubles' worth of photographic equipment and chemicals.

43. Lenin, *Directive on Cinema Affairs*, 17 January 1922, quoted in Taylor and Christie (1988), p. 56.

44. Lenin in conversation with Lunacharsky, 1922, quoted in Taylor and Christie (1988), p. 57.

45. Kepley (1991), p. 73. The following discussion of Goskino's subsequent history is based largely on the same source, pp. 73–5.

46. The report was made in August 1923 (quoted in Taylor (1979), p. 77).

47. The Commissariat of Enlightenment and the Petrograd and Moscow Soviets jointly bought 55 per cent, the Commissariat of Foreign Trade 30 per cent.

48. The term here is used to describe those cinemas in which films were exhibited for profit – in contrast to the West, as late as 1928, 98 per cent of such cinemas were owned and run by a variety of 'public' institutions like the Commissariat of Enlightenment, trade unions or local government. I am indebted to Richard Taylor for drawing my attention to this – so far unpublished – finding of his research into the period.

49. Vance Kepley, Jr, 'Cinema and everyday life: Soviet workers clubs of the 1920s', in Robert Sklar and Charles Musser (eds), *Resisting Images: Essays on Cinema and History*, Philadelphia, 1990, pp. 108–25. Hereafter Kepley (1990).

50. The data summarized here derive from Kepley (1991), p. 76, and Kenez (1985), p. 206.

51. Kepley (1990), p. 110. Kepley's essay provides a detailed discussion of the part played by the workers' clubs in Soviet film exhibition, and what follows derives from the same source.

52. In effect, Sovkino simply covered its administrative costs, making little or no profit from this form of exhibition.

53. Kenez (1992), p. 84.

54. By the first Congress of Teachers of Natural History (Taylor (1979), p. 8); the term was used to describe a process of equipping the schools with the new technology of cinema.

55. Kenez (1992), pp. 85–6. The remainder of this discussion of rural cinefication derives from Kenez (1992), pp. 83–90, and Taylor (1979), pp. 87–92.

56. *Zhizn iskusstva*, 27 September 1927, quoted in Taylor (1979), p. 102.

57. The film is variously dated as 1925 or 1926. Leyda describes a screening to an invited audience on 21 December 1925 at the Bolshoi Opera Theatre, although the public première took place nearly a month later (Leyda, *op.cit.*, pp. 196–7).

58. Kenez (1992), pp 72–5.

59. Paxton Hibben, writing in *The Nation* in November 1925, quoted in Leyda, *op. cit.*, p. 185.

60. Vance Kepley, Jr, and Betty Kepley, 'Foreign films on Soviet screens 1922–1931', *Quarterly Review of Film Studies*, Vol. 4, No. 4, Fall 1979, p. 437.

61. Namely, Eisenstein's *The Strike* (1924), *The Battleship Potemkin* (1926), *October* (1929) and *The General Line* (1929); Pudovkin's *The Mother* (1926), *The End of St. Petersburg* (1927) and *Storm over Asia* (1928); Vertov's *A Sixth of the World* (1926) and *The Man with a Movie Camera* (1929); Shub's *The Fall of the Romanov Dynasty* (1927); Dovzhenko's *The Arsenal* (1929) and *The Earth* (1930).

62. This and the following discussion of the circumstances of the film's production are based on David A. Cook, *A History of Narrative Film*, London, 1981, pp. 149–50.

63. The role of editing was, in Eisenstein's judgement, at the very heart of the language of cinema, and his theoretical formulation of the idea of dialectical montage was often illustrated by reference to *The Battleship Potemkin* – see for example his essay 'The dramaturgy of film form' (1929), reproduced in Richard

Taylor (editor and translator), *S.M. Eisenstein: Selected Works*, London, 1988, pp. 161–80.

64. Alexei Gvozdev, 'A new triumph for Soviet cinema', 26 January 1926, quoted in Taylor and Christie (1988), p. 140.

65. Kristin Thompson, 'Eisenstein's early films abroad', in Ian Christie and Richard Taylor (eds), *Eisenstein Rediscovered*, London, 1993, p. 57. Hereafter Christie and Taylor (1993).

66. Taylor and Christie (1988), p. 5.

67. *Ibid.*, pp. 1–17.

68. Taylor (1979), p. 95.

69. Katsigras' observations about peasant audiences are discussed in Denise Youngblood, *Soviet Cinema in the Silent Era, 1918–1935*, Ann Arbor, 1985, p. 50.

70. Protazanov's work is discussed in Denise Youngblood, 'The return of the native: Yakov Protazanov and Soviet cinema', in Taylor and Christie (1991), pp. 103–23, and Ian Christie and Julian Graffy, *Protazanov and the Continuity of Russian Cinema*, London, 1993.

71. Richard Taylor, 'Ideology as mass entertainment: Boris Shumyatsky and Soviet cinema in the 1930s', in Taylor and Christie (1991), p. 195.

72. Taylor and Christie (1988), pp. 208–15.

73. Petrov-Bytov's article was published on 21 April 1929 (*ibid.*, pp. 261–2).

74. See for example Richard Taylor, 'Ideology and entertainment: Boris Shumyatsky and Soviet cinema in the 1930s', in Taylor and Christie (1991).

75. Once again, recent scholarship has challenged the over-simple view that the 1930s were a period of unremitting terror in which no one dared to question, let alone challenge, anything that the Party did – see in particular, Sarah Davies, *Popular Opinion in Stalin's Russia: Terror, Propaganda and Dissent, 1934–1941*, Cambridge, 1997; and Sarah Davies, 'Stalin, propaganda and Soviet society during the Great Terror', *The Historian*, No. 56, Winter 1997, pp. 24–9. Even in the light of such work, however, it remains clear that the political culture of the 1930s was profoundly different from that which had existed a decade before.

CHAPTER 3

National Socialist Film
Propaganda in Germany,
1933–1945

The Bolsheviks' very particular emphasis on propaganda derived from the potent combination of Lenin's confidence in its singular ability to mobilize popular support, and a Marxist analysis which required nothing less than the revolutionary transformation of the ideology of the mass of the people, and to a remarkable extent these same imperatives are at the root of a comparable commitment to propaganda within German National Socialism. Certainly, Hitler shared Lenin's assumptions about its power (as the two chapters on propaganda in *Mein Kampf* make clear), and his analysis of effective propaganda bears more than a passing resemblance to Lenin's earlier assessment, notably in its emphasis on simple ideas that the masses can easily understand. Thus propaganda would only be successful when 'its intellectual level [is] adjusted to the most limited intelligence among those it is addressed to', and it must always avoid a 'many-sided approach'; the complexities of 'scientific instruction' play no part in successful propaganda – it must be direct, simple, clear. Drawing an analogy with advertising, Hitler argues that just as an advertisement for soap which pointed out the qualities of other brands would be unsuccessful, so too with propaganda. Its function is:

> ... not to weigh and ponder the rights of different people, but exclusively to emphasise the one right which it has set out to argue for. Its task is not to make an objective study of the truth ... its task is to serve our own right, always and unflinchingly.

Moreover, he was convinced that the 'great masses', whose 'intelligence is small, but their power of forgetting is enormous', were 'so feminine by nature and attitude that sober reasoning determines their thoughts and actions far less than emotion and feeling'.[1] In short, effective propaganda must be clear and simple, appealing primarily to the emotions of its target audience.

That said, Hitler's approach to propaganda derived just as much from the ideas that the propaganda was to convey. For he did not see the world in shades of grey – the complex pattern of ideas out of which his particular *Weltanschauung* (philosophy of life) had been constructed resulted in a singularly black-and-white view of the world, where virtue and sin, good and evil, heroes and villains were all too easily delineated.[2] Drawing on a variety of traditions, including early German *völkisch* (nationalist) writing, later nineteenth century racial theory, anti-Semitism and Social Darwinism, Hitler both idealized the past and demonized the present. He looked back to a mythical, medieval past in which the German *Volk* (people) had fulfilled its true destiny: a stable, racially pure, rural community, rooted in the soil of the homeland, entirely at one with its natural environment. Over succeeding generations, however, that original, idyllic community had been destroyed by a process of economic and social modernization that culminated in nineteenth-century industrial capitalism. Traditional German values had been replaced with the values of the market-place, a capitalism that was increasingly associated with notions of liberalism and parliamentary democracy.

Moreover, these changes had not been the result of anonymous, impersonal forces – quite the contrary, it was the Jews above all others who had subverted and undermined the original German tradition. Indeed, in early *völkisch* thinking, the very definition of what it was to be German was conceived in part in contradistinction to the Jews. The *Volk* was stable and settled – the Jews were wandering and rootless; the *Volk* was spiritual, the Jews were materialist; the *Volk* was the epitome of healthy rural life, the Jews embodied the decadence and corruption of the life of the city. Moreover, the Jews were not a separate group in open conflict with the *Volk*: they had penetrated into the very heart of German society and culture, and it was this penetration that had undermined the strength and the purity of the German people. While the positive characteristics of the original German tradition had not been entirely destroyed (they could still be found in rural Germany), the only way forward, however, was to exterminate what George Mosse in a memorable phrase called 'the snake at the root of the tree'.[3] In short, the Jews were the enemy, and it was only through their destruction that Germany could ever be reborn.

From such assumptions, Hitler and other radical nationalists developed their own explanation for the German situation in the years immediately after the First World War. The German armies had not been defeated on the battlefield – they had been 'stabbed in the back' by civilian politicians, who had dismantled the Wilhelmine monarchy and put Weimar democracy in its place. Weimar Germany and everything that it stood for represented the very antithesis of true German values; it was only with the total destruction of Weimar – its democratic politics, its liberal ideas, its experimental culture – and the complete exclusion of the Jews, that the *Volk* could ever be reborn. Moreover, in addition to the Jewish 'enemy within', the Jews outside

Germany posed a parallel threat, whether in the form of bankers and financiers who controlled the world economy, or the Bolsheviks who controlled Russia. Thus, it was the twin forces of international capitalism and Soviet Bolshevism that represented the most potent threat to contemporary Germany – the first responsible for the devastating economic crises which gripped Germany in the years 1919–1923 and 1929–1933; the second posing a direct military threat to the very survival of the German state.

Given such an analysis, there was only one way forward. The first step must be to purge the enemy within, for only then would Germany be able to develop the power to defeat her enemies abroad. The new Germany would then emerge triumphant out of the violent destruction of her enemies, powerful enough to construct a vastly enlarged German *Reich*, extending deep into Central and Eastern Europe. And in all of this, the people would be led to their new destiny by an entirely new kind of leader, presiding over an entirely new kind of politics. *Völkisch* writers had constructed the idea of a leader who combined the power of the philosopher with the courage and endurance of the medieval German knight, his values rooted in the values of the *Volk;* his mission, the racial mission of reclaiming the race's former greatness.[4] Hitler was convinced that he was that leader, a twentieth-century *Führer*, characterized by qualities that set him apart from all other Germans, who would lead the *Volk* to victory in the decisive final war with its racial enemies.

These then were the black-and-white ideas that were so important to Hitler. They provide an additional explanation for his emphasis on clear, simple propaganda: there was no ambiguity in the ideas and there should, therefore, be no ambiguity in the propaganda that would carry those ideas to the German people.

IDEOLOGY INTO PROPAGANDA

While there was nothing ambiguous about Nazi propaganda, Hitler and Goebbels[5] proved especially skilful in forging direct links between these ideas and the contemporary concerns of the German people and, in the propaganda campaigns of the mid- and late 1920s, these connections were constantly made. Thus, for example, they exploited working-class resentment of the wealth and power of the business classes by claiming that the enemy was not financiers and bankers, but an international conspiracy of *Jewish* financiers and bankers; for middle-class Germans worried about the rise of socialism, the enemy was not socialism itself, but international Jewish Marxism; Jews, it was claimed, had caused the Depression. In foreign policy, even the traditional nationalist dream of *Grossdeutschland* (a much larger German state in which the people would be able to expand and prosper) was linked to contemporary preoccupations with the defeat of Bolshevism;

National Socialism would deliver *Lebensraum* (living space), but it would be in Central and Eastern Europe, carved out of the defeat of the Slavs – another lesser race which must be destroyed if German culture was to triumph. In short, the translation of National Socialist ideology into the reality of the Nazi state manifested what Martin Broszat tellingly called a 'Janus-like quality', an ability to tap into powerful traditional ideas and link them explicitly to a new, contemporary reality. Thus:

> ... romantic pictures and clichés of the past ... were translated into the popular and the avant-garde, into the fighting slogans of a totalitarian nationalism ... the princely 'theory of divine right' gave way to the popular national *Führer*.[6]

A mythical vision of the past is translated into the terrifying contemporary reality of racial selection and the gas chambers.

In addition, Hitler's insistence on the importance of an emotional appeal to the target audience is repeatedly illustrated in the propaganda that helped to build popular support for National Socialism. The enormous emphasis on military symbols – parades, flags, uniforms, forms of address – triggered deeply felt emotions associated with Germany's former military might[7] while, on the streets, the violence of the uniformed SA[8] provided a powerful indication of just how far the Nazis were willing to go to defeat their enemies. In the carefully orchestrated set-piece occasions, music, flags and elaborate ritual served to arouse the audience in eager anticipation of the (invariably late) arrival of the *Führer*. The use of an aeroplane to transport Hitler from one location to another in the 1932 election campaign served not simply to allow him to visit many more locations: it powerfully dramatized and glamorized the 'coming' of the *Führer*. Certainly the intensity of the emotional response of his audiences testifies not just to Hitler's oratory, but also to the skill with which these events were staged. While there was a tendency in much early historical writing to overstate the importance of propaganda in explaining Hitler's rise to power, there can be little doubt that it was not favourable circumstances and political skill alone that explained his success – propaganda often served to translate the potential of such a situation into the actuality of enlarged support.[9]

Moreover, just as for the Bolsheviks before them, propaganda was no less important once the Nazis took power in 1933. Within days, Hitler had established the Ministry for Popular Enlightenment and Propaganda, with Goebbels as Minister, evidence in itself of just how important propaganda remained. The most obvious explanation was that, although they had won the support of 37 per cent of the electorate, 63 per cent had not supported them;[10] the job of mobilizing the mass of the German people behind the Nazi programme was far from complete. Moreover, while part of the Nazi response to that situation would be the banning of the other political parties and the systematic use of state terror to break their will to resist, contrary to the early historiography of Nazi Germany, this regime never governed by force alone – as Goebbels put it at the 1934 Nuremberg Party Rally: 'It may be a good thing to possess power that rests on arms. But it is better and more gratifying to win and hold the heart of the people.'[11] The reason was clear: the transformation the Nazis were attempting to achieve went far beyond the winning of conventional political support. Centuries of subversion and infiltration had led the people away from their true values, and those very values had to be restored if the new *Völkischer Staat* (People's State) was ever to be achieved. Thus it is no coincidence that the word 'Enlightenment' was used in the title of Goebbels' new Ministry, an unmistakable echo of the Bolshevik Commissariat of Enlightenment, with just the same revolutionary mission of ideological transformation.

What then was this 'enlightenment' which Goebbels' Ministry was required to achieve? In a wealth of historical analysis of this topic, one short essay by Ian Kershaw sets out, with exemplary economy and clarity, the interlocking objectives that would prepare the German people for the crucial battles that were to come.[12] Hitler had always understood that the new Germany could only be built after the violent destruction of its enemies, and therefore the nation had to be transformed into a 'fighting community' if it was ever to achieve those goals; nothing less than the complete reconstruction of German values would effect that transformation. Thus, where Germans were divided one from another by class, region, religion, or party political affiliation, a new sense of *Volksgemeinschaft* (national community) would be created. In the new Germany, all would derive their identity exclusively from their sense of belonging to that community – they would be Germans first and last. Moreover, this new oneness would find literal expression in the recovery of that 'racial purity' which, in the *völkisch* myth, had been the original condition of the people, and that in turn would mean the 'exclusion' of all those who were not classified as racially pure. And, while it was primarily the Jews and the gypsies who would be the victims of such a policy, many other minority groups (including homosexuals, social misfits, the mentally and physically disabled) were deemed racially degenerate and would thus suffer the same fate.

In another political culture, the regime might have been content with implementing policies to achieve these objectives without reference to public opinion, but it was the essence of Nazi ideology that the people should understand and welcome them. Thus, it is in their determination to secure that active support that the truly revolutionary character of Nazi objectives becomes clear, for it required nothing less than the destruction of any religious, ideological or ethical system that found such objectives unacceptable: it was a formidable task indeed. Hugely ambitious as such goals were, however, the construction of the *Völkischer Staat* also identified other propaganda goals that were perhaps more attainable. Thus, it was important to maximize hatred for those who would be the victims of the Nazi revolution, with propaganda representing them as enemies of the *Volk*. Moreover, while racial enemies in general, and the Jews in particular, were the primary targets of such a strategy, it was by no means limited to them alone. At home, all political opponents were characterized as enemies – outside Germany, any nation that opposed the new Reich was *ipso facto* an enemy. Running through all of this was the construction of a very particular idea of the leader. The *Führer* would embody in his person everything that was at the heart of the German tradition for, in Hitler, the people would find the complete expression of all the German virtues, the one man uniquely capable of acting only in ways that would serve the true interests of the nation. Thus, in presenting this god-like figure, the propaganda would lead the people not merely to accept his leadership, but rather to develop passionate adulation and uncritical obedience, to worship their one true saviour. As Rudolf Hess was to put it at the very end of the 1934 Party Rally: 'The Party is Hitler. But Hitler is Germany, just as Germany is Hitler.'[13]

That claim, that the whole project of transformation came together in the person of Hitler, provides an important reminder of the essentially interlocking character of these different objectives. In the new Germany, the only source of personal identity would derive exclusively from a deeply felt sense of nation, embodied (quite literally) in the person of Adolf Hitler. That new sense of national identity carried an equally clear sense of the nation's enemies which, in turn, created a recognition of the need to purge Germany of the enemy within and to defeat the enemy without. In recognizing the necessity of the battles ahead, the nation would indeed become the 'fighting community', capable of destroying all its enemies and securing for ever Germany's 'true' role in the world. Thereafter, the task of propaganda would become more conventional: as war approached, psychological mobilization would parallel military mobilization; in war, the people's morale would be strengthened and reinforced until, through the very process of conflict, the triumphant nation would finally realize its full potential, its destiny complete.

Thus propaganda was at the very heart of the National Socialist revolution, and Goebbels had no illusions about the scale of what was being attempted. In an early speech to representatives of the press he argued that the new regime had no intention of 'abandoning the people to their own devices and locking them up in an airless room'; rather it was the role of propaganda to forge an entirely new relationship between government and people:

> It is not enough to reconcile people more or less to our regime, to move them towards a position of neutrality towards us, we want rather to work on people until they are addicted to us.[14]

'We want to work on people until they are addicted to us': it was an extraordinary use of words, conveying all too accurately the scale of the ambition which animated Nazi propaganda.

THE ORGANIZATION OF PROPAGANDA

How then did Goebbels set about translating these objectives into practice? Any effective answer to that question has to take account of the complex and contradictory character of the state and Party apparatus in Nazi Germany for, while historians once characterized this as a monolithic, totalitarian regime, such a view is over-simplified and, in part, misconceived. Hitler's own position was indeed unchallenged and unchallengeable, but the policies over which he presided were characterized by conflict and division, a complex web of overlapping institutions, very many of which were in more-or-less open conflict one with another. This situation derived partly from the enormous gulf between the Party's rhetoric and its actions in power, for while the Nazis had promised a revolutionary restructuring of the whole of German society, in practice their ambitions were more limited. Thus, while Weimar democracy was dismantled, while all other political parties and the trade unions were destroyed, while state terror was used deliberately and systematically to destroy any overt political opposition, in marked contrast to the Soviet Union the regime did little to alter the deeper fabric of German society. German industrial capitalism continued to function much as it had always done, vital institutions such as the churches, the civil service, and, above all else, the army were left largely intact.

Thus this contested political culture was, in part, a product of the way in which the institutions of the Party were overlaid on top of existing, well-established and powerful German institutions. But that situation was further complicated by the fact that the Party itself was not a single, unified institution. Its various different sections enjoyed considerable autonomy, and the ambitious individuals who led them were left free to develop their own 'empires' almost as they saw fit, even if this brought them into direct conflict with some other Party institution or the state. All of this is illustrated by the administrative structure that Goebbels created during 1933 for, while the Party's own propaganda office continued to function, in March 1933 it was supplemented by the new Ministry of Propaganda and, in September 1933, by the Reich Chamber of Culture. Each had a slightly different role – the Party was responsible for 'spreading the National Socialist ideology and the achievements of the Party leadership'; the Ministry for 'the spiritual direction of the nation'; the Chamber of Culture for 'furthering German culture and regulating economic and social aspects of cultural affairs'.[15] The resulting competition and conflict was mitigated to some extent by the fact that all three institutions were led by Goebbels and, in both the Ministry and the Party Propaganda Office, many of the key posts were held by the same men.[16]

On the other hand, the relationship with existing departments of state was rather less harmonious, and the Ministry of Education successfully resisted repeated attempts by Goebbels to assume control over propaganda in schools. The Foreign Ministry also resented the fact that Goebbels was given responsibility for the control of news and information abroad, although, throughout the years that Neurath served as Foreign Minister, it proved unable to resist Goebbels' growing power. When Neurath was succeeded by Ribbentrop in 1938, however, the Foreign Ministry fought back, and by the summer of 1939 the two ministries were in open conflict, a conflict that was not fully resolved until late in 1941.[17] Thus at least some of Goebbels' energies were diverted into the competition and conflict that was so characteristic of Third Reich politics and administration.

Yet none of this stopped him from constructing a propaganda empire of considerable proportions. As early as 1934 the Party propaganda apparatus employed some 14,000 people spread throughout the Reich.[18] The Ministry's staff grew to nearly 2000 in 1941, while its annual expenditure rose from 14 million marks in 1933 to some 95 million on the eve of war, a total that had almost doubled by 1942, all funded (according to Goebbels) by the sale of radio licences.[19] Such dramatic growth might suggest that Goebbels had constructed (as some Party ideologues wanted) a bureaucracy large enough to control every aspect of German cultural and media production. But Goebbels' strategy was rather more sophisticated than this. For, while he was determined that all cultural and media production would conform to National Socialist ideology, he understood that such a transformation would be severely compromised if the true extent of political direction became clear. It was necessary to intervene, but he wanted the extent of that intervention to be concealed from the public, except where it would serve in itself to convey an important propaganda message. Thus no attempt was made to conceal the fact that Jews and other *entartete Künstler* (literally 'degenerate artists', but in effect a term used to describe anyone of whose ideology or aesthetics the Nazis disapproved) would no longer be allowed to work – the process of 'cleansing' was in itself a way of signalling the rebirth of true Aryan culture.

On the other hand, the extent to which the new Party and state agencies orchestrated cultural production was a much more closely guarded secret. Goebbels was reportedly furious when a magazine published a photograph of a man putting on a record of a triumphal bell chime after a special announcement and, at a subsequent press conference, journalists were told that 'problems of stage management should not on principle come before the public'.[20] The decision in 1936 to require critics to write only descriptive reviews may have been intended to serve a similar purpose, even if it was primarily concerned to remove the possibility of any negative comment about work which had been officially approved. Finally, Goebbels was determined that only a small proportion of cultural production should take the form of explicit and open propaganda. Just like Lenin before him, he understood that too much propaganda would be counter-productive and, while nothing that in any way subverted National Socialist values was allowed into the public domain, much cultural production in Nazi Germany was designed essentially to entertain and amuse.

Much of the burden of implementing this strategy fell on the Reich Chamber of Culture, with its seven Chambers for each area of cultural production.[21] The Chambers played the leading role in commissioning cultural or media products, but their most important function was to determine who was entitled to work in each particular field – the refusal of a permit brought an abrupt end to a professional career. On the other hand, those approved by the appropriate Chamber enjoyed a new measure of professional security – unless and until they acted in such a way as to incur disapproval. In this way Goebbels established a structure which achieved the maximum degree of control with the minimum public awareness that any such control was being exercised. With the important exception of the exclusion of Jews and others publicly condemned by the Nazis, Goebbels was determined to preserve the fiction that little had changed, and a more detailed examination of the way in which this policy was implemented in the film industry will reveal how this worked in practice.

Film was clearly a critically important medium for Goebbels. When he first addressed the assembled representatives of the German film industry at the end of March 1933, he claimed that he was 'a passionate devotee of the cinematographic art',[22] and for once he was speaking the truth. Thus he took a much more direct and time-consuming interest in the cinema than any of the other media, surrounding himself with the stars whom he had for so long admired from afar, and it is clear that he relished his position at the heart of the *Filmwelt*. Moreover, Goebbels shared his passion for cinema with no less a person than the *Führer* himself – one Christmas, for example, Goebbels gave Hitler 30 'serious films' and 18 'Mickey Mouse films'.[23] Yet, if the two shared a personal enthusiasm for cinema, it has often been argued that there were important differences in their understanding of how film could best be used for Nazi propaganda.

Thus, Hitler is represented as someone who preferred his film propaganda 'straight', repudiating the notion that propaganda could ever be effective when it was disguised as art; Goebbels, on the other hand, is seen as taking the contrary position, believing that propaganda would be at its most effective when it was least obvious – propaganda disguised as entertainment perhaps the most effective propaganda of all.[24] While there is much to be said in defence of this claim, notably the steps taken by Goebbels to ensure the closest possible supervision of *all* German films, the vast majority of which took the form of so-called 'entertainment' films with little if any explicit propaganda content, Goebbels' position was not quite as black-and-white or as consistent as this contrast suggests. Certainly he recognized that the cinema was a medium of entertainment and thus understood only too well that it must continue to fulfil that function – film programming that consisted of an unremitting diet of propaganda would surely drive the audiences away. Equally, as the Nazis were engaged in the construction of a new, all-embracing *völkisch* culture, even so-called entertainment films had to conform to that culture. At the very least they must not contain anything which would in any way subvert or challenge it; at best, they too would be imbued with National Socialist values. Indeed, Goebbels argued that films in which the propaganda remained in the background as 'a tendency, as a characteristic, as an attitude', would be 'effective in every respect'.[25]

However, he also recognized the central importance of a small number of films which would deliver their propaganda in just that direct, explicit register of which Hitler so warmly approved. Just like Hitler, Goebbels recognized the central role of the newsreel. Traditional claims that he strongly disapproved of Leni Riefenstahl's films of the 1933 and 1934 Party rallies, *Victory of Faith* (1934) and *Triumph of the Will* (1935), derive almost entirely from Riefenstahl's long-running attempts to rehabilitate her own reputation; Goebbels' own diaries present a very different view.[26] Most striking of all, recent research into the origins of *The Eternal Jew* (1940), the most explicit example of anti-Semitic film propaganda and, arguably, the clearest possible example of that direct, unashamed propaganda so favoured by Hitler, demonstrates Goebbels' role at the very heart of the film's production.[27] In short, Goebbels' position was rather more complex than many have claimed; while he understood the value of propaganda embedded in the narrative of films with no obvious propaganda purpose, he also saw a very important role for direct, explicit film propaganda.

THE GERMAN FILM INDUSTRY

In any event, Hitler and Goebbels were agreed that the propaganda potential of the cinema must be exploited to the full and, in marked contrast to the Bolsheviks, the German film industry in 1933 presented the Nazis with enormous opportunities. In the first place, this was an industry with a substantial pedigree, for while film production had grown slowly in Germany before the First World War, the wartime disruption of trade stimulated domestic film production and, in the latter part of the war, the German government increasingly recognized the propaganda potential of the medium. Partly as a result of that recognition, a major new film company, *Universum Film AG* (UFA), was founded at the end of 1917 in order that it could undertake, in General Lüdendorff's words, 'planned and energetic measures for influencing the masses in the interests of the state'.[28] UFA brought together a number of production, distribution and exhibition companies to achieve an unprecedented vertical integration (a model also being explored by those American studios that were ultimately to dominate Hollywood in the 1920s), and this, combined with a considerable injection of public and private finance, put the new company in an immensely powerful position. Much of that new capital was invested in the construction of new studios at Neubabelsberg, near Potsdam, and while this was too late to make any dramatic difference to wartime propaganda, Germany ended the war with a film industry especially well placed to compete successfully in post-war markets.[29] By the end of the war UFA had emerged as the dominant company within the German film industry; very soon thereafter, it would become the dominant company in the European film industry as a whole.

On the other hand, the spectacular success of the German film industry in the immediate post-war years was not simply the product of new wartime investment. It derived just as much from the remarkable achievements of German film-makers of the period, whether in producing lavish costume dramas like Lubitsch's *Anne Boleyn* (1920) or in innovative and experimental films like Wiene's *Cabinet of Dr. Caligari* (1919), many of which were not produced by UFA. Moreover, the German film industry's ability to sustain ever higher production values, ever more innovation, was also a product of the very favourable circumstances in which Germany traded in the immediate post-war period.[30] As the international value of the mark declined, any industry able to sell its products abroad secured disproportionately high returns. A German film that achieved even modest international success was assured of a healthy profit and, in the years up to 1924, the German film industry was unique in world cinema in being able to sustain much the same volume of film production as Hollywood.[31] It was in fact a large, thriving industry, with technical and aesthetic standards rivalling the very best that world cinema had to offer.

Yet, almost as quickly as it had risen, the German film industry began to decline. Problems arose partly from over-confident producers committing themselves to ever more ambitious and expensive films, but the essence of the changed situation is the mirror image of the earlier economic situation. Thus Germany's new currency stability removed the special advantages previously enjoyed by export industries; in negotiating the Dawes Plan, which redefined the level of German post-war reparations and helped to underpin the new economic stability, the Western powers (notably the Americans) insisted on a substantial reduction in Germany's exports and a greater opening up of the German market to foreign imports. Hollywood immediately saw an opportunity to cripple its one major competitor and American films flooded the German market. Many small German production companies went bankrupt and, by the end of 1925 even the mighty UFA was on the brink of collapse. Indeed, it was only saved by two American studios (Paramount and Metro-Goldwyn-Mayer) agreeing to subsidize its debt in exchange for access to its studios, cinemas and personnel, a deal which strongly favoured the American companies and which led to a large number of German film-makers going to work in Hollywood.[32] The 'Parufamet' deal demonstrated in unmistakable terms the extent of Hollywood's domination of world cinema – its one major rival had been eliminated.

For all that, it did not resolve UFA's continuing crisis and, with debts still rising, the company was forced to look for a new source of support. It came from Alfred Hugenberg, who already controlled an important cross-media empire with interests in advertising, publishing, the press, the cinema and a news agency. Initially giving UFA a substantial loan,

Hugenberg subsequently bought out the American studios, becoming chairman of the UFA board in 1927; a year later he became leader of the nationalist German National People's Party. At a stroke, the single most powerful company in the German film industry became committed to an extreme nationalist agenda and, while the immediate consequence was that the Nazis achieved a new prominence in UFA newsreels, the more important result was that the Nazis knew that if and when they took power, many within the German film industry would be favourably disposed towards them. Indeed, one historian argues that Hugenberg's deal with UFA provides especially clear evidence that the transformation of German cinema under the Nazis was simply the culmination of an interlocking series of economic, political and military developments which were already in place by the end of the First World War,[33] a view partly endorsed by other scholars who argue that some of the most important German films of the Weimar years disseminated ideas that were intrinsically sympathetic to National Socialism.[34]

Whatever the truth of such claims, when the Nazis came to power they confronted a very different situation to that which had faced the Bolsheviks 16 years before. While a small minority of film-makers were committed to left-wing parties or ideologies that were opposed to National Socialism, many more were employed by a company that had explicitly aligned itself with extreme nationalist policies five years earlier. At the very least this suggests a willingness to tolerate such an ideology – it may mean that by 1933 many German film-makers were already broadly sympathetic to Nazi ideology. In the event, the Nazis came to power in circumstances that were even more favourable than this, for by 1933 the industry was in the grip of a major crisis which made it even easier for the new regime to establish a successful relationship with the industry. That crisis was the product of both the Depression and the high cost of introducing the new technology of synchronized sound, and between 1928 and 1932 the total number of films produced fell from 224 to just 132; gross takings from 274.9 million marks to 176.4 million marks; annual audiences from 352 million to 238 million. Indeed, in 1932 the situation was so serious that only UFA made an overall profit and no fewer than 59 film companies went bankrupt.[35] In such a situation, a government that took positive steps to restore this once-successful industry would surely win enthusiastic support. And this is precisely what Goebbels did.

GLEICHSCHALTUNG [36]

Before that could be done, however, a detailed strategy for the film industry would have to be determined and when the Nazis came to power that job was still not complete, not least because Goebbels had first to establish control over the Party's own film-making activities. Starting in 1928, the Party had made a number of low-budget, somewhat amateur projects, focusing largely on its own activities and intended entirely for Party audiences; it was not until October 1932 that Goebbels finally achieved complete control over this aspect of the Party's work.[37] That achieved, he could concentrate his energies on the incomparably more important task of extending that control to the German film industry as a whole although, in seeking to do this, Goebbels had to negotiate his way through the profound divisions within both his own Party and the film industry itself. In the Party, policy proposals ranged from those which canvassed complete nationalization, to those which favoured greater centralization, albeit within a capitalistic structure, while others argued that the only practical way forward was to negotiate an accommodation with the existing industry.

In the industry, the divisions were even more profound. On the one side stood the *Spitzenorganisation der Deutschen Filmindustrie* (SPIO), the industry's main representative body dominated by the large companies like UFA. On the other, the German Cinema Owners' Association, representing the much larger numbers of small cinema owners, many of whom were facing bankruptcy in the worsening economic situation.[38] Relations between the two organizations had deteriorated to such an extent that in 1932 the Association's representatives were excluded from the SPIO board and, when SPIO published its own plans for the regeneration of the film industry in 1932, it blamed the cinema owners for much of the current crisis. Its solution was a radical rationalization of the industry, to be implemented by a new ministry of film, which would cut the number of cinemas by two-fifths, while incorporating SPIO and the association which represented the first-run cinemas into its new bureaucracy. All of this further antagonized the Cinema Owners' Association, and they instinctively looked to the National Socialists for support, not least because the Nazis had so often blamed the country's economic crisis on the large corporations – surely the Party would give them its support? Indeed, it was within the Cinema Owners' Association that the Nazis had made most progress, and a Nazi faction led by Adolf Engl finally acquired control of the organization in March 1933. Thus Goebbels faced a difficult choice: did he follow the radicals in his own Party and pursue policies designed to rescue the film industry through supporting the small cinema owners; or did he work instead with that small number of large film companies which already exercised considerable power in the industry?

To begin with, the position was unclear. SPIO engaged in discussions with the Ministry of Economic Affairs but, when knowledge of these talks became public in February, it provoked considerable opposition from both the Party's own paper (the *Völkischer Beobachter*) and the Cinema Owners' Association. Indeed, it was in the following month that Engl won control of the latter organization, and it looked for a moment as if the new regime would support the radicals. In fact, almost exactly the opposite happened. When Goebbels addressed the representatives of the film industry at the end of March, he took great care to reassure those who were anxious that the Nazis might be about to embark on a radical programme of restructuring the film industry. A speech which might, in other circumstances, have been interpreted simply as a reassuring statement to an industry anxiously grappling with a serious economic crisis was accurately seen as demonstrating Goebbels' willingness to ally himself with SPIO and the big battalions. Significantly, the full text of the speech was not made public – indeed, a carefully edited version appeared in the *Völkischer Beobachter*, misleadingly suggesting a more radical approach.[39]

Goebbels' intentions became even clearer in the months that followed. In May he dissolved DACHO, the industry's trade union; in June he adopted one of SPIO's key proposals, establishing the *Filmkreditbank* (Film Credit Bank) to provide much-needed new capital to fund film production. A week later, the entertainment tax on average film earnings was reduced from 11.5 to 8 per cent, and finally in July, he set up the *Reichsfilmkammer* (Reich Film Chamber). Significantly, the new Chamber immediately absorbed the Cinema Owners' Association, removing at a stroke any remaining opposition from that section of the industry and, because the Association had been linked to radicals within the Party, this aspect of *Gleichschaltung* served as much to 'co-ordinate' disparate strands within the Party, as to 'co-ordinate' the larger world with the Party. In all, this rescue package won Goebbels' many new friends in the boardrooms of the German film industry, although it soon became clear that it was a rescue that benefited some rather more than others. Thus, whereas before 1933, small- and medium-sized companies accounted for 60 per cent of the films on the market, by 1934/35 this figure had been halved to less than 30 per cent – by 1935/36 it was below 20 per cent. By that time, the market was dominated by just four firms (UFA, Tobis, Bavaria and Terra) – UFA and Tobis alone accounted for no less than 60 per cent of total German film production.[40] As in so many other areas of the German economy, it was the large corporations that were the primary beneficiaries of Nazi policy, and in return they willingly co-operated in realizing Goebbels' vision for cinema in the Third Reich.

On the other hand, Goebbels' was not content to rely on that goodwill, and the operation of the Film Credit Bank makes this abundantly clear. For, while it appeared to represent simply a much-needed initiative for generating new investment in the industry, in reality it served to extend Goebbels' control. At first it drew its capital from UFA and four commercial banks but, as early as June 1933, UFA's shares were transferred to SPIO; when SPIO was subsequently incorporated into the Film Chamber, its shares went with it. When the banks transferred their shares to the Film Chamber in the spring of 1934, the Film Credit Bank was effectively state owned. The scale of its operations grew quickly and, by 1936, it financed no less than 73 per cent of all German feature film production and, while it had to be persuaded that the films it supported were commercially viable, it also set out to encourage films that showed the way towards 'a truly German art'. In other words, its decisions were not simply commercial. The criteria against which potential projects were judged were always both ideological and commercial and, by the time the Film Chamber assumed total control of the Bank, its investment decisions provided Goebbels with a powerful instrument with which to influence the future shape of German film production.

None of this was obvious to the cinema-going public, although, in contrast, strenuous efforts were made to make them aware of another change that was initiated in this period, namely the exclusion from the industry of Jews and other film-makers designated as *entartete Künstler*. Thus it was not enough merely to emphasize that they would no longer be allowed to work in the film industry, the cinema audience had to be persuaded that these changes were positively desirable and fake statistics were produced deliberately to exaggerate the number of Jews in the industry. Prominent film-makers publicly declared their commitment to National Socialism and the public was even encouraged to name anyone whose racial origins were 'suspect', even the most prestigious stars were not immune from the resulting investigations.

While all of this represented an important start for Goebbels, the extent of his ambitions was such that further measures were necessary, and they came in the Reich Cinema Law of February 1934, which imposed much stricter censorship and control at every stage of the production process.[41] A new pre-production censorship required that all initial proposals be submitted to the new Reich Film Director; armed with his approval, a full script could be developed, although it too was subject to his scrutiny. Moreover, once the script had been approved, he could intervene at any stage in the production process and any changes required by him would be binding. The Law also gave the Reich Film Director responsibility for advising film-makers whose projects had been rejected, envisaging that this would 'prevent in time the treatment of themes contrary to the spirit of the times'.[42]

Once complete, films would be subject to the closest possible censorship. Weimar's two independent Censorship Offices were combined into a single Office, incorporated into the Film Chamber. All films were now subject to censorship, with no distinction drawn between private and public screenings – even the advertising of films was subject to the same scrutiny. Films were classified according to the age groups which were to be allowed to see them, and children under the age of six were allowed to attend only those films that had been approved by Goebbels himself. Strict penalties of fines and up to a year's imprisonment were introduced for any contravention of the censorship regulations. Most important of all, however, was the basis on which a film could be rejected, which was fundamentally changed. Thus, whereas the Weimar rules precluded the banning of a film 'out of political, social, religious, ethical or ideological tendencies', allowing censorship only when a film 'endangers public order and safety ... or endangers the German image or the country's relationship with foreign states',[43] under the 1934 Cinema Law a film could be banned if it:

> ... is liable to endanger the interests of the State or public order or security, or to offend National Socialist, religious, moral or artistic feeling, or to have a

brutalising or immoral effect, or to jeopardise German prestige or the relations of Germany with foreign countries.[44]

It does not take much imagination to understand just how elastic these new criteria were. Moreover, the Law also gave Goebbels the right to ask for any film to be re-examined, even after it had been approved; an amendment in June 1935 gave him the power to ban any film without reference to the Censorship Office.

The 1934 Law gave Goebbels one further weapon with which to influence the shape of future film production. In Weimar Germany, *Prädikate* (marks of distinction), with associated tax benefits, were awarded to films of exceptional merit. The awards were made on artistic grounds, and were determined by an independent Chamber for Film Evaluation. Under the new Law, the awards would be made by the Censorship Office, and the acquisition of a *Prädikat* became a precondition for public exhibition – without it, the exhibition of a film required special permission. Most important of all, the original artistic criteria were redefined, and the 11 *Prädikate* in place by 1939 were predominantly political: thus, three were designed for films which achieved varying degrees of political value, while others identified films variously as culturally valuable, valuable for youth, nationally valuable, a 'Film of the Nation', an instructional film, or a film of national education – just two identified films which were artistically valuable. From 1938, cinema owners were not allowed to refuse to exhibit a film that had been awarded a political *Prädikat*. A film that was awarded the *Prädikat* 'Valuable for Youth' or 'Film of the Nation' did not attract tax relief, but these were in many ways the most highly desired awards of all, as they substantially enhanced a film's status and were decisive in the selection of films for schools and Nazi youth organizations.

Thus the 1934 Cinema Law gave Goebbels a complex range of weapons with which to influence German film production but, because these new powers built on well-established Weimar practices, it preserved the fiction (at least as far as the public was concerned) that little had changed. Goebbels had acquired much the same degree of influence over film production that would have resulted from nationalization, but he had managed to avoid the disadvantages which would have been the inevitable consequence of public ownership. Indeed, as far as the public was concerned, apart from the exclusion of the Jews and the *entartete Künstler,* the film industry operated much as it had always done and, perhaps in consequence, the cinema audience began to recover from the decline of the Depression years. By 1934 the annual audience stood at 245 million; by 1938 it had risen to 430 million, surpassing the previous highest annual total of 352 million in 1928.[45] Audiences grew even more spectacularly in the war years, with annual admissions exceeding a thousand million for the first time in 1942 and, while part of this rise can be explained by reference to the enlarged territory of the wartime Reich, it was also the product of a marked increase in the frequency with which adult Germans visited the cinema. Thus annual cinema visits (for those over the age of 15) averaged 8.4 in 1938; by 1944, they had risen to 14.4. By any standards, film in Nazi Germany was reaching a substantial proportion of its target audience, a clear vindication of Goebbels' strategy of reaching the population through the existing forms of commercial distribution and exhibition.[46]

Young people constituted an especially important part of that audience, for it was widely assumed that they were more profoundly influenced by cinema than adults.[47] Thus, it was recognized that there were limits to the extent to which adults could be persuaded to abandon long-held ideologies and beliefs, but it was assumed that children exposed to propaganda from a very young age could be wholly persuaded of the virtues of Nazi ideology. Moreover, these young people constituted the coming generation and, if National Socialism was to survive, it was theirs and the generations that would follow that would sustain the thousand year Reich. In consequence, in addition to reaching young people in the cinemas (where they were in any event disproportionately well represented), the regime developed two further approaches. First, and most obvious, was the use of film in schools. Schools had been equipped with 16mm projectors in the Weimar years, and teachers were thus already experienced in using film in the classroom. Moreover, teachers as a group were especially well disposed to the new regime – 97 per cent were members of the Nazi Teachers' Association and, as early as 1936, no less than 32 per cent were members of the Party as well. Therefore, this should have been an especially fruitful venue within which Nazi film propaganda could be directed at young people, and as early as June 1934 the Reich Office for Educational Films was set up to organize the production and distribution of appropriate films for schools. In practice, however, film propaganda in schools was bedevilled by that internal competition so typical of the Nazi state apparatus – the Ministry of Education refused to hand over responsibility for this work to Goebbels, and continuing competition between the two ministries always undermined the effectiveness of this particular initiative.

Probably more important, therefore, was the second approach: working through the Hitler Youth organization. Film Hours for the Young were first organized on a monthly basis in April 1934 in Cologne – by 1936, regular Sunday shows were being held across the Reich. In 1938/39 some 2.5 million young people attended these shows, and by 1942/43 that number had increased by almost 500 per cent to 11.2 million.[48] Notwithstanding their title, Film Hours invariably included a number of activities: there was often a guest speaker who introduced the film and led the discussion after it was shown; in addition there was community singing, flag hoisting and sometimes a short political drama as well. That said, the film was the central attraction and, in contrast to film shows in schools (where the silent films were specially produced for 'educational' purposes, with the teacher providing an appropriate commentary), Film Hours for the Young included feature films and newsreels, as well as films made specially for this audience.

So successful were these film shows that, during the war, the practice of taking films to the people outside the cinemas was used for adult audiences as well. Goebbels equipped no less than 1500 mobile film units, taking film shows (predominantly of newsreels) to those parts of the population who lived outside the reach of the urban cinemas.

Thus, in all these ways, Goebbels' film propaganda strategy worked well. He achieved considerable control over German film production and, in marked contrast to the Bolsheviks and the British propagandists during the First World War, he did ensure that those films were seen by the mass of the population at whom they were targeted. All of this required the closest possible collaboration between the Propaganda Minister and the commercial film industry, and just such a close, collaborative relationship was established within the first 18 months of Nazi rule. Goebbels had every reason to be satisfied with the *Gleichschaltung* which he had effected within the German film industry.

FILM PRODUCTION COSTS AND PROFITABILITY

But there remained one important aspect of this strategy which had not been successful. The original plan for the regeneration of the German film industry formulated by SPIO in 1932 had intended to put the industry once again on a profitable basis, and Goebbels was just as committed to achieving that financial objective, if only because his film propaganda strategy required a thriving and profitable industry. As it turned out, however, this financial objective proved extraordinarily elusive for, notwithstanding the substantially increased audience, the profitability, even the viability, of individual film companies did not improve – indeed, in many cases, the difficult situation of 1933 only deteriorated further as many small- and medium-sized companies went into bankruptcy. The core of the problem lay with an inexorable rise in film production costs, amounting to no less than 200 per cent over the 10 years from 1927 to 1937.[49] This sharp rise in costs can be explained in a number of ways, of which the dramatic increase in top stars' salaries was perhaps especially significant.[50] Their bargaining power increased, both because the total number of actors remaining in Germany declined as a result of the Nazis' own policies, and also because the very nature of Goebbels' strategy demanded that wherever possible 'Nazi' films should feature the same stars as films made before 1933. Moreover giant companies like UFA were able and willing to pay these inflated salaries, and it was this that put medium or small studios in such a difficult situation.

Alongside this rise in costs, however, the German film industry witnessed an equally dramatic decline in the revenues earned from exports. Before 1933 no less than 40 per cent of the industry's income had come from foreign distribution; by 1934/35 this was down to below 15 per cent, and by 1936/37, below 7 per cent. Once again, the Nazis' own policies were to blame, both because knowledge of Nazi racial policy made American film distributors increasingly reluctant to take German films, and also because, in a period where trade quotas were widely applied, Goebbels' determination to reduce the number of films imported into the German market had an inevitable impact on German companies' ability to sell into those overseas markets. Overall, the industry's losses, which were running at between eight and ten million Reichsmarks in 1935/36, had risen to over ten million Reichsmarks the following year. Once again, the industry was facing a serious economic crisis, raising many of the same questions that had so exercised the industry when Hitler first came to power.

One answer would have been nationalization, for it would have given Goebbels that ability to manage costs that he presently lacked, but once again that option was rejected. Goebbels remained convinced that nationalization would fatally undermine the credibility of film propaganda, while making film exports even more problematic. The alternative was to embark instead on a strategy which would deliver a much greater degree of control over the film industry, without the public understanding the scale of the change that was taking place. The opportunity to pursue such a strategy was provided by Max Winkler, a former delegate to the Prussian *Landtag* who, working with the active support of the Weimar government, had bought controlling interests in a large number of German newspapers in those areas in the east of Germany which had been ceded after the war. When the Nazis came to power, he worked with the new government massively to extend his newspaper holdings, buying closed-down Communist or Jewish papers, and any others that were financially weak. By 1939 he had either bought outright, or had achieved controlling interests in, over 2000 newspapers.

Winkler was thus ideally placed to pursue precisely the same strategy with the film industry. The economic crisis which confronted the German film industry in 1936 created the opportunity, and Winkler started by acquiring no less a company than UFA itself. While the principles of such a strategy were tried and tested, pursuing the same strategy in the film industry demanded very much larger capital sums and, in all, Winkler needed some 64 million Reichsmarks of public money to acquire majority share-holdings in all Germany's major film companies. The companies retained their individual identities and the very nature of the strategy preserved the fiction of their private ownership. Moreover, Winkler did not exercise his new power with a heavy hand – the whole purpose of the strategy was to try to control costs by moderating competition between the various companies, while at the same time exercising an even stricter control over the nature of the films that were produced. At much the same time, Goebbels took a further initiative to strengthen the industry. In 1938 he set up a film school, the *Deutsche Filmakademie*, to ensure that any shortfall in personnel would be made good, that the new generation of film-makers would be entirely loyal to the regime and that the industry would have at its disposal the best-trained workforce outside Hollywood.

Both these initiatives had only begun to make an impact on the industry when the situation was transformed by the outbreak of war – at home, cinema-going became more popular than ever, while Germany's early military successes substantially enlarged the market for German films. In these changed circumstances, the new priority was to increase the number of films being made; Winkler estimated that the industry needed to produce at least 100 feature films a year to satisfy the new enlarged market. However, by 1941 it became clear that this target was not going to be reached, and Winkler re-examined the situation once more. He found that production was 29 per cent down on 1939/40; costs had risen by 68 per cent, while the gross profits of the companies he controlled had fallen by 12 per cent. Films were taking too long to make. The Propaganda Ministry was commissioning too many films with excessively high production values, and was intervening too often, thereby slowing the production process down still further. It was, in short, a deeply unsatisfactory situation, and Winkler concluded that if radical action was not taken, production would continue to decline.

In the event, just such radical action was taken and the new strategy, introduced at the end of 1941, went very much further than any of the earlier attempts to restructure the industry. In November 1941, the *Deutsche Filmtheater GmbH* was formed to take control of all German cinemas; two months later, the *Deutsche Filmvertriebs GmbH* was set up to take over film distribution; and finally, on 10 January 1942, a new giant trust company, *UFA-Film GmbH* (UFI) was created, to serve as a single umbrella organization for the entire German film industry. Nationalization had come at last, although even at this eleventh hour Goebbels concealed the extent of the change from the cinema-going public, and films continued to be released under the names of the old production companies. What evidence there is suggests that this final restructuring of the industry did achieve the financial objectives that had animated Winkler's activities ever since 1936. At long last, the inexorable rise in production costs came to an end: 1942 was the peak year and, in both the following years, small but appreciable reductions were achieved. In 1941/42 and 1942/43 UFI recorded net profits of 18 million Reichsmarks, which meant that the film industry was no longer dependent on state aid. In all, Petley calculates that the state was now achieving an annual return of some 200 per cent on the 80 million Reichsmarks which it had invested. On the other hand, Winkler's production targets were never met – in 1942 only 57 films were completed, and while this grew to 78 in 1943, it fell back once again to 64 in 1944.[51]

In the closing months of the war all of this became increasingly irrelevant. Allied bombing raids had a devastating impact on the cinemas, and the overriding imperative became one of maintaining sufficient capacity for the mass audience. Thus, in those towns that suffered the heaviest bombing, a number of legitimate theatres were converted into cinemas, and throughout the latter months of the war Goebbels gave the highest priority to the repair of damaged cinemas – in Berlin alone, for example, no less than 174 cinemas were repaired, or were in the process of being repaired between June 1943 and June 1944. In the end, however, it was a losing battle and, by the time the war ended, only about 35 per cent of the cinemas remained open.[52] Goebbels' great ambition for a powerful, popular cinema of propaganda, just like the larger ambition for a powerful, popular thousand-year Reich lay, quite literally, in ruins.

But that was, of course, only true in the closing months of the war. Looking at the history of the Third Reich as a whole, Goebbels had gone a very long way towards realizing almost all the goals of his film propaganda strategy. Within 18 months of the Nazis' coming to power he had achieved effective control of the industry while sustaining the illusion (in the minds of the public at least) that the free-market German film industry continued to serve its audience just as it had always done. From then until 1945 he ensured both that no film of which he disapproved was ever shown in Germany and, more important, that all the films that were shown conformed precisely to his vision of what was appropriate for the new *Völkischer Staat*. While that meant that the vast majority of films did not overtly or explicitly preach National Socialist ideology, none challenged that ideology, and an important minority of films set out explicitly and overtly to present that ideology to the mass cinema audience. Moreover, in contrast to the experience of the Bolsheviks in the 1920s, with only a handful of exceptions, these films did reach their target audiences. German films were popular with German audiences throughout the Nazi years, and year on year those audiences grew larger and larger, with the most dramatic increases being achieved during the war years. If the widely-held assumptions about the power of film as a medium of propaganda were true, then Goebbels had surely created the ideal set of circumstances in which that potential could be realized. Just as in the Soviet Union of the 1920s, Nazi propaganda films (clearly and unambiguously identifiable as such) constituted a small proportion of the total number of films which made up the regular diet of the growing number of people who went to the cinema; but, in stark contrast to the Soviet Union, the majority of those propaganda films did achieve large audiences. Surely, in those circumstances, the propaganda must have been successful?

THE FILMS AND THEIR AUDIENCE

But was it? Did the propaganda films achieve that transformation in ideology which was the very *raison d'être* for their production? Much of the early writing on Nazi propaganda argued that they did, but recent scholarship has increasingly challenged that view, both by looking more closely at what evidence there is of the way in which audiences responded to the films, and by setting that knowledge within a broader historical understanding of public opinion in Nazi Germany. None of this is easy. The evidence of audience response to the films is fragmentary, incomplete and always so much less detailed than even the least industrious historian would want and, in this particular case, much of the data appears to be especially problematic. The effective banning of public criticism of films in 1936 denies us access to that source of evidence; the growing power of the various internal security agencies, the emergence of a political culture that was increasingly dominated by fear, suspicion, anxiety and insecurity, and which encouraged everyone to denounce anyone suspected of opposition to the state, all served to create a situation in which most people were extremely reluctant to express honestly held opinions.

However, one of the most striking features of the regime was its highly developed awareness of public opinion – almost every relevant organization of the Party or the state monitored public opinion, and the data which survives contains a mass of information. Especially useful here are the reports on civilian morale and public opinion prepared from 1939 onwards by the *Sicherheitsdienst* (Security Service) of the SS (hereafter referred to as the SD) which, on occasion, provide explicit discussion of audience reception of individual films. Moreover, the mass of data that originated from the regime can be supplemented by the detailed reports which were made to the *Sopade* – the exiled leadership of the Social Democratic Party. While the absence of opinion polls makes it impossible to quantify the precise extent of particular views, the careful and rigorous application of well-established methods of historical investigation can lead to a remarkably full and well-founded analysis of this most difficult topic.[53]

In drawing on work of this kind to try to assess the efficacy of Nazi film propaganda, this analysis will explore what was achieved in four important areas. First, the attempt to construct representations of Adolf Hitler as the supreme, all-powerful, all-wise, god-like leader; secondly, the attempt to mobilize a virulent, fanatical anti-Semitism among the audience, which would give its active support to ever-more radical anti-Semitic policies; thirdly, the attempt to change attitudes towards what the Nazis euphemistically called their programme of 'euthanasia action'; and finally, the attempt to construct a particular representation of war, both before and during the war. These four examples have been chosen, because they provide the opportunity to examine film propaganda facing different challenges, notably the difference between, at one extreme, simply reinforcing existing attitudes while, at the other, attempting to challenge established views, putting a new ideology in their place. As early as 1936, Aldous Huxley had emphasized the importance of such a distinction, arguing that:

> Political and religious propaganda is effective, it would seem, only upon those who are already partly or entirely convinced of its truth ... The propagandist is a man who canalizes an already existing stream. In a land where there is no water, he digs in vain.[54]

The analysis that follows provides an opportunity to test the validity of Huxley's claim.

IMAGES OF LEADERSHIP

It has long been understood that the construction of a very particular set of attitudes towards the *Führer* was at the heart of the National Socialist project. The proposition that Adolf Hitler was uniquely capable of effecting that revolutionary transformation that would enable Germany once more to achieve its 'true' destiny was so important, not only because it encapsulated a positive, optimistic vision of the future, but also because it presented a powerful icon of unity in an otherwise deeply divided political culture. Moreover, popular as Hitler was when he took power in 1933, he became even more popular in the years that followed. The absence of free elections and public opinion polls makes it difficult to be absolutely certain, but an analysis of changing attitudes towards Hitler demonstrates a remarkable rise in popularity right through the first six years of Nazi rule; by the time Hitler celebrated his fiftieth birthday in April 1939, a *Sopade* report accepted that the extent of popular devotion to Hitler was not a figment of the propagandists' imagination: it derived 'from a naïve faith which is not so easily destroyed'.[55]

Further, the spectacular military victories in the early months of the war served only to intensify that adulation and, by the early summer of 1941, Hitler was more popular than ever. An SD report commented on 'the childlike trust [with which] the most ordinary people in particular look up to the *Führer*',[56] and this and other reports repeatedly demonstrate that any anxieties which people had about the future of the war were dissipated by their unquestioning faith in Hitler. The Party, other Nazi leaders, even the military commanders, were fallible and capable of making mistakes – Hitler alone could be relied on to do only what was in the best interests of the nation. Hardly surprising, then, that Goebbels commented at the time that 'the creation of the *Führer* myth' was, indeed, his greatest propaganda achievement.[57] Thereafter, of course, as the first news of military setbacks on the Eastern Front began to reach Germany, the position started to change, although criticism of the Party grew much more quickly than criticism of the *Führer*. Up until the deep trauma of the Stalingrad defeat in February 1943, most people were willing to attribute every setback to 'the King's evil advisers', but after Stalingrad the position began to change and, by the end of the war, adulation of Hitler had all but disappeared. When a memorial service was held in the little Bavarian town of Markt Schellenberg in March 1945, the call for a *'Sieg Heil'* for the *Führer* was met with silence, soldiers and civilians expressing in their silence more eloquently than any words the scale of the transformation that had taken place over the preceding two years.[58]

For all that, Goebbels' earlier claim appears to have been well-founded. The uninterrupted growth in Hitler's popularity during the first 10 years of Nazi rule was truly remarkable, and Goebbels gave the construction of the *'Führer'* myth the highest possible priority in Nazi propaganda of this period. Certainly this was as true of film as any other medium, and throughout the Third Reich the newsreel always focused special attention on Hitler, so much so that it was reported in 1941 that 'a newsreel without pictures of the *Führer* was not regarded as up to standard'.[59] But in addition to the newsreel footage, a small number of feature films played their part as well. Most famous of these was the two-hour documentary of the 1934 Party Rally, *Triumph of the Will* (1935), although Leni Riefenstahl's earlier film *Victory of Faith* (1934) had also celebrated Hitler's leadership.[60] Thereafter no further major documentary film about Hitler was ever made, and Leiser may well be right in arguing that 'after *Triumph of the Will* there was no need to make another film about Hitler',[61] although Hitler did, of course, appear regularly in newsreels and some other documentaries.

A number of other films, however, served to underpin the 'Hitler myth', albeit in a less direct way, by examining the achievements of a remarkable individual who could be seen as illustrating some of the *Führer*'s special qualities. Occasionally such films had a contemporary narrative, as for example in *The Ruler* (1937), whose central character was a powerful industrialist, but more commonly the parallels were drawn with important historical figures, reinforcing the notion that Hitler embodied everything that was best in the German historical tradition. The films did not concentrate exclusively on political leaders, but included anyone who could be represented as having triumphed over the prevailing assumptions of his generation. The most important examples were *Friedrich Schiller* and *Bismarck*, both released in 1940, and *The Dismissal* (a further film about Bismarck) and *The Great King* (a film about Frederick the Great), both released in 1942. Goebbels returned to this theme in the dying months of the war, with *Kolberg* (1945), a film that attempted to revive faith in Hitler by celebrating the resistance of the fortress town to the invading Napoleonic armies, under the courageous leadership of its mayor.[62] But although the film was completed before the war ended, its release was overtaken by events – it ran for only a few days in Berlin.[63]

If *Kolberg* made little impact, the earlier historical films all played to large audiences – *The Dismissal* and *The Great King* proved especially successful, sharing seventh place among the fifteen most profitable films of 1940 to 1942.[64] Not that this was, in itself, especially remarkable, for lavish costume dramas with high production values had long been a popular *genre* at the German box office. But what evidence there is does suggest that audiences understood the political message of these films. Thus the SD reported that audiences for *Bismarck* found 'direct parallels between Bismarck's struggle to establish a united German Reich and the unifying work of the *Führer*', while many in the audience for *The Great King* found '*a mirror image of our own age*' (original italics).[65] But the fact that audiences drew these conclusions demonstrates that they already saw Hitler in terms which enabled the parallel to be made. If the all-important connection was to be made with Schiller, or Bismarck, or the industrialist of *The Ruler*, then the audience had to supply the Hitler element in that equation. Thus if these films did achieve their objectives, all this demonstrates is that the 'Hitler myth' was already well-established by the time that they were seen. Indeed, such a conclusion is entirely consistent with the chronology of Hitler's growing popularity for, by the outbreak of war, all the important foundations of the 'Hitler myth' were in place.

On the other hand, Riefenstahl's two documentaries were seen much earlier, and it is possible therefore that they made a more proactive contribution to the construction of that myth. Energetic efforts were made to promote both Riefenstahl's documentaries and, although *Victory of Faith*'s emphasis on Ernst Röhm (the SA leader who was killed in the purge of June 1934), restricted its exhibition to the seven months up to his death, it was widely seen during those months.[66] Cinema owners were encouraged to screen *Triumph of the Will* as the main feature, although it did not prove to be especially popular, and in many cinemas it was replaced after a week. In the years that followed, it was shown to both Party and Hitler Youth audiences.[67] *Victory of Faith* served as the model for Riefenstahl's later film, but *Triumph of the Will* was undoubtedly the more important of the two. It won considerable critical acclamation: one month after its première it was awarded the German National Film prize, and later the same year it won the Gold Medal at the 1935 Venice Film Festival in fascist Italy; more surprisingly, it also won the Gold Medal at the Paris World Exhibition of 1937. Nor did the film lose its audience after 1945 – probably no other Nazi film has been so frequently screened since the war, and many of the most enduring images of the regime and its leader derive from Riefenstahl's film.

Following an apparently chronological narrative, *Triumph of the Will* presents a record of various aspects of the Party rally held at Nuremberg, 4–10 September 1934, although no one can fail to understand that this is first and foremost a film about the *Führer* himself. After an overture (which is played against a blank screen), and a title sequence which tells us in a series of short statements (presented in a distinctive Gothic typeface) that 'nineteen months after the beginning of the rebirth of Germany' Hitler flew to Nuremberg 'to muster his faithful followers', the film opens in the clouds. The clouds part and we see an aeroplane and subsequently, medieval Nuremberg below, through whose streets thousands march in perfect formation. The plane touches down and Hitler emerges to the cheers and adulation of the crowd and we follow his triumphal progress into the heart of the city, with a series of breathtaking tracking shots both alongside and immediately behind the open limousine in which Hitler stands. The *Führer* has descended from the clouds to greet his faithful followers, their facial expressions and body language revealing only too clearly the intensity of their passionate adoration.

Already in these opening 11 minutes, the two interlocking ideas that are at the heart of the film have been established, for Nazi ideology required not just a singular representation of the *Führer*, but also that he be seen as the embodiment of the nation. The nation, therefore, must have a clear and tangible identity and in these opening sequences that identity is found in the richness of the German past. The aerial shots of Nuremberg reveal the full glory of its medieval splendour, and although the film soon moves to the realities of contemporary Nazi power, this happens only after the most lyrical sequence in the film has given the audience a series of idyllic images of Nuremberg at first light. Thereafter the main body of the film offers countless sequences in which serried ranks of uniformed men with all the associated Nazi paraphernalia (flags, belts, boots, burning torches, drums, banners) construct a persuasive sense of the apparently limitless extent of the Party's power. And yet Riefenstahl is always careful to link these images back to the person of Hitler himself in a manner which emphasizes the bond between *Führer* and nation, while always stressing Hitler's separateness.

Nowhere is this clearer than in the sequences which are at the political heart of the film. For this particular Nuremberg rally took place just two months after the purge of Röhm and the other SA leaders, and the occasion that brought together 100,000 SA and SS men in the Luitpold Stadium on 9 September was designed both to reassure the SA and to establish Lutze as their new leader. It opens with a huge Nazi eagle, a recurring icon in the film, and this is immediately followed by an extraordinary overhead shot as we look down at the huge numbers of men assembled in the stadium. For a moment the scale is so vast that it is difficult to be certain what we are watching, but as our eyes adjust to the spectacle we see that the men are arranged in two vast rectangles, divided by a space in which just three men are walking. These three men are Hitler, Lutze (the new head of the SA) and Himmler (head of the SS) and, as the camera descends, we see just how carefully this formation has been choreographed. Hitler walks a couple of paces in front of the other two and this distance is maintained as they move towards the fires that burn in memory of martyred Nazi heroes. They stand and salute the flames and then turn and walk again through the serried ranks of men, the choreography of leadership sustained throughout. Once again Riefenstahl encapsulates the twin themes of the film: the new nation, personified in the tens of thousands of uniformed men; and the *Führer*, deriving his power from the mass, yet separate, unique, solitary.

After this extraordinary introduction, the film continues with a sequence in which the men regroup, the complex and sweeping movements of the men and their flags echoed in the cinematography, as the camera sweeps and tracks overhead. Hitler then addresses the men, a solitary figure on a massive concrete rostrum, whose physical separateness is emphasized by the position of the camera as it looks up, reverently, at the leader. The words of his speech seek to heal the tensions which might, in other circumstances, have been the consequence of the Röhm purge, but important as those words are, they are immediately overshadowed by what follows: the consecration of the flags and banners, in which Hitler solemnly touches each of the new flags with the old 'blood flag'.[68] While the facial expressions and body language of both Hitler and the men speak powerfully of the realities of leadership and the led, what makes this sequence so special is the fact that Riefenstahl's cameras now take the audience right into the heart of the action. A combination of the staging and the location of the camera brings us closer and closer to Hitler until, in the end, he is almost presenting the flag to us. It is, by any standards, a remarkable moment.[69]

Thereafter the film never again achieves such emotional intensity, and the 18 minutes of the penultimate section of the film, covering the military march-past in the streets of Nuremberg, is probably 15 minutes too long! Yet, for all its repetition, Riefenstahl's film achieves its political objectives in almost every frame, constructing an ideology consistent in all important respects with the central tenets of Nazi ideology. For the Party faithful it serves the immediate short-term goal of re-affirming unity in the wake of the Röhm purge, while at the same time offering enormously powerful images of the Party and its leader; for the German people, the film constructed a complex and powerful portrait of the new National Socialist nation – masculine, disciplined, loyal, rooted in its medieval past, yet looking forward with confidence and optimism to its brave new future. And in and through it all is Adolf Hitler, Riefenstahl offering her audience both images of the all-powerful *Führer*, and also images that are altogether more intimate and personal. Of the two central themes, it is the representation of the *Führer* that is, in the end, more powerful, and Hess's words, the last words spoken in the film, accurately sum up this most political of films: 'The Party is Hitler. But Hitler is Germany, just as Germany is Hitler. Hitler! Sieg Heil!'

Now that it is clear that Goebbels' apparent disapproval of the film and its director is just one more part of Riefenstahl's campaign to rehabilitate her reputation, his public praise for the film ('steel-like in its conviction and fired by a passionate artistry'[70]) probably expressed his own assessment – no other documentary film of Hitler was ever made because *Triumph of the Will* gave him what he wanted. Thereafter it was simply a matter of reminding the cinema audience of that construction of the *Führer*, and this was a role for which the newsreel was ideally suited. The film fulfilled every one of Goebbels' ideological and cinematic objectives, but does that mean that, together with its predecessor (*Victory of Faith*) and all the newsreel footage that followed, it was responsible for creating the 'Hitler myth'? Was Goebbels' faith in film as a medium of propaganda vindicated by *Triumph of the Will*?

To answer that question, we need to examine the evidence of changing attitudes towards Hitler in the months following the film's release, for it was in the months following the première on 1 May 1935 that it was most widely seen, and its potential impact was largest, and yet in precisely that period there was a marked *decline* in Hitler's popularity. The year had started very well with the Saar Plebiscite in January[71] and the reintroduction of universal military service in March, powerful evidence of the regime's willingness to turn its back on one of the most resented provisions of the Versailles Settlement. Both decisions served enormously to strengthen Hitler's growing popularity – as *Sopade* observers were forced to report, 'Hitler has again won extraordinary popularity. He is loved by many ...'[72] The following month Hitler celebrated his birthday, and one month later *Triumph of the Will* was released.

But thereafter attitudes changed. The promulgation of the notorious anti-Jewish laws at the 1935 Nuremberg Party Rally was one source of a new unease with the leadership, which led the Stettin Gestapo to write of 'a tone of command ... which is more off-putting than attractive', with increasing evidence of 'a mood of opposition'. Mounting economic problems – low wages, rising living costs, food shortages and still high levels of unemployment – were an even more important source of dissatisfaction with the regime, and much of that dissatisfaction now focused on Hitler himself. By July *Sopade* commentators were writing that 'the Hitler cult is visibly in decline', and were even beginning optimistically to speculate about the end of the Nazi regime. Conditions and attitudes continued to deteriorate throughout the winter of 1935/36; by early March 1936 the Berlin Gestapo reported that one could go for days without hearing the 'Heil Hitler' greeting; there was no longer 'a general trust in the State leadership and Movement' and while much of the responsibility for this rested with the behaviour and lifestyle of Party leaders and functionaries, Hitler was not immune from this radical change in public opinion – 'the confidence of the population in the person of the *Führer* is also undergoing a crisis'.

In the event the crisis proved short-lived. German troops marched into the Rhineland on 7 March 1936, and this spectacular and unexpected success provoked almost uniform celebration and approval, with Adolf Hitler once again the supreme beneficiary. But what this demonstrates is the marginal role played by *Triumph of the Will* in shaping attitudes towards Hitler. His growing popularity before the film's release derived from the achievements of the preceding months; the rapid decline in his popularity, at the very time when the film was most widely seen, was the result of mounting problems in the world outside the cinemas. At a time when the 'Hitler myth' was facing a serious challenge, with many Germans questioning their support for their *Führer*, the film appeared powerless to defend the myth; it was not the film that solved this problem, but the very tangible achievement of the reoccupation of the Rhineland. Moreover, the rise in Hitler's popularity over the next six years must also be explained above all else by reference to his perceived achievements. As the *Sopade* explained in the spring of 1939, it was Hitler's success in solving the scourge of mass unemployment, coupled with dramatic successes in foreign policy (the Austrian *Anschluß*, the acquisition of Czechoslovakia), that led so many Germans to believe that Hitler was indeed the demigod of Nazi propaganda – the achievements were so extraordinary that they could only have been achieved by a leader of equally extraordinary qualities. The even more dramatic *blitzkrieg* victories of the early months of the war served only to intensify the myth – as the Governor of Swabia put it in July 1940, all 'well-meaning' citizens recognized 'wholly, joyfully and thankfully the superhuman greatness of the *Führer* and his work'.[73]

But, having said all that, it is important not to exaggerate the failure of the film propaganda. Most obviously, the opportunity for Hitler's achievements to make such a profound impact on public opinion was a direct product of the extent to which the people were informed about those achievements, and while the press and the radio carried the primary responsibility for this, the newsreels did play an important supporting role. Actuality footage of German troops in the Rhineland, of Hitler entering Vienna, of the defeat and occupation of Poland and France made its own distinctive impact. In addition, the fact that those who accepted the 'Hitler myth' did so in terms which largely reflected Goebbels' own definition of that myth, is in itself a product of the particular iconography and imagery of Nazi propaganda, which can be identified in all important respects in Riefenstahl's films. While much of this has its roots in a much earlier German tradition, it was arguably Riefenstahl's and Goebbels' particular achievement to tap into those well-established cultural and historical traditions and present them anew in the 'modern' formulations of Nazi culture. Goebbels had constructed a very particular 'Hitler myth', and Riefenstahl's films made a powerful contribution to that achievement. And yet, as the events of 1935 and 1936 revealed, without real success in domestic or foreign policy, not even propaganda as powerful as *Triumph of the Will* was capable of manufacturing support for Hitler. Many historians have drawn attention to Hitler's apparently excessive preoccupation with the changing shape of public opinion – this particular example suggests that those preoccupations may have been well-founded.

ANTI-SEMITIC FILM PROPAGANDA

The fanatical anti-Semitism which was central to Nazi ideology manifested itself almost at once in the systematic exclusion of the Jews from the film industry, but it did not lead to the immediate production of anti-Semitic films. In fact it was not until 1939 that Jews were featured as central characters in Nazi films, although both *Robert and Bertram* and *Linen from Ireland* were comedies and, not least because of what was to follow, have been characterized as 'relatively innocuous'.[74] What came the following year was three very different films: two feature films, *The Rothschilds* and *Jew Süss*,[75] and the documentary film, *The Eternal Jew*. The timing of these films has been explained in terms of preparing public opinion for the mass killing of the Jews which was to begin at the end of March 1942,[76] but such an explanation is immensely problematic. Leaving aside the intense debates about the chronology of decision-making in the 'Final Solution of the Jewish Question', in which many argue that the key decisions to exterminate the Jews were not taken until 1941,[77] the origins of these films go back very much earlier. In October or November 1938 an order was issued to German film companies to produce anti-Semitic films, and Goebbels ordered work to begin on *The Rothschilds* on 17 November 1938, a rejoinder to Twentieth Century Fox's 1934 film *The House of Rothschild*.[78] *Jew Süss* originated early in 1939 when Metzger (a scriptwriter at the Terra film company) took his proposal for a Nazi version of the 19th-century Hauff *novella* of the same name to the Propaganda Ministry, where it was enthusiastically received.[79] Work on *The Eternal Jew* began soon afterwards, although Goebbels' first attempt to film in the Jewish ghettos in Poland was blocked by the Polish authorities, and it was not until October 1939 that shooting in Poland began.[80]

Why then did Goebbels decide to embark on a new campaign of anti-Semitic film propaganda at the end of 1938? Following the promulgation of the Nuremberg Laws of 1935, the pace of anti-Semitic measures slowed, not least in order to preserve appearances during the 1936 Berlin Olympic Games. At the end of 1937, however, the situation changed, with renewed attempts to 'Aryanize' Jewish businesses, and in the following year, both the Austrian *Anschluß* in March and the Sudeten crisis in the summer provoked new waves of violence towards the Jews. In July, Jews were required to carry special identity cards and in October, 17,000 Jews with Polish citizenship were expelled from the Reich. Finally, on 9–10 November 1938, came the 'Crystal Night' pogrom, in which Jewish shops were looted, houses, schools and synagogues burned down, a number of Jews killed, many more bullied and intimidated and tens of thousands arrested.

The pogrom was initiated by Goebbels in a somewhat desperate attempt to restore his earlier close relationship with the *Führer*, for he had fallen from grace that summer when Hitler had learnt of his affair with the film star Lida Baarova. In the event, Hitler still demanded that Goebbels save his marriage by ending the affair, and it was only after a new marriage contract was agreed in January 1939 that the damage began to be repaired[81] – indeed, many argue that it was not until the outbreak of war that the original close relationship with the *Führer* was fully restored.[82] There is, moreover, considerable irony in the fact that Goebbels had promoted the Crystal Night pogrom for, as propaganda, it was a disastrous failure. Not only did it provoke predictable international protest, it was widely condemned in Germany as well, and Goebbels drew the important conclusion that much more vigorous anti-Semitic propaganda was necessary. Certainly the new direction in film propaganda was now clear, and was soon publicized by no less a person than Hitler himself. Thus in the notorious speech of 30 January 1939, promising the destruction of international Jewry in the event of war, Hitler also indicated that the fact that some American film companies were to make anti-Nazi films would 'cause us in our German industry to produce anti-Semitic films'.[83]

The first of the 1940 trilogy of anti-Semitic films was *The Rothschilds*, a costume drama of the rise to power and influence of the Rothschild family in early nineteenth-century England. When Nathan Rothschild arrives in

England in 1806 he is ostracized and despised by the English financiers and bankers, but through a combination of unscrupulous behaviour and the international contacts provided by other members of the family, he is able to turn the tables on those who had so despised him on his arrival. Thus not only does he outwit his financial rivals, but his underhand manipulation of the Stock Market makes his personal fortune, while simultaneously impoverishing everyone else; the Rothschild victory is complete. Although the film received unanimously enthusiastic reviews,[84] historians agree that it was a signal failure. Most explain this by reference to its twin attack on the Jews and the British, and its attempt to demonstrate the emergence of the 'Jewish-British plutocracy', for by attacking both targets simultaneously, the film missed both. The film certainly failed. It was withdrawn just two months after its première, by which time it had been shown only in Berlin and a few other towns. It was re-issued a year later under the revised title *The Rothschilds' Shares in Waterloo*, but Goebbels remained unhappy with the film and, even in this revised, more clearly anti-British form, it received no *Prädikat* and the press was forbidden from discussing it in any detail.[85]

If *The Rothschilds* failed, the film that was released just two months later was immensely successful. *Jew Süss* was premièred at the Venice Film Festival on 8 September, followed two weeks later by the Berlin première, where it enjoyed a most enthusiastic reception. It had taken nearly 20 months to complete – indeed, at least two complete scripts were prepared before the Propaganda Ministry was satisfied that the narrative was, in fact, sufficiently anti-Semitic.[86] Soon after, Goebbels changed his mind about the film's director, and Peter-Paul Brauer was sacked and replaced by Veit Harlan, an experienced director whom Goebbels had come to know well during his affair with Lida Baarova. The film proved extremely difficult to cast: the exclusion of Jews from the industry meant that it was very difficult to persuade non-Jewish actors to play the key roles in the film – at best they were in danger of being typecast, at worst the audience might suspect that they were in fact Jews and treat them accordingly. Thus Ferdinand Marian, the actor who played Süss, was only confirmed in the role a week before shooting began and, on the day of the German première, Goebbels instructed the press to publish a statement to the effect that all the 'actors playing Jewish roles do not have any Jewish blood; rather they are very good actors'.[87]

Having said all that, however, all these difficulties were vindicated in the end result. The final version of the film was, indeed, as Goebbels noted in his diary, 'the first truly anti-Semitic film'.[88] The revised script, while still loosely based on the career of Joseph Süss-Oppenheimer, who had served as financial adviser to the unpopular Duke of Württemberg in the 1730s, distorted and embellished the historical realities in order to construct a narrative better suited to Goebbels' purpose. Thus, while the historical Süss-Oppenheimer was ultimately executed for his part in helping the Duke govern in defiance of the fiercely independent Diet of Württemberg, in the film he is presented in incomparably blacker terms than this. Thus his financial success derives directly from the exploitation of the good, honest citizens of Württemberg on whom he imposes exorbitant tolls and taxes; playing on the Duke's greed and insatiable sexual appetite, Süss persuades him to open the city to the Jews, whose arrival in their hundreds horrifies the German inhabitants; most significant of all, when the beautiful Dorothea Sturm (daughter of the Chief Minister) comes to Süss to plead on her husband's behalf (who has been arrested for plotting against Süss), he brutally rapes her – in shame and despair Dorothea drowns herself. After the Duke's sudden death, Süss is arrested and charged with 'extortion, profiteering, trading in offices, sexual misconduct, procuring and high treason'.[89] Through most of the film he has been presented as the assimilated Jew *par excellence*, elegantly dressed, his speech modelled on the prevailing manners of the Court – in the court-room scene he is once again the Jew seen at the outset, even reverting to his original Jewish accent. Süss is found guilty and, after he is hanged, the Chief Minister announces that all Jews have just three days in which to leave Württemberg, concluding: 'May our descendants honour and adhere to this decree, that they may be spared great harm to their property and to their lives and to their blood and that of their children and their children's children.'

All the surviving evidence suggests that the film was hugely popular. It was awarded both the *Prädikat* 'Of Particular Value Politically and Artistically' and also 'Valuable for Youth', and was thus shown extensively at Film Hours for the Young, in spite of reservations expressed by both parents and teachers that its sex and violence made it unsuitable for a young audience. Himmler was so impressed that he ordered that it be screened to all members of the SS and the police during the coming winter and, at the post-war Auschwitz trial, a former SS officer admitted that showing the film prompted maltreatment of prisoners.[90] Even more important, it enjoyed enormous commercial success, proving to be the sixth most profitable film released in the years 1940 to 1942,[91] and the SD found that the response of the audience was 'extraordinarily favourable', many comparing it explicitly to *The Rothschilds*, especially in relation to the quality of the acting.[92] Even more striking, a report by the Strasbourg Security Police claimed that the film provoked members of the audience to shout out:

> 'Dirty pig Jew!', 'You Jewish swine!', 'Filthy Jewboy!' ... particularly from women; and the rape scene, linked as it is with the only just bearable torture scene, really outrages people. While the expulsion of the Jews and the execution of Süss ... is greeted with great satisfaction and relief ('Serves him right, dirty Jew', 'They should all be hanged!').

Moreover, heated discussion continued outside the cinema and the report concluded, '*Jud Süss* is *the* best film in a long time'.[93] Goebbels must surely have been delighted when this particular report landed on his desk.

Yet we must be careful not to assume that in describing the response of *some* members of the audience, the Security Police were in fact recording the views of all – by definition, anyone sympathetic to the Jewish characters in the film would not have expressed such views publicly in a German cinema in 1940. Moreover, we know that some members of the audience did indeed respond warmly to the most important Jewish character of all, or at least to the actor who played him – Ferdinand Marian (who played Süss) received 'baskets full of love letters from every cinema in Germany'.[94] The fact that a minority of the audience responded in this way raises real doubts as to how persuasive the ideology of the film could have been. Certainly *Jew Süss* had many other features which could explain its popularity, and it could be argued that it encompassed *all* the qualities which characterize box-office success: lavish production values, major stars, accomplished performances and, perhaps most significant of all, a particularly strong narrative. Indeed, the two staple ingredients of popular cinema, sex and violence, are at its very heart, albeit handled with considerable restraint.[95] Perhaps the film was popular not because of its anti-Semitism but in spite of it?

The answer to that question may perhaps be found in audience responses to *The Eternal Jew*, the third and final film of the 1940 trilogy, and the one in which Goebbels took the closest personal interest. He commissioned the first footage shot in the Jewish ghettos in Poland in the autumn of 1939 and went to Lodz in November of that year to supervise shooting personally.[96] Moreover, the fact that it was a further year before the film was ready for exhibition is explained by his obsessive determination to ensure that this film really would do the job required of it. Thus while a first rough cut was ready in January 1940, in a matter of days, after showing the film to Hitler, Goebbels determined that further work was required. This was completed in March, and the new version was given a test screening before a carefully selected audience of over a hundred Party officials, academics and military men; the only result was that it went back to the editing table once more. A third version was ready in April and once again it was shown to Hitler. Still Goebbels was not satisfied, and a fourth version was produced in May, with yet another version ready a month later. Still unsure, version number six was produced at the beginning of September, and Goebbels was at last sufficiently confident to arrange a further test screening. Reactions this time were more intense: some argued that the film was so powerful that it should only be used at closed Party screenings, while others argued that it was only suitable for those with a strong constitution. In the event, Goebbels determined to produce two versions of the film, with a new, shorter version (omitting the scenes of ritual slaughter at the end) intended for children and women, and it was in this dual form that the film was premièred in Berlin on 28 November 1940; the shorter version was shown in the afternoon and the full version at 6.30 p.m.

The Eternal Jew opened with footage shot in the Polish ghettos which, it was claimed, showed 'the Jews as they really are, before they conceal themselves behind the mask of the civilized European'.[97] This is followed by an account (complete with animated maps) of the historical expansion of the Jews, which ends with footage of packs of rats devouring food and grain, while the commentary rams home the point – 'Wherever rats appear they bring ruin ... They represent craftiness and subterranean destruction – just like the Jews among human beings.' Thereafter the film sets out to expose the ability of the Jews to assimilate into German society by contrasting bearded men in traditional dress with the same men, clean-shaven and wearing contemporary suits. Jewish financial practices are attacked by using an extract from the 1934 Hollywood comedy, *The House of Rothschild*, with judicious use of subtitles and commentary to subvert the meaning of the original film. Evidence of Jewish success is conveyed by images of prominent Jews and hugely exaggerated claims about the extent to which the Jews had penetrated the professions. So-called Jewish art is caricatured as 'unnatural, grotesque, perverted, or pathological', with Jewish critics blamed for the fact that 'German cultural life was niggerized and bastardized'; science, the theatre and cinema were all subverted in the same way. Thereafter, the film turns to religion. Worship is caricatured, Jewish religious schools presented as institutions for the political indoctrination of the young and finally, in footage which many still find unbearable, the audience is shown the ritual slaughter of cattle and sheep. A title asserts that the footage is genuine, 'among the most horrifying ever photographed'; any 'objections on grounds of taste' have been set aside in order that 'our people should know the truth about Jewry'. The commentary emphasizes that the Nazis had always campaigned against Jewish ritual slaughter, and that soon after Hitler came to power it was banned. Thereafter an extract from Hitler's Berlin speech of 30 January 1939 is shown, in which he promises that if 'Jewish financiers' succeed in 'plunging the nations once more into world war,' then the result will be 'the annihilation of the Jewish race in Europe'. The film ends with a short sequence of young, blond Aryans, with flags and banners, with the commentary proclaiming, 'the unified German people march on into the future'.

For many years discussion of *The Eternal Jew* started from the assumption that it was an example of the way in which, in Hull's words, 'the medium of film can be used as a propaganda tool far greater than the printed or spoken word alone'.[98] More recently, however, such claims have been re-examined, and the most detailed recent scholarly analysis of the film reaches very different conclusions.[99] In the first place, in spite of the fact that it was cheap (free of the normal entertainment tax) and vigorously promoted by the Party, the film was not successful at the box office – probably no more than a million people paid to see it in the cinemas (compared to over 20 million for *Jew Süss*). In consequence, Goebbels quickly turned to non-theatrical distribution in an attempt to reach his target audience, with a special promotion to those who organized Film Hours for the Young – prints were also made available to the army. Moreover, the qualitative data on audience reception of the film, notably a detailed SD report prepared in

January 1941, explains why the film was so unsuccessful.[100] The initial promotion of the film did provoke considerable interest, but audience interest declined quickly thereafter for, while it was successful with 'the politically active sections of the population', the mass cinema audience (the primary target of the propaganda) was deeply alienated by it. Much of the film (particularly the scenes of ritual slaughter) was perceived to be so 'repulsive' as to keep people away; the film was 'repeatedly described as an exceptional "strain on the nerves"', and many of those who did go to see it left the cinema 'in disgust in the middle of a performance'. It was in this context that the report commented: 'Statements like "We've seen *Jud Süss* and we've had enough of this Jewish filth" have been heard', adding that there were 'isolated cases' of women and younger men fainting during the ritual slaughter scenes.

That reference to *Jew Süss* has often been seen both as further evidence of the extent of the earlier film's success, and as an endorsement of Goebbels' claimed aversion to explicit, overt propaganda; audience responses to *The Eternal Jew*, in contrast, the decisive proof that his hostility to overt propaganda was indeed well-founded. But an accurate understanding of Goebbels' personal role in the production of *The Eternal Jew* makes the broader claim difficult to sustain and, more important, a careful reading of the SD report reveals less black-and-white conclusions – it might even be argued that the reference to *Jew Süss* indicated that audiences enjoyed the film in spite of its anti-Semitism. Whether or not that is correct, the report certainly demonstrates *Jew Süss*'s failure to indoctrinate its audience with an extreme anti-Semitism, for if it had achieved those political objectives, then the mass audience would surely have been only too eager to see *The Eternal Jew*, with its promise of the documentary 'proof' of the realities of Jewish history, culture and contemporary life. Goebbels, a passionate anti-Semite, described the film as 'absolutely splendid' and 'a sublime creation', and all those test screenings before carefully selected audiences had ensured that the film was effective in preaching to the converted – indeed, the SD report makes it abundantly clear that the 'converted' (perhaps the same minority who had responded so vocally to *Jew Süss*?) did respond enthusiastically to the film. The problem lay with the mass audience who had so enjoyed *Jew Süss*, but who had not as a result been converted to the fanatical excesses of Nazi anti-Semitism and who refused to go to see *The Eternal Jew* – to that extent, its box-office failure is testimony to the ideological failure of *Jew Süss*. *The Eternal Jew* offered audiences the clearest possible exposition of Nazi anti-Semitism, with all its grotesque exaggerations and lies presented without qualification or hesitation, and the film's rejection by the mass of the German cinema audience suggests that the mass of the German people had not, in fact, been persuaded to accept that obscene ideology.

Nor should we find any of this surprising. Most recent work on the history of popular anti-Semitism in Germany during the Third Reich is consistent with the conclusions that emerge from an examination of these three films. In particular, the proposition that by the time the Nazis started to kill the Jews, the mass of the German population had been persuaded actively to support that genocide has been widely discredited.[101] This does not, of course, mean for a moment that anti-Semitism played no part in German life. When Hitler took power in 1933, it was already pervasive, and Kershaw's investigation of public opinion in Bavaria during the Nazi years demonstrated that the propaganda did intensify that already existent anti-Semitism. Very many, probably a majority of, Germans opposed the Jews, welcomed their exclusion and saw them as outsiders against whom it was legitimate to discriminate. But it is also clear that very many, probably a majority, 'would have drawn the line at physical maltreatment'.[102] More-over, David Bankier's broader analysis reaches essentially the same conclusion – as long as the Nazis were carrying out 'traditional' programmes of political anti-Semitism, they could carry the majority of the population with them; once they moved away from that approach (and the 'Crystal Night' pogrom was a clear example of their doing just that), then they encountered substantial resistance: 'the conflict between the regime and the population evolved not around anti-Semitism ... but around the measures adopted ... The majority reacted by opposing not anti-Semitism itself but the terror.'[103] More important, in terms of Nazi ideology, there is a world of difference between those two positions. Given the central, defining nature of National Socialism's fanatical and obsessive anti-Semitism, the regeneration of the German people could only be fully achieved as and when the people were persuaded of the necessity of both purging Germany of the last trace of Jewish tradition and culture and, ultimately, of carrying through the same process of 'cleansing' in the world as a whole. And in this, truly radical, objective, Goebbels clearly failed.

Indeed, it could be argued that the contrast in audience responses to the two major works of Nazi anti-Semitic film propaganda mirrored this broader position. *Jew Süss* was largely consistent with traditional German anti-Semitism, for while Süss is hanged, the nature of the crimes he has committed is such that he would almost certainly have been punished in this way even if he had not been a Jew. For all other Jews, the 'punishment' is exclusion (three days to leave Württemberg), precisely that kind of *apartheid* solution which had been popular with so many Germans for so long. Moreover all this takes place off screen – we are simply told in the final moments of the film that it will happen; the audience leaves the cinema without having to observe the human consequences of that decision. In contrast, *The Eternal Jew* is remorselessly explicit, and by the time Hitler's speech is reached, there can be no doubting the terror which will be visited on the Jews in consequence. And, in terms that are entirely consistent with Bankier's broader analysis of German public opinion, *The Eternal Jew* is rejected by all but the fanatical minority who were already committed to Nazi ideology. In much the same way, it could be argued that these three films demonstrate again how easy it is to reinforce existing attitudes, but how difficult to overthrow them.

While it is clear that the film propaganda fell far short of achieving Goebbels' hugely radical objectives, the more limited success that was achieved did have real political benefits for the regime. It was enough to win acceptance of the various measures that were taken systematically to exclude the Jews from every aspect of German life, the end result of which made them even less visible to most Germans than they had been when the Nazis took power. The majority of Germans had never met a Jew, and the combination of that ignorance and the remorseless propaganda did create what has been called 'a fatal degree of indifference'[104] within which the regime could carry out the mass killings. It is a supreme irony that in the years when anti-Semitic propaganda was at its most intense, the so-called 'Jewish Question' became less and less important to the mass of the population: the war went from bad to worse, and the people had a host of other things on their minds. Yet, while that did create a situation in which almost no one protested against the horrors of the gas chambers, it must also be remembered that the regime went to extraordinary lengths to conceal those horrors from the German people. The killing of the Jews was, as Himmler put it, the 'never to be written glorious page of our history';[105] it was kept so secret precisely because the regime understood that it could not carry the people with it. With all the data at its disposal, the regime was very well-placed to judge the efficacy of its propaganda, and the very fact that even after eight years of remorseless and skilful anti-Semitic propaganda, it dared not tell the German people the truth of the 'Final Solution of the Jewish Question' is, in the end, the most convincing evidence of all that the propaganda had failed.

FILM PROPAGANDA IN FAVOUR OF THE POLICY OF 'EUTHANASIA ACTION'

In both the previous examples, all the films (with the possible exception of *The Eternal Jew*) sought to build on existing attitudes but, in this third example, all the films attempt to confront and overturn existing attitudes – in this case, a deeply entrenched ethical code, grounded in the centuries-old Judaeo-Christian tradition, supplemented by more recent secular traditions. Nazi eugenics was almost as well-established within the ideology as anti-Semitism and, at the 1929 Nuremberg Party Rally, Hitler had praised ancient Sparta's policy of selective infanticide as a model for Nazi Germany. Soon after taking power the regime introduced the legal sterilization of people suffering from so-called hereditary diseases (including such ill-defined conditions as 'feeble-mindedness' or 'chronic alcoholism'), and it soon became clear that this was only the first step along a much more radical road. The new programme, which the Nazis euphemistically called 'euthanasia action', began early in 1939 when, without seeking the consent of parents or anyone else, over 5000 mentally or physically handicapped children were killed.[106] With the outbreak of the war, the policy was expanded with the killing of thousands of adult patients in Polish mental hospitals to provide barrack space for German soldiers, and thereafter patients in German mental hospitals were systematically reviewed to determine whether they should be killed. The victims were taken to a specially equipped asylum where they were gassed: some 70,000 people had been killed by August 1941.

The fact that the programme was not launched until the start of the war was not accidental, for it was hoped that in the highly charged atmosphere of war the killings might go unnoticed. On the other hand, there was little optimism that public opinion would approve of the programme, and the regime therefore went to very great lengths to hide what was being done. Patients were collected in grey postal vans, their relatives only notified after the 'transfer' had taken place; some time later they received a letter of 'condolence', informing them that the patient had died in the new institution. Not least because of the ineptitude of those who were administering the programme, however, news of what was happening soon began to leak out: families with just one relative in an asylum would receive two urns of ashes; people who had had their appendix removed years before would be certified as having died from appendicitis; staff made unguarded remarks. While none of this provoked any collective protest from either the legal profession or the churches, individual lawyers and clerics did protest, most famously Bishop Galen of Münster. In a passionately outspoken sermon on 3 August 1941, he attacked euthanasia as a violation of the Fifth Commandment, condemning the murder of the mentally ill as a breach of both God's Law and the secular German law. While some urged Hitler to hang Galen, on Goebbels' prompting, Hitler's response was very different – just three weeks later the programme was publicly halted, although in reality it was only the mass gassings that stopped; many patients continued to be murdered through starvation or lethal injection. Moreover, the experience gained in 'euthanasia action' was soon put to a different purpose: in October, personnel who had worked in the programme were transferred to the East, and in December the first gassings of Jews took place at Chelmno. Yet Hitler's 'retraction' in August 1941 represented an extraordinary and unparalleled victory for public protest during the Third Reich, a clear indication of just how sensitive this regime was to public opinion.

Indeed, it had been attempting for some time to win public acceptance of these policies, and between 1935 and 1937 the Party's Racial and Political Office made five 16mm silent films to justify euthanasia, although these films were apparently intended for internal ideological 'education', and do not seem to have been screened publicly. In 1937, however, a sound film, *Victim of the Past*, produced jointly by the Party and the Propaganda Ministry, was shown in German cinemas. Following the approach used in the earlier 16mm films, it drew parallels with methods used in animal breeding and plant cultivation to argue that the prevention of the spread of hereditary disease was a moral law – 'To prevent the growth of weeds is to promote the plants of value.'[107] The law of natural selection had been 'frighteningly transgressed' and precious economic resources were being squandered which could be put to much better use helping 'strong, healthy, talented children'. But time and again the film also claimed that euthanasia could be justified on moral grounds, and it concluded that reinstating 'the great law of natural selection' would respect 'the law of the Creator'. Thus, rather than confront existing moral codes, the film attempted to justify the policy in just those terms.

Nothing is known of audience response to the film, or indeed how many people saw it. Following Hitler's personal intervention, every German cinema was ordered to show it, although Michael Burleigh claims that the public stayed away.[108] Indeed, it may be that the regime knew that the film had not been well received, for in October 1939 it was decided that a new film was required.[109] Once again, the intention was to make a documentary, but in December 1940 that approach was dropped, apparently as a result of a letter from Himmler arguing that the local population knew what was going on in one particular asylum and 'the mood there is very ugly' – film propaganda was needed to 'enlighten people there intelligently and rationally'. Soon after, the decision was taken to make a fiction film, and after two false starts, it was decided to base it on Unger's novel *Mission and Conscience*, although it was only after Wolfgang Liebeneiner (an established Tobis director) was appointed that real progress was made. A workable script was finally produced and shooting began in March 1941. The film was called *I Accuse* and its narrative concentrated on the beautiful Hanna Heyt, very much in love with her husband Thomas, a pioneering professor of pathology. While playing the piano at a party, Hanna's left hand suddenly fails her and, as there is no improvement in the days that follow, Heyt asks his friend (and former admirer of Hanna), the doctor Bernhard Lang, to examine his wife. Lang immediately diagnoses multiple sclerosis and he does his best to nurse his patient, while Hanna's husband works night and day to try to develop a cure for the disease. But the illness makes its inexorable progress and the healthy young woman deteriorates, soon unable to accomplish even the most simple physical tasks. Increasingly overwhelmed by the severity of her condition, she pleads with Lang to help her die; Lang, opposed to euthanasia on principle, refuses to help. In the scene which is at the emotional heart of the film, Hanna turns instead to her husband. Arguing that she will soon become 'deaf, blind and idiotic' she urges him to promise 'that you will deliver me before that happens'. With Lang playing the piano downstairs, Heyt administers the fatal overdose and, as she dies, they both affirm their undying love. With Hanna dead, Lang bursts into the room and accuses Thomas of murder.

Thereafter the film becomes increasingly didactic. Thomas is put on trial for murder, and the unfolding trial is intercut with a sub-plot which explores the case of one of Lang's patients, Trude Günther, a handicapped baby whose life had been saved by Lang, and who has now grown into a terribly deformed child. Her parents, once so grateful that their baby's life had been saved, are now resentful and angry. Lang goes to see Trude in an institution, and although the audience never sees the child, Lang is so horrified by what he has seen that he abandons his long-held objections to euthanasia. Meanwhile, the trial provides an opportunity to debate the issues head on, and the ideological climax of the film comes in the discussions between the various jury members, whose occupations represent a cross-section of German society, and whose points of view represent all possible sides of the debate. One by one the objections to euthanasia are voiced and 'overcome', until the jury reaches a consensus articulated by the Prussian major: 'It is my view that the state which can command us to die should also afford us the *right* to die.' But finally, it is Heyt himself who articulates the film's ideology most explicitly. Lang arrives in court to testify on behalf of his friend, but Heyt interrupts. He confesses to killing his wife and continues:

> Here I stand, the accused, and now I accuse. I accuse the proponents of outmoded beliefs and antiquated laws. This is not just about myself, but about the hundreds of thousands ... whose lives we unnaturally prolong, and whose suffering we unnaturally increase ... it is about those millions of healthy people, who cannot be protected against illness because everything that is needed to do so has to be employed keeping beings alive whose death would be a deliverance for them and a liberation from a burden for the rest of humanity.

I *Accuse* was released at the end of August 1941, and it attracted a very large audience, ranking 11th in the most profitable 15 films of the years 1940 to 1942; by January 1945 it had been seen by over 15 million people.[110] Nor is this surprising, for this is another film grounded in the conventions of popular narrative cinema: a triangular love story given melodramatic emphasis by the intensity of Hanna's suffering, and the conflict between Heyt's willingness to help his wife to die and Lang's principled opposition to euthanasia. Moreover, as all that is combined with the particular qualities of the court-room *genre*, with its special opportunities for drama and debate, the end result is an accomplished piece of narrative cinema. Strong performances (especially from the popular film star, Heidemarie Hatheyer as Hanna) are underlined by a powerful musical score written by Norbert Schultze, although at just over two hours' long, the more or less constant dialogue must have taxed the attention of some.

All the appropriate agencies examined the way in which audiences responded to the film, and amongst many surviving reports, two are especially interesting. Thus a report from East Hanover revealed that the impact of the film was completely undermined by Galen's sermon; in Carinthia, people who were at first favourably impressed by its arguments, quickly changed their minds after being exposed to the contrary argument.[111] Moreover, a summative SD report demonstrated that audience response was deeply divided.[112] The strongest opposition came from members of the audience with religious convictions, although here too there were divisions, with Catholics more opposed than Protestants – some Catholic priests, for example, tried to stop their congregations going to the film. Equally, while doctors were broadly sympathetic, younger doctors were more enthusiastic than older doctors, and the SD identified class differences as well: working-class audiences were more favourable than others, apparently because they were 'more concerned about their own financial obligations'. In sum, the report concluded: 'from the wealth of material it emerges that in general the practice of euthanasia is approved, *when decided by a committee of several doctors with the agreement of the incurable patient and his relatives*' (original italics).

Assuming for the moment that this was a legitimate reading of the data (and the remainder of the report throws some doubt on this), it nevertheless reveals just how unsuccessful the Nazis had been in winning support for a programme on which they had actually embarked. For the film tackles only the softest of soft targets in this area, exploring the case of a deeply sympathetic individual, dying painfully of an incurable disease who, in full possession of her faculties, makes the decision to end her own life and seeks help so to do. And yet, even with such a compelling justification for euthanasia, the film could only win limited support; even in *these* circumstances, significant sections of the audience were not persuaded. It does not take any imagination to recognize how much more hostile that response would have been if the film had examined the kind of 'euthanasia' that was, in fact, being practised – the killing of people, few if any of whom were threatened by terminal illness, and none of whose relatives, let alone the patients themselves, had ever given their consent. Indeed, it may be that the film reconfirmed to the regime the complete hopelessness of trying to carry public opinion with it in this area, and to that extent Liebeneiner may not have been entirely disingenuous when he claimed that its purpose was to test public reaction to a law legalizing euthanasia.[113] Certainly no such law was introduced, the programme of 'euthanasia action' was publicly suspended, and when the gassings of the Jews began at the end of the year, they took place outside Germany and in conditions of the greatest secrecy.

In short, on the evidence of *I Accuse*, the attempt to challenge existing moral and religious attitudes proved almost wholly unsuccessful. Those systems of ethics were rooted in centuries of religious and secular experience, and it is surely not at all surprising that they proved more than a match for a single feature film, no matter how popular, how potentially persuasive, it may have been. Indeed, only someone as convinced as Goebbels of the power of film propaganda would ever have imagined otherwise.

IMAGES OF WAR

The final example concerns the attempt to prepare the people for war and to sustain their support for war once it came. While the war years saw the production of a small number of feature-length documentaries, it was the newsreels that were always at the heart of this propaganda. Thus, from October 1938, a newsreel had to be included in every cinema programme, and the rental charges were changed so that it was no longer cheaper to hire old, out-of-date newsreels. Until the outbreak of war, the four separate newsreels continued to exist, although they were subject to closer and closer supervision – by 1939 the responsibilities of the supervising agency included 'the arranging of film reports according to the political and cultural points of view of the State'.[114] Nevertheless, in November 1940, a new company was formed subsuming all the other newsreels: the new newsreel was to be known simply as *Deutsche Wochenschau (German Newsreel)*, and it was produced until the very end of the war.

In 1939 the newsreels played an important supporting role in attempting to mobilize public support for the coming war. Military subjects became more and more common, with a number of reports, for example, focusing attention on the war in Spain; in the weeks leading up to the invasion of Poland, there were repeated claims of Polish atrocities against Germans living in Poland and the wider assertion that, despite Hitler's best diplomatic endeavours, the Poles were forcing Germany into war. However, in making the case for war, the newsreels and the other news media faced a very difficult task, for one key component in the 'Hitler myth' had always been his claimed commitment to peace – as a 17-year-old German girl later recalled, while rumours of war were spreading throughout the summer of 1939, 'We were convinced that Hitler was a man of peace and would do everything he could to settle things peacefully.'[115] Throughout the years of peace, while people welcomed the various dramatic steps towards Germany's regeneration, they remained resolutely opposed to war and a key component of Hitler's popularity was the fact that so much had been achieved without a shot being fired. Thus, if the intention had been to recreate the mood of 1914, the propaganda clearly failed, for in contrast to the optimism and excitement at the outbreak of the First World War, the mood in 1939 was one of great anxiety and a distinct lack of enthusiasm.

On the other hand, Hitler led his people into war without protest or opposition. When faced with the reality of the invasion of Poland, most Germans may have accepted the propaganda claim that the war had been forced on Germany by the Poles and their Western Allies. Moreover, building on foundations that went back to the very birth of the modern German state, the propaganda had characterized anti-war sentiments as unpatriotic and, when there seemed to be no alternative, the mass of the people were willing to fight. Moreover, as soon as war broke out, the situation was totally transformed – patriotic imperatives demanded support for Hitler; war was war, and opposition had no part to play in the new situation. On balance it is therefore clear that the propaganda (of which the newsreels were a part) did just enough to enable Hitler to negotiate the dangerous and difficult transition from peace to war.

Thereafter, the newsreels really came into their own, a role for which they were certainly well prepared. For it had been decided as early as 1936 to establish *Propaganda Kompanie Einheiten* (hereafter referred to as PK Units), appointed by the Ministry of Propaganda but under the command of the service to which they were assigned. Some 13 such units were established at the start of the war – seven for the army, four for the airforce and two for the navy – each with over a hundred personnel, and it is clear that the investment of such large resources in the 'soldier cameramen' (as Goebbels later described them) paid handsome dividends. Abundant high quality war footage was produced from the very beginning of the Polish campaign, and the newsreels were well placed to make the very most of a succession of German victories in the opening phase of the war. Certainly they were hugely popular, and the SD reported in June 1940 on the 'enormous success' achieved by the fifth war newsreel, which was 'followed breathlessly by spectators'.[116] Goebbels was not slow to take advantage of this situation. Already in May the length of the newsreel had been extended to 40 minutes and, in the short term at least, the quality of the footage and the message which it conveyed was more than enough to carry this heavier burden. Moreover, in an attempt to take the newsreels to rural areas, Goebbels equipped 1500 mobile units, with the aim of ensuring that all Germans had access to the newsreel at least once a month. Saturday newsreel shows, with specially low ticket prices, were added and, after 1940, newsreels were also shown in schools and at the Film Hours for the Young.

However, this huge popularity did not last long. As early as March 1941 the SD reported that the newsreel had become so unpopular that film-goers waited outside the cinema until after it was over before buying their ticket, prompting Goebbels to respond by ordering the box office closed as soon as the newsreel began; the newsreels had not yet lost their audience, but the high point of their popularity had clearly passed. The final and terminal decline set in with defeat at Stalingrad, and the SD was soon reporting that the newsreels could not 'regain their former popularity ... wide sections of the community are not allowing themselves to be influenced by the newsreel'.[117] There were still exceptional moments, as with the newsreel of Goebbels' remarkable 'total war' speech at the Berlin *Sportpalast* on 18 February 1943, but while this made a short-term impact, its effect quickly receded once it was set against the realities of the military situation.[118] Indeed, that response illustrates precisely the problem that was at the heart of all Nazi propaganda in the second half of the war: once the military realities changed, and increasingly the cinema audience *knew* that they had changed, then the remorseless optimism of the propaganda fell on increasingly deaf ears. Goebbels' response to the changing military situation was to use the newsreel to deny the realities of the situation, a strategy that derived from decisions made much earlier in the war. As early as May 1940, cameramen and editors had been told not to use any footage that would produce 'fear, horror or revulsion' at the war,[119] and thus even at the time of the greatest Nazi victories, the newsreels constructed a strictly sanitized image of war. Audiences were not to be disturbed by anything that might give them a real sense of what their soldiers were enduring – the human and material losses of the enemy could be represented (in part), but the newsreels gave no sense of the huge scale of German casualties, nor even much sense of the destruction of military hardware. Hardly surprising then that, when the nature of the military realities changed, there was even less appetite for accurate reporting.

The newsreels were only truly popular when they were reporting good news, and it is therefore clear that it was the news and not the newsreels that achieved that response. Of course the newsreels were photographed and edited with very great skill, but once again, the power of the medium to enthuse and excite the audience seems paltry in comparison to the realities it sought to reflect. While spectacular victories were being won at small cost, people flocked to the cinemas to see the dramatic footage of the daring deeds of the soldiers and airmen. Once the victories turned sour, people would continue to go to the cinemas, but they would do their best to avoid the newsreel – the appeal of cinema in these very different circumstances was that it offered a few precious hours *escape* from the realities of the war outside. Once again, the medium was wholly subservient to the message.

An even clearer illustration of the constraints within which German war reporting functioned is provided by the feature-length documentary, *Baptism of Fire*, released in April 1940, and focusing on the pivotal role of the air force in the defeat of Poland.[120] After the usual Nazi exposition of the origins of the war, blaming the Poles and the British for the war, the film set out to construct a powerful, romantic image of the youthful *Luftwaffe* pilots, and the extraordinary technology at their disposal. Thus the pilots are young and blond, full of energy and enthusiasm for their task, invariably smiling as they go about their work. This sense of war as a hugely exciting and enjoyable adventure is underlined in a number of ways in the film, not least in the repeated use of the pilots' songs. For while they provide a peculiarly direct way of communicating much of the film's ideology (the concluding song, for example, anticipates the next stage of the war with the refrain 'Bombs, bombs, bombs on England!'), they also underline the sense of an exclusively masculine culture which is such a marked feature of the film. As so often in Nazi war films, German women are conspicuous by their absence and, just in case anyone failed to understand the point, a refrain in an early song made it all too clear – 'Comrade, comrade, all the girls must wait...'

The film also constructs a very particular image of the technology which is at these young men's disposal. Remarkable actuality footage is used to construct images of the precision and awesome power of the aircraft featured in the film, which must have seemed to contemporary German audiences not unlike the images of technological precision and power which were so dominant in Western television reporting of the Gulf War of 1991. The commentary explains that the aeroplanes will hit particular kinds of military targets – a troop train, railway lines, a bridge – and the footage shows the bombs doing just that. Moreover, while the latter part of the film offers detailed and explicit footage of the material havoc wreaked by the bombs, and some footage of dead and wounded Poles, there are no images of dead Germans – the one brief sequence of the wounded is used simply to emphasize how quickly they are flown back to Germany for treatment. Thus, the film offers a very particular image of the German experience of war: young, fit, good-looking pilots wreak havoc on the enemy, deploying their hugely superior technology to devastating effect, at almost no cost to themselves. The title of the film describes war as a baptism of fire: in the film itself, it is presented as a painless and glamorous adventure.

Baptism of Fire was in the cinemas at precisely the same time as Germany was achieving even more spectacular success in Western Europe, and it must have been expected that its celebration of an earlier victory would have struck a potent chord with the mass audience; in reality the response was rather different. For while the SD reported that some wanted more explicit actuality footage, others (mainly women) were powerfully moved by the footage of the defeated Poles; shots of a devastated Warsaw in particular led to feelings of 'depression and anxiety about the "horrors of war", rather than one of heroic pride';[121] even at the height of Germany's success, anxieties about the character of modern war continued to persist.

This analysis of the way in which war was represented in Nazi film propaganda serves, yet again, to highlight the limits rather than the extent of the power of film propaganda. Pre-war attempts to whip up positive enthusiasm for war were not successful, although the newsreels did underline the message (carried primarily by other media), that this was a war forced on a reluctant Germany. In the event, that was enough to sustain support for Hitler as he led Germany to war once more. The experience of the war, however, demonstrated even more clearly the limited power of film propaganda when the message it seeks to convey goes against the knowledge and experience of the target audience. Thus, while Germany was winning the war, footage of German victories won large audiences but, as soon as the military situation changed, such actuality footage quickly lost its audience. The evidence of their own eyes, accounts from soldiers back on leave from the Eastern Front, a growing audience for BBC radio, all told the German audience that the war was going badly; the newsreels tried to tell them something very different and, with only very limited and short-lived exceptions, that message was rejected.

CONCLUSION

In contrast to the experience in Britain during the First World War and the Soviet Union in the 1920s, the preconditions for successful film propaganda were achieved in Nazi Germany. All the important logistical problems were solved and the film industry was managed in such a way as to ensure that the required films were produced – even the vexed problem of costs was eventually solved in the final years of the Third Reich. Moreover, the mass audience remained largely ignorant of the changes that had taken place, believing that, with the one important exception of the exclusion of the Jews, entertaining German films, with many of the same stars as before the Nazi takeover, were still being produced by the major German studios. More important, the films so carefully supervised by Goebbels (including the small number of all-important fiction and factual films that carried the primary burden of the propaganda) did reach the mass cinema audience, which grew consistently during the Nazi years. Nor was access to the target audience limited to the mainstream cinemas – Goebbels reached young people outside the cinemas as well, both in schools and in the hugely popular Film Hours for the Young and, in wartime, this non-theatrical distribution was extended through the mobile cinemas that toured rural Germany.

On the other hand, even with these preconditions met, Goebbels fell far short of achieving his vision of a film propaganda so popular, so powerful, so contagious that it would effect radical, even revolutionary transformations in the attitudes and ideology of the mass of the German people. Instead, Nazi film propaganda demonstrated that it was incomparably better at reinforcing existing attitudes than it was at changing them. Thus, the propaganda aimed at winning support for 'euthanasia action' encountered significant opposition; propaganda designed to counter a fast-growing pessimism about the eventual outcome of the war proved even less successful; even the attempt to transform long-established German anti-Semitism into a more virulent racial hatred failed largely to achieve its objectives. Yet, the propaganda was successful in reaffirming existing attitudes, even adding a distinctively Nazi gloss to those established traditions. Goebbels was always convinced that the construction of the 'Hitler myth' was his greatest propaganda achievement, and the *Führer* certainly did achieve a unique position in German society. The extent of Hitler's popularity was unprecedented, and the nature of that popularity went far beyond that which is normally associated with a political leader; he secured that kind of intense personal adulation that is usually associated with stars in the world of entertainment and sport. Moreover, Goebbels was able to graft these attitudes on to a long-established respect for the German military, exploiting to the full the resurgence of patriotic pride in Germany's reborn armed services. All this came together triumphantly in the opening months of the war, where the immensely popular newsreels celebrated the extraordinary achievements of the German forces, and gave the audiences their brief but singularly precious moments of access to their *Führer*.

Yet even this conclusion has to be qualified. Notwithstanding Hitler's huge popularity, attitudes soon changed when it became clear that he was no longer able to sustain the apparently uninterrupted pattern of success that had characterized the years 1933–1941. Exultation in Germany's new military prowess proved extremely short-lived and, as audience responses to *Baptism of Fire* made clear, even at the height of Germany's wartime success, a significant minority of the cinema audience sustained grave reservations about what was happening. In short, attitudes towards the regime were always determined above all else by what the regime was doing: as long as its achievements broadly coincided with the aspirations of the German population, it enjoyed very considerable support; once that changed then, no matter how powerful the propaganda, attitudes towards the regime changed too. For all its considerable skill, Nazi film propaganda was only truly successful when it was giving its audience a message that it wanted to hear. The target audience is not the passive recipient of powerful propaganda messages; it always decides what it will do with those messages and it is even capable of refusing to expose itself to messages of which it strongly disapproves, as both *The Eternal Jew* and the newsreels of the later war years reveal. All too often historians have ascribed popular enthusiasm for Hitler to Goebbels' skills as the supreme manipulative propagandist. In reality it was Hitler's achievements that provoked the enthusiasm and, when the achievements went sour, no amount of propaganda could rebuild the 'Hitler myth' which Goebbels, with such skill and invention, had so painstakingly constructed.

NOTES

1. Adolf Hitler, *Mein Kampf*, translated by Ralph Mannheim, London, 1972, pp. 164–7.

2. Historians have sometimes had difficulty with the proposition that Hitler's views were clear and consistent enough to constitute such a *Weltanschauung*. For a powerful response to such reservations, see Eberhard Jäckel, *Hitler's World View: A Blueprint for Power*, translated by Herbert Arnold, Cambridge, Mass., 1972.

3. George L. Mosse, *The Crisis of German Ideology: Intellectual Origins of the Third Reich*, London, 1968, p. 29.

4. The notion of the medieval German knight personifying all the true *völkisch* values had been most effectively popularized in a sixteenth-century engraving by Dürer, *The Knight, Death and the Devil*. Hitler was to be represented in precisely the same terms in a famous painting by Hubert Lanzinger, titled *The Protector of German Art* (1934), reproduced in David Elliott, 'The battle for art in the 1930s', *History Today*, Vol. 45, No. 11, November 1995, p. 14.

5. Joseph Goebbels – appointed as head of party propaganda by Hitler in April 1930.

6. Martin Broszat, *The Hitler State: The Foundation and Development of the Internal Structure of the Third Reich*, translated by John W. Hiden, London, 1981, p. 22.

7. Many of these devices served skilfully to bring together radical traditions of both left and right – the party adopted the Communist form of address, 'comrade'; traditional revolutionary songs were rewritten with Nationalist words; the red flag of the revolution formed the background to the black swastika on the Nazi flag, while red, white and blue were also the colours of imperial Germany.

8. *Sturmabteilungen,* literally 'Storm Troopers', the paramilitary wing of the National Socialist Party.

9. For a thoughtful discussion of the role of propaganda in the Nazi rise to power see Richard Bessel, 'The rise of the NSDAP and the myth of Nazi propaganda', *The Wiener Library Bulletin*, 1980, Vol. 33, New Series, Nos. 51/52, pp. 20–9.

10. This was in the first of the two elections of 1932 – the percentage given is of those who actually voted; the percentage of the electorate entitled to vote was substantially smaller at 31 per cent. The Nazis did increase their share of the vote to nearly 44 per cent (nearly 39 per cent) in March 1933, but this was of course after Hitler had been appointed Chancellor, and in the wake of the dramatic changes which followed the Reichstag Fire of February 1933.

11. Quoted in David Welch, *Propaganda and the German Cinema*, Oxford, 1983, p. 20. Hereafter referred to as Welch (1993).

12. Ian Kershaw, 'How effective was Nazi propaganda?' in David Welch (ed.), *Nazi Propaganda: The Power and the Limitations*, London, 1983.

13. The speech which ended with these words comes right at the end of the final event in the 1934 Nuremberg Rally.

14. Goebbels on 15 March 1933, quoted in David Welch, *The Third Reich: Politics and Propaganda,* London, 1993, p. 138. Hereafter referred to as Welch (1993).

15. *Ibid.,* p. xv.

16. Z.A.B. Zeman, *Nazi Propaganda*, London, 1973, p. 21.

17. *Ibid.,* pp. 65–70.

18. *Ibid.,* p. 38.

19. R.E. Herzstein, *The War That Hitler Won: The Most Infamous Propaganda Campaign in History*, New York, 1978, pp. 124–6. *Prima facie* the claim seems improbable and yet the mass production and sale of radio sets was one of Goebbels' most striking achievements, with over 70 per cent of German households owning a set by 1939.

20. Zeman, *op. cit.,* p. 36.

21. One each for literature, theatre, music, radio, film, fine arts and the press.

22. Welch (1993), p. 150.

23. Ralf Georg Reuth, *Goebbels,* translated by Krishna Winton, London, 1993, p. 195.

24. This view has been developed by David Welch on more than one occasion – see, for example, Welch (1983), pp. 44–5.

25. Goebbels in his diary for 15 May 1943, quoted in Welch (1983), p. 45.

26. Thus Goebbels wrote very warmly about Riefenstahl on many occasions. For further discussion of this issue, see Martin Loiperdinger and David Culbert, 'Leni Riefenstahl, the SA and the Nazi Party Rally films 1933–1934: *Sieg des Glaubens* and *Triumph des Willens*', *Historical Journal of Film, Radio and Television*, Vol. 8, No. 1, 1988, pp. 3–38, and David Culbert, 'Leni Riefenstahl and the diaries of Joseph Goebbels', *Historical Journal of Film, Radio and Television*, Vol. 13, No. 1, 1993, pp. 85–93.

27. Stig Hornshøj-Møller and David Culbert, ' "Der ewige Jude" (1940): Joseph Goebbels' unequalled monument to anti-Semitism', *Historical Journal of Film, Radio and Television*, Vol. 12, No. 1, 1992, pp. 41–68.

28. Quoted in Julian Petley, *Capital and Culture: German Cinema 1933–45*, London, 1979, pp. 31–2.

29. At the end of the First World War, the government sold its shares in UFA and it became an entirely private company.

30. Notwithstanding the fact that some European countries banned German imports, Germany's overall trading position in the immediate post-war period was very favourable.

31. In 1925 German feature film production totalled 228; in the same year France produced 74 feature films and Britain 44.

32. While few of the leading directors (with the exception of Lubitsch and Murnau) stayed in Hollywood, a large number of minor directors, actors and technicians did remain.

33. See Petley, *op. cit.*

34. Such a view was first advanced by Siegfried Kracauer in *From Caligari to Hitler: A Psychological Study of the German Film*, Princeton, 1947; another approach argued that the tragedy and despair of many German films of the period helped to construct an environment within which National Socialism could more readily take root (Lotte Eisner, *The Haunted Screen*, Berkeley, 1969).

35. Petley, *op. cit.*, pp. 41–2.

36. The word means co-ordination and is used to describe the process whereby existing institutions and practices were remodelled along Nazi lines.

37. Welch (1983), pp. 6–7.

38. For more detailed discussion of this situation and the developing relationships between the new regime and the industry see Petley, *op. cit.*, pp. 44–51.

39. The speech is reproduced in full in Welch (1993), pp. 150–4.

40. Petley, *op. cit.*, p. 55. The following discussion of the changing structure of the industry and the role of the Bank derives from the same source, pp. 52–4.

41. Welch (1983) offers further discussion of the Cinema Law, pp. 17–24; the text of the Law is reproduced in Welch (1993), pp. 156–67.

42. Clause 2(e) of the Law (Welch, 1993, p. 159).

43. Welch (1983), p. 19.

44. Welch (1993), p. 160.

45. Petley, *op. cit.*, p. 59.

46. Welch (1983), p. 31. The following discussion of the audience derives largely from the same source, pp. 24–35.

47. This assumption was made in most countries in which cinema had established

itself as the dominant medium of popular entertainment and broadly echoes late-twentieth-century assumptions about the power of television to influence the same age group.

48. Welch (1983), p. 28.

49. The actual figures are RM 175,000 in 1927 to RM 537,000 in 1937 (Petley, *op. cit.*, p. 59). The remainder of this discussion of the financial problems of the industry and Goebbels' response derives largely from this source, pp. 59–94, and from Welch (1983), pp. 30–8.

50. Becker suggests that their salaries rose by 200 per cent after the Nazis came to power (Wolfgang Becker, *Film und Herrschaft*, Berlin, 1973, pp. 115–16, cited in Petley, *op. cit.*, p. 59).

51. Petley, *op. cit.*, pp. 86–7.

52. Herzstein, *op. cit.*, p. 421.

53. An outstanding example of work of this kind is provided in Ian Kershaw, *Popular Opinion and Political Dissent in the Third Reich: Bavaria 1933–1945*, Oxford, 1983; his introduction provides an especially thoughtful analysis of the strengths and weaknesses of the kinds of evidence referred to in this paragraph.

54. Aldous Huxley, 'Notes on propaganda', *Harper's Monthly Magazine*, Vol. 174, December 1936, quoted in Richard Taylor, *Film Propaganda: Soviet Russia and Nazi Germany*, London, 1979, p. 22. A revised edition of Taylor's book was published in 1998 by I. B. Tauris.

55. The study is Ian Kershaw, *The 'Hitler Myth': Image and Reality in the Third Reich*, Oxford, 1987 (hereafter Kershaw (1987)); the *Sopade* report is quoted on p. 140.

56. *Ibid.*, p. 158.

57. Quoted in Welch (1983), p. 147.

58. The incident is described in Kershaw (1987), p. 224.

59. *Ibid.*, p. 159.

60. For a detailed discussion of the earlier film see Loiperdinger and Culbert, *op. cit.*

61. Erwin Leiser, *Nazi Cinema*, London, 1968, p. 29.

62. In the film their resistance is successful, although in reality the town was overwhelmed by the French forces.

63. For more detailed discussion of the film, see Taylor, *op. cit.*, pp. 216–29; Welch (1983), pp. 221–35; Leiser, *op. cit.*, pp. 121–33; and David Culbert, '*Kolberg*: film, filmscript and Kolobrzeg today', *Historical Journal of Film, Radio and Television*, Vol. 14, No. 4, 1994, pp. 449–66.

64. Gerd Albrecht, *Film in Dritten Reich*, Karlsruhe, 1979, p. 251.

65. Both quoted in Welch (1983), pp. 171, 181.

66. Loiperdinger and Culbert, *op. cit.*, p. 16.

67. I am indebted to David Welch for this information about the mixed reception of *Triumph of the Will*.

68. The 'blood flag' was the flag which, it was claimed, was stained with the blood of Nazi martyrs in the abortive *putsch* in Munich in November 1923.

69. By and large those who have written about the film share this view of its visual power. One interesting dissenting view is provided by Brian Winston, 'Reconsidering "Triumph of the Will": was Hitler there?', *Sight and Sound*, Vol. 50, No. 2, Spring

1981, pp. 102–7.

70. Goebbels on the occasion of presenting Riefenstahl with the National Film prize in May 1935, quoted in Welch (1983), p. 158.

71. In which 90 per cent of the Saar population voted for integration into the Reich.

72. *Sopade* report for 14 March 1935, quoted in Kershaw (1987), p. 71. The remainder of this paragraph and the following paragraph derive from the same source, pp. 73–7.

73. Quoted in Kershaw (1987), p. 155.

74. Welch (1983), p. 283.

75. Following the conventions adopted throughout this book, the German title *Jud Süss* is here translated as *Jew Süss* – this should not be confused with an earlier British production, *Jew Süss*, directed by an expatriate German director (Lothar Mendes) for Gaumont British in 1934.

76. Thus, for example, Welch (1983), p. 283: the 1940 films 'were released in this manner ... to prepare the German people for the full-scale extermination'.

77. For a remarkably concise introduction to those debates see Ian Kershaw, *The Nazi Dictatorship: Problems and Perspectives of Interpretation*, 3rd edn, London, 1993, pp. 80–107.

78. Hornshøj-Møller and Culbert, *op. cit.*, p. 55.

79. Metzger claimed that his script was based on the earlier Hauff *novella* and not the much better known 1925 novel *Jud Süss*, written by Lion Feuchtwanger. For a detailed discussion of the origins of the films see Susan Tegel, 'Veit Harlan and the origins of "Jud Süss", 1938–1939: opportunism in the creation of anti-Semitic film propaganda', *Historical Journal of Film Radio and Television*, Vol. 16, No. 4, 1996, pp. 515–19.

80. Hornshøj-Møller and Culbert, *op. cit.*, p. 41.

81. Marsha Howard, *Anti-Semitic Film Propaganda in the Third Reich and the 'Final Solution'*, unpublished MA dissertation, Thames Valley University, 1995, pp. 24–5.

82. See, for example, Tegel, *op. cit.*, p. 521.

83. Quoted in Tegel, *op. cit.*, p. 516.

84. Although, ever since 1936, any element of criticism in a published review was forbidden – see above, p. 138.

85. Howard, *op. cit.*, p. 39.

86. For a detailed discussion of the origins of the film see Tegel, *op. cit.* The remainder of this discussion of the origins of the film derives from the same source.

87. Quoted in Tegel, *op. cit.*, p. 525.

88. Quoted in Tegel, *op. cit.*, p. 523.

89. This and all other quotations from the dialogue of the film are taken from Susan Tegel, *Jew Süss/Jud Süss*, Trowbridge, 1996.

90. Leiser, *op. cit.*, pp. 84–5.

91. Albrecht, *op. cit.*, p. 251.

92. *Ibid.*, pp. 152–3.

93. *Ibid.*, pp. 153–4.

94. The words are Veit Harlan's and they are quoted in Regine Mihal Friedman,

'Male gaze and female reaction: Veit Harlan's *Jew Süss* (1940)', in S. Frieden, R.W. McCormick, V.R. Petersen and L.M. Vogelsgang, *Gender and German Cinema: Feminist Interventions. Volume II: German Film History/German History on Film*, Oxford, 1993, pp. 120–1.

95. We see only the very beginning of the rape, and Dorothea's suicide takes place off-screen.

96. The majority of this footage was shot in the Lodz ghetto, although Nazi cameramen were at work in the Warsaw ghetto in October 1939 (Hornshøj-Møller and Culbert, *op. cit.*, pp. 41–2). The remainder of this discussion of the production of the film derives from the same source.

97. This, and all subsequent quotations from the commentary, are taken from David Culbert's translation of the commentary, reproduced as Appendix B in *ibid.*, pp. 56–67.

98. David Stewart Hull, *Film in the Third Reich: A Study of the German Cinema 1933-1945*, Berkeley, 1969, p. 173.

99. Hornshøj-Møller and Culbert, *op. cit.*

100. The report is reproduced in Leiser, *op. cit.*, pp. 157–8.

101. For a recent discussion of the effectiveness of anti-Semitic propaganda see David Bankier, *The Germans and the Final Solution: Public Opinion under Nazism*, Blackwell, Oxford, 1992.

102. Kershaw (1983), p. 371.

103. Bankier, *op. cit.*, pp. 155–6.

104. The phrase is Kershaw's – see for example 'How effective was Nazi propaganda?' (1983), p. 191.

105. Quoted in Kershaw (1983), p. 371.

106. For a detailed discussion of this topic see Michael Burleigh, *Death and Deliverance: 'Euthanasia' in Germany 1900–1945*, Cambridge, 1994. A brief introduction is offered in Michael Burleigh, 'Euthanasia and the Third Reich', *History Today*, Vol. 40, February 1990, pp. 11–16. The discussion of the policy derives from these two sources.

107. Quoted in Leiser, *op. cit.*, p. 90. Succeeding quotations from the commentary of the film are taken from the same source.

108. Burleigh (1990), p. 14.

109. *Ibid.* The following discussion of the origins of the film derives from this source and Burleigh (1994). The quotations from the dialogue are all from Burleigh's translation.

110. Burleigh (1994), p. 216.

111. *Ibid.*, p. 217.

112. The report in January 1942 is reproduced in its entirety in Leiser, *op. cit.*, pp. 146–9.

113. In conversation with Leiser in 1965 (Leiser, *op. cit.*, p. 92).

114. Welch (1983), p. 194 – what follows derives largely from the same source, pp. 191–6.

115. Quoted in Kershaw (1987), p. 142.

116. Quoted in Welch (1983), p. 197.

117. A report dated 4 March 1943; quoted in Welch (1983), p. 201.

118. David Welch, 'Goebbels, Götterdämmerung and the Deutsche Wochenschauen', in R.M. Short and Stephen Dolezel, *Hitler's Fall: The Newsreel Witness*, London, 1988, p. 87.

119. Welch (1983), p. 200. In practice, a good deal of such footage was shot, and it was the editors who were primarily responsible for seeing that none of that footage was seen by the public in the finished newsreels.

120. It followed two months after *Campaign in Poland*, which had concentrated on the role of the army.

121. Quoted in Welch (1983), pp. 213–14.

CHAPTER 4

Official Film Propaganda in Britain during the Second World War

In the twenty years that separated the wars, significant changes took place in British society that had profound implications for propaganda during the Second World War. Electoral reform introduced full adult suffrage for the first time[1] and, as early as 1922, even before it was fully implemented, the Labour Party had secured a larger share of the popular vote than the Liberals. Thereafter, Labour presented the only real challenge to Conservative pre-eminence and, in both 1924 and 1929–1931, it formed minority governments. At the same time, the mass media developed a much more central position in British culture. Fleet Street finally established its national readership at the expense of the provincial morning newspapers, massively extending the size of that readership at the same time – by 1939 almost the whole literate population read a Sunday newspaper, and most read a daily newspaper.[2] While much of the expansion in the popular press resulted from a move away from *news*papers towards publications that sought to entertain as much as to inform, from a late-twentieth-century perspective the British popular press of the inter-war years looks remarkably serious and, notwithstanding the realignment in party politics, it still adopted a broadly conservative political position. That said, the Communist Party launched the *Daily Worker* in 1930; the year before, the Trades Union Congress gave financial backing to the pro-Labour *Daily Herald*, and by 1939 it was one of just three papers selling more than a million copies a day. The market for magazines grew just as dramatically, with publications directed at women achieving particularly high sales and, in 1938, *Picture Post* pioneered a completely new form. Mixing titillation with photojournalism and serious, invariably left-wing, political comment, it proved enormously successful, achieving a circulation of over two million within a year.

The cinema also became more important in these years. American films and their stars were just as popular in Britain as anywhere else, and

Hollywood's colonization of the British market was such that, by the middle 1920s, over 90 per cent of the films shown in British cinemas were American. Devastating as this was for British film production, it stimulated yet further growth in audience numbers. Some decline in the later 1920s was reversed by the introduction of synchronized sound in 1928, and by 1939 weekly admissions exceeded 20 million.[3] Hundreds of new cinemas were built to keep pace with this growing demand, with no less than 715 built between 1927 and 1932 alone[4] and, while many were super-cinemas in major urban centres, new suburban cinemas were also built, adding a new, middle-class (and predominantly female) element to the long-established working-class audience.

While the fortunes of the press and the cinema were driven largely by market forces, the new medium of radio developed very differently. To avoid the chaos of private broadcasting in the United States, a monopoly British Broadcasting Company was formed in 1922, funded by an annual licence fee administered by the Post Office.[5] Through most of these years, the BBC was led by John Reith, who gave the organization a unique view of its mission. Far from being a medium of entertainment, Reith believed that radio could be a powerful force for education and enlightenment and, in complete contrast to newspaper proprietors and film producers who attempted to respond to the needs and desires of their consumers, Reith was determined that he, not the listeners, would shape the form and content of programming – 'few know what they want and very few what they need'.[6] As a result, in an attempt to introduce the mass audience to high culture, classical music and serious drama were initially dominant. Reith even insisted on the careful elocution of BBC announcers, with the result that an upper-middle-class London accent was increasingly perceived as 'Standard English'.

Reith believed that the BBC could play an important role in creating an informed and enlightened electorate, and it began covering the important issues of the day. Almost at once, however, this led to accusations of bias from both left and right, and increasingly the BBC retreated from this objective. However, the General Strike of 1926 revealed that, in a crisis, the BBC would co-operate actively with the government, even if Reith did resist Churchill's demands for even more partisan news coverage.[7] Yet in spite of that experience, the avoidance of controversy, coupled with the authoritative tone of its news broadcasts, gave the BBC a national, even an international, reputation for objective, disinterested news reporting and, whether or not such a reputation was deserved, that is how most of its listeners regarded the BBC at the time. In all, it proved hugely successful: where only 10 per cent of households had radio licences in 1924, by 1939 over 70 per cent did. The medium had indeed achieved a national audience and, at least in its coverage of the royal family and some major sporting events, it had made a real impact on the nation's sense of its own identity.

PLANNING FOR WARTIME PROPAGANDA

The political culture that confronted the government on the eve of the
Second World War was profoundly different from that which had existed in
the First World War. Mass society, characterized by a mass electorate and
truly mass media of communication was now a reality; 'the people'
constituted an incomparably more important part of the equation of politics
than ever before, and politicians had to find ways of coming to terms with
this new reality. The success of Reith's 'top-down' approach suggested that it
was not impossible for Britain's traditional ruling establishment to respond
effectively to this changed situation, but no one could be certain that the
same would be true in the very different circumstances of the coming war.
All assumed it would be incomparably more devastating than the last war,
particularly in the widespread bombing of urban centres in which civilians
would suffer the most appalling casualties. Whitehall estimated that there
would be over a million civilian casualties in the first six months of war,[8]
while a committee of psychiatrists anticipated over three million cases of
acute panic, hysteria and neurosis in the same period.[9] With such apocalyptic
assumptions, it seemed extremely unlikely that the relative stability of
peacetime politics could be sustained – indeed, many believed it was
necessary to plan for nothing less than a complete breakdown in domestic
morale. Accordingly, in October 1935, secret guidelines for the establishment
of a wartime Ministry of Information (MoI) were prepared, and in July 1936
Sir Stephen Tallents was appointed as MoI Director-General Designate.

It was an eminently sensible choice: Tallents was in charge of public
relations at the BBC and had extensive experience of public service
propaganda, having served at both the Empire Marketing Board and the
General Post Office. He would need all that experience in the coming
months, for the problems confronting him were formidable. Very little was
known of First World War propaganda: almost all the relevant papers were
inaccessible and, what information there was, was often misleading. With
the exception of Tallents and one other, none of the team had any experience
of publicity and all had to fulfil their new brief while continuing in their
existing jobs. Moreover, the government (led since May 1937 by Neville
Chamberlain) apparently lost enthusiasm for their work. Chamberlain had
real difficulty persuading any member of the Cabinet to become involved,[10]
and when (in the aftermath of the Munich crisis) Tallents complained about
the lack of Cabinet backing for his work, he was sacked. Thereafter progress
was even slower. Tallents' successor, Sir Ernest Fass, the Public Trustee, had
no aptitude for the job and lasted just four months; he was replaced in April
1939 by a retired diplomat, Lord Perth – an almost equally inappropriate
appointment.[11]

However, the core principles of wartime propaganda were identified in
this pre-war period. The original brief had argued that, in addition to
propaganda, the MoI would have to 'provide for ... the issue of "news" and

for such control of information ... as may be demanded by the needs of security',[12] and it was this twin emphasis on news and censorship that proved most problematic. The heart of the problem, as Nicholas Pronay has so persuasively argued, derives from the fact that news and censorship are driven by contradictory imperatives: news is about making information available, censorship about restricting access to that information.[13] Moreover, while the BBC had a monopoly over domestic broadcasting, there were five separate newsreel companies, and literally hundreds of companies engaged in the production of print news. How could 'control of information' be achieved? Direct control would have been one solution,[14] but then all news would have been perceived as official propaganda, irrevocably undermining its credibility. Moreover, a plurality of opinions was a vital characteristic of Britain's democratic politics, and any restriction of that plurality would undermine the very values that were apparently at stake in the war. It was indeed a formidable conundrum.

In the event the solution was remarkably simple. All news would be controlled at source, and thus with no news of which the government disapproved finding its way into the public domain, the media could be allowed to function essentially as before. The practicalities of day-to-day newsgathering made such a solution comparatively easy to implement: national newspapers relied on specialized news agencies for most of their international news; the provincial press relied on a cable network run by the Press Association for national news as well. To a considerable extent, therefore, it was the agencies that set the news agenda – control of their output would deliver control of that agenda. Moreover, the cables for both the Press Association and Reuters (the most important of the international news agencies) originated in the very same building, making it even easier to exercise such control. Nor was the power of the news agencies limited to the print media: the newsreel companies subscribed to their services (although they shot their own footage), and, from 1931, the BBC relied on the agency services as well. Thus, the news originated from a very limited number of sources that, in time of war, the MoI would control; its News Division would 'tell the truth, nothing but the truth and as near as possible the whole truth',[15] but it would determine what that 'truth' was.

It was a brilliant solution, but it had its own very particular Achilles' heel that was, in itself, a product of the changed political culture. The nation had become accustomed to a regular supply of news and, while it would make some concessions to the imperatives of war, it would nevertheless expect to be kept properly informed. Thus if news was to serve as the 'shock-troops of propaganda',[16] the supply of news would have to be plentiful and accurate – and that was the problem. In war, access to most important news was controlled by the service ministries, and they were committed to keeping news out of the public domain; if the MoI strategy was to work, it would have to overcome that secretiveness. But on this issue Tallents made no progress at all. Neither Chamberlain nor any of his ministers was willing to support him in tackling such powerful adversaries – indeed, when he dared to question the lack of Cabinet support for the emerging MoI, he was dismissed. None of his successors fared any better.

THE MoI IN THE FIRST TWO YEARS OF THE WAR

Thus, on the outbreak of war, the MoI found itself in the worst of all worlds: its strategy of news management was implemented without any agreement with the service ministries about the release of news, thereby creating a vacuum which the media quickly found intolerable. The initial crisis reached absurd proportions on 11 September when, after French radio announced that the British Expeditionary Force had arrived in France, the War Office agreed to lift the ban on the story. Then, just before midnight, the ban was re-imposed, on the grounds that the press was printing too much detail: the police were ordered to confiscate first editions from trains and astonished readers. Finally, at 2.55 a.m. the ban was lifted once more – it was, as Ian McLaine accurately observes, 'the very stuff of farce'.[17] In the following weeks the new Ministry was pilloried by the press. Jokes about its 999 staff were quickly followed by more serious charges: officials were woefully lacking in appropriate experience; the administrative structure was unnecessarily complex; the Ministry lacked a clear sense of direction – a judgement apparently shared by the Minister himself, the elderly Scottish lawyer Lord Macmillan.[18] Macmillan was out of his depth, and when he failed to persuade the Cabinet to allow his Ministry proper access to war news, he proposed that responsibility for press and censorship be removed from the MoI. Not only did Chamberlain accept this proposal (establishing a separate Press and Censorship Bureau), he even considered abolishing the Ministry altogether. In the event, it survived, albeit in a much reduced form: a third of the staff were sacked, including the whole of the Home Intelligence Division.

Early in the New Year, Sir John Reith replaced Macmillan, finally accepting the role that many believed he should have taken a year earlier. He immediately set about reversing the decision on censorship, and by April 1940 it had been restored to the MoI – a month earlier, the decision to scrap Home Intelligence had also been reversed. A new Division was launched, led by Mary Adams (a broadcaster in the infant BBC television service) and, using a remarkably wide range of sources, it rigorously monitored wartime public opinion thereafter.[19] But on the critical issue of access to news, Reith made no progress at all and in May he fell foul of Churchill's wholesale reconstruction of government. The new Minister was Duff Cooper[20] and, while he lasted over a year, he too failed to make any headway on MoI access to news.[21] By May 1941 the situation was so bad that two of Duff Cooper's most senior colleagues threatened to resign unless a solution was found, but when the matter came to the War Cabinet in June, Churchill still refused to be moved. Duff Cooper resigned on 20 July.

In his place, Churchill appointed Brendan Bracken[22] and at last, after nearly two years of war, the MoI acquired an effective Minister. Indeed, in a few short months, he had so transformed the position that the Ministry came to be seen as one of the most successful innovations of wartime administration. Central to Bracken's success was his access to Churchill. His long-standing close personal relationship meant that he never hesitated to stand up to the Prime Minister (or indeed any other Minister) whenever MoI interests demanded it. Moreover, his long years as an MP enabled him quickly to restore the reputation of the Ministry in Parliament while, as the proprietor of a number of publications, he was equally well-placed to repair damaged relations with the press. Most important of all, from an incomparably stronger position than any previous Minister, Bracken was able to bring the service ministries into line. The Foreign Office proved more resistant, but in the end most of the MoI's objectives were achieved. By 1942 all departmental publicity campaigns (with the exception of the Ministry of Health) went through the MoI, and the strategy of news management, with its central emphasis on keeping the people properly informed, was at last put into practice.

It is possible, however, that the implementation of the strategy would have been delayed, even if the policy issues had been resolved more quickly. For, throughout most of this period, MoI officials remained trapped in their pre-war, class-bound assumptions. They looked down disdainfully on the mass of the population, invariably attributing to 'the people' the most negative characteristics. Thus, while they recognized at the start of the war that 'the public is stolidly facing a catastrophe', they concluded: 'There is a danger that this attitude may degenerate into defeatism.'[23] Indeed, the Ministry's very first poster offered remarkably public evidence of the assumptions that dominated its approach: '<u>Your</u> courage, <u>your</u> cheerfulness, <u>your</u> resolution will bring us victory.'[24] *The Times* scornfully described it as 'insipid and patronising'; Mass-Observation found that many ordinary people saw it as confirmation that they would be expected to make the sacrifices for the benefit of the privileged few.[25]

To be fair to the officials, the circumstances that confronted them in these early months of the war were almost entirely different from those for which they had planned. Thus, rather than the chaos of mass urban bombing, almost nothing happened. After Hitler's defeat of Poland, there was no further military action – even domestic mobilization was extraordinarily slow. Food rationing did not begin until January 1940, and the recruitment of labour into war industries was so slow that over a million men were still unemployed in April 1940. In consequence, the public mood fluctuated between half-hearted patriotism and boredom or apathy – indeed, as Angus Calder has noted, the term used by contemporaries to describe these opening months was the 'bore war'.[26] People were convinced that Hitler had to be stopped; what they found intolerable was a 'war' in which nothing apparently happened. In such circumstances, the need for clear, detailed information was paramount, but with the service ministries obdurate and the government unwilling to articulate its war objectives, the MoI could only resort to exhortation. 'Freedom is in Peril – Defend it with all your Might!' or 'It all depends on me' were the slogans emblazoned on posters all over the country. Notwithstanding its best endeavours, public morale remained low. More and more radio listeners tuned in to the Nazi propaganda broadcasts in which 'Lord Haw-Haw' (William Joyce) provided his own version of the news, and this caused considerable alarm in official circles.[27]

The mismatch between MoI perceptions and the realities of the situation became even more pronounced when the 'bore war' finally came to an end with Hitler's invasion of Denmark in April 1940, followed by the defeat of the Netherlands and Belgium in May, and that of Norway and France in June. At first the public mood did worsen – many were outraged that they had been misled about Britain's abortive attempt to come to Norway's aid, and for a moment it looked as if the pessimists at the MoI might have been right. But when the ensuing House of Commons debate acted as the catalyst for Chamberlain's resignation on 10 May, the situation quickly changed. In Winston Churchill, Britain acquired a war leader whose determination to prosecute the war successfully was expressed in a tone that accurately mirrored the public mood; where Chamberlain could never conceal his deep sense of regret that war had come once more, Churchill's defiant and dogged determination gave expression to a very different voice. Thus, while his first speech as Prime Minister offered 'nothing ... but blood, toil, tears and sweat', he nevertheless promised to lead the nation to victory: 'Victory at all costs, victory in spite of all terror, victory however long and hard the road may be ... ' Moreover, as the crisis deepened, he unerringly found the words to articulate popular emotions. By July, an opinion poll found that approval of Churchill had reached the extraordinary level of 88 per cent – thereafter, or at least up to May 1945, it would never fall below 78 per cent.[28]

On the other hand, this dramatic change in the public mood was not simply a product of a new style of leadership. Churchill led a coalition government which represented a decisive break with the previous decade of Tory rule, caricatured almost immediately as a period when Britain had been ruled by 'guilty men'.[29] There is therefore a real sense in which the war began anew in May 1940: a new coalition government spoke for the people as a whole, and Labour ministers would soon make their mark on the objectives of the war itself. Even before that happened, however, the BBC invited the popular Yorkshire playwright, J.B. Priestley, to broadcast after the Nine O'Clock News, and not only did his Yorkshire vowels represent an unprecedented break with the standard BBC voice, the views he expressed were even more novel. He was soon arguing that the inescapable logic of a war against Nazism was a war for a better Britain, in which the traditional emphasis on 'property and power' would be replaced by a new emphasis on 'community and creation'.[30] Priestley's common-sense socialism struck a powerful chord with his audience and he enjoyed huge popularity, second only to Churchill himself – as Siân Nicholas observes, Priestley came to represent 'the Voice of the People', the ideal foil for Churchill, 'the Voice of the Nation'.[31]

Even more important, however, was the experience of the war itself for, in startling contrast to MoI fears, the desperate events of the summer of 1940 served only to reinvigorate morale. The so-called 'myth' of Dunkirk, the claim that it was not an ignominious defeat but rather a triumphant manifestation of Englishness, in which (in Priestley's words) 'when apparently all is lost, so much was gloriously retrieved',[32] was so powerful because it fitted so closely with the way in which so many contemporaries themselves understood these events. As early as 4 June, the very day that the last troops were being evacuated, Home Intelligence found that Dunkirk was being seen as a 'Victory' and 'a lasting achievement'.[33] Moreover, when the war finally came to Britain itself, with the Battle of Britain, quickly followed by the Blitz, morale remained high. Home Intelligence monitored the situation with daily reports, which repeatedly recorded the remarkable way in which the population adapted to the new situation. Thus, an early report noted that:

> The Public continue to take the bombing in good heart ... An increasingly fatalistic attitude towards the effects of bombing is reported, and this appears to be coupled with a high state of morale ... Co-operation and friendliness in public shelters are reported to be increasing.[34]

Indeed, at the end of September (when the Blitz was at its height), Home Intelligence reverted to weekly reports, an indication of just how stable it judged the new situation to be. The people had developed their own strategies for surviving the raids and 'morale in general continues good'.[35] Pre-war anxieties about a dramatic increase in psychological breakdown proved totally unfounded; the war saw no appreciable increase in mental illness, and the number of suicides actually fell.[36]

Yet, because those convictions had been so deeply held, it took the MoI an extraordinarily long time to accept what was actually happening. Any slight hint of wavering morale or defeatism or pessimism was seized upon as an indication that all was not well. MoI officials assumed that it was the working classes who would crack first under the strain of war, and therefore argued that only an unequivocal commitment to post-war social reform would maintain working-class morale – ordinary people would have to be bribed to support the war by the promise of a better Britain after the war was over.[37] Accordingly, throughout the summer and autumn of 1940 they attempted to persuade the Cabinet to commit itself to post-war social reform and, equally consistently, Churchill resisted the pressure. He was not going to be rushed into premature action, and throughout the critical months of the Blitz no major formulation of post-war policy was ever made; the 'bribe' was never offered. Instead, the MoI had to fall back again on patriotic exhortation with, for example, a poster of British battleships and aircraft with the two words 'Mightier Yet'. At best, vague exhortations like this fell on deaf ears;[38] at worst they probably provoked that same kind of irritation that had been the response to the MoI's very first wartime poster.

A NEW APPROACH TO PROPAGANDA

Thus, in spite of the inappropriate character of so much official propaganda, morale remained resolute: the people were tested and were not found wanting. In the end, even the officials at the MoI had to recognize that they had been wrong and, some time during the early months of the Blitz, they abandoned their pre-war prejudices. Almost from the outset this had been characterized as the 'People's War' and now, at last, the MoI began to understand what this meant: by their courage and composure the people had proved that they were indeed the informed and reliable citizens that pre-war propaganda planning had assumed them to be. Those who had endured so much deserved nothing less than accurate and reliable information about the way in which the war, *their* war, was being fought; it was intolerable that the service ministries, and even the Prime Minister himself, were still treating them with such caution and suspicion. It is no coincidence that the issue of access to news came to a head in May 1941 – with its new-found faith in the people, the MoI could not prevaricate any longer. In sum, Bracken's arrival in July and his new approach to the provision of news encapsulated that new trust in the people. No longer would they be patronized with vague exhortations but, accepted as full partners in the project of winning the war, they would be given clear and accurate information about its progress.

On the other hand, the inordinate delay in reaching this position had changed fundamentally the relationship between the propagandists and their target audience. Indeed, in the new situation propaganda followed rather than led public opinion, and nowhere is this clearer than in the vexed area of post-war reconstruction. The MoI's original assertion that such propaganda would bribe the working-classes into a continuing commitment to the war was clearly no longer tenable, but the issue had not gone away. As early as January 1941 (in part at the MoI's urging), *Picture Post* devoted a whole issue to 'the Britain we hope to build when the war is over'; it proved enormously popular, with over 2000 readers writing to the editor to express their approval. When it proposed a further edition two months later on 'A Plan for Britain', the Ministry's initial support was soon abandoned in deference to Churchill's unwillingness to tolerate any discussion of post-war reconstruction. *Picture Post* went ahead anyway, and the second edition proved even more popular than the first.[39]

In the months that followed, Home Intelligence charted continuing public interest in these issues, and in April 1942 it concluded that, while there was a widespread expectation that post-war Britain would put the inter-war problems of poverty, disease and unemployment behind it, few believed that any of the political parties could be trusted to implement the required changes. The MoI understood the importance of counteracting this scepticism, but Churchill's continuing unwillingness throughout 1942 to commit the government to a clear programme of post-war reform made it impossible to develop appropriate propaganda. All that could have changed with the publication of the Beveridge Report at the end of the year although, in the event, Churchill's reluctance again prevented the Ministry from exploiting this opportunity to the full. Thus, it was only agreed at the very last moment that the MoI should publicize the Report and, just a few days later, a pamphlet on the Report distributed by the Army Bureau of Current Affairs was withdrawn. Doubts about the government's lack of commitment to Beveridge were reinforced by the long delay in bringing the Report to Parliament – when it was finally debated in February 1943, the government simply welcomed it in principle; a hundred Labour MPs were so incensed that they broke ranks and tabled an amendment demanding a more urgent commitment to its implementation.[40]

If Churchill's response to Beveridge may have been ambivalent, the people's response could not have been more different. The Report itself achieved extraordinary sales of 635,000 copies, and no less than 86 per cent of the population believed that it should be implemented.[41] Beveridge had articulated a consensus that had been gaining ground since the mid-1930s and which now commanded support right across the political spectrum.[42] Moreover, this enthusiastic response to Beveridge was part of a broader movement to the left that can be traced back to the months after Dunkirk. It manifested itself in various ways, including the passionate denunciation of the 'guilty men', the huge personal popularity of J.B. Priestley and William Temple (the new 'people's' Archbishop of Canterbury) and the surge of support for the Soviet Union, brought into the war by Hitler's invasion in June 1941. Opinion poll data suggests that, by the end of 1942, two out of every five voters had changed their political allegiances since the beginning of the war, and a study by Mass-Observation earlier the same year suggests that the Conservative Party then was considerably less popular than it proved to be in the 1945 landslide Labour election victory. Indeed, Paul Addison goes even further, arguing that 'it is very difficult to believe that the Conservative Party would have won a general election at any point after June 1940'.[43] In the wake of such a sea change in British politics, the leftward drift of official propaganda seems slow and cautious, and it was not until 1944, with Butler's Education Act and the publication of a series of White Papers relating to post-war policy in the fields of health, employment and Social Insurance, that the MoI was able unreservedly to engage in post-war reconstruction propaganda.

Setting this example within the wider context of changing MoI attitudes towards domestic public opinion, the overall shape of the history of official wartime propaganda becomes clear. There was little in the first 18 months in which the MoI could take pride, for, while its strategic approach was well-founded, its failure to achieve an adequate supply of war news, coupled with the class-bound assumptions of so many of its officials, created a situation in which official propaganda was at best irrelevant, at worst offensive, to the majority of its target audience. There followed, in the early months of 1941, a gradual re-evaluation of that approach, driven by the constant flow of data supplied by the Home Intelligence Division, and it was this which eventually convinced the propagandists that the people could in fact be trusted. Once this new understanding had been reached, the Ministry (under the much more effective leadership of Brendan Bracken) set about implementing a radically different approach to propaganda, in which news and information largely replaced patriotic exhortation. The work of Home Intelligence was just as important in the implementation of the new approach as it had been in its formulation, and it ensured (by and large) that the MoI never again committed those errors of judgement which were so common in the early months of the war. While this respect for public opinion restricted the propagandists primarily to the role of reinforcing and strengthening existing attitudes, propaganda is probably best suited to just such a limited role.

As a result, after the summer of 1941 official propaganda was largely appropriate to the needs of wartime British political culture. The nation was broadly united in its commitment to a war which it was determined should be fought to a successful conclusion, but that did not mean that it would simply do whatever the government told it to. Quite the contrary: these informed and critical citizens required information and explanation as much as leadership. With sufficient information, proper explanation and appropriate leadership they were willing to give their active support to the war effort, but that support could never be taken for granted. They had to be taken seriously as full partners in the war, and it was only when wartime propaganda did this that it was well received. The clearest possible illustration of what this meant is provided by changes implemented at the wartime BBC, the institution at the very heart of official propaganda. It was transformed from a monolithic, upper-middle-class station of news, education and high culture, into a pluralist radio network which, through the addition of the Forces Programme at the beginning of 1940, for example, began to reflect the preferences and tastes of the population as a whole. As the *Listener*'s Grace Wyndham Goldie accurately recognized at the time: 'For the first time the quality of the programmes is being decided from below rather than from above ... the box-office, so to speak, is dominant.'[44] It was not simply that *Music While You Work* was a popular new programme; its very presence on the network signalled an entirely new recognition of the importance of popular culture in the life of the nation, and thus represented a new and important recognition of ordinary working people themselves. This was indeed the People's War, and in accepting and celebrating the all-important role of the people in prosecuting the war, the propaganda eventually found a tone and a voice that met the needs of the nation at war.

BRITISH CINEMA ON THE EVE OF THE WAR

The pre-war planning of film propaganda started from the devastating assumption that, in the event of war, cinemas and all other public places of entertainment would immediately be bombed, with resulting levels of casualties too terrible to contemplate. Accordingly all cinemas, theatres and sports venues would be closed at the onset of war and, while there was an expectation that they would eventually re-open, the circumstances in which that would happen were entirely unclear; there was therefore little point in wasting precious time and energy in planning for such an unpredictable situation. However, on the assumption that the newsreels would constitute the single most important form of film propaganda, some pre-war consideration was given to their wartime role. It was agreed that the general principles for news management would apply to the newsreels and, in war, they would be scrutinized by the British Board of Film Censors (BBFC) for the first time.[45] Moreover, largely as a result of a misunderstanding of the way in which the War Office Cinematograph Committee had worked during the First World War, it was assumed that all military footage (which would be so important to the wartime newsreels) would be supplied by the War Office's own cameramen.[46]

In the event, the war did not bring the expected bombing raids and the cinemas quickly re-opened. It took some weeks, but by early November even cinemas in London's West End were open,[47] and it was therefore in these very different circumstances that the MoI Films Division had to formulate a strategy for wartime film propaganda. The British cinema in 1939 presented the propagandists with very considerable opportunities. Cinema-going was firmly established at the heart of British popular culture and, while cinema still retained its traditional, predominantly young, working-class audience, an important suburban, middle-class audience had been added during the 1930s; in all, some 20 million people visited the cinemas each and every week. Equally, while Hollywood competition had threatened to destroy the film production industry, the protectionist regime introduced by the two Cinematograph Acts of 1928 and 1938 had made a real difference. Thus, where domestic feature film production had fallen to just 37 in 1926, the quota system introduced by the 1928 Act raised this to 128 in 1929, and 212 by 1936.[48] Moreover, while it has traditionally been argued that these larger volumes were achieved at the expense of quality, with the production of inferior, low-budget films, singularly ill-equipped to compete with Hollywood products, John Sedgwick has shown that undue attention to these 'quota quickies' is misplaced. A significant part of British film production in the 1930s was good enough to meet the Hollywood challenge head on, demonstrating a rather more fundamental recovery in British film production.[49] That said, over-expansion in the mid-1930s did lead to a slump in 1937, and in 1939 just 103 British feature films were registered.

Precise levels of film production may have varied during the inter-war years, but the narrative range of the films (especially after the introduction of synchronized sound) was much more narrowly consistent. Jeffrey Richards has shown that British studios concentrated on a limited range of genres (comedies, crime films, musicals and detective films), in which only a very small part of the population was usually represented.[50] Working-class characters were few and far between; middle-class characters almost non-existent. Instead, films focused on the privileged lives of the upper-middle-classes, with the occasional working-class caricature by way of light relief. The only real exception to this was the group of films featuring the two truly working-class stars of the period, Gracie Fields and George Formby.[51] Yet, while they were unmistakably working-class, the extravagant worlds which they inhabited in their films had almost nothing in common with the lives of their working-class audiences – indeed, it was that very lack of realism, coupled with their huge personal popularity, that accounted for their success. In sum, British cinema offered a peculiarly narrow diet of British feature films and, while many of these films were popular, American films continued to prove even more popular.

The reasons for this exceedingly narrow range were both ideological and pragmatic. Ideologically, the BBFC followed a deeply conservative approach – in matters of politics quite as much as morality. Established before the First World War, by 1930 the censors had developed an extensive set of prohibitions.[52] Wholly excluded topics included 'references to controversial politics' and 'relations between capital and labour', a prohibition that was subsequently extended to include 'subjects calculated or possibly intended to foment social unrest or discontent'. Pre-production censorship was added in 1933, with the studios expected to submit their 'scenarios' to the BBFC before they went into production. In all, the President of the BBFC could proudly boast that 'there is not a single film showing in London today which deals with any of the burning questions of the day'.[53] Yet it was not censorship alone that had created this situation. Synchronized sound brought a new problem of the intelligibility of regional and local accents, a problem already solved by the BBC by largely excluding everything except an urban, upper-middle-class voice[54] and, perhaps because of the limitations of the technology,[55] the film studios opted for precisely the same solution. With much the same voice dominating the legitimate theatre as well, actors could move freely between all three media. Thus, as John Ellis argues, the dominant voice in British films of the 1930s was 'not so much a classless accent ... as a class-bound accent ... the accent of the metropolitan urban upper middle-class, given an extra inflection towards clarity of enuncia-tion'.[56]

Such were the characteristics of British feature film production on the eve of the war, but the cinema programme always included a newsreel as well. By 1939, five different newsreels competed for business in British cinemas, with even the least popular reaching an audience larger than the most popular daily newspaper.[57] Moreover, factual films made by the commercial studios (notably travelogues and natural science films) also featured intermittently in cinema programmes. But cinemas only very rarely showed those other factual films, proudly and self-consciously described as 'documentary films', in the language of the founding father of the British documentary film movement, John Grierson.[58] Grierson had persuaded Sir Stephen Tallents (Secretary of the Empire Marketing Board at the time) to allow him to make a factual film about the men working in the Scottish herring-fishing industry, and the resulting film, *Drifters* (1929), served as the model for this entirely new form of factual film-making. In the years that followed Grierson trained a number of film-makers, instilling in them all his deep convictions about the potential role of the documentary film in a modern democracy. Much influenced by Walter Lippmann's claim that ordinary people lacked the knowledge with which to exercise their proper democratic role,[59] Grierson was convinced that appropriate factual films could remedy this situation, giving back to the people just that knowledge and understanding that would enable them to fulfil their democratic responsibilities. Moreover, he saw in the work of contemporary Soviet film-makers an example of films that were serving just such a serious role, even though his moderate left-wing views were far removed from the ideology of the Soviet films.

Grierson certainly made a powerful mark on British film culture. When the Empire Marketing Board was closed down in 1933, Tallents took Grierson and his film-makers with him to the General Post Office, and the GPO Film Unit became the best-known documentary film unit in the country.[60] Moreover, in addition to the public patronage of the GPO, a number of private companies set up documentary film units as well, the most important being the Shell Film Unit. Finally, there were a number of very small, independent documentary film units and, although few established a permanent existence, firms like Realist, Strand and Paul Rotha Films did endure. In all, some 60 or so documentary film-makers were at work by the end of the 1930s, collectively responsible for the production of some 300 films, many of which had achieved substantial critical recognition. Indeed, in the eyes of the cultural establishment, the 'art' of British cinema existed almost exclusively in the form of the documentary film – in their judgement, the mainstream, commercial film industry was of almost no aesthetic importance.

Yet, notwithstanding its critical success, the documentary film movement could never persuade the commercial cinemas that there was a mass audience for their films. Cinema owners unanimously argued that documentary films had no appeal for ordinary cinemagoers and, although the films were invariably offered on exceptionally generous terms, cinema owners would not take them. Thus, with one or two exceptions (like *Night Mail* (1936)), the films did not reach the mass audience and were seen instead by a much smaller audience outside the commercial cinemas. This alternative, non-theatrical audience was drawn from the film enthusiasts who belonged to the film societies that grew up in this period, and a wide variety of other groups (including the Women's Institute, trade unions, schools and other young people's organizations), that would, on occasion, include a documentary film in their programme. In all, hundreds of thousands saw the documentary films each year – by any standards other than those of the commercial cinema, a not insignificant achievement.

THE MoI FILMS DIVISION'S POLICY FOR WARTIME FILM PROPAGANDA

The resources available to the MoI Films Division in 1939 were thus incomparably larger than those that had been open to propagandists during the First World War. The Division was led by Sir Joseph Ball and, at first glance, Chamberlain's choice had much to commend it. Trained initially as a lawyer, Ball joined MI5 in 1914 and worked there until he moved to the Conservative Party in 1927, first as director of Publicity and then, from 1930, as head of the Research Department. He organized the Party's successful film propaganda during the 1935 election campaign, commissioning films (which were exhibited by mobile projection vans) and working with the newsreel companies to ensure plentiful and positive coverage. Thus Ball had extensive experience of propaganda and had developed close links with the film industry. On the other hand, his was an unashamedly partisan appointment. He had been a loyal servant of the Conservative Party for over a decade[61] and his appointment provoked inevitable party political criticism, Clement Attlee (leader of the Labour Party) claiming that it proved that Chamberlain viewed the MoI as 'part of the Conservative machine'.[62]

However, it was not just his appointment that caused problems; the policies he introduced proved quite as unpopular. He started from the reasonable assumption that, as the mass audience that the MoI wanted to reach was to be found in the cinemas, the Division should concentrate above all else on reaching that audience. Feature films would play an important part, but even more important would be the newsreels, supplemented where appropriate by specially commissioned factual films. On the other hand, Ball was apparently not convinced that the documentary film-makers should make such films – certainly, in the pre-war planning, it was the newsreels and the companies that produced advertising and publicity films that were consulted, not the documentary film-makers. In such circumstances they concluded that Ball was intransigently opposed to them and, once the war began, they complained vociferously that Ball totally ignored the GPO Film Unit. After six weeks of war, they took the initiative themselves and shot the footage that became *The First Days*.[63] Many years later, the documentary film-maker Paul Rotha even claimed that those responsible for pre-war MoI planning did not even know of the Unit's existence.[64]

But was Ball really so intransigently opposed to the documentary film-makers? Rotha's claim is clearly indefensible for, as Nicholas Pronay has demonstrated, many of those who had planned wartime propaganda had first-hand experience of the documentary film-makers – indeed, it could be argued that Tallents' patronage of Grierson had given birth to the whole movement; the claim that he was ignorant of their work is patently absurd. Moreover, the documentary film-makers seriously exaggerated the extent of their exclusion from wartime propaganda. It had been decided before the war that the GPO Film Unit would become the official wartime film production unit and, notwithstanding considerable GPO reluctance, it was agreed in August 1939 that its resources would be made available to the MoI; its costs were charged to the Ministry from 24 August. Finally, the traditional account of the origins of the *The First Days* is simply disingenuous – far from being an act of protest by film-makers denied a role, it originated in a proposal made by the GPO Film Unit on 8 September; the Films Division authorized it to 'proceed at once' with a budget of £1500.[65] Thus, even if Ball gave priority to the newsreel companies and the commercial film agencies, he did envisage a supporting role for the documentary film. The problem was that the documentary film-makers would not accept such a minor role, and they mobilized their extensive contacts in the literary and critical establishment to mount an attack on the Films Division. The novelist and film critic Graham Greene, for example, demanded a much greater role for the documentary film-makers who, in his judgement, were the only real artists working in film. The nature of their art was such that it gave unique voice to ordinary people and Greene contrasted the pioneering use of the interview in Edgar Anstey's *Housing Problems* (1935), in which ordinary people living in the slums spoke of their experiences in their own voice, with the condescending style of the newsreels: 'Above all we do not want the old commentators with their timid patronising jokes; this is a people's war.'[66]

Nor was it only the documentary film-makers and their friends who attacked the Films Division. Given the MoI's overall emphasis on news, Ball assumed that the newsreel companies would enjoy proper access, and he was probably as horrified as they were to discover that the blanket ban on photographing military subjects applied to film footage as well. Prevented from filming the departure of the British Expeditionary Force, the newsreel editors went immediately to Ball, who in turn protested in the strongest possible terms to the censors. The reply was courteous but intransigent – footage of troops leaving, or even preparing to leave, was 'absolutely forbidden'.[67] Moreover, as if to rub salt in the wound, War Office cameramen subsequently produced footage of such poor quality that it was unusable. Nor was there much progress in the weeks that followed, as officials pursued the (ultimately pointless) quest of producing their own newsreel. The newsreel companies also became increasingly critical of the MoI and the man who led its Films Division.

Ball did not fare any better with the cinema owners and the production studios either for, although the cinemas reopened and audiences recovered, there was great anxiety about the future. Much of this derived from the fact that the industry had to deal with many different government departments – the cinemas had been closed by the Home Office; American imports (crucial for the distributors) were decided by the Board of Trade; the Ministry of Labour determined who would be exempt from military service; the Ministry of Works resolved competing demands for industrial or commercial premises. It was a complex and confused situation and, while the MoI ought to have been able to co-ordinate policy towards the industry, its poor relationships with the rest of Whitehall made that enormously difficult. Instead, confusion and uncertainty persisted, and Ball was blamed for a situation over which he had little control. As for feature film production, while he recognized its importance, little was accomplished in these early months. On the outbreak of war, the film producer Alexander Korda decided to make a feature-length propaganda film about the RAF and, while *The Lion Has Wings* was very much his own personal project, Ball was very closely involved in its production.[68] But he played no role in the production of any other feature films in this period, and his friends in the film studios may well have been as unhappy with his leadership as everyone else.

Criticized on all sides, Ball's position became increasingly untenable and he finally resigned at the end of 1939. He was succeeded by Kenneth Clark, Director of the National Gallery. Clark had no background in the film industry, but this urbane and talented art historian was at least entirely acceptable to the literary and critical establishment, and Ball's departure certainly signalled a fresh start. Thus, during Clark's short period of office progress was achieved across a number of fronts: by the middle of January, for example, all ideas of producing an MoI newsreel were finally set aside, as the Division recognized that it needed 'the co-operation of the newsreel companies more, possibly, than that of any other part of the film industry'.[69] More importantly, at the end of January Clark presented a comprehensive 'Programme for Film Propaganda' to the Co-ordinating Committee of the MoI.[70] This marked a crucial departure from the *ad hoc*, improvised approach that had characterized Ball's leadership of the Division, setting out a cogent exposition of the Division's strategy. Moreover, if there had been an earlier prejudice against the documentary film, it had disappeared by the time this policy paper was produced: its potential contribution explored alongside that of feature films, cartoons and newsreels. The different roles which the different forms of film might play were explored in relation to the three propaganda themes that had been identified in an MoI Policy Committee paper the previous month, namely, 'What Britain is fighting for', 'How Britain fights' and 'The need for sacrifice if the fight is to be won'.

Three separate examples illustrated the way in which feature films might effectively convey what Britain was fighting for. First, films representing 'British life and character' would demonstrate 'our independence, toughness of fibre, sympathy with the under-dog, etc.', suggesting that in addition to films with a contemporary setting, 'histories of national heroes' might also be used. Secondly, films of 'British ideas and institutions' (defined, somewhat tersely, as 'ideals such as freedom, and institutions such as parliamentary government') could either be treated in an historical narrative 'on the history of British Liberty and its repercussions in the world' or by 'a film about a part of the British Isles (e.g. Isle of Man) that the Germans had cut off, showing the effect of the Gestapo on everyday life'. This was then taken further in the third example: films about 'German ideals and institutions in recent history', in which the Germans are seen to be sinister (but not sadistic) and also capable of making 'absurd errors of judgement'. While all this refers to feature films, documentary films could also help to convey what Britain was fighting for, although the fact that many such films has been made in the recent past meant that there would be little need to commission new work here.

On the other hand, 'a long series' of new documentary films would be needed to demonstrate 'How Britain was fighting'. Newsreels would, of course, make an especially important contribution to this second theme, and the overriding emphasis on 'realism' as the method by which audiences would understand the nature of the war was illustrated by the suggestion that even feature films working in this area would incorporate a 'documentary element' within the 'dramatic story'. The objectives of the third theme ('The need for sacrifice if the fight is to be won') would be met by the manner in which films serving the needs of the first two themes were made. Thus, for example, the British character would be shown as 'capable of great sacrifices', while audiences would be shown that British institutions had been 'won and retained by sacrifices'; films about the way in which the war was being fought would stress the enormous sacrifices involved. Finally, the Programme recognized that film would also be used on occasion to convey specific, immediate messages 'e.g. to prevent gossip, to induce greater caution in pedestrians, to explain the shortage of food etc.', and this could best be done by 'short dramatic films' or cartoons.

In addition to identifying the ideas which film propaganda would seek to convey, however, the Programme revealed a sophisticated understanding of the requirements for successful film propaganda. Thus, only 'in a few rare prestige films, reassurance films and documentaries should the Government's participation be announced', and it was imperative that 'the influence brought to bear by the Ministry on the producers of feature films ... must be kept secret'. Most important of all, film propaganda 'must be good entertainment if it is to be good propaganda – a film which induces boredom antagonises the audience to the cause which it advocates ... film propaganda will be most effective when it is least recognizable as such'. This concluding observation made explicit an approach that was implicit throughout. The Lady Vanishes, for example, was recognized as a more subtle exposition of what Britain was fighting for than Goodbye Mr Chips; 'histories of national heroes ... may easily become too obvious'; feature films about the nature of the war should incorporate 'the documentary element' but *The Lion Has Wings* was merely 'three documentaries strung together'. The Programme also demonstrated a very early recognition that the people who were are at the heart of this People's War could be trusted. Its discussion of 'How Britain fights' emphasized the need to:

> ... stress the sacrifices made by merchantmen, fishermen (as minesweepers) and ... by railwaymen and all classes of workers. These sacrifices can be shown not as something which the Government is afraid to ask, and the public expected to resent, but as something to be accepted with courage and pride.[71]

At a time when most other MoI officials remained decidedly pessimistic about working-class morale, the Films Division seems to have been persuaded that ordinary people would respond positively to the enormous demands of war.

In sum, within just four months of the outbreak of war, the Films Division had defined its strategy for wartime film propaganda with singular clarity, and Clark set about implementing this strategy with considerable energy; by February 1940, he had commissioned 32 documentary films, showing 'various aspects of our part in the war'. At much the same time he started discussions with the director Michael Powell that ultimately led to the production of *49th Parallel*, the only commercial wartime feature film financed (at least in part) by public money, and some progress was also made in resolving the anomalous position of the GPO Film Unit: the MoI assumed complete control in April, albeit without prejudice to a review of its longer-term future.[72] Yet Clark was still subject to a good deal of public criticism, notably on the grounds that he epitomized that amateurishness that was seen to be the defining characteristic of the Chamberlain administration and, in April, he was promoted to a more senior position in the MoI.[73]

His successor was Jack Beddington, formerly director of publicity at Shell Mex and BP Ltd., where he had created the Shell Film Unit, the most successful of the pre-war commercial documentary film units. Beddington held this post to the end of the war, a sharp contrast with the rest of the MoI, where change and reorganization remained endemic until Bracken's appointment over a year later. With such close links with the documentary film-makers, Beddington's appointment might have been expected to lead to a much greater emphasis on the documentary film, and two different initiatives were launched to increase the audience for such films. Cinema owners were persuaded to set aside ten minutes in each programme for the screening of short MoI films, and a Non-Theatrical Distribution Department was established to enlarge the market outside the commercial cinemas. This Department commissioned 76 mobile film units to exhibit documentary films in places where no regular film shows took place, while also expanding distribution within established venues.[74] Moreover, Beddington went out of his way to consult with the documentary film-makers and some key personnel were recruited into the Films Division.[75] Yet, none of this represented a radical change of direction. The January Programme had identified a role for all the different forms of film (newsreels, feature films and documentary films), and it was that strategy that continued to guide the work of the Films Division throughout the remainder of the war.

Before the Programme could be fully implemented, however, the Division faced a formidable challenge in the form of a report to the Select Committee on National Expenditure from the sub-committee on Home Defence Services. Investigating the Films Division in the spring and early summer of 1940, the sub-committee's assessment could not have been more critical. It claimed that there was no clear definition of propaganda objectives, only an inappropriate emphasis on 'a vague theme of re-assurance' when what was needed was 'messages to the people precisely related to particular needs'.[76] Moreover, it was equally critical of the Division's methods for, while it did approve of the new policy of including short informational films within the ordinary cinema programme, it was not convinced of the need to commission longer documentary films. Persuaded by the trade view that such films were too esoteric for the mass audience, it urged that resources be committed to the newsreel instead, 'the most important for propaganda purposes of the three principal kinds of film'.[77] It was equally critical of Clark's support for *49th Parallel*, arguing that the MoI should not engage in risky ventures of this kind and recommending that no further funding of this kind should take place. These criticisms provoked a series of difficult debates within the MoI until, in the end, a compromise was reached. There would be no further funding of large-scale feature films, and the Division would be restricted to initiating projects that would only go into production if and when a studio took them up. But the sub-committee's reservations about documentary films were not upheld. The Films Division would continue with this form of film production (albeit on a reduced scale) and would develop the non-theatrical exhibition of such films. A subsequent internal review concluded that the GPO Film Unit should remain, and its new permanent position was recognized in a change of name to the Crown Film Unit.[78]

With these new ground rules finally agreed, Beddington could at last implement the strategy formulated at the beginning of the year. Documentary films represented perhaps the easiest part of the equation, for part of the growing demand could be met in-house by the Crown Film Unit, under the energetic leadership of Ian Dalrymple,[79] who replaced Alberto Cavalcanti[80] in August. Dalrymple successfully negotiated a move out of cramped facilities in central London, first to Denham Studios and ultimately to Pinewood, where the Unit enjoyed a level of resources unheard of in pre-war documentary film-making. Crown was primarily involved in the production of short films, but within a year it had produced its first feature film, *Target for Tonight*, and it was on this film and the small number of subsequent feature-length productions that much of its favourable wartime reputation was based. These feature-length films were part of a group of 47 documentary films that achieved general theatrical distribution,[81] a remarkable achievement given the extent of pre-war trade hostility to the documentary film. And yet, as James Chapman has shown, after Dalrymple resigned in May 1943, the Unit lost some of its original impetus, and many of the productions inaugurated in 1944 failed to reach completion.[82]

While the Crown Film Unit was the single most important source of wartime documentary film production, in terms of numbers its output represented little more than 5 per cent of the 1400 or so official documentary films that were produced during the war, and thus many were made by independent documentary production companies and, where appropriate, by commercial film studios. While the majority of these films did not reach the mass cinema audience, from the summer of 1940 the cinemas did agree to screen a series of short, five-minute official films. Released weekly, these films were made available to cinemas without charge, and some 86 had been completed when the policy was changed in 1942; thereafter, fifteen-minute films were issued monthly, with short 'trailers' incorporated into the newsreels.[83] The Films Division also made determined efforts to reach its target audience outside the cinemas. From 1940 to 1942, the number of mobile 16mm film units almost doubled to 130, with a dozen 35mm units added later in the war. The resulting film shows accounted for about half the total non-theatrical audience, with the remainder made up of shows organized by organizations that possessed their own projectors.[84] Claims about the size of the non-theatrical audience vary wildly, but at the very least it amounted to four million a year,[85] and while this is very small in comparison to the 30 million who went to the cinema *each week*, by any other standards it is a substantial number of people.

From the outset, the newsreels had been given pride of place within the MoI's film propaganda strategy and, with that status endorsed in the 1940 sub-committee's report, the newsreel companies were secure – their personnel safe from conscription, their access to film stock guaranteed. On the other hand, that very importance brought its own price. Exempt from film censorship before the war, they now enjoyed the unhappy distinction of being the only news medium that was subject to both pre- and post-production censorship, in part because of the way in which meaning is constructed in newsreels. The precise form of a particular newsreel (the order, for example, in which the stories are presented) can be as important in determining the way in which the material is understood as the content, and the censor therefore needed to have access to the reel as a whole, as well as vetting individual stories. Thus, in addition to struggling with the same problems of access as the other news media, the newsreels had to work within a much stricter regime. From the outset, a list of prohibited subjects was issued,[86] and this was systematically extended in the months that followed. Moreover, in addition to agreeing the topics to be covered, all the footage was censored, frame by frame if necessary. Commentaries had to be submitted in writing, in advance and, where this was not practical, they were dictated over the telephone. Finally, each Monday and Thursday morning, the completed newsreel was brought to the MoI for a final 'Scrutiny Viewing', as a result of which alterations could still be required.[87] In practice, post-production censorship was rare and even censorship of the original footage became increasingly uncommon.[88] Patriotic newsreel editors willingly accepted MoI instructions and they became so skilled in anticipating the nature of those instructions, that there were fewer and fewer disagreements over the footage that had been shot.

There remains feature film production, and the supporting structures of distribution and exhibition that ensured that the films reached the millions who went to the cinema each week. At the very beginning of the war, the commercial film industry briefly faced a devastating situation, with the closure of the cinemas threatening to bring the whole industry to a halt. When the cinemas re-opened, however, in spite of the continuing blackout, new restrictions on opening hours and fears of air raids, audiences came flocking back. Box office receipts were back to normal by the end of October 1939, and grew dramatically thereafter. By the end of the war, the weekly audience had grown by 50 per cent to over 30 million, a clear indication of the increased importance of cinema-going in the social life of wartime Britain. Indeed, it was a recognition of the importance of this social role, together with an assumption that the supply of Hollywood films would be uninterrupted, that led government initially to give film distribution and exhibition a much higher priority than production. Thus, when conscription began in 1940, cinema staff were treated much more favourably than actors or technicians[89] and this, coupled with the growing employment of women, meant that no cinema ever closed through lack of staff. In the summer of 1940 the Board of Trade planned to decentralize film distribution so that supplies would be maintained even if transport was severely disrupted. However, only a few months earlier it had not acted to halt the growing crisis in film production. By the spring of 1940 a combination of conscription and the requisitioning of studio space had reduced the 19 pre-war studios to just six – four more worked part-time. A further four were requisitioned in the summer, with even Denham (the largest still in production) threatened as well. It was only then, with the very future of film production in peril, that the Board of Trade intervened, insisting that the remaining studios be protected from any future requisitioning.[90] The government was finally persuaded of the need to maintain a 'healthy nucleus', a slimmed-down production industry with the capacity to make perhaps 50 feature films a year, less than half the pre-war output.[91] While the role that these studios might play in the production of propaganda films was one factor in creating this situation, anxieties that the supply of Hollywood films might not be sustained, and the need to save dollars after the war were probably more important.

On the other hand, the Films Division understood only too well the propaganda potential of the feature film and, while it had been forced to abandon its initial policy of direct funding, it remained determined to create a situation in which all feature film production would conform to its strategy for wartime propaganda. It was this objective that Beddington now sought to pursue and, to a remarkable extent, he followed the approach used by Goebbels in Nazi Germany. Feature film production would be closely supervised by the Ministry, but that supervision would be kept strictly secret, ensuring in particular that the audience would know nothing of its extent. Moreover, just as in Germany, the MoI did not exercise direct control over the studios, but rather used a mixture of threats and rewards to ensure that its objectives were met, working where appropriate with the active assistance of other government departments. At the heart of the approach were two inter-linking objectives: no inappropriate films should be screened, while the films that were produced should, where necessary, actively sustain and support the war effort. In meeting the first of these objectives, the MoI was in the happy position of inheriting an extremely strict censorship policy, long since accepted by the industry and, aside from extending its scope to include newsreels, no other extensions of film censorship were necessary. The second objective, however, was more problematic, not least because indiscriminate conscription and the requisitioning of studio space had suggested that, far from recognizing the importance of the industry, the government was doing everything it could to destroy it. To cap it all, film stock was designated as a strategic material, and the studios had to apply to the Board of Trade for permission to use it.

On the other hand, provided the Films Division could secure the co-operation of the appropriate Ministries, the very existence of these controls would give it just the leverage it required. Accordingly, it was agreed early in 1940 that the Board of Trade would seek MoI advice in determining the allocation of film stock and the studios quickly realized that if they won the support of the Films Division at the start of each project, they would ensure that their application for film stock would be successful; in time, to be certain of that support, they would engage script consultants nominated by the Films Division. Moreover, the Division could help in other ways as well, securing travel permits, the release of personnel and even access to service facilities where appropriate.[92] Such close collaboration did not emerge overnight, and it took time for the Films Division to recognize that co-operation was preferable to compulsion.[93] But, by the end of 1940, all recognized the extent of their mutual self-interest and this newly established close co-operation between the Films Division and the industry was to last until the end of the war.

The new co-operation resulted in the studios taking their ideas to the Films Division for approval, but the MoI was also keen to play a more proactive role, identifying those topics that it would like to see addressed in future films. At first, this new role worked on an entirely informal, perhaps even one-to-one basis until, in late 1941, at the instigation of the Screenwriters Association, it was formalized in the shape of an Ideas

Committee, where film-makers and MoI officials 'met round a table over beer and rather lousy sandwiches'.[94] While these meetings took the form of a mutual exchange of views, it was the Films Division that had most to gain from the exchanges, although the claim that the Committee was 'the fount of feature film production ideology'[95] caricatures the complex realities of the situation. For, while the Films Division's broad objectives had been formulated very early on in the war,[96] in common with the rest of the MoI, its approach was also always informed by Home Intelligence data about (changing) public opinion. Thus, it was more than willing to listen to the industry's own views about what films would prove most popular, and Beddington also attended meetings of the British Film Producers' Association.

The complex nature of the relationship between the Films Division and the industry is revealed most clearly by the circumstances surrounding the production of *The Life and Death of Colonel Blimp* (1943).[97] Drawing on the cartoon character (first created by David Low in the *Evening Standard* in 1934) who personified reactionary politics and military incompetence, the film set out to demonstrate that such figures had no place in the modern British army. The project initially met with a mixed reception in the MoI, but fierce opposition from both the War Office and the Prime Minister forced the MoI to modify its original position. Yet, while it was willing to convey the extent of official displeasure to the film-makers and to deny them access to service facilities, the MoI stopped short of banning the film, arguing indeed that it did not have the power so to do. Whether or not that was the case is a matter of some dispute, but the key point is that, even faced with Churchill's very considerable anger, it chose not to. Beddington and Bracken understood only too clearly just how damaging such a ban would be to a wartime propaganda that constantly asserted that the war against Nazism was a war in defence of democracy and free speech. Even more important, it was of the essence of its own approach that, wherever possible, it should work closely and co-operatively with the film studios – personal objections to one particular film, even from the Prime Minister himself, could not be allowed to jeopardize this very special relationship that enabled the MoI to exert such influence over feature film production.

What then were the films that the MoI wished to see produced? Given its sensitivity to changing public opinion, the answer to that question changed over time. Discussions early in 1940 about the need for 'Publicity about the British Empire' led ultimately, to the production of *49th Parallel* (1941); anxieties in 1942 that the public had become unduly complacent about the danger of invasion resulted in *Went the Day Well?* (1942). Such changing short-term imperatives were developed within the context of the broad objectives set out in the 1940 Programme for Film Propaganda, although the Films Division never believed that *all* film production should directly serve those objectives. Cinema had a very important social function as well that could only be sustained if cinemas continued to screen the films the public wanted to see and, given that Hollywood films continued to be seen in British cinemas throughout the war, British films had to be able to compete with Hollywood on its own terms. Indeed, as early as July 1940, Clark had stressed how important it was to maintain 'entertainment as such'.[98] At times, the Films Division and the industry clearly took different views about the proper balance between propaganda and entertainment but when, in July 1942, the industry called for fewer war films on the grounds that the public was 'getting tired of this type of picture and asking for films which took their mind off the tragedy now taking place',[99] the Films Division immediately took notice. Its response, less than a month later, is especially interesting for, while it agreed that it was important to 'support all types of pictures, including entertainment of a dramatic and comedy kind', it insisted that all films should be of 'the highest quality'; the 'non-war propaganda' which it was very happy to support must, nevertheless, take the form of 'realistic films about everyday life ...'[100]

In effect, the MoI wanted to promote a new realism in British cinema and, in the context of the pre-war tradition, such 'realism' could only be achieved by substantially widening the scope of British films; the pre-war, upper-middle-class straitjacket must be set aside in new narratives that focused on the lives of all the people. Part of the way in which the Films Division sought to effect this change was to suggest to film-makers in the commercial film industry that there was an alternative to studio-bound production, and one simple way of doing this was to show them documentary films. The divide between the two sectors of the industry had been so fundamental that many commercial film-makers were unfamiliar with the way in which documentary film-makers worked and thus, more often than not, meetings of the Ideas Committee ended with a screening of documentary films.[101] Yet there was an even more important obstacle to the production of the kind of films that the Films Division wished to encourage, namely the character of pre-war film censorship. In 1936, for example, two different British studios had tried to film Walter Greenwood's enormously successful social realist novel *Love on the Dole*, but both proposals were turned down. Yet, when British National submitted a treatment that was even more faithful to the original novel to the wartime BBFC, it was immediately accepted and the film was released early in 1941.[102] In other words, the production of People's War films required a significant *relaxation* of film censorship, and the production of *Love on the Dole* demonstrates just how quickly it was achieved.

The war, therefore, saw unprecedented co-operation, both between the Ministry and the industry and within the various constituent elements of the industry itself, even if, at times, some of the old tensions and conflicts resurfaced. The newsreels, for example, resented the rota system imposed on them by the MoI, and the commercial studios constantly complained about the extent to which public money was distorting the free market. Occasionally the industry was openly critical and Michael Balcon at Ealing even threatened at one time to break off all co-operation with the

Ministry.[103] In the event, however, he did not, and he subsequently described the objectives of wartime film propaganda in terms of which the Films Division would surely have approved:

> The aim in making films during the war was ... first and foremost, to make a good film, a film that people would want to see, and at the same time to make it honest and truthful and to carry a message, or an example, which would be good propaganda for morale and for the war effort.[104]

Thus, the policy that the MoI Films Division had put in place by the end of 1940 was well suited to the circumstances of wartime Britain. It allowed the Ministry to exercise considerable influence over wartime film production, without having to resort to compulsion or instruction. It was flexible enough to take account both of changing wartime public opinion (as measured by its own Home Intelligence Division), and of the changing desires of wartime cinema audiences (as measured by the box-office returns of the films). Indeed, as many have argued, the war period represents something of a Golden Age in British cinema, with innovations in almost every form of film and the production of a significant body of films which achieved both critical and commercial success.

THE FILMS AND THEIR AUDIENCE

Impressive as that achievement may have been, however, the Films Division had been set up to develop effective film propaganda, to ensure that appropriate films reached their target audiences and that the audiences took from those films the messages which the MoI wanted to convey. To determine whether or not these objectives were met, it makes sense to distinguish between the different forms of film (newsreel, documentary and feature), the different audiences they reached and the changing context within which the films were seen at different times in the war. In particular, it is necessary to take account of the leftward shift in public opinion that took place during the first year of the war, and the relationship which that may have had with the film propaganda that was orchestrated by the MoI Films Division in that period. For it is at least possible that the Division may have committed itself rather more quickly to People's War propaganda than the rest of the MoI. Many of the documentary film-makers who worked for the Crown Film Unit during the war were left-wing, and its films may therefore have played a more proactive role in stimulating a change in political attitudes than MoI propaganda as a whole. Certainly many Conservative MPs were persuaded that it had been a powerful source of left-wing wartime propaganda and, when they finally regained power in 1951, the Crown Film Unit was soon disbanded.[105]

NEWSREELS

If the left-wing sympathies of many documentary film-makers were clear, however, no one could level that charge at the newsreels that had so consistently supported Conservative governments throughout the 1930s. It had been assumed from the outset that they would constitute the single most important form of wartime film propaganda, and the character of their reception by the mass audience is therefore a matter of some consequence. They undoubtedly reached the target audience, for every cinema in the country included the twice-weekly newsreel (produced by one of five separate newsreel companies) in all of their programmes. But how did those audiences respond to what they saw? Did the newsreels justify the faith which the planners had put in them? Wartime newsreels remained broadly faithful to the style of presentation that had been developed in the pre-war years: a variety of short items, many light-hearted in character, always accompanied by an insistent commentary, delivered in an upper-middle-class male voice, painstakingly instructing the audience in the way in which the footage was to be understood. Behind a veneer of objectivity, they pursued a broadly conservative political agenda, although the proportion of time taken up with overtly political items was always less than in other news media.

By and large, this strident, sometimes jokey, always patronizing approach seems to have been well-received by many in the pre-war audience, and the newsreels entered the war with a respectable, if not outstanding, approval rating – measured by Mass-Observation in January 1940 at over 60 per cent.[106] Very soon thereafter, however, they began to lose that popularity and, by September, approval had dropped to under 25 per cent.[107] Mass-Observation reported that audiences complained that the newsreels 'contain[ed] no news', a striking illustration of that problem of access to news with which the MoI struggled so ineffectively throughout this early part of the war. The report highlights other issues as well, notably the fact that the commentary had become 'far more dramatic and emotionalized', with 'vituperative' comments about the enemy and a marked increase in 'patriotic sentiments'. Thus Gaumont News had presented Dunkirk as 'almost ... a patriotic victory' and now finished every reel with a Union Jack. On the other hand, 'criticism or satire is now less prominent than ever before'.[108] In short, the dramatic decline in popularity was also the product of a more nationalistic, propagandist approach to the news.

Certainly, the increasingly strident and exhortatory tone of the newsreels is all of a piece with the kind of approach which the MoI was pursuing in other media at this time and, as we have already seen, propaganda of that kind was invariably badly received. Interviewed in February 1940, a Pathé newsreel cameraman strongly criticized the overly propagandist character of newsreel commentaries, arguing that what was needed was the straightforward presentation of actuality footage, with the minimum of additional exposition,[109] a view that accords almost exactly with the conclusions which the MoI itself reached later in the year in the light of its own public opinion data. Reflecting on the wartime experience many years later, Tom Harrison of Mass-Observation suggested that 'the newsreels, on our evidence, gravely over-played the war emphasis'; the audience simply became 'fed up with ... over-commentary, too much talk, the inability to stop spouting heavy words'.[110] Nicholas Pronay, on the other hand, has suggested that this growing disenchantment may also have been a product of the bad news which the newsreels had to report – 'people hate bad news and the bearer of bad news is never popular'.[111] Certainly, the news was unremittingly bad throughout the summer and early autumn of 1940, and we have already seen that the German newsreels quickly lost their popularity when Germany's victories came to an end; it may well be that the British newsreels suffered much the same fate.

Whether they regained any of that lost popularity during the remainder of the war is unclear, for Mass-Observation did not investigate audience attitudes to the newsreel again. Pronay has no doubt that they did not, explaining this by the fact that there was little good news to report until almost the end of 1942 (El Alamein) and that, even thereafter, progress was painfully slow. What is clear, however, is that the newsreels stuck doggedly to an approach that had been developed in the years before the war, even though the world in which their audiences lived had changed out of all recognition. Nowhere is this more clear than in the way in which they reported on women. Thus a typical pre-war item reporting on a fashion show at Le Touquet prompted the *Pathé* commentator to mock the young women modelling swimwear: one stumbles as she walks away from the pool and the commentator remarks, 'Ah. I hope you enjoyed your trip'; a shot that lingers over another's body provokes the comment, 'Hasn't she got a charming face'.[112] Nearly two years later, a wartime story about the introduction of compulsory registration for young women suggested that the women were eager to co-operate because they 'like the idea of a uniform, anxious to cock a military cap over the eye no doubt', adding that anyone unsure about their girlfriend's age could 'see what call-up she attends'.[113] Even more extraordinary, stories about those working women who now made up such a large part of the wartime audience were used yet again as an opportunity to poke fun. Thus the commentator explains that a woman riveter working in a shipyard was good at her job because 'riveting must be done in the heat of the moment'; women repainting a railway bridge were 'giving that old bridge a new coat so that they can buy themselves a new one'.[114] In a story about women flight mechanics, a close-up of an attractive young woman servicing an aircraft engine provoked the comment: 'Look at this lovely bit of work. She's a peach. Air cooled with 350 horsepower in her cylinders.'[115]

In short, the newsreels failed completely to respond to the immense changes that had taken place in women's wartime lives. By 1943 over seven million women were working in direct support of the war effort, with many younger women having been conscripted into the women's armed services and important industrial jobs. For married women with children, outside the paid workforce, the burdens of war weighed especially heavily. They struggled to sustain some form of normal family life without their husbands and in the face of the almost intolerable stress engendered by bombing, evacuation, rationing and the myriad other changes in everyday wartime life. Yet the newsreels continued to see stories about women simply as the opportunity, at best, for light-hearted humour, at worst, for patronizing and sexist comment. What makes this so remarkable is that of all the wartime media, it was the newsreels that were the most closely supervised by the MoI, and yet that it was the MoI that was responsible for a wealth of other propaganda that sought both energetically to recruit women into these new wartime roles, and to celebrate their many wartime achievements. Thus, a newsreel in November 1942 included an MoI recruitment trailer that climaxed in a sequence in which images of war were superimposed on images of women in the cinema audience, with the commentary: 'There is a job waiting for you. A job that must be filled ... You are needed in the ATS, the WRENS, in the WAAF. You are vital to the offensive.'[116] The irony would surely not have been lost on the women in the audience and, in the context of such rapid and far-reaching social and cultural changes, many must have seen the newsreel as an increasingly anachronistic vestige of a world long gone.

On the other hand, in the absence of detailed empirical data, it is important not to overstate the extent of the newsreels' failure. Guy Morgan's powerful firsthand account of the wartime experience of London's Granada cinemas suggests that once the news from the war started to improve at the end of 1942, the newsreels did regain their popularity. Many Granada cinemas showed the newsreel again at the end of the programme for the benefit of latecomers and, by 1944, the cinema audience had become sufficiently relaxed to greet the newsreel appearance of their particular heroes (Churchill, Stalin, Montgomery) with an enthusiastic cheer.[117] As such a claim is the mirror image of Pronay's explanation for the newsreels' earlier unpopularity, it is in all probability well-founded. But even if the newsreels did increasingly regain their popularity in the closing months of the war, their failure in the incomparably more difficult circumstances of the earlier war years demonstrates, yet again, the inability of film propaganda to counter the dominant public mood. When the newsreels were in tune with that mood they were well received; when they were not, the audience simply rejected them.

DOCUMENTARY FILMS

If the newsreel seemed somewhat out of touch with wartime Britain, surely the same would not be true of the documentary film? With ten years of focusing attention on those ordinary men and women who were at the heart of the People's War, it should have been comparatively easy for documentary film-makers to develop the 'long series' of films chronicling Britain at war envisaged in the Films Division's original Programme. Moreover, *The First Days*, completed by the GPO Film Unit at the very end of 1939 represented a promising start. For the first time it gave audiences some sense of the way in which war was changing the face of London: barrage balloons overhead, air raid shelters and sirens, city workers with gas masks over their shoulders, special trains loaded with evacuees, strips of paper pasted across shop windows to limit blast damage, women driving ambulances. There is even a rare moment of humour as the camera dwells momentarily on the face of a painter as a bus runs over the white line he has just painted in the road, an aspect of the film that Mass-Observation found to be especially popular with audiences.[118]

Yet, notwithstanding this early success, it took the Films Division and its documentary film-makers almost another year to develop an approach that was truly in tune with the emerging culture of wartime life. To begin with, many of its early ventures came to nothing simply because the films could not be produced quickly enough – by the time the film was ready, the circumstances for which it had been designed had changed out of all recognition. As a result, in the first ten months of the war, no less than 60 per cent of the 28 planned documentary films had to be abandoned. In response, from the summer of 1940, it began to commission five-minute films, released weekly, free of charge to the cinemas; the first, *Westward Ho!* (designed to reassure parents anxious about the evacuation of their children) was premièred just two weeks after shooting began. In the early months of the five-minute film programme, films dramatized the dangers of 'careless talk', urged audiences to work in munitions factories, purchase National Savings certificates or dispose properly of their refuse. However, the two films that attracted the most attention were both films which, in the aftermath of Dunkirk, confronted fears of invasion. *Britain at Bay* (seen in the cinemas in July 1940) emphasized that Britain was already prepared, while urging its audience to volunteer for essential wartime services, its message carried primarily by the commentary written and narrated by J.B. Priestley. *Miss Grant Goes to the Door* (released in August), set out to demonstrate that even the most unlikely citizens could successfully thwart German invasion plans. Its two central characters, two middle-aged and distinctly prosperous women, unmask a German paratrooper disguised as a British officer, and although they are eventually saved by the Local Defence Volunteers,[119] their vigilance and courage is perhaps the most striking feature of the film.

The launch of the five-minute films represented the beginning of a more successful period for the Films Division, for Mass-Observation found that they were much more popular than the newsreels.[120] But the same report identified a major unresolved problem – all too often, the films revealed that same class-bound view of the world that was so prevalent in the MoI at this time. Thus, the spies in the 'careless talk' films were always working-class, while the heroes of these and many other films (including *Miss Grant*) were invariably prosperous and middle-class, characteristics which prompted class-differentiated audience responses, with the highest approval coming from middle-class members of the audience. The one exception was *Britain at Bay*, where Mass-Observation found that Priestley's commentary was 'the most remembered and commented on feature of any film', precisely because he provided 'a bridge [between] middle and working-classes'. While Priestley's Yorkshire vowels played their part in this, his words articulated that same sense of the People's War that had been so well-received in his radio broadcasts. Thus, although the defence of Britain would depend on the armed forces, it would also depend 'on all of us'; the words, 'these people of ours ... are now hurrying to man this island fortress', are followed by footage of industrial workers, skilled men and women making their own vital contribution to the war effort.

Britain at Bay is also important in the way in which it started to develop a visual construction of the nation that was to become central to the wartime documentary film. Thus, in the opening sequence, images of the rural landscape are contrasted to, but also combined with, industrial images of the urban north, bringing together the rural and the urban in a peculiarly powerful representation of the nation for wartime audiences. For while rural images serve as a metaphor for Britain's past freedom ('these hills and fields and farmsteads' have been free from foreign invasion for nearly a thousand years), in the context of a newly isolated Britain ('alone at bay') the fields are also a vital source of food. Workers on the land make their own crucial contribution to the war, alongside equally vital contributions by factory workers, service personnel, ambulance drivers, firemen and so on. In short, *Britain at Bay* had begun to find a way of representing the whole nation, and the Mass-Observation data demonstrates just how positively cinema audiences responded. *The Front Line* (a film about the three-month old bombing of Dover), took this a stage further, emphasizing the contribution made by all the people of Dover, allowing some of them to speak about their experience in their own voices.

Important as these early examples were, however, People's War propaganda found its first truly confident expression in *London Can Take It*, released in November 1940.[121] It took the form of a film report from London in the Blitz by the American journalist, Quentin Reynolds. Like Priestley's commentary, Reynolds' words break away from that upper-middle-class voice that had so dominated pre-war culture; his is the voice of a classless observer, an independent outsider, reporting on the Blitz to his fellow Americans. Nicholas Cull has argued that for some months before this the American correspondents in London had been persuaded that Britain had 'cast off its old ways and was now fighting a "People's War"',[122] and Reynolds' commentary provides vivid evidence of just such a view. Thus he claims not simply that London is surviving the Blitz, but that the bombing has provoked an extraordinary response from the ordinary men and women who live and work in the capital. They are 'members of the greatest army ever to be assembled'; 'these civilians are good soldiers'; they are the 'People's Army ... they are the ones who are really fighting this war'. There is 'no panic, no fear, no despair ... nothing but determination, confidence and high courage', and although German bombs destroy hundreds of buildings and kill thousands of people, they cannot 'kill the unconquerable spirit and courage of the people of London'.

Alongside these powerful words, *London Can Take It* offered images and sounds that were to become central to the iconography of wartime Britain: St Paul's Cathedral standing resplendent amidst the ruins of bombed buildings, searchlights piercing the blackness of the night sky, sirens and anti-aircraft gunfire, explosions, firemen fighting the ensuing blazes. But in addition to these 'public' images, the film includes equally memorable footage of the everyday lives of ordinary people. Thus, Reynolds' claim that the sign of a great fighter is that he can 'get up from the floor after being knocked down', is demonstrated by two ordinary moments made extraordinary by the context in which they take place. A woman looks out of her first-floor window, but the window out of which she looks has been shattered by bombing; she actually puts her head through the hole in the glass, but just as if it were an ordinary open window. In the next shot, another woman opens her front door and bends down to collect the morning milk; as she stands up, without looking down, she kicks away the shards of glass on the step. In both cases, it is the absence of drama, the persistence of everyday routines that substantiates Reynolds' claim – 'no panic, no fear, no despair'.

The film enjoyed enormous success. A report presented by Mass-Observation in July 1941 found that it was, far and away, the most popular MoI film to date and 'received nothing but praise';[123] an itinerant projectionist explained its success by reference to 'the neutral reporter, the emphasis on the common people and the fact that it showed what the war was like'.[124] It had taken 15 months, but with *London Can Take It* the Films Division and its documentary film-makers had at last found an approach that properly met the needs of its wartime audience. Its ideology was entirely consistent with the people's ideology and, as such, won their warm approval. To that extent, it does reveal that the Films Division embraced People's War propaganda a little earlier than the rest of the MoI, although not early enough to suggest that it was leading rather than following public opinion. Five months earlier, the extraordinary popularity of Priestley's radio broadcasts had revealed just how well-established those views already were and thus, even in its documentary films, the MoI's role was one of reinforcing and strengthening already established views. That is why the ideology of the hundreds of documentary films that followed remained remarkably consistent for, between them, *Britain at Bay* and *London Can Take It* had set out a vision of Britain's historical traditions and contemporary realities which would make sense throughout the years that followed. Britain had an historical tradition in which she could take great pride; it was the values at the heart of that tradition which were at stake in the war and, in its struggle to defeat those who would threaten those values, all the people would play their part. This indeed was the People's War, and wartime documentary films paid powerful tribute to their remarkable achievements.

If there is an ideological consistency in most documentary films after *London Can Take It*, however, the style and quality of the films did not remain unchanged. Unprecedented public investment gave rise to unprecedented innovation and experiment and, perhaps most remarkable of all, some of the most innovative films were also the most popular. In this too, *London Can Take It* is crucial, for it initiated a collaboration between the film editor Stewart McAllister and the writer, painter, poet and film director, Humphrey Jennings, a collaboration that produced some of the war's most remarkable films. For many years, McAllister's contribution to these films was ignored until, nearly 40 years later, Dai Vaughan (an editor himself) demonstrated just how important it had been, a salutary reminder of the inherently collaborative character of the art of the film.[125] Their collaboration gave rise to many remarkable films, of which *Listen to Britain* (1942) and *Fires Were Started* (1943) are especially interesting, illustrating two very different forms of wartime innovation.

Listen to Britain was probably the most complete expression of their vision of wartime Britain, not least because, in its determination to allow the people of Britain to speak in their own voice, it dispenses with commentary altogether.[126] Indeed, the structure of the film is more musical than narrative (even if its separate movements do follow a 24-hour sequence), with sounds and images overlaid one on top of another to produce a work of unparalleled richness and complexity. Thus in a short, 20-minute film, the audience is taken, for example, from the cornfield to the factory floor, from Flanagan and Allen in a factory canteen to Mozart at the National Gallery, from the Blackpool ballroom to a troop train, from a rural village school to the world served by the BBC foreign service. More important than this diversity is an overwhelming sense of the interdependence of these disparate elements, a society completely united in the common cause of war. Occasionally the different elements are integrated into the same image as, for example, in the extraordinary moment when armoured cars power their way through a picture-book English village, watched quizzically by a little girl in a swimsuit. But more commonly it is achieved by the way in which sounds and images are linked together, sequences often linked by sounds that derive from either the preceding or the following sequence. Thus we start to hear Flanagan and Allen several shots before we finally reach them in the factory canteen; the Mozart Piano Concerto continues long after the camera has moved out of the National Gallery, and it is only some way into the footage of the tank factory that it is finally drowned out by the sounds of the factory.

But the integration derives quite as much from the attitude which the film takes towards every one of its very many different subjects. The two lunchtime concerts are accorded precisely the same respect, Flanagan and Allen fulfilling just as important a role in the lives of their audience as Myra Hess playing Mozart does for hers. In a society in which culture was equated with high culture, such respect for popular culture was remarkable, a potent metaphor for the transformation which war had effected in British society. Moreover, precisely the same attention is accorded to the most ordinary events as well: the little girl who moves too soon in the round dance in the school playground; a munitions worker smiling as she sings along to 'Yes, My Darling Daughter'; servicewomen waiting in the station concourse. In each and every case the film celebrates the value of the particular people it observes, while emphasizing their common membership of the disparate family that is the nation. More than this, the absence of commentary coupled with this subtle and complex mixing of images and sounds, gives the film that 'rich ambiguity'[127] that is, perhaps, its most important political achievement. The essence of the MoI's propaganda strategy was that the people of Britain deserved to be treated as intelligent and sophisticated democratic citizens, and nowhere was that confidence vindicated more than in the response that *Listen to Britain* provoked from its audience. As a contemporary later observed:

> All sorts of audiences felt it to be a distillation and also a magnification of their own experience of the home front. This was especially true of factory audiences. I remember one show in a factory in the Midlands where about 800 workers clapped and stamped approval.[128]

The complex representation of wartime Britain that is constructed in *Listen to Britain* derives predominantly from actuality footage; *Fires Were Started* (1943), by contrast, consists almost entirely of material that was specially staged for the camera. Yet contemporary documentary film-makers saw no conflict between these two approaches, provided that it was real events that were being reconstructed and that the reconstruction was achieved, not by actors, but by men and women re-enacting their own real-life roles. Thus to reconstruct the work of the Auxiliary Fire Service during the Blitz, a number of serving firemen from stations around London were seconded to the film unit.[129] The film examines the work of one dockland fire crew during a period of just 24 hours, but whereas such a structure enabled *Listen to Britain* to develop an almost entirely non-narrative approach, here the narrative closely follows the conventions of the fiction film, using its 65 minutes[130] to follow a dramatic narrative in the lives of its central characters. A new recruit, Bill Barrett, joins the existing six-man team, his introduction to the men and their work introducing them to the audience as well. These daylight hours are presented in an informal, almost leisurely manner and it is only with the onset of night and the ensuing bombing raid that the pace starts to quicken. The crew are sent to battle with a particularly virulent warehouse fire which threatens a nearby munitions ship. At the height of the fire, one of them is killed, and in the closing moments of the film, footage of his funeral is intercut with shots of the munitions ship, saved by the firemen and now sailing triumphantly down the river.

If the narrative structure of *Fires Were Started* is very different from *Listen to Britain*, the film is, nevertheless, securely grounded in People's War ideology; the fire crew (which includes one Scotsman) an unmistakable surrogate for the nation. Yet, unlike *Listen to Britain*, where all the classes of Britain are represented, the nation here is essentially working-class. Thus, even if the occupations of only two members of the original fire crew are clearly delineated (one a taxi-driver, the other a tobacconist), and the Scottish fireman reads poetry aloud more than once in the film, the reaction of the other men, coupled with the way in which they fill their leisure time (snooker, darts, table tennis), firmly establishes the dominant working-class culture. Indeed, this is contrasted strongly with the middle-class commander (one of the weakest performances in the film) and, more importantly, with the middle-class newcomer (Barrett), an advertising copywriter. Moreover, while all the fire-fighting is presented in an heroic style, the one unmistakable act of heroism is achieved by Jacko, the Cockney tobacconist. One of the three men fighting the blaze on the top of the warehouse is wounded: Jacko insists on staying behind so that he can hold the rope steadying the ladder down which Barrett carries the wounded man. In the end, the flames become too intense, Jacko lets go of the rope and falls to his death. His death marks the dramatic climax of the film, but the sequence that charts the aftermath of the fire is, perhaps, at its emotional heart. The firemen are devastated, physically exhausted by fighting the fire, emotionally shattered by Jacko's death, but rather than simply focus all its attention on them, the film reminds us forcefully of the community that they serve. Thus, in a grey dawn, as they wearily reassemble their equipment, ordinary civilians pick their way through the mass of fire hoses that criss-cross the street. Like so many of McAllister's and Jennings' most enduring sequences, the meaning is complex and ambivalent, stressing simultaneously the importance and the ordinariness of the work that has been done, the courage and the despair, the exhaustion and the heroism.

While *Fires Were Started* represents their first and only excursion into mainstream dramatic narrative, it is a most accomplished piece of film-making. Contemporaries praised its authenticity: a serving fireman claimed that, allowing for 'the absence of foul language', the film was 'true to life in every respect',[131] while a wireless operator suggested that 'never have ordinary people been more convincingly done',[132] a judgement echoed by the *Documentary News Letter*, 'the best handling of people on and off the job that we've seen in any British film'.[133] Other published reviews were almost all equally enthusiastic, although the *Daily Telegraph* echoed the claim of a publicity manager employed by the film's distributor that the opening half-hour of the film was 'deplorably slow'.[134] The film was distributed as a first feature and probably did better box office than Ealing's *The Bells Go Down* (released soon after), which shared precisely the same subject matter and starred Tommy Trinder and James Mason. Ideologically, it is perhaps the most radical of the mainstream wartime documentary films, at least in its representation of the essentially working-class character of the nation, although it is difficult to escape the conclusion that such a sense of radicalism was essentially a middle-class conceit – working-class audiences did not need to be told just how important their contribution to the war effort had been!

A small group of documentary films did pursue a more overtly left-wing agenda, partly by reiterating that critique of contemporary Britain that had been commonplace in pre-war documentary films, partly by arguing that the unprecedented transformation that war had effected in British society made post-war radical reconstruction a realistic possibility. Moreover, an initial scholarly analysis of these films by Nicholas Pronay appeared to lend academic weight to the claim made by many post-war Conservative MPs that the Films Division had prepared the ground for Labour's post-war election victory.[135] Since then, however, Toby Haggith's rigorous reappraisal has demonstrated just how mistaken such claims are.[136] These 'left-wing' films 'had no radical programme to offer': there is no mention of nationalization, no discussion of the role of the trades unions or the co-operative movement and their discussion of social and industrial policy was developed within the terms of the wartime coalition government's consensus position. Indeed, when the film-maker Reg Groves presented a script for *Manpower* (1944) that included 'an unequivocal plea for proper planning and reconstruction', he immediately ran into such serious opposition within the MoI that he withdrew from the project; the finished film made no mention of post-war planning. In sum, the claim that this small minority (about 2 per cent) of the Films Division's wartime documentaries acted as a potent pre-emptive strike in the post-war electoral battle derives rather more from party political myth-making than any solid grounding in historical reality.

Any final assessment of the impact which home-front documentary films made on the wartime audience, however, must engage with the problematic issue of the size and character of the audience reached by such films. For while the short MoI films were seen in the cinemas, the vast majority of all other home-front documentary films were never seen in the commercial cinemas at all, reaching only those non-theatrical audiences that represented such a small proportion of the cinema audience. Moreover, historians have tended to emphasize the difficult circumstances within which such screenings took place (cold, draughty halls, noisy equipment, competition with other distractions during factory lunchtime screenings), invariably using the post-war claim made by the film critic Dilys Powell, that she had attended a mobile film show at which 'miners and their wives sat rapt and silent through a documentary record of the making of an airscrew', as a way of mocking the idea that such screenings served any purpose at all.[137]

In fact, Powell's claim related to people who had never encountered cinema before, and there is abundant evidence from the early history of the cinema of comparable audiences being enthralled by the technology, regardless of the images on the screen. Moreover, in precisely the same paragraph, she describes a very different audience:

> ... women workers in their hundreds clattered from the sheds into the canteen rooms where, while they ate their sandwiches and drank their strong tea, documentary films about air training in Canada and the British Army health service were shown on the screen. The noise was incessant and savage, a third of the audience paid little attention to the performance, and of the rest probably the majority were tolerant rather than interested. Yet something was communicated ...[138]

Hers is no rose-tinted view from a documentary film apologist, but rather an honest account of the circumstances in which such factory screenings (which amounted to about a third of all non-theatrical screenings) took place, and her conclusions that 'something was communicated' is both modest and well-founded. For, once the class prejudices of early Films Division films had been overcome, the films did present a view of wartime Britain that corresponded closely with the views of their audience. In such circumstances, even the most mundane film was tolerated, while, as we have already seen, the very best (*Listen to Britain*) provoked another factory audience to clap and stamp its approval.

When the Films Division first formulated its Programme for Film propaganda at the start of 1940, it assumed that battlefront documentary films would parallel those recording the impact of the war at home. Yet, the nature of the war and the long-running problems associated with access to war news, meant that there was a long delay before such films were made. Indeed, all the early battlefront films took the form of documentary reconstructions, using 'real people' to re-enact their wartime roles. Thus, the GPO Film Unit made two short films in 1940, *Squadron 992* (about the men who manned the barrage balloons) and *Men of the Lightship*; these were followed in 1941 by a third short film, *Merchant Seamen*.[139] However, it was a fourth film, the incomparably more ambitious *Target for Tonight*, that achieved the first real success in this area. This 50-minute film, produced by the Crown Film Unit and released in the summer of 1941, enjoyed extensive publicity before its commercial release, and some cinemas ran it as a first feature. Screened so soon after the end of the Blitz, its account of the experiences of the crew of one RAF bomber came at a particularly timely moment, and its message that the RAF was beginning to strike back at Germany was one that audiences wanted to hear. Certainly, Harry Watt, the director of the film, had no doubt that timing was critical to the film's success,[140] a view endorsed by Guy Morgan in his explanation of its popularity in London's Granada cinemas.[141] That said, the low-keyed, unsensational character of the film provides an additional explanation for its popularity and, while there is at least some evidence that its particular form of realism did not convince all its audiences,[142] it proved to be the most successful of all Crown's wartime films.[143]

In the light of that success, there was every reason to develop further documentary reconstructions of this kind and, before the end of 1941, Crown began work on a new project about the merchant seamen who were keeping Britain's vital transatlantic supply lines open. In the event, it took over three years to translate that initial idea into the feature film that became *Western Approaches*,[144] the delay a direct consequence of the scale of the film's ambition. Its account of the fate of the survivors of a torpedoed boat and their long ordeal in a lifeboat, was set within the wider narrative of the continuing battle between the convoys and the German U-boats, and wherever possible the film was shot on location; the decision to shoot the film in Technicolor added enormous additional logistical and financial burdens. Pre-production lasted nine months and, while location shooting off Holyhead finally began in September 1942, all filming was not finally completed until the very end of 1943. Yet, even though a rough cut was ready a month later, that was not the end of the film's problems. Almost every element of post-production proved problematic and the film did not go out on general release until January 1945, a full year later. Thus a film that would have served as excellent propaganda at any time during the Battle of the Atlantic became, as a result of all the delays, a retrospective celebration of the achievements of the men whose battle had been already won. While none of this should detract from its undoubted qualities (the extraordinary colour photography, the persuasive performances by serving seamen, the powerful drama of the narrative), all of which were recognized by almost all the contemporary film critics, C.A. Lejeune in the *Observer* was surely right to argue that 'a good deal of its message has already been conveyed'.[145] The time and resources taken up in its production ensured that no other feature-length documentary reconstructions were produced during the war.

However, actuality battlefront films were made right to the end of the war. A number of such films had been produced during the First World War, and in 1941 the Army Film and Photographic Unit (AFPU) started at last to release short films constructed from actuality footage. Few films followed in the next two years, however, and none made any very great impact on the audience. Yet, in a striking parallel with the First World War, that situation was transformed in March 1943 with the release of the feature-length *Desert Victory*, an actuality record of the dramatic defeat of Rommel's German and Italian forces in November 1942 – the first important British victory of the war. It is commonplace in documentary films to make special claims for their authenticity – *Target for Tonight* had proudly announced that each part was played 'by the actual man or woman who does the job'. The pre-publicity material for *Desert Victory* emphasized the numbers of cameramen who had been killed or wounded in making the film,[146] asserting a quite different order of authenticity. *Desert Victory* amply fulfilled the high expectations created by such claims for, while a small number of sequences were reconstructed,[147] it offered a rich variety of actuality footage of every aspect of the war in the desert. It also included useful captured footage of Rommel and Hitler, and of German and Italian troops in action, and all these disparate sources were welded together into a battlefront narrative, exemplary in its clarity, drama and pace.

Desert Victory professed precisely the same People's War ideology as the home-front films: its opening titles dedicating the film not only to the armed services, but also to 'the workers ... without whose efforts victory could not have been achieved'; a radio report of the initial successes prompts an enthusiastic response from listening women munitions workers. The ideology of the film is found, above all else, however, in the commentary, written by the journalist J.L. Hanson. Not only does it avoid rhetorical excess, being both eloquent and economical at the same time, it powerfully involves the audience in the action of the film. The first person plural is used consistently, not only to represent the men serving in the desert, but all the people at home as well, with the words delivered in a male voice that avoided the connotations of class that so dominated pre-war cinema, and that still dominated the newsreels.[148] Thus, where commentaries had so often alienated cinema audiences, this commentary served powerfully to identify the audience with the men whose victories were being celebrated. It had been a long time in coming, but in *Desert Victory* the AFPU had produced a film that achieved for its audience what *Battle of the Somme* had achieved 27 years earlier. It enjoyed enormously enthusiastic reviews, and fully justified its release as a first feature, winning remarkably large audiences for a documentary film.[149] Released just four months after the victory it celebrated, timing certainly played its part in its success at the box office, but that popularity also derived from its remarkable quality, with the film achieving the unprecedented distinction of winning a Hollywood Oscar for best documentary feature film. Indeed, the extent of its success (especially in America) was such that those responsible for the production of American film propaganda were determined never to allow a British film to achieve such success again, and when a rough cut of *Africa Freed* (AFPU's follow-up to *Desert Victory*) was screened in July 1943, American pressure ensured that it was not released on the grounds that it did not do justice to America's role.[150] In the event, the film was reworked in the form of a joint Anglo-American production, and was finally released as *Tunisian Victory* in March 1944, a year after the events on which it reported had ended. It was not a great success.

A quite different fate, however, awaited the final Anglo-American production, *The True Glory*, which charted the history of the final stages of the war in Western Europe, from the preparations for the Normandy landings through to the unconditional German surrender in May 1945. This time there was no delay, and the film was first shown in August 1945, where it had considerable success in the cinemas, and subsequently won a second

Oscar for a wartime documentary feature. Notwithstanding the fact that it was in every sense a joint Anglo-American production, *The True Glory* adopted just that People's War ideology that had so dominated British wartime documentary films, using the voices of 160 combatant service men and women to comment, in the first person, over actuality footage that had been shot by cameramen from no less than nine different allied countries.[151] Aside from a brief introduction by General Eisenhower, the narrative exposition took the novel form of short passages of blank verse, backed up by maps to illustrate the changing geography of the campaign. While the poetry sometimes strikes an overly rhetorical note, its presence underlined the power of the ordinary, everyday character of the personal testimony, and it is the interaction between these words and the battlefront images that so often gives the film its special force. Thus while we watch an extraordinarily rich and varied visual record of each and every element in the campaign, the tiny fragments of spoken personal narrative serve as a powerful bridge between the audience and the events that are being recorded in the film, allowing the audience to identify closely with this rich and complex narrative. Nowhere is this more clear than in the sequence recording the liberation of the Belsen concentration camp. The voice over the initial horrific images is that of a British medical orderly, who explains that while he had served through the Blitz and had 'lost count of all the arms and legs I pulled out of the wreckage', nothing had prepared him for what he found in Belsen:

> But this was different. Very different. I don't know any words big enough to make you understand what we all felt. All I can say, and I'm proud of this, is that I had to fall out and be quickly sick in the courtyard. As I say I'm not squeamish but, well, I'm human and thank God for it.

By the time *The True Glory* was released, audiences had already seen newsreel footage from the concentration camps and, while the character of the images is such that they can never lose their enormous power to shock, their juxtaposition with comments as particular and personal as these made this extraordinary sequence truly memorable.

Battle of the Somme had launched a tradition of battlefront reporting which finds its triumphant conclusion 29 years later in *The True Glory*. At the heart of that tradition was a determination to put the ordinary serviceman or woman at the very centre of the narrative and, while *The True Glory* does give its audience some limited sense of the role of the most senior officers and politicians, it is the ordinary service personnel who are its true heroes. To that extent it can stand also for Second World War documentary films as a whole for, at their best, they constructed powerful representations of a People's War that celebrated the remarkable achievements of all the people who had made the victory possible. But *The True Glory* encapsulates the wartime tradition in another way also for, by the time it reached the cinemas in August, the war was already over and thus, like so many films before it, it served to reconfirm and validate an already firmly established view of recent events. This should in no way diminish its achievement or the achievement of the many documentary films which preceded it. The people had been called on to make huge sacrifices in the cause of defeating fascism, and what evidence there is suggests that they derived both pleasure and satisfaction from the public recognition accorded them in wartime documentary films.

FEATURE FILMS

Important as such films were, however, only very few documentary films reached the mass cinema audience where, of necessity, they constituted a very small proportion of the feature films that those audiences watched so avidly throughout the war years. What then was the character of those British feature films? A number of contemporaries clearly believed that the war years witnessed radical changes in British cinema and, in 1947, Dilys Powell (the *Sunday Times* film critic) spoke for the whole critical establishment when she argued that the war years had seen:

> ... a certain sharpening of public taste ... Themes which would once have been thought too serious or too controversial for the ordinary spectator are now accepted as a matter of course... We have seen how the semi-documentary film has gained a hold over British imaginations. We have seen too how even in the film of simple fiction, the demand has grown for knowledge and understanding. The British no longer demand pure fantasy in their films; they can be receptive also to the imaginative interpretation of everyday life. The serious British film has thus found an audience as well as a subject.[152]

At first sight, there is much to be said in defence of such claims. Films like *Love on the Dole* (1941), that were unable to find a way past the pre-war censor, did go into production and enjoyed some modest success at the box office.[153] A new kind of realism, drawing strongly on approaches pioneered by documentary film-makers before the war, did make its mark on a number of film genres, although perhaps most obviously in films about the war. Thus the melodrama and artificiality of *Convoy* (1940) and *Ships with Wings* (1942) gave way to the more realistic approach of *In Which We Serve* (1942) or *The Way Ahead* (1944). But, perhaps most striking of all, the extraordinarily narrow class confines of pre-war British cinema were breached. It became more common for films to draw characters from across the British classes, and the family at the centre of the hugely popular *This Happy Breed* (1944) was lower-middle-class.

Yet, in its enthusiasm for those changes of which it approved, the contemporary critical establishment constructed a highly selective history of wartime British cinema. As Jeffrey Richards has properly emphasized, the most popular British star from 1938 to 1943 was the former music hall comedian George Formby, and when he was finally displaced in 1944, his place was taken by James Mason, the striking new male star of the Gainsborough costume melodramas.[154] Neither Formby nor Mason bore any marks of the new realism in British cinema, and their huge wartime popularity serves as a salutary reminder of both the enduring appeal of comedy and melodrama, and also the clearest possible evidence of the diversity of wartime film production. Nor did the new realism carry all before it. *Ships with Wings* demonstrated an enormous public appetite for a war film of the most traditional kind – patriotic, melodramatic, stagey – and it was released at the start of 1942, six months after *Target for Tonight*, a film that was claimed to demonstrate the public's enthusiasm for the new documentary approach.[155] Wartime feature film production reveals considerable evidence of continuity alongside the much-trumpeted evidence of change.

On the other hand, there was no necessary conflict between this diversity of production and the strategy which the MoI pursued in respect of feature film propaganda. From the outset, the Films Division recognized that cinema's ability to attract mass audiences was directly related to its ability to screen films that would prove popular with those audiences. And it followed that, just as in the Soviet Union or Nazi Germany, there was never any intention to flood the market with propaganda films. Censorship would ensure that no film would be screened that would harm the war effort and the Films Division would ensure that at least some of the feature films that were made would directly serve its propaganda objectives. Moreover, it was vital that these films had sufficient popular appeal to win audiences in competition with both Hollywood imports and other British films, less burdened by propagandist imperatives – 'a film which induces boredom antagonises the audience'.[156]

Any assessment of this aspect of the work of the MoI encounters two difficult problems of definition. First, after the production of *49th Parallel*, no other feature film produced by a commercial studio was directly funded by the MoI, and there is therefore some difficulty in deciding which films can properly be used to assess whether or not MoI objectives were met. In a small minority of cases, surviving departmental papers reveal close government involvement in the initiation of a particular project, yet the influence of the MoI stretched far beyond these few films; in reality, the complex web of disincentives and opportunities that had been put in place by 1941 created a culture within which the Films Division was able to exert considerable influence over all commercial film production. Moreover, the MoI's growing emphasis on the importance of taking proper account of public opinion in the formulation of propaganda brought it closer to the commercial imperatives that drove the studios. Thus, for example, it was clearly in the MoI's interest to initiate a project like *Millions Like Us* (1943), to encourage more young women to serve in munitions factories and reinforce public recognition of the importance of their work, but those same young new women workers constituted a growing part of the cinema audience, and there was therefore commercial sense in producing a film which would have a special appeal for them. In short, in a People's War, the MoI and the film studios shared a common interest in giving the people what they wanted. Therefore it makes sense to test *all* feature film production against the MoI's own stated objectives, excluding only those rare films (like *The Life and Death of Colonel Blimp*) that were made in the face of unmistakable government opposition.

Secondly, film propaganda that does not reach its target audience is of little use, and it is therefore important to take the films' popularity into account. Yet, the industry did not record accurate national box office statistics, and historians have to grapple with a variety of less than complete sources. Pride of place must go to R.H. 'Josh' Billings' annual survey in *Kine Weekly*, an impressionistic but extremely well-informed trade view that, in all probability, identified all the most successful films, albeit lacking the statistical base to enable precise measurement of their success. Box office statistics do exist in the form of the records of just one cinema, The Majestic in Macclesfield,[157] and this microcosm of the wartime audience provides a useful cross-check for Billings' broad brush analysis. When these sources are combined with a variety of personal and anecdotal evidence, a reasonably clear picture emerges of just which films secured the largest audiences in wartime Britain, and by concentrating primarily on those most popular films it becomes possible to make some assessment of the extent to which the Films Division was able to achieve its objectives for feature film propaganda.

The Films Division was not in any position to influence feature film production before the summer of 1940, and the first films bearing the unmistakable marks of its influence did not therefore reach the cinemas until the following summer. Thus, during the most difficult period of the war, it was cast in the role (as far as feature film production was concerned) of passive observer. It had to work on the assumption that the war would not be lost and its attempt to influence the shape of future feature film production would, in the end, bear fruit but, in the short term, there was nothing it could do to influence the character of the films that audiences would see.[158] Thereafter, however, the Films Division had good reason to feel satisfied with what was achieved. At the start of 1940 it had indicated how the feature film might serve the three primary themes of official propaganda (namely, 'What Britain is fighting for', 'How Britain fights' and 'The need for sacrifice if the fight is to be won'), and in the months that followed these themes were further refined as the MoI committed itself to the ideology of the People's War. If we then test the most popular British film of each year after 1940 against the template of these objectives, we find a remarkable correlation. With the exception only of *The Seventh Veil* in 1945, each of the most successful British films of the four previous years fulfilled one or more of the MoI's objectives.

The most popular British film in 1941 was Michael Powell's *49th Parallel*, a film about a German U-boat crew attempting (unsuccessfully) to make their escape across Canada to a still neutral United States, in the course of which the brutal Nazis variously encounter opposition from a remarkably disparate group of people, ranging from a French Canadian trapper to an English author. In 1942 came *The First of the Few*, a biography of R.J. Mitchell (the designer of the Spitfire fighter plane) who, as realized by Leslie Howard, becomes the very essence of an understated, diffident, middle-class English hero. The most popular film of 1943 was the very different *In Which We Serve*, for while Coward's film originated as a tribute to Lord Louis Mountbatten, its central focus was on the ship and its company, a unmistakable surrogate for the whole nation at war. Finally, while the most popular British film of 1944 – David Lean's *This Happy Breed* – ignored the war altogether, its exploration of the inter-war history of one lower-middle-class family acted as a vehicle for an even more intimate examination of the character of British society.

If the focus is widened to include all those films singled out as being especially successful in the *Kine Weekly* annual surveys, together with those that did better than average business at The Majestic, Macclesfield,[159] then a further 11 films serving one or more of the Films Division's themes also achieved considerable success. These included the three films which focused attention on the other armed services – the RAF in *Ships with Wings* (1942) and *The Way to the Stars* (1945), the army in *The Way Ahead* (1944); the two films which concentrated on the new wartime roles of women – the ATS in *The Gentle Sex* (1943), munitions workers in *Millions Like Us* (1943); the 'careless talk' film *The Next of Kin* (1942); a film about the Resistance in occupied Holland, *One of Our Aircraft Is Missing* (1942); *Pimpernel Smith* (1941), a film starring Leslie Howard as an English university professor helping refugees escape Nazi tyranny in pre-war Germany; and finally, Laurence Olivier's lavish production of Shakespeare's *Henry V* (1945). What this data also reveals, however, is that at least some of the films which clearly served the MoI's needs were not well-received in Macclesfield. Thus historical films fared badly with this particular audience: John Gielgud's portrayal of Disraeli in *The Prime Minister* (1941) secured only 41 per cent of the audience for the most popular British film of the year, and *The Young Mr Pitt* (1942) did only slightly better business with 53 per cent of the audience. In the case of the latter film, however, the Macclesfield audience was clearly out of step with the country as whole, for *The Young Mr Pitt* was identified by *Kine Weekly* as one of the four most popular films of the year. Similarly, *The Foreman Went to France* (1942), the third most popular film in the *Kine Weekly* survey, reached only 51 per cent of The Majestic audience.

What did always prove popular with the Macclesfield audience was comedy – in 1940, 1941 and 1942 George Formby topped The Majestic bill with *Come on George*, *Spare a Copper* and *Somewhere in Camp* respectively, while in 1943, Frank Randle's low-budget slapstick comedy, *Somewhere on Leave*, proved more popular than *In Which We Serve*. In the last two years of the war, however, Gainsborough melodramas overtook the comedies in audience popularity (*Fanny by Gaslight* and *They Were Sisters* respectively), even though *This Happy Breed* did just beat *Fanny by Gaslight* into second place in 1944. While it is extremely unlikely that the Films Division took any satisfaction from the success of the Gainsborough films, it is not difficult to argue that these films did explore important contemporary issues of gender and class, albeit through the refracting lens of historical melodrama,[160] and at least to that extent made some contribution to People's War propaganda. Moreover, very many wartime comedies were given a contemporary setting, and while it would be quite wrong to suggest that this accounted for their huge popularity, the way in which (within the conventions of slapstick comedy) they so often caricatured the enemy accorded only too well with the Films Division's emphasis on showing Germans 'making absurd errors of judgement', in addition to stressing their 'sinister ... aspect'.[161] Thus, all in all, the MoI was remarkably successful in fulfilling the two preconditions for effective feature film propaganda: it did secure the production of films that were consistent with its objectives, and many of those films did reach their target audience. But the most important and most difficult question of all remains: what were the messages that the films were intended to convey, and were those messages received and understood by their target audience? In sum, did the propaganda work?

The easiest way of answering that question is to look at those films that were designed to meet specific needs at a particular moment in the war. For the problems of timing that had beset so many documentary films proved even more intractable with the longer lead times of feature film production, and many such films were simply overtaken by events. For example, MoI anxieties about public complacency about the dangers of invasion led to various publicity campaigns in 1941 and 1942. The feature film which addressed the same problem, *Went the Day Well?*, was not released until November 1942, by which time its powerful message about the ruthless brutality of a potential Nazi invasion lacked any real contemporary resonance.[162] The ATS experienced real difficulties in recruitment and, not least because of the large numbers of young women who went regularly to the cinema, it was decided that a feature film could make an important contribution to a recruitment campaign that also involved a wide range of other media. What evidence there is suggests that *The Gentle Sex* was indeed just such a film – a 36-year-old stenographer, for example, told Mass-Observation that it made her wish 'that I could join one of the Women's Services'.[163] But by the time it reached the cinemas in the summer of 1943, the ATS' recruitment crisis was over and the film became, in the words of one of Mass-Observation's other respondents, simply 'a film about life as it is now for many girls'.[164] Very much the same fate awaited *Millions Like Us*, the film designed to recruit women into munitions: it was not released until September 1943, the very month in which the wartime mobilization of women reached its peak. Thereafter the pressures eased, and by the middle of 1944 the first of the women newly recruited into the engineering industry began to be laid off.

Vincent Porter and Chaim Litewski argue persuasively that much the same charge can be levelled at The Way Ahead (1944), Carol Reed's remarkable exploration of the way in which a disparate and, initially, discontented group of conscripted men are forged into a united and effective platoon.[165] The first recognition that such a film was needed came in the summer of 1942, before the army had achieved any significant successes; by the time it was released two years later, the situation could not have been more different. No one any longer doubted the need for conscription and the film opened in London's West End on the very day that the first Allied troops landed in Normandy; the doubts and anxieties of the summer of 1942 seemed a very long way away. Much the same might be said of The Way to the Stars (1945). The original idea for a film about the transformation of a British airfield from an RAF to a USAAF base was developed in March 1943, at a time when the MoI was anxious to promote better Anglo-American co-operation and mutual understanding. For a variety of reasons it did not go into production until 1944, and was not released until June 1945, after the end of the war in Europe.[166] Thus in each and every one of these cases, films designed to meet a particular need could not be produced quickly enough to serve that original purpose. Attitudes did change, the need for conscription (whether in the services or the factories), for the support of the American airforce, were accepted, but those attitudes were changed by the imperatives of the war, not by the film propaganda. The very most that the films could do was reinforce and reconfirm the very views that they had been designed to create.

In reality the feature film is too unwieldy a weapon to deploy in these kind of propaganda campaigns and, almost without exception, films that were designed to play a part in such particular, time-specific campaigns failed to meet their original objectives. That said, early in the war the Films Division had understood that this was not the most important role which feature films would play in wartime propaganda. Rather, they would construct an ideology for a nation at war, an ideology that was defined rather broadly at first, but which gained a sharper focus as the MoI committed itself more and more wholeheartedly to the imperatives of the People's War. Its purpose was to reinvigorate commitment to the war effort, but because the strategy emerged out of an experience of the Blitz that had taught the propagandists just how determined and resilient the people were, its emphasis was invariably on celebration (of the people's achievements), rather than exhortation (to achieve more). The nation's own sense of its identity (past and present) would be reflected back to it in the cinema and, in the pride of that recognition, it would renew once more its commitment to the war effort. Indeed, in such a strategy, the very failure of films that had been designed to meet particular, earlier wartime needs became a source of success, their ability to reinforce existing views yet another potent contribution to the ideology of the People's War.

The first clear exposition of this ideology in a truly popular British film came in the spring of 1942 with the release of Ealing's *The Foreman Went to France*. Like so many subsequent films, it looked back to an earlier period in the war, namely the fall of France in the summer of 1940, following the adventures of a British foreman who decides to rescue British machinery (vital in the production of anti-aircraft guns) that had been loaned to a French factory. The foreman, Fred Carrick, embarks on this mission in the face of determined opposition from his managers, who are wholly dismissive of his fears for the safety of the machinery and, in his retrieval of the equipment, he is aided and abetted by an American secretary (working at the French factory) and two ordinary British soldiers whose lorry has become separated from their unit. In conception, the film clearly intended to celebrate the insight and common-sense of ordinary working men in contrast to the smugness and naïvety of their middle-class 'betters', but its ability to sustain this message convincingly is undermined not a little by Clifford Evans, singularly implausible as the working-class foreman, and Constance Cummings' performance as the glamorous American secretary. Although she had been born in America, Cummings proved curiously unable to sustain her American accent throughout the film. In contrast, Tommy Trinder and Gordon Jackson bring a good deal of credibility to the roles of the two soldiers (the one a bus conductor, the other a garage hand in civilian life), and the integration of newsreel footage of Belgian refugees provides one of the strongest moments in the film. In all, the film signalled a clear departure from the class-bound conventions of pre-war cinema and, for at least one Mass-Observation respondent, it clearly achieved its purpose: 'a useful little documentary [*sic*] of the war. Inspiring in its heroism of ordinary people and its emphasis on the best in British character.'[167]

Powell and Pressburger's *One of Our Aircraft Is Missing*, also released in 1942, represents a less whole-hearted exploration of the new ideology of war, following the experiences of the crew of a Wellington bomber who bail out over Holland, and eventually escape back to England thanks to the bravery and boldness of the Dutch Resistance. Nevertheless, the film does emphasize the different class backgrounds of the crew of the bomber (ranging from a professional footballer to a middle-aged knight) and the extent to which their service experience destroys those divisions. The notion of cross-class unity is perhaps reinforced by the fact that the different members of the Dutch Resistance also come from very different social backgrounds, from the school-teacher (played by Pamela Brown) to the very wealthy society lady (played by Googie Withers). Nevertheless, the primary appeal of the film surely lay in the strength of its narrative and its extremely strong cast, which included (in addition to the two actresses already mentioned) Eric Portman, Bernard Miles, Peter Ustinov and Robert Helpmann.

Two further films released that year served further to reinforce notions of a People's War, albeit in narratives that were primarily intended to serve quite different purposes. Thus Thorold Dickinson's brutally effective *The*

Next of Kin was designed first and foremost to warn against the dangers of 'Careless Talk', in a gripping narrative which showed how a network of German spies and fifth columnists collected vital information about a British commando raid on the French coast. As a result, the Germans were better prepared for the raid than they would otherwise have been and resulting British casualties were very high – 'the next of kin have been informed'. In its exposé both of those servicemen who unthinkingly divulge information and of the German spies who so convincingly conceal their identity, the film carefully draws its characters from across the class spectrum, insisting that in even this least desirable aspect of the war, all the people are involved. Moreover, the German spies and fifth columnists are of course civilians, and the film's equally clear message is that if vital information is not to be divulged to the enemy, civilians quite as much as service personnel must be constantly on their guard.

In all this there is a strong element of exhortation, warning the audience against the dangers of 'Careless Talk'. Cavalcanti's *Went the Day Well?* explores some of the same ground, but reverts to the usual, celebratory style. It retells the story of German paratroopers (disguised as British soldiers) who, with the help of an already resident fifth columnist, occupy the fictional village of Bramley End over the 1942 Whitsun weekend. Once the villagers understand what has happened, they demonstrate remarkable courage and resourcefulness in defeating the brutal occupying force. As we have seen, its original purpose was not especially relevant when it finally reached the cinemas in November 1942, but it did play its part in strengthening notions of wartime cross-class unity. Thus, it stresses the selfless way in which all the villagers, from the postmistress to the lady of the manor, play their part in defeating the enemy, several, indeed, dying in the cause. The nation, as represented in *Went the Day Well?* was wholly united in its determination to defeat Nazism. It was also singularly resolute, more than willing to repay the brutality of the invaders in kind, and one of the most remarkable aspects of the film is the way in which that violence is represented. For while, within the conventions of the day, it is remarkably explicit, in stark contrast to late-twentieth-century film representations of violence, the film never dwells on these acts, and it is the very pace with which the narrative moves on after each of the killings that makes them so powerful. The image of a forgetful and rather bumbling middle-aged postmistress killing a German soldier with an axe struck a real chord with audiences that had learnt, so recently, of the British army's ability to strike back successfully at the enemy at El Alamein.

If all these films had gone some way towards translating the ideology of the People's War into the form of the feature film, it was a film released right at the end of the year that gave it its most complete and most popular realization. Noel Coward's *In Which We Serve* had originated over a year earlier at a dinner party at which Coward had heard Lord Louis Mountbatten describe the sinking of *HMS Kelly*, the destroyer that he had commanded during the Battle of Crete.[168] Yet, Coward's film went to considerable lengths to shift the emphasis away from Mountbatten – indeed, partly at Mountbatten's insistence, the character of Captain Kinross in the film is an ordinary, upper-middle-class Captain, not a fabulously rich member of the royal family. More important, the film has three central characters: Kinross himself, played by Noel Coward; the lower-middle-class Chief Petty Officer Hardy, played by Bernard Miles; and the working-class Ordinary Seaman Blake, played by John Mills. By structuring the narrative in this way, it is abundantly clear that the ship (renamed *HMS Torrin* in the film) is a surrogate for the nation.

Much of the narrative takes the form of flashbacks after the ship has been sunk. The men await rescue in a liferaft, and their reflections provide the opportunity to explore the history of the ship up to the Battle of Crete, which (with some manipulation of the truth) gave Coward an opportunity to recapitulate the history of the war.[169] But important as these public events are, the film concentrates even more on the family lives of the three central characters. It is full of careful observation of their different worlds, making no attempt to gloss over the differences that separate the classes, nor indeed to claim that those differences are forgotten in wartime. Rather, it suggests that the existence of class, so often a source of division in the past, serves in wartime powerfully to strengthen and invigorate the now united nation. Not least because all understand and accept the position of their own class, they can work co-operatively and collaboratively together, all equally important members of a national family, wholly united in the common task of winning the war.

In almost every conceivable way *In Which We Serve* breaks free from the conventions of the traditional British war film, so clearly exemplified in earlier wartime films like *Convoy* and *Ships with Wings*. Coward[170] wholeheartedly adopted the new realism so favoured by the Films Division: documentary footage is seamlessly integrated into the film, and location shooting is paralleled by studio work in which considerable attention is paid to details of furniture, décor and design. There is even some limited attempt to capture the realities of ordinary speech, with the occasional use of words like 'bloody' and 'bastard', a practice wholly outlawed by the pre-war censor and thus embarrassingly unfamiliar to the contemporary audience.[171] Far from celebrating a glorious victory, the *raison d'être* of the narrative is the sinking of the ship, itself part of the wider defeat inflicted in the Battle of Crete, and this had prompted some initial MoI reservations about the project. Even more interesting is the role of women in the film. At first glance they play conventional, minor, supporting roles, and they are certainly on screen much less than the men. But in each and every case, the wives of the three leading male characters (played by Celia Johnson, Joyce Carey and Kay Walsh) are properly developed, convincing characters, and Coward is careful to emphasize the particular burdens which war imposes on them. Significantly, the only major character in the film who is killed is Hardy's wife (in an air raid on Portsmouth) and, in a further interesting reversal of gender stereotypes, Coward focuses considerable attention on Hardy's pain in learning of her death in a letter which he receives when the ship docks in Scotland.

In Which We Serve was hugely popular, by far the most popular British film of 1943 and, in all probability, the most popular propaganda film of the war as a whole. It won almost unanimous critical praise and, while it failed to win the 1943 Oscar for Best Picture (for which it was nominated), Coward himself was presented with a special Oscar for his 'outstanding production achievement in the film'. The Russian director Pudovkin described it as 'profoundly national ... The Picture is English through and through. You can see the real face of England in it,'[172] and it is clear from the comments collected by Mass-Observation at the end of the year that this is just how the audience saw it too. Again and again they make reference to the film's realism, to its truthfulness: a 38-year-old welfare officer praised it for being 'truly British, I could visualise it happening to me, or any of my friends ...', while a 23-year-old RAF accounts clerk described it as 'a film of things as they are, and not just a string of hashed up ideas from the back-room boys of the film world with false heroics and sentiment'.[173] The Films Division may have initially had some doubts about the film, but in fact it would be difficult to find a more convincing endorsement of their particular approach to People's War propaganda.

While the women in *In Which We Serve* may have been more important than they appeared at first sight, their role was still fundamentally subsidiary to that of the men. All that changed with two films released in 1943: *The Gentle Sex*, which explored the work of the ATS, and *Millions Like Us* which looked at the conscription of women into the munitions industry. By definition, both films served the needs of People's War ideology, their emphasis on the novel and important wartime roles of women an unmistakable sign of the way in which war demanded commitment and sacrifice from every part of society. Both films also draw attention to the way in which women, divided by pre-war divisions, eventually found a new camaraderie and unity in the common cause of their new war work. Of the two, it is *Millions Like Us* which makes the more determined attempt to engage with the issues of class that had been so central to *In Which We Serve* while, in contrast, Leslie Howard in *The Gentle Sex* puts rather greater emphasis on confronting traditional male views of women. This is achieved both within the narrative as the characters encounter the prejudices of male soldiers, and also by the novel and not wholly successful device of putting himself into the start and finish of the film in the character of an anonymous middle-class male observer. The device is designed to confront the deeply prejudiced view of 'the gentle sex' at the outset with the varied and demanding experiences which the women undergo during the film, but given that in the end Howard praises the women as 'strange, wonderful, incalculable creatures', it is far from clear that the lessons of the film have in fact been learnt!

Millions Like Us had its service equivalent in *The Way Ahead* (1944), with Carol Reed's film exploring the way in which a group of disparate and discontented conscripted men are welded into an effective platoon, under the intelligent and subtle leadership of their officer (David Niven) and sergeant (William Hartnell). The different backgrounds, attitudes and personalities of the seven recruits are clearly established in a film that presents an honest view, not just of the rigours of military training, but of the boredom and waiting which invariably follow it. Indeed, front-line action is conspicuous by its absence, concentrated entirely in the closing sequences of the film. This honest, adult approach to the subject matter is exemplified by the very last sequence in the film, for while we watch the men march steadily towards the enemy, bayonets fixed, disciplined and determined, it is far from clear whether their counter-attack will succeed; the two words 'The Beginning' bring the film to a close. Too long in production to fulfil its original objectives, *The Way Ahead* was nevertheless well-received by audiences who, in the aftermath of the D-Day landings, were only too happy to accept its tribute to the citizens' army.[174]

Wartime ideology was most obviously constructed in war films, but the narrative of one of the most popular films, David Lean's *This Happy Breed* (scripted once again by Noel Coward), ended just as the war began, reconstructing the history of inter-war Britain through the experience of one lower-middle-class family. By putting the Gibbons family right at the centre of a narrative which included some of the important public events of the period (the British Empire Exhibition, the General Strike, the Abdication, Munich), the film made it abundantly clear that it was precisely families such as these that were at the core of that 'happy breed' that was the nation. It was their values, their moderate, centrist politics, their commitment to evolution rather than revolution, that were central to British culture, the source of everything that made Britain great. Not that this was an anodyne, romantic view of lower-middle-class England. Frank and Ethel Gibbons (played by Robert Newton and Celia Johnson) have much to endure, including the presence of Ethel's irritable mother and her neurotic sister-in-law Sylvia, their son's flirtation with radical politics at the time of the General Strike, their elder daughter leaving home to live with a married man and the death of their son Reg and his wife in a car crash. And yet they survive all these challenges, and while it would be wrong to suggest that the film ends on a triumphant or smug note, it nevertheless represents a most eloquent tribute to middle England. And middle England loved it. The *Observer's* film critic reported that the film had prompted more letters of appreciation than any other wartime film – 'the film about the suburbs has gone out into the suburbs and the suburbs have take it to their hearts'.[175]

Thus in these (and other) films, ideas that were at the heart of the ideology of the People's War were forcefully and clearly communicated to British cinema audiences and, what evidence there is suggests that they were both understood and accepted. Indeed, given the close coincidence between the ideology of these films and the ideology of many of those in the target audience, it would have been not a little curious had this not been the case. And yet not all the most popular propaganda films shared the populist ideology of the feature films discussed so far. Nothing could have been further removed from the People's War films than Ealing's 1942 film, *Ships with Wings* but, as Jeffrey Richards has shown, it was a huge success with just that same mass audience.[176] Stylistically, its use of crude models and painted backdrops could not have been further removed from the new realism so favoured by the Films Division; ideologically, its almost exclusive preoccupation with gallant officers confronting comic-book German and Italian enemies, was almost the antithesis of representations of the war which were at pains to stress the all-important contribution made by the other ranks.

Incomparably more subtle, yet equally firmly rooted in a more traditional ideology, were Leslie Howard's hugely popular constructions of the quintessentially English gentleman-hero. Howard's role in British wartime propaganda was unique, not only in its range (his radio broadcasts were arguably as important as his films), but also in the fact that he brought to his wartime roles an already established star *persona* that was ideally suited to constructing a particular form of Englishness. This 'thinking man as hero'[177] had been developed in a series of roles in the 1930s, most importantly in *Pygmalion* in 1938, although in the first of the two wartime propaganda films which he directed – *Pimpernel Smith* released in the summer of 1941 – he drew even more directly on his 1935 film *The Scarlet Pimpernel*, based on Baroness Orczy's novels about an English gentleman who rescues French aristocrats from the Terror in revolutionary France. In the 1941 film, Howard is an English university professor in pre-war Germany helping refugees escape Nazi tyranny, and the film provided an ideal means by which to demonstrate that precisely those qualities so often seen as signs of weakness (the highly educated, cultured voice; the donnish, absent-minded demeanour; the powerful awareness of and interest in spiritual matters), could in fact co-exist with a passionate commitment to ideals of justice and freedom, in the defence of which the individual would reveal remarkable resources of audacity and courage. Indeed, in some especially English way, the two sets of characteristics were seen to be inextricably linked together. Described like that it all appears hugely improbable: in Howard's inimitable style, it achieved a remarkable credibility. Thus his Professor Horatio Smith, the quintessential 'absent-minded professor', stands in total opposition to the boorish, uncivilized, humourless Nazis, whom he is of course able to outwit at every turn. Certainly audiences responded enthusiastically to what *The Times* perceptively called Howard's remarkable ability to 'flick sentiment and feeling away from him at the same time as he is cunningly arranging them in his buttonhole',[178] and even though the *Monthly Film Bulletin* thought that 'the propaganda is laid on with a somewhat heavy hand',[179] the film proved to be one of the two most popular British films of the year.

Howard followed this a year later with *The First of the Few*, the most popular British film of 1942, and here the contrast with the People's War films is even more clear. The film tells the story of R.J. Mitchell, the designer of the Spitfire fighter plane, who learns on a trip to Germany of the progress being made in designing a new German fighter plane, and determines that he must design an even better fighter for Britain. Fulfilling that ambition is not just a matter of solving the design problems, but quite as much one of overcoming commercial indifference, political hostility (in a climate dominated by appeasement), and the cancer which finally kills him in 1937 at the age of 42. The real Mitchell had been apprenticed as an engineer at 17, but in *The First of the Few*, the character is constructed entirely within the terms of Howard's screen *persona* – middle-class, diffident, absent-minded, a visionary inventor with a formidable (though rarely articulated) sense of patriotic duty. In the hands of a less skilful actor, all this could have easily descended into caricature but, once again, Howard brings subtlety and warmth to a performance which carries real conviction. Time and again Mass-Observation respondents commented explicitly on the quality of Howard's performance, one suggesting that what made the film so special was because it showed 'without heroics ... how men can be truly great without bullying others just seeing their duty and doing it in spite of every obstacle'.[180]

Thus a Films Division that was committed to the ideology of the People's War was equally happy to see the production of films which all but ignored the role of the people, concentrating on the extraordinary achievements of one or a small number of (invariably middle- or upper-class) heroic individuals. Occasionally, as in *The Young Mr Pitt* (1942), some attempt would be made to put a People's War gloss on the all-important role of an individual (emphasizing the extent to which Pitt's interests coincided with those of the people as a whole), but more often than not these films simply tapped into a quite different, more traditional form of English patriotism, which found expression in the heroic achievements of the extraordinary individual. Thus at the end of 1944 came *Henry V*, Laurence Olivier's lavishly funded and richly opulent celebration of the warrior king, and the last war film of the war, *The Way to the Stars*, concentrated almost exclusively on the lives of its middle-class officers. In that respect it was a direct successor to such traditional films as *Convoy* or *Ships with Wings*, although in every other way (the quality of the writing, the acting, the *mise-en-scène*, the cinematography, above all else the mature and adult narrative) it could not have been more different. Yet the measure of continuity with the earlier films does illustrate the ideological variety of the Films Division's propaganda; powerful as the new wartime populism was, the MoI understood that very many still subscribed to a more conventional patriotism and it was important to reinforce their commitment to the war as well.

There is therefore no direct parallel between the ascendancy which People's War ideology gained in the documentary films and the more varied ideology which can be found in the most popular propaganda feature films. In part this may have been a product of the different relationship between the Films Division and the commercial film studios, where there was never the opportunity to exercise that kind of direct control over production that was commonplace with documentary films. But it may also have a good deal to do with the film-makers themselves, for whereas many documentary film-makers were left-wing, very few feature film-makers were. To be fair, the war did create opportunities for that small minority. John Baxter was able to make *Love on the Dole* (1941), a powerful exploration of social and economic deprivation in pre-war Britain, which ended with the promise that a new and better Britain must be constructed after the war was over. That expectation was then reinforced in a handful of other films, including *Let the People Sing* (1942), *The Shipbuilders* (1943) and *They Came to a City* (1944). Yet, just like the small number of overtly left-wing documentary films, the left-wing ideology of these films was moderate and consensual, and even the most popular enjoyed only modest box-office success.

Thus, once again, the claim that the Films Division secretly orchestrated a campaign of radical left-wing film propaganda in the feature films which it supported and encouraged is clearly misplaced. Taken together, the most popular wartime feature films did not follow a single, MoI-defined line, but rather reflected back to their mass audience its own ideological diversity. Indeed, some of the most successful films themselves adopted a complex, even ambiguous position, leaving audiences free to construct their own ideological meanings in the film. Nowhere is this more clear than in Noel Coward's two hugely popular wartime films, where initial appearances are surely deceptive. *In Which We Serve* appears to be the more conservative film, presenting a traditional England, irrevocably divided into classes, each of which understands and accepts the rights and responsibilities of its particular situation. All the classes play their part, but no one can fail to recognize the central, decisive part played by the ruling class, personified in the film by Coward himself. *This Happy Breed*, on the other hand, abandons such a conventional view. The ruling class, even the upper-middle class, is conspicuous by its absence: in its place, Coward and Lean construct a film in praise of lower-middle class Britain, celebrating its values, its achievements, with barely a reference to those who governed them. Closer examination, however, reveals that both films are rather more complex than these readings might suggest.

In Which We Serve featured prominently in the responses elicited by Mass-Observation in its request for comment on the respondents' six favourite films of 1943 and, amongst the fulsome praise, there are recurring criticisms of Coward's own performance as Captain Kinross. These range from arguing that 'Noel Coward was a little too much to the fore', to 'Noel Coward spoiled it. I never once was able to forget that I was watching Noel Coward, an actor, and not a naval officer'; others pointedly praised the way in which the film represented 'lower-class service and artisan parts' without making any reference to Coward.[181] This irritation at Coward/Kinross inevitably affected the way in which the audience constructed meaning in the film, at the very least raising doubts about the character of the ruling class he so unmistakably personifies. Those doubts are then enormously reinforced by the way in which the other classes are represented, not simply because the performances of both Bernard Miles (as Chef Petty Officer Hardy) and John Mills (as Ordinary Seaman Blake) are incomparably more persuasive, but because there is a warmth and affection about the film's attitude to these two characters (strikingly absent in its attitude towards Kinross), with which the audience inevitably identifies. Thus, while the film does on occasion poke gentle fun at Hardy's pomposity, or his idiosyncratic use of language, such comment falls far short of mockery, and the fact that it is his wife who is killed serves powerfully to reawaken our affection for him. Blake, in contrast to both his superiors, is presented in wholly sympathetic terms and, alone amongst all the major characters, he performs the one unmistakably heroic act in the film: he continues to man his gun after suffering concussion, earning Kinross' approbation 'You did damn well. I'm very proud of you.' Throughout the film, he demonstrates a directness and openness which is not simply a product of his youth, but is entirely consistent with the culture of the family to which he belongs, most obviously represented by his mother (Kathleen Harrison), whose uninhibited joy at her son's unexpected return home on leave, or at the telegram bringing news of his survival at the end of the film, remains one of the enduring images of the film.

On the other hand, Coward's somewhat strained characterization of upper-middle-class England, is powerfully mitigated by Celia Johnson's extraordinary performance as the Captain's wife. One of the key moments in the film contrasts the very different Christmas Day celebrations of the families of the three central characters and, while the Blake and Hardy households are, if anything, dominated by the men, the Kinrosses' lunch (on board the ship) is entirely dominated by Alix Kinross, forced reluctantly to make a speech at the end of the meal. What follows is perhaps the most startling sequence in the film, for the essence of her speech is that she and all other naval officers' wives must live with the fact that her husband's ship constitutes an unavoidable rival for his affections; it is, in effect, 'her implacable enemy'. The sentiments are far from novel, yet the manner of delivery is simply electrifying for, concealed beneath her impeccable intonation, is an almost overwhelming sense of the frustration and the pain of her situation; her final 'God bless this ship and all who sail in her', redolent of the complex mixture of emotions which she feels towards the ship (the nation) that her husband serves. The complexity of that moment is, in fact, representative of the complexity of the film as a whole which, while it celebrates the traditional class system, suggests both that this places enormous, almost intolerable, burdens on individuals and that traditional notions of the relative value of the different classes are misplaced.

Celia Johnson is even more important to *This Happy Breed*. As the lower-middle-class Ethel Gibbons, her performance is central to the film in precisely the same way that, as wife and mother, she is central to the life of the family. Frank Gibbons may speak the words which make explicit the film's political ideology, but it is Ethel Gibbons who is at the film's emotional heart. And this is crucial, for it is in her changing role and in the film's changing attitude towards her that its real complexities are to be found. For much of the first half of the film, she is presented in entirely positive terms, her apparently limitless energy and boundless good humour warmly endorsed by the celebratory approach of the film. But all that changes when her elder daughter Queenie (played by Kay Walsh), increasingly at odds with what she sees as the dull, narrow-minded life of middle England, leaves home in the middle of the night to live with a married man. Ethel's response is bitter and angry – 'I don't want her back. She's no child of mine. I never want to see her again as long as I live' – and our shock at her response is immediately put into words for us by her husband Frank: 'I've never seen you like this before. Hard as nails you are.'

Very soon thereafter Frank and Ethel learn that their son Reg and his wife Phyllis have been killed in a car crash, and it soon becomes clear that these two events have scarred Ethel deeply. Not that there is any dramatic or sudden transformation: she continues to play her role at the heart of the family, life goes on apparently much as before. But we nevertheless begin to recognize changes. The once ebullient and energetic Ethel now seems tired, even, at times, dispirited; everyday chores take more of a physical toll; her face is now invariably dominated by a slight but unmistakable frown. It is this very different woman who then experiences something of a renewal in the closing part of the film: Queenie returns, married at last to the boy next door, and Ethel quickly settles into her new role as grandmother. But even here Lean emphasizes the way in which the new baby simply adds to Ethel's burden (a kitchen strewn with drying nappies), and the closing sequences of the film emphasize the limits of that renewal even more clearly. Throughout the film, Frank's passion for cultivating his small suburban garden has provided opportunities to explore gardening metaphors for the nation and the circumstances in which it would flourish. Now Ethel and Frank are moving on: they are leaving their house and garden for a flat, and Ethel attempts to console Frank, partly by reminding him that it was his decision to move, partly by pointing out that there will at least be a balcony which he can fill with window-boxes. They leave the now empty house, claiming that they are both 'glad to be out of it' and, with all that has happened to them, the sentiment carries some force. But their unspoken regrets are quite as eloquent, and it is with this deep ambivalence that the film leaves us. Ethel buttons up her coat, and leaves the house, apparently ready and willing to face the next challenge that life will present to her. Yet this is such a different Ethel from the woman who had so triumphantly led the family into the house at the start of the film; far from broken, she is nevertheless an incomparably less happy, more damaged woman than she had been those 20 years before. Of course, she believes that her next challenge is to start a new life in a flat, while we (the audience) know that it is in fact six long years of war. Once again, the film's celebration of lower-middle-class England is modulated by its honest recognition of the burdens which that class imposes on those who serve its values so faithfully.

The complexities and ambiguities of both the Coward/Lean wartime films demonstrate once again the difficulties of attaching neat and tidy party political labels to the politics of such films. Of course they are imbued with a deep love of country, a powerful sense of what Englishness is and where it has come from, but their formidable emphasis on the pain and suffering of the human condition, in peace quite as much as war, protects them entirely from any romantic nationalism, any self-satisfied jingoism. For the generation who first watched these films, they constructed a remarkably truthful representation of the world in which they lived, a truthfulness so far removed from the dominant conventions of pre-war British cinema that one, slightly bemused, 15-year-old schoolgirl commented that *This Happy Breed* 'was so ordinary and so natural that it seemed a little odd'.[182] But it was in that very ordinariness that the film's great strength lay, presenting the nation with a mirror in which to look at itself, not entirely unlike the very different mirror that McAllister and Jennings were able to construct in their documentary films. Just like the documentary films, the openness of meaning which was at the heart of such ordinary, everyday narratives, provided further proof that the MoI's confidence in the people was such that it was willing to allow its target audience to draw its own conclusions from films such as these. And it was for that reason, as much as any other, that that audience took these films to their heart.

There is, however, one final aspect of the history of wartime British cinema that deserves attention. For while MoI-inspired films played no part in the most difficult period of the war, the same cannot be said for the cinema itself. Right through the Blitz, cinemas in London and other bombed cities remained open, and it is abundantly clear that in these most desperate circumstances, they fulfilled a real and important social need. Guy Morgan's history of London's Granada cinemas during the war provides a striking account of cinemas staying open all night, offering their patrons not just a re-run of the main programme, but also stand-by features, recitals on the cinema organ, and even impromptu variety shows in which staff and patrons together improvised instant entertainment until, at four or five in the morning, everyone finally fell asleep.[183] Of course there was a limit to which even Granada staff could sustain this kind of response, and eventually the cinema managers had to close at the usual time and advise their patrons to move to the local air raid shelter. But exceptional as these experiences were, they demonstrate only too graphically cinema's extraordinary wartime appeal. Even in the most dangerous times, audiences remained remarkably loyal. In Morgan's words:

They queued patiently in the dark when aircraft were droning overhead; they sat through films while the building was rocked by near misses, and glass and plaster showered into the auditorium, while the film jumped on the screen or the spotlight bounced from the stage to the ceiling; they put out incendiaries in the stalls and went on with the show; they came with rugs and hot-water bottles when the heating failed, and when part of the roof was blown off and the rain came in, they moved into a part of the theatre where it was dry; when their homes were hit, they came back the next morning with the bomb-dust still in their hair, and when the cinema was hit they climbed over the rubble in the street to ask when it would re-open ... So far from subscribing to the pre-war official view of a cinema as a potential death trap, patrons came to regard it as a refuge, a strength and an escape.[184]

Morgan was writing about the exceptional circumstances of the Blitz, and yet throughout the four long remaining years of the war, cinema continued to act as 'a refuge, a strength and an escape'. In a society turned literally upside down by war, in which a combination of bombing, evacuation and conscription totally transformed the lives of tens of millions of people, the familiarity of the experience of going to the cinema provided an all-too-rare reminder of the everyday realities of pre-war life. Moreover those few short hours in the cinema offered a brief but important respite from the hard work, the anxieties, the boredom, the terror and the shortages that made up the everyday experience of war. What is perhaps most remarkable of all, however, is that British films proved able to fulfil this need, even when they did not turn their back on the world outside, demonstrating once and for all that films do not need to be escapist for the act of going to the cinema to fulfil that need to escape which is such a vital part of the medium's appeal to the mass audience. To that extent, Dilys Powell's claim that the war years witnessed a certain 'sharpening of public taste' was not entirely misplaced, as audiences came to discover that the pleasures and satisfactions of going to the cinema could be experienced with The First of the Few or This Happy Breed just as well as Let George Do It or Bambi. The anonymous filmgoer whose 'War Diary' provides such a rich additional element of Morgan's study of wartime cinema,[185] had it exactly right in claiming that: 'They love to be honestly entertained by films that are glamorous, romantic, truthful, adventurous, preposterous, and clearly removed from any semblance of everyday life.'[186] The war years had shown that truthful films could indeed play their part alongside glamorous, adventurous and preposterous films.

That same anonymous filmgoer, however, provided the most eloquent and accurate summation of the role which 'the pictures' had played in wartime Britain:

They have kept our spirits up. They have taken the worst strains off mind and body. No other form of relaxation has been quite so successful in helping people to bear the burdens they had – burdens of fear and loneliness, discomfort and overexhaustion; anxiety for husbands and sweethearts, and sons and little children. Consciously or sub-consciously, it was the firm determination of the people to keep on top, not to let themselves get depressed, so that they could stand the bombs and bad news when they came. So they went to the pictures and enjoyed the pictures and were all the better for the pictures.[187]

This was indeed the role which the cinema had played in wartime Britain and, perhaps most extraordinary of all, propaganda films (for which the MoI Films Division could take some real credit) had played their part in fulfilling that role. It was, by any standards, a formidable achievement.

CONCLUSION

Thus, there can be little doubt that, in contrast to all the other examples of film propaganda that we have discussed, films produced in Britain during the Second World War did achieve much success. Newsreels represent the one important exception and, in so far as the MoI always considered newsreels to be a critically important weapon in its film propaganda armoury, their inability to sustain their pre-war popularity must be seen as an important failure. With both documentary and feature films, however, the Films Division did ensure that films that served the needs of its propaganda objectives were made; many of those films did reach their target audiences and, to an incomparably greater extent than in any of the other examples discussed in this book, those audiences took from the films the messages that the propagandists had set out to communicate.

On the other hand, it took some time before the propaganda strategy agreed in outline even before the war began was properly implemented, and that delay was critical in two very important ways. First, it meant that the people worked their way through the most difficult period of the war without the support of appropriate propaganda, and secondly, and in no small part in direct consequence, appropriate film propaganda (when it was finally produced) was designed to reinforce and strengthen ideas and attitudes that were already well-established. In that way, the task that faced People's War propaganda was incomparably easier than that which had confronted Bolshevik or Nazi propaganda, and that represents an important qualification to its undoubted success. Moreover, as we have seen, the MoI never made the mistake of flooding the cinemas with propaganda films, and even those films that most closely served its propaganda objectives did not remorselessly push a 'party line', but presented different constructions of nationalism and the nation, directly mirroring the pluralism of the audience. If Huxley had been right that successful propaganda 'canalises an already existing stream', then British film propaganda during the Second World War is the clearest possible example of just such propaganda in practice.

NOTES

1. The 1928 reforms created a total electorate in 1929 of 28.9 million, in stark contrast to the mere 7.9 million enfranchised in 1911.

2. By 1939, 69 per cent of the population over 16 years of age read a daily newspaper, while 82 per cent read a Sunday paper – see John Stevenson, *British Society 1914–45*, Harmondsworth, 1984, pp. 402–3.

3. The absence of precise data before 1934 makes the issue of the size of cinema audiences before that time problematic. An inventive attempt to estimate the size of the audience suggests that admissions may have been as large as 20 million in 1916, before a sharp rise in the level of Entertainment Tax effected a dramatic reduction (Nicholas Hiley, 'The British cinema auditorium', in Karel Dibbets and Bert Hogenkamp, *Film and the First World War*, Amsterdam, 1995, pp. 160–70).

4. Margaret Dickinson and Sarah Street, *Cinema and State: The Film Industry and the British Government 1927–84*, London, 1985, p. 36.

5. The Company became a public corporation in 1927, answerable to a Board of Governors appointed by the government.

6. Reith quoted by Stevenson, *op. cit.*, p. 410.

7. For a brief introduction to these issues of political bias, see Andrew Davies, 'Cinema and broadcasting', in Paul Johnson (ed.), *Twentieth Century Britain: Economic, Social and Cultural Change*, London, 1994, pp. 265–9.

8. In fact, civilian deaths for the whole war totalled just 60,000.

9. Ian McLaine, *Ministry of Morale: Home Front Morale and the Ministry of Information in World War II*, London, 1979, p. 26.

10. In the end the Home Secretary, Sir Samuel Hoare, had it 'thrust upon him' – Hoare's own words in his memoirs, quoted in McLaine, *op. cit.*, p. 17.

11. To be fair to the government, the job had been offered to Sir John Reith, who had left the BBC the previous year, but he had turned it down.

12. McLaine, *op. cit.*, p. 12.

13. Pronay has developed this argument several times – see, for example, 'The news media at war', in Nicholas Pronay and D.W. Spring (eds), *Propaganda, Politics and Film 1918–1945*, London, 1982, pp. 173–208: hereafter Pronay, 'News' (1982). Much of this discussion of the pre-planning of news and censorship is based on Pronay's analysis.

14. Up until the Munich crisis this was precisely what was intended for the BBC, although in the light of those events, the policy was substantially modified – see Siân Nicholas, *The Echo of War: Home Front Propaganda and the Wartime BBC, 1939–45*, Manchester, 1996, pp. 18–22.

15. The words are taken from an agreement between the MoI and the service ministries in March 1940, but they accurately summarize the pre-war approach (McLaine, *op. cit.*, p. 26).

16. The phrase was Reith's, coined when he briefly served as Minister of Information in 1940 – quoted in Pronay, 'News' (1982), p. 174.

17. McLaine, *op. cit.*, p. 38.

18. He confessed in the House of Lords on 26 September 1939 that 'he had considerable difficulty in ascertaining what were its functions'; quoted in McLaine, *op. cit.*, p. 40.

19. In addition to using the Ministry's own Regional Information Offices, and organizations like BBC Listener Research, Mass-Observation and the Wartime Social Survey, Adams enlisted the help of branch managers of W.H. Smith (the bookseller) and the cinema chains, officials of the London Passenger Transport Board, officials of political parties and voluntary agencies, as well as the secret sources of police duty reports and the postal censors.

20. A former First Lord of the Admiralty who had resigned over the Munich agreement.

21. Probably for that reason he too was assailed mercilessly in the press, with an especially vicious attack using the phrase 'Cooper's Snoopers' to conjure up images of an overweening and intrusive bureaucracy prying into the private lives of its citizens – in reality, less than one-half of one per cent of those asked by the Wartime Social Survey to give interviews refused.

22. An MP, publisher and long-standing and close personal friend of Churchill, who served as his Parliamentary Private Secretary from 1939–41.

23. Home Publicity Division Paper, September 1939, quoted in McLaine, *op. cit.*, p. 34.

24. The poster is reproduced in McLaine, *op. cit.*, facing p. 86.

25. *Ibid.*, p. 31.

26. The phrase 'phoney war' was a later, American, expression; see Angus Calder, *The People's War: Britain 1939–1945*, London, 1969, p. 57 (hereafter Calder, 1969).

27. In fact, subsequent investigation by BBC Listener Research revealed that the audience proved remarkably resistant to Haw-Haw's propaganda – a mere 17 per cent of those who listened to his broadcasts believed that they contained even a grain of truth (Nicholas, *op. cit.*, p. 61).

28. Peter Clarke, *Hope and Glory: Britain 1900–1990*, London, 1996, p. 197.

29. In the title of a popular book published anonymously by three left-wing journalists in the summer of 1940: 'Cato' (Michael Foot, Peter Howard and Frank Owen), *Guilty Men*, London, 1940; republished by Penguin Books, 1998.

30. The phrases come from a broadcast on 21 July 1940, quoted in Vincent Brome, *J.B. Priestley*, London, 1988, p. 251.

31. Nicholas, *op. cit.*, p. 60.

32. Priestley's first *Postscript*, broadcast on 5 June 1940, quoted in Angus Calder, *The Myth of the Blitz*, London, 1991, p. 199 (hereafter Calder, 1991).

33. Quoted in Calder (1991), p. 123.

34. Report for 6 September 1940, quoted in Calder (1991), p. 126.

35. Report for 8 October 1940 (*ibid.*, p. 127).

36. Calder (1969), p. 223.

37. McLaine, *op. cit.*, pp. 93–107.

38. McLaine includes a photograph of tube shelterers on Aldwych station underneath just that poster, and it is not difficult to imagine the comments they would have made about it (McLaine, *ibid.*, illustration 7, between pp. 86 and 87).

39. *Ibid.*, pp. 174–6.

40. *Ibid.*, pp. 176–83.

41. According to a British Institute of Public Opinion Poll in 1943, quoted in Paul Addison, *The Road to 1945: British Politics and the Second World War*, London, 1977, p. 217 (hereafter Addison, 1977).

42. The extent to which it was the war that created this consensus has been the subject of intense historical debate. For a concise introduction to that debate see Harold L. Smith (ed.), *War and Social Change: British Society in the Second World War*, Manchester, 1986.

43. Addison (1977), p. 162.

44. Quoted in Nicholas, *op. cit.*, p. 52.

45. In playing this all-important role, the BBFC would be strengthened by the presence of officials from the MoI Censorship Division (James Chapman, *The British at War: Cinema, State and Propaganda 1939–1945*, London, 1998, p. 17).

46. Nicholas Pronay and Jeremy Croft, 'British film censorship and propaganda policy during the Second World War', in James Curran and Vincent Porter (eds), *British Cinema History*, London, 1983, pp. 146–7. Hereafter Pronay, 'British film censorship' (1983).

47. Outside urban areas, cinemas reopened as early as 11 September; down-town cinemas (outside London) reopened four days later; some West End London cinemas opened on 4 October, with full reopening a month later (Anthony Aldgate and Jeffrey Richards, *Britain Can Take It: The British Cinema in the Second World War*, Oxford, 1986, p. 1).

48. Dickinson and Street, *op. cit.*, pp. 13, 65.

49. John Sedgwick, 'The market for feature films in Britain, 1934: a viable national cinema', *Historical Journal of Film, Radio and Television*, Vol. 14, No. 1, 1994, pp. 15–36.

50. Jeffrey Richards, *The Age of the Dream Palace: Cinema and Society in Britain 1930–1939*, London, 1984 – especially pp. 245–56.

51. Both Fields and Formby had established their audiences in the first place in the music halls.

52. Thus as early as 1917 it had established a set of 43 rules, identifying both those topics which could not be discussed at all, as well as setting out the limits within which acceptable topics could be discussed; by 1930, the 43 rules had become 90. This discussion of the political censorship of films in the period derives largely from Pronay, 'The political censorship of films in Britain between the wars', in Nicholas Pronay and D.W. Spring (eds), *Propaganda, Politics and Film 1918–1945*, London, 1982, pp. 98–125. Hereafter referred to as Pronay, 'Political censorship' (1982).

53. Lord Tyrrell, speaking to the Cinema Exhibitors' Association in 1937 (*ibid.*, p. 122).

54. A slightly more flexible approach was followed in drama with the inclusion of some working-class voices.

55. The quality of sound reproduction was such as to put a very great premium on clarity of enunciation.

56. John Ellis, 'Victory of the voice', *Screen*, Vol. 22, No. 2, 1981, p. 71.

57. That paper was the *Daily Express*; Pronay, 'News' (1982), p. 176.

58. Grierson had used the term 'documentary film' for the first time in 1926 in a review of *Moana*, Flaherty's factual film about the South Sea Islands. For an introduction to Grierson's work, see Ian Aitken, *Film and Reform: John Grierson and the Documentary Film Movement*, London, 1990.

59. Lippmann was an American political commentator who served as chief editorial writer on the *New York World* from 1921 onwards.

60. Grierson himself left for Canada in 1938, where he established the National Film Board of Canada the following year.

61. Ball was especially close to Chamberlain, having worked with him at both the Treasury and Downing Street – he had even used his earlier experience in MI5 to place agents within Labour Party Headquarters, although whether this was known to the Labour Party at the time is unclear.

62. Quoted in F. Thorpe and N. Pronay, *British Official Films in the Second World War*, Oxford, 1980, p. 24.

63. In an account of the film given by the documentary film-maker, Harry Watt, in Elizabeth Sussex, *The Rise and Fall of the British Documentary: The Story of the Film Movement Founded by John Grierson*, London, 1975, p. 117.

64. On the other hand, Rotha footnoted this claim with a reference to MoI files (Paul Rotha, *Documentary Diary*, New York, 1973, p. 233).

65. Toby Haggith, 'Post-war reconstruction as depicted in official British films of the Second World War', *Imperial War Museum Review*, No. 7, p. 37; Charles Barr, 'War record', *Sight and Sound*, Vol. 58, No. 4, Autumn 1989, p. 265; Chapman, *op. cit.,* pp. 117–19.

66. Greene writing in the *Spectator* on 29 September 1939, quoted in Thorpe and Pronay, *op. cit.*, p. 34.

67. Pronay, 'News' (1982), p. 183.

68. For a detailed discussion of the origins and production circumstances of the film, see Chapman, *op. cit.*, pp. 59–65.

69. Sir Edward Villiers writing on 19 January 1940 – quoted in Pronay, 'News' (1982), p. 186.

70. Chapman, *op. cit.*, p. 53. It is reproduced as an Appendix to Ian Christie (ed.), *Powell, Pressburger and Others*, London, 1978, pp. 121–4.

71. Christie, *op. cit.*, p. 123.

72. The circumstances of production of *49th Parallel* are discussed in Chapman, *op. cit.*, pp. 70–4; the position of the GPO Film Unit in *ibid.*, p.120.

73. Clark became Controller of Home Publicity *(ibid.*, pp. 28–9).

74. For a more detailed discussion see Helen Forman, 'The non-theatrical distribution of films by the Ministry of Information', in Nicholas Pronay and D.W. Spring (eds), *Propaganda, Politics and Film 1918–1945*, London, 1982, pp. 221–33.

75. For example, Thomas Baird (who had pioneered non-theatrical exhibition at the GPO) was recruited to supervise MoI non-theatrical distribution (Chapman, *op. cit.*, p. 33).

76. Quoted in Dickinson and Street, *op. cit.*, p. 115.

77. Quoted in Aldgate and Richards, *op. cit.*, p. 31.

78. Chapman, *op. cit.*, pp. 125–6.

79. Dalrymple had worked before the war as a screenwriter in the commercial film industry.

80. Cavalcanti was a Brazilian film-maker who had led the Unit ever since Grierson left for Canada; he left to join Ealing Studios in August 1940. For speculation as to why, see Barr, *op. cit.*, p. 265.

81. The Arts Enquiry, *The Factual Film. A Survey Sponsored by the Dartington Hall Trustees*, Political and Economic Planning, London, 1947, p. 73.

82. Chapman, *op. cit.*, pp. 135–6.

83. Jeffrey Richards and Dorothy Sheridan (eds), *Mass-Observation at the Movies*, London, 1987, p. 424.

84. Forman, *op. cit.*, p. 224.

85. Thus, William Farr (the head of the Central Library) estimated that in 1943–44 there were four million regular viewers (i.e. people who saw MoI films at least three times a year), while the post-war report, *The Factual Film*, claimed that the annual audience was over 18 million (Paul Swann, *The British Documentary Film Movement*, Cambridge, 1984, p. 169).

86. These ranged from the location of evacuated children, to the IRA, to references to King Farouk's visit to the western desert – in all, some 38 topics were 'stopped' (Pronay, 'News' (1982), p. 192). The remainder of this discussion of the newsreels derives from the same source, pp. 192–208.

87. Pronay draws attention to a particular occasion in June 1941 when the company concerned inadvisably printed 131 copies of a particular newsreel *before* this final screening – the MoI then insisted on a further cut of 43 feet and all 131 prints had to be recut!

88. The surviving Paramount records reveal that almost 90 per cent of original footage proved acceptable to the censors, demonstrating just how effectively the companies came to understand what was required of them.

89. Chief projectionists were exempted from the age of 18, while senior production technicians were only exempted from the age of 30; actors and some junior grades of technicians were not exempted at all.

90. Dickinson and Street, *op. cit.*, pp. 106–7.

91. Although precisely what form that nucleus should take remained a matter of contention for some considerable time – see Margaret Dickinson, 'The state and the consolidation of monopoly', in James Curran and Vincent Porter (eds), *British Cinema History*, London, 1983, pp. 74–82.

92. Pronay, 'British film censorship' (1983), pp. 152–3.

93. As late as June 1940 it was considering compelling cinema owners to show short MoI films although, in the end, good sense prevailed and it sought (and obtained) their voluntary agreement instead (Aldgate and Richards, *op. cit.*, p. 7).

94. In the words of Paul Rotha – quoted in Aldgate and Richards, *op. cit.*, p. 10; see also *ibid.*, p. 297, n. 13.

95. Vincent Porter and Chaim Litowski, 'The way ahead. Case history of a propaganda film', *Sight and Sound*, Vol. 50, No. 2, Spring 1981, p. 110.

96. See the Programme for Film Propaganda discussed above, pp. 152–5.

97. The film and, more particularly, the circumstances of its production have recently been the subject of a rigorous and perceptive re-examination (James Chapman, 'The Life and Death of Colonel Blimp (1943) reconsidered', *Historical Journal of Film, Radio and Television*, Vol. 15, No. 1, March 1995, pp. 19–54).

98. Minutes of the Policy Committee for July 1940, quoted in Aldgate and Richards, *op. cit.*, p. 11.

99. C.M. Woolf, President of the British Film Producers Association, quoted in Aldgate and Richards, *op. cit.*, p. 11.

100. As reported by *Kinematograph Weekly* on 30 July 1942, quoted in Aldgate and Richards, *op. cit.*, p. 12.

101. Paul Rotha claims that it was the screening of his *Night Shift* (a documentary film about women working in a factory in South Wales) to Launder and Gilliat, that led to their developing the script for *Millions Like Us*; Sussex, *op. cit.*, pp. 140–1.

102. Richards, *op. cit.*, pp. 119–20.

103. Balcon's hostility to the MoI may have originated from the fact that in the summer of 1940 he made an unsuccessful attempt to bring the GPO Film Unit under the control of his (Ealing) studio – see Chapman, *op. cit.* (1998), pp. 121-4.

104. Charles Barr, 'Projecting Britain and the British character': Ealing Studios, Part I, *Screen*, Vol. 15, No. 1, Spring 1974, p. 99.

105. Nicholas Pronay, "The Land of Promise": the projection of peace aims in Britain', in K.R.M. Short (ed.), *Film and Radio Propaganda in World War II*, London, 1983, pp. 52–72. Hereafter, Pronay, 'Land of Promise', (1983).

106. Of those questioned, 61.5 per cent 'liked' the newsreels, 19 per cent were 'doubtful', 15 per cent 'disliked' them and 4.5 per cent 'don't know': *Newsreel Content (29 January 1940)*, reproduced in Richards and Sheridan, *op. cit.*, pp. 381–94.

107. *Newsreel Report 3 (6 October 1940)*, reproduced in Richards and Sheridan, *op. cit.*, p. 418.

108. *Ibid.*, p. 417.

109. *Interview with Kenneth Gordon*, reproduced in Richards and Sheridan, *op. cit.*, pp. 422–3. Gordon was a trade union activist and part of his objections to the ideology of the newsreels can be explained in those terms.

110. Tom Harrison, 'Films and Home Front – the evaluation of their effectiveness by "Mass-Observation" ', in Nicholas Pronay and D.W. Spring, *Propaganda, Politics and Film 1918-1945*, London, 1982, pp. 238–9.

111. Pronay, 'News' (1982), p. 203.

112. *Pathé Gazette*, July 1939, reproduced in the Parkfield *Pathé* collection *A Year to Remember 1939*.

113. *Pathé Gazette*, April 1941, reproduced in the Parkfield *Pathé* collection *A Year to Remember 1941*.

114. *Pathé Gazette*, July 1942, reproduced in the Parkfield *Pathé* collection *A Year to Remember 1942*.

115. *Pathé Gazette*, October 1942, reproduced in the Parkfield *Pathé* collection *A Year to Remember 1942*.

116. *Pathé Gazette*, November 1942, reproduced in the Parkfield *Pathé* collection *A Year to Remember 1942*.

117. Guy Morgan, *Red Roses Every Night. An Account of London Cinemas under Fire*, London, 1948, pp. 26, 71.

118. *The Cinema in the First Three Months of War*, reproduced in Richards and Sheridan, *op. cit.*, p. 167.

119. The Local Defence Volunteers were renamed the Home Guard in July 1940.

120. *Fifteen Ministry of Information Shorts*, Mass-Observation Report prepared by Len England, 16 October 1940, reproduced in Richards and Sheridan, *op. cit.*, p. 425.

121. Commissioned for exhibition in America, where it did extraordinary business, being exhibited in some 12,000 cinemas; a slightly shorter version was distributed at home with a tactful change of title to *Britain Can Take It*.

122. Nicholas John Cull, *Selling War: The British Propaganda Campaign Against American Neutrality in World War II*, Oxford, 1995, p. 99.

123. Mass-Observation, *Preliminary Report on Opinion about Ministry of Information Shorts*, 24 July 1941, reproduced in Richards and Sheridan, *op. cit.*, pp. 442–3.

124. Report in *Documentary News Letter*, July 1941, quoted in Dai Vaughan, *Portrait of an Invisible Man: The Working Life of Stewart McAllister, Film Editor*, London, 1983, p. 69.

125. His study was published in 1983 (Dai Vaughan, *op. cit.*).

126. The film is in fact preceded by a curious and rather pompous introduction by Leonard Brockington which serves above all else to demonstrate just how redundant it is to the audience's understanding of the film.

127. The phrase is Jim Hillier's, in a short essay on Jennings in Alan Lovell and Jim Hillier, *Studies in Documentary*, London, 1972, p. 87.

128. The comment was made by Helen Forman who, as Helen de Mouilpied, had been deputy head of the MoI's non-theatrical distribution (Helen Forman, *op. cit.*, p. 230).

129. This discussion of the circumstances of the film's production derives from Aldgate and Richards, *op. cit.*, pp. 230–40.

130. The film originally ran 75 minutes and was titled *I Was a Fireman* – pressure from the distributor resulted in the cutting of 10 minutes and the change of title to *Fires Were Started*.

131. William Sanson writing many years later – quoted in Aldgate and Richards, *op. cit.*, p. 237.

132. A response to the directive Mass-Observation issued to its respondents in November 1943, asking them to list their six favourite films of the year, together with their 'reasons for liking them'; hereafter referred to as Mass-Observation 1943 Directive. Quoted in Richards and Sheridan, *op. cit.*, p. 225.

133. *Documentary News Letter 4*, 1943, quoted in Aldgate and Richards, *op. cit.*, p. 242.

134. Arthur Jarratt, quoted in Aldgate and Richards, *op. cit.*, pp. 242, 239.

135. Pronay, 'Land of Promise' (1983), pp. 52–72.

136. Haggith, *op. cit.*, pp. 34–45.

137. The claim is made in Dilys Powell, *Films since 1939*, London, 1947, p. 39. An example of the disparaging way in which historians use this claim is provided by Peter Stead, *Film and the Working-class: The Feature Film in British and American Society*, London, 1989, p. 123. That said, the most recent study argues that the short documentary films 'had an important role to play' and that 'in their way [they] were no less important than commercial feature films; they just served a different purpose' (Chapman, *op. cit.* (1998), p. 113).

138. Powell, *op. cit.*, p. 39.

139. Clive Coultass, *Images for Battle: British Film and the Second World War 1939–1945*, Cranbury NJ, 1989, pp. 29–30.

140. Harry Watt, *Don't Look at the Camera*, London, 1974, p. 152.

141. Morgan, *op. cit.*, p. 70.

142. Leonard England, the author of many of Mass-Observation's reports on wartime

cinema, was stationed at an army ordnance camp in Wellington and he suggested that the vast majority of them were disappointed in the film, not least because much of the film was 'thought to look unreal' (quoted in Coultass, *op. cit.*, p. 59).

143. Chapman, *op. cit.* (1998), p. 131.

144. For a detailed discussion of the circumstances of the film's production see Aldgate and Richards, *op. cit.*, pp. 246–76.

145. Reviewing the film on 10 December 1944, quoted in Aldgate and Richards, *op. cit.*, p. 272.

146. In the print released in America a title was inserted claiming that four cameramen had been killed, seven wounded and six captured by the enemy. In fact this claim was a little misleading, for these figures related to total AFPU casualties in action, and not just in the filming of *Desert Victory* (Anthony Aldgate, 'Creative tensions: *Desert Victory*, the Army Film Unit and Anglo-American rivalry, 1943–5', in Philip M. Taylor (ed.), *Britain and the Cinema in the Second World War*, London, 1988, p. 150).

147. Notably the night-time infantry advance on the opening evening of the battle (see Coultass, *op. cit.*, p. 110).

148. These issues are explored in two articles: Annette Kuhn, '*Desert Victory* and the People's War', and John Ellis, 'Victory of the voice', *Screen*, Vol. 22, No. 2, 1981, pp. 45–68 and pp. 69–72 respectively.

149. No national box-office wartime records survive, but in the one cinema for which records do survive *Desert Victory* secured 75 per cent of the audience for the most popular film of the year, the Frank Randle slapstick film *Somewhere on Leave*; its audience was exactly the same size as that for Arthur Askey's *King Arthur Was a Gentleman*. See Julian Poole, 'British cinema attendance in wartime: audience preference at the Majestic, Macclesfield, 1939–1946', *Historical Journal of Film, Radio and Television*, Vol. 7, No. 1, 1987, pp. 23–4.

150. In reality, the Americans had refused to allow the British film-makers access to appropriate American footage (Aldgate, 'Creative tensions', *op. cit.*, pp. 155–8).

151. In fact, many of these service personnel were actors in real life and their comments were carefully scripted, albeit by men who were also serving in their respective armies at the time (Coultass, *op. cit.*, p.183).

152. Powell, *op. cit.*, 1947, pp. 39–40. A very similar analysis of wartime changes in British film can be found in Roger Manvell, *Twenty-five Years of British Film 1925–1945*, London, 1947.

153. It is often argued that *Love on the Dole* was a box-office disaster, yet the one cinema for which we have detailed records reveals that it achieved a respectable enough audience of 7,734, compared to 8,847 for *Pimpernel Smith*, *Kine Weekly*'s British Runner Up for the year (Poole, *op. cit.*, p. 21).

154. Richards and Sheridan, *op. cit.*, pp. 14–15.

155. For a detailed discussion of the film and its reception see Jeffrey Richards, 'Wartime British cinema audiences and the class system: the case of '*Ships with Wings* (1941)', *Historical Journal of Film Radio and Television*, Vol. 7, No. 2, 1987, pp. 129–41.

156. A Programme for Film Propaganda – see note 70 above.

157. The Majestic was one of six cinemas in Macclesfield, charging the highest seat prices in the town; it mainly showed first-run features. The data deriving from these records are carefully analysed in Poole, *op. cit.*

158. That said, the most popular British film of 1940 was *Convoy*, a naval film constructed firmly within the traditions of pre-war British heroic drama, a clear example of the way in which British studios quickly attempted to tap into the newly patriotic mood of wartime Britain.

159. Taken here to be indicated by achieving 60 per cent or more of the audience for the most popular British film of the year.

160. See, for example, Jeffrey Richards' analysis of the films in Aldgate and Richards, *op. cit.*, pp. 158–65.

161. Programme for Film Propaganda, see note 70 above.

162. Further discussion of the problems of the film's timing can be found in Aldgate and Richards, *op. cit.*, pp. 114–37.

163. Response to Mass-Observation 1943 Directive, quoted in Richards and Sheridan, *op. cit.*, p. 267.

164. *Ibid.*, p. 261.

165. Vincent Porter and Chaim Litewski, 'The Way Ahead. Case history of a propaganda film', *Sight and Sound*, Vol. 50, No. 2, Spring 1981, pp. 110–16.

166. For detailed discussion of the circumstances of its production, see Aldgate and Richards, *op. cit.*, pp. 280–2.

167. Thirty-year-old male tax inspector, Mass-Observation 1943 Directive (Richards and Sheridan, *op. cit.*, p. 240).

168. The circumstances of the film's production are discussed in detail in Aldgate and Richards, *op. cit.*, pp. 193–9.

169. *HMS Kelly* had not in fact taken part in rescuing troops from Dunkirk although, in the film, *HMS Torrin* does.

170. While Coward produced, scripted, starred in and wrote the music for the film, his credit as director is somewhat misleading. David Lean (who also edited the film) increasingly took over that role as the production developed, although given Coward's role in initiating the film and the multiplicity of other roles which he did play, the film remained very much his.

171. Roger Manvell reported that audiences laughed in embarrassment at their inclusion (Coultass, *op. cit.*, p. 103).

172. Writing in the *Documentary News Letter* in 1944: quoted in Aldgate and Richards, *op. cit.*, p. 210.

173. Mass-Observation 1943 Directive (Richards and Sheridan, *op. cit.*, pp. 223, 264).

174. There is some discussion of the film's reception in Porter and Litowski, *op. cit.*, p. 116.

175. C.A. Lejeune writing in 1947 and quoted in Aldgate and Richards, *op. cit.*, p. 213.

176. Jeffrey Richards, 'Wartime British cinema audiences', *op. cit.*

177. The phrase is Jeffrey Richards' (Aldgate and Richards, *op. cit.*, p. 53). The essay in which it is used, 'The Englishman's Englishman. *Pimpernel Smith*', offers a thoughtful exploration of Howard's wartime role (*ibid.*, pp. 44–75).

178. *The Times*, 2 July 1941 – quoted in Aldgate and Richards, *op. cit.*, p. 64.

179. *Monthly Film Bulletin*, 8, 1941, quoted in Aldgate and Richards, *op. cit.*, p. 63.

180. Unidentified 57-year-old respondent, Mass-Observation 1943 Directive (Richards and Sheridan, *op. cit.*, p. 248).

181. A 26-year-old estate agent, a 42-year-old chemist and a 55-year-old university lecturer respectively. Mass Observation 1943 Directive, reproduced in Richards and Sheridan, *op. cit.*, pp. 228, 233, 246.

182. Quoted in Aldgate and Richards, *op. cit.*, p. 213.

183. Morgan, *op. cit.*, p. 31.

184. *Ibid.*, p. 11.

185. Probably C.A. Lejeune, the *Observer* film critic.

186. Morgan, *op. cit.*, p. 73.

187. *Ibid.*, p. 67.

CHAPTER 5

Italian Neorealist Films

So we're in rags? Then let us show our rags to the world. So we're defeated? Then let us contemplate our disasters. So we owe them to the Mafia? To hypocrisy? To conformism? To irresponsibility? To faulty education? Then let us pay all our debts with a fierce love of honesty, and the world will be moved to participate in this great combat with truth. This confession will throw light on our hidden virtues, our faith in life, our immense Christian brotherhood. We will meet at last with comprehension and esteem. The cinema is unequalled for revealing all the basic truths about a nation.[1]

In those remarkable words, written in June 1945, the Italian film director Alberto Lattuada encapsulated the huge ambitions which animated a small group of Italian film-makers at the end of the Second World War. Just like those many governments before them that had put such faith in the cinema as a means of propaganda and persuasion, these film-makers were convinced that cinema was uniquely placed to effect that transformation in the hearts and minds of the Italian people that, in their judgement, was a precondition for its successful post-war recovery. For Italy was not just a country that had suffered ignominious military defeat, it had experienced that defeat after over 20 years of extravagant propaganda that had claimed that Fascist Italy was a formidable world power, more than able to hold its own in military conflict with other powers. While many Italians remained sceptical about the excesses of Fascist rhetoric, their unwillingness to oppose Mussolini (at least until the gulf between reality and rhetoric was finally exposed in a series of military defeats), constituted a tacit support for the regime, a manifestation of the 'hypocrisy' and 'conformism' to which Lattuada refers. Faced with such a legacy of rhetoric and self-delusion, these film-makers were convinced that there was only one way forward: the nation must confront the truth about itself, and it was the cinema that was uniquely equipped to reveal that truth. Moreover, such a mission would be greeted with 'comprehension and esteem': cinema would reveal the truth and, not only would the people understand that truth when they saw it, they would value and appreciate the film-makers who revealed it to them.

Aspirations like these mirrored the high expectations that had animated Bolshevik film-makers over 20 years earlier, and that measure of continuity is important because, in almost every other regard, this final case study is very different from the four that have preceded it. For the Italian neorealist films are not the work of a party, still less of a government; they are not even the product of a group of film-makers who had a precisely defined aesthetic and ideological position that would strictly define the parameters within which their films would be made. Rather, they are the work of film-makers who had shared a common film culture in Fascist Italy, who had shared the same devastating experience of war, invasion, resistance and liberation and who, in the confusion and disorganization of Italy immediately after the war, set out to make films that would meet the needs of this society at this very special moment in its history. Thus, at least to begin with, their films were shown with no labels attached to them; they laboured under none of the disadvantages that so often bedevil propaganda – no associations with a political party or a government. To that extent, they represented an especially important test of the power of the medium of film for effective propaganda for, whatever else they may have disagreed about, these film-makers all shared Lattuada's conviction that cinema could play a crucial role in this critical moment of Italian rebirth and renewal. And while that conviction was in part the product of the role which cinema played in Fascist Italy, it was also a product of the wider Italian experience of the inter-war years.

FASCISM, WAR AND LIBERATION

At the very heart of Italian fascism was a disjunction between appearance and reality. In spite of the grandiloquence of its propaganda slogans, notably the claim 'Everything within the State, Nothing outside the State, Nothing against the State', Mussolini's transformation of Italian society fell far short of that achieved by other authoritarian regimes. There were of course important changes. Italy's democratic constitution was set aside: political parties and trade unions were dissolved and their leaders sent into exile; locally elected mayors and councils were replaced by appointed officials; freedom of speech, of association and of the press was abandoned; a special Tribunal for the Defence of the State was established, with extensive powers to punish anyone who challenged the regime. And yet, much of traditional Italian political culture remained unchanged. With the exception of the purging of Freemasons, the bureaucracy (which flourished under the new regime) was still controlled by career civil servants. The appointed officials who now controlled local government were recruited almost entirely from the old ruling class. Most striking of all, the new regime made no attempt to challenge the power of either the monarchy or the Catholic Church, both of which institutions saw in fascism a powerful defence against revolution and modernization. Indeed, in the case of the Church, its new relationship with the state was codified in the Lateran Treaty of February 1929 and, while this represented a considerable propaganda coup for the regime, the regime's recognition of the continuing role of the Church in Italian society provided clear evidence of the extent to which the Party's revolutionary ambitions had been abandoned.

In fact, the character of the Fascist Party changed out of all recognition once Mussolini took power. Many of its original (ideologically committed) members were purged; hundreds of thousands of new members were recruited, the vast majority of whom were clearly motivated by personal ambition rather than any clear commitment to fascism. Indeed, by the end of the 1920s, many parodied the initials of the party (PNF) as *per necessità famigliari*, for family reasons.[2] Moreover, in marked contrast to other authoritarian regimes, Fascist Italy made very little use of state terror – the Special Tribunals administered just 31 death sentences, invariably preferring to send political opponents into exile. They imposed fewer than 4000 sentences altogether in the years up to 1939 and, as the Tribunals also tried members of the Mafia, homosexuals and others, the extent of political persecution was clearly limited.[3] In sum, while the regime may have claimed that it represented a twentieth-century Roman Empire, inspired by the vigorous, militaristic values of classical Rome, in reality it governed not by force but by consent and, at least until Italy's entry into the war in 1940, it was able to secure the support of most of the people.

If the character of Fascist rule was one important source of that support, it was reinforced by aspects of both foreign and domestic policy. Within two years of taking power, Mussolini had resolved the vexed problem of Fiume, persuading the Yugoslavian government finally to recognize that it was a part of Italy, and an increasing emphasis on colonial policy began to lend some substance to the nationalist rhetoric of the regime. Mussolini's ambitions centred on North Africa and, having consolidated and strengthened his position in Libya, Italian forces invaded Ethiopia in October 1935, defeating this last independent African state the following May. The Italian victory precipitated almost universal international disapproval, but that found its mirror image in huge levels of domestic approval, marking the high point of the regime's popularity. In domestic policy, Mussolini benefited from the economic recovery that was already beginning to take place when he took power in 1922. As elsewhere, the Depression at the end of the decade provoked a sharp rise in unemployment and a fall in standards of living, but this did not result in any significant increase in opposition to the regime. State intervention in the economy, especially in the form of grandiose public works schemes, provided visible evidence of the government's attempts to counter the impact of the Depression and this, coupled with some improvement in welfare benefits, may have been the reason. Moreover, in the later 1930s the economy recovered, and by 1938 industrial production had recovered to its 1929 level.

Propaganda clearly played its part in securing support for the regime and, throughout the Fascist period, the press was always subject to the strictest censorship, ensuring not simply that it was full of the good news of the 'achievements' of the new order, but also that any hint of bad news (crime, suicides, even traffic accidents) was never reported. Yet propaganda was never as important in Fascist Italy as it was in the Soviet Union or Nazi Germany, and it was not until 1937 that a full department of state (the Ministry of Popular Culture) was set up to oversee work in this area. Even then, while the regime did take advantage of the propaganda opportunities presented by the one million radio sets in use by 1938, it did not make extensive use of film (other than the newsreel) for explicit propaganda. By and large it was content (as we will see below) to allow the commercial cinema, dominated until 1938 by Hollywood imports, to meet the needs of its growing audience much as it had always done.

Indeed, that emphasis on providing entertainment for the masses can be found even more clearly in the regime's enthusiastic support for competitive sports: motor racing, skiing, cycling, boxing and, above all, football, came to occupy a central role in popular culture – Italy staged and won the World Cup in 1934, winning it again in 1938. That emphasis on competitive sport was also a feature of another Fascist innovation, namely the *dopolavoro* (literally 'after work'), or social clubs for ordinary working people. Membership grew from just 280,000 in 1926 to some 4 million in 1939 and, in addition to sports facilities, the clubs provided bars, billiard halls and libraries; they organized concerts and plays, charabanc trips, ballroom dancing and days at the seaside; they even provided summer holidays for children. Given that such opportunities for mass leisure had never existed in Italy before, it was hardly surprising they were hugely popular for, as Martin Clark accurately observes, this was 'fun not propaganda: it was recreation, not self-improvement'.[4]

Thus, the popularity of the regime cannot be explained in terms of its ideology, still less in its ability to effect a radical transformation in the character of Italian society. Rather, the radical veneer of the propaganda concealed a regime that had secured support by appeasing the old ruling class, entertaining the masses and pandering to the nationalist aspirations of all Italians. For so long as this was all that it did, it was secure but, in the later 1930s, not least because of the diplomatic isolation which followed the invasion of Ethiopia, Mussolini moved closer and closer to Germany. Thus, the 1936 Rome–Berlin axis, which may have been intended to frighten the French and the British into making concessions to Italy, served only to antagonize the Western powers still further. Intervention in the Spanish Civil War led only to the defeat of Italian troops, and Hitler's annexation of Austria in 1938 demonstrated just how little influence Mussolini had gained from his new relationship with Berlin. Mussolini, however, continued to strengthen his ties with Nazi Germany: in 1938, he introduced anti-Semitic laws for the first time, and in May 1939 entered a formal military alliance with Hitler. Yet, in spite of all this, when Hitler invaded Poland in September, Mussolini held back, recognizing that Italy was in no position to go to war; against all the odds, he remained neutral.

In the event, however, it was only a short-lived respite. The following June, with France nearly defeated, Mussolini judged that it was finally safe to join the war on Germany's side. The Italian war began in earnest with the invasion of Greece in October 1940, but it proved to be the first of a series of disastrous military campaigns, culminating in the surrender of all Italy's North African forces in May 1943. Woefully under-trained and ill-equipped, the appalling defeats suffered by Italian troops in North Africa, Russia and ultimately the Italian peninsula itself, exposed once and for all just how empty Fascist military rhetoric had been. Even before this happened, however, opposition to the regime had begun to grow. Mussolini's new, close relationship with Nazi Germany was unpopular from the start, not least because it was assumed that it would inevitably draw Italy into war. The anti-Semitic laws provoked some opposition from the Church and, while the extent of Italian hostility to racism has been over-emphasized in the past, the legislation did serve further to undermine the consensus on which the regime was based.[5]

With the onset of war, the situation quickly worsened. Within days police informers in Milan were reporting that there were already major problems with morale – support for the regime declined steadily with the news of each new military defeat. The crisis came to a head when the Allies embarked on the widespread bombing of the northern cities at the end of 1942. By the following spring, industrial production was down to two-thirds of its 1938 level, standards of living were seriously undermined by inflation and rationing and, with food shortages intensifying, hundreds of thousands of people fled to the countryside. In March 1943, Fiat workers in Turin went on strike and the strikes quickly spread to Milan and other major northern cities. Over the same period, a number of anti-Fascist movements began to gain ground: the Communist Party (which had maintained a small underground presence throughout the Fascist years) helped organize the strikes; leading Roman Catholics formed a Christian Democratic Party; a new Party of Action was formed by republicans and radical liberals. By April 1943, these very disparate parties had agreed to work together to overthrow fascism.

Three months later, in July 1943, the Allies landed in Sicily and that was the signal for the old ruling class to take action. Within days, the king had dismissed Mussolini and installed Marshal Badoglio as Prime Minister in his place; Mussolini was arrested, Fascist institutions were dissolved and the army took over Rome. While Badoglio assured the Germans that Italy would continue to fight, it was obvious to all that the position was hopeless, and by September an armistice had been agreed with the Allies. The king and his government fled to Brindisi, the army disintegrated and the Germans took control of Rome and most of northern Italy, rescuing Mussolini and installing him in Salò on Lake Garda as leader of the Italian Social Republic. In fact, both the king and Badoglio in the south, and Mussolini in the north watched almost as spectators as the real battles in a long and bloody war were fought by the Allied and German forces. Rome was not liberated until June 1944 and it was almost a further year before Allied forces reached the northern cities, in April 1945. At the end of that month, Mussolini fled towards Switzerland, but he was captured and shot by Communist partisans.

While the brunt of the fighting was borne by Allied and German troops, this final period of the war made a formidable impact on Italian society, not simply because these battles were all fought on Italian soil, but also because tens of thousands of Italians intervened directly in the struggle – 40,000 partisans and 10,000 civilians were killed in the last 19 months of the war. The first partisan groups had formed in central and northern Italy in the autumn of 1943, and by the following summer some 80,000 Italians were under arms. The anti-Fascist parties immediately recognized the huge political potential of this situation and worked hard to forge links with the partisans. Most successful were the Communists, who won the support of about 60 per cent of the partisans; the Party of Action accounted for a further 25 per cent, with Christian Democrats, Socialists and Liberals accounting for the remainder.[6] Nevertheless, in spite of such clear party political differences, the various partisan groups normally co-operated in local Committees of National Liberation (CLN) and, as they made progress, it was these Committees which took over administration in liberated areas.

With the war finally at an end, it was the parties most closely associated with the partisans that formed the first post-war government, led by the Resistance hero and leader of the Party of Action, Ferruccio Parri. The situation that confronted his government was desperate indeed: prices were 24 times their 1938 level; over three million houses and much of the transport infrastructure had been destroyed or seriously damaged; industrial production stood at just 25 per cent of what it had been in 1941; average income per head was lower than it had been in 1861.[7] Economic and social dislocation on this scale could not be resolved overnight, but an impatient population soon began to blame the government for the lack of progress. Moreover, Parri's tough determination to purge everyone who had collaborated with the Fascist regime quickly provoked a bitter backlash – the terms of the purge were such that anyone who had not actually been a partisan could be convicted of collaboration. The courts increasingly refused to convict, the Liberals withdrew their support from the government and, in November, Parri was forced to resign. The new government, led by the Christian Democrat leader Alcide De Gasperi, abandoned the purge altogether and, more importantly, replaced CLN-appointed officials in the north. By January 1946 state power was back in the hands of career civil servants.

Nevertheless, 1946 saw important constitutional developments that appeared to confirm the ending of the old order. In a referendum, the Italian people dispensed with the monarchy, and a Constituent Assembly was elected by universal suffrage (enfranchising women for the first time), with constitutional guarantees for civil and political rights. At first the wartime coalition was sustained, but in the context of a rapidly intensifying Cold War, relations between the Christian Democrats and the Communists became increasingly difficult to maintain. Both the Church and the United States made their opposition to the Communists more and more clear and this, coupled with De Gasperi's recognition of the deeply conservative character of the southern electorate, persuaded him to exclude both the Communists and the Socialists from the coalition in May 1947. In the months that followed, the United States and the Vatican joined ever more enthusiastically in the campaign to defeat communism, and the parliamentary election in April 1948 was held in an atmosphere of hysterical claims and counter-claims. In the event, the Christian Democrats won nearly 49 per cent of the vote, while the Popular Front of Communists and Socialists secured just over 35 per cent. In January 1949, Italy applied for admission to NATO and, in the following July, the Vatican excommunicated Communist voters. Just two years after they had defeated fascism and established their new Italian Republic, the left-wing parties of the North had been defeated: the Christian Democrats, with support from the smaller pro-western parties, would govern Italy for the next 40 years.

FASCIST CINEMA AND THE ORIGINS OF NEOREALISM

In the culture of the Resistance that dominated Italy at the end of the war, the neorealist film-makers set out to distance themselves completely from fascism: their cinema, they asserted, was brand new, born out of a total rejection of the practices and traditions of Fascist film culture; their films, the very antithesis of the lavish escapism and mendacious propaganda that characterized the Fascist film. The reality was rather more complex than this, with the roots of neorealism firmly based within the practices and institutions of Fascist film culture. This does not mean that neorealism was not new, but it does mean that any attempt to make sense of what it was that neorealist film-makers were trying to do, must take account of this longer historical context.

Before the First World War, not least because of its success in pioneering the historical epic with films like *Quo Vadis?* (1912), Italian cinema briefly occupied a powerful international position – indeed by 1914, it was the third largest exporter in the world.[8] That pre-eminence, however, proved short-lived. Even before the war, protectionist measures had sharply reduced Italian film exports to the USA[9] and, during the war, many other markets were lost, with Hollywood exploiting this situation to its own advantage. After the war, many Italian producers resumed the costly productions that had been so successful before the war, but the market had changed. American films now represented much more serious competition, and Italian films found it increasingly difficult to compete, even in their domestic market. Thus, while nearly 371 features were produced in 1920, three years later this had dropped to 114; by 1930, production had almost ceased altogether, with just eight films completed.[10] Thereafter, production recovered slowly, reaching 30 films in 1935 and 67 in 1938;[11] after 1938 it grew more quickly, with 87 in 1940 and a peak of 120 in 1942.[12]

Through the whole of this period, however, audiences grew. Gross box office receipts doubled between 1924 and 1927, by which time cinema accounted for more than half of the takings of all forms of commercial entertainment (including sport); by 1941 this proportion had reached 83 per cent.[13] By 1936 the annual audience stood at 260 million – by 1942, it had nearly doubled to 470 million.[14] With low levels of Italian production for most of this period, such growth was only achieved by a comparable growth in imports and thus, for the majority of the Fascist years, the films that Italian audiences saw were predominantly foreign (American and, to a much smaller extent, German) – as late as 1938, foreign films accounted for no less than 87 per cent of the market.[15] While that in itself provides a vivid indication of the limits of Fascist hegemony, what is more extraordinary is that, for many years, the regime was quite unconcerned about this situation. Indeed, its only important intervention in the 1920s came in 1926, when it nationalized the Light Institute, a firm that specialized in the production of educational films. Under state control, the Institute was given the additional responsibility of producing newsreels which all cinemas were required to screen. But, beyond that, the regime was content to allow the cinemas to continue to show the (largely foreign) films that were so popular with their audiences. As Giuseppe Bottai, the Minister of Corporations, explained in 1930: 'the public is invariably bored when the cinema seeks to educate them. The public wants to be amused ...'[16] The newsreel was a useful vehicle for Fascist propaganda, but cinema's primary purpose was to entertain and, consistent with fascism's wider emphasis on entertaining the masses, the regime was content to allow it to do just that.

As the Depression began to intensify, however, it become clear that, without state aid, the cinema might not be able to continue to fulfil this function; for the first time, companies engaged in distribution and exhibition began to fail. The regime's first response came in 1931: 10 per cent of all box-office takings would be allocated to those 'with a proven ability to cater for the tastes of the public';[17] limited protection was also introduced, with the requirement that one in ten films shown in Italian cinemas must be Italian. That proportion was raised to one in four in 1933, and in the same year it became illegal to show any foreign language film that had not been dubbed into Italian – a tax levied on the dubbing of foreign films provided additional revenues for the industry. In spite of all these measures, however, Italy's largest film studio, Cines, went bankrupt in 1933 and, while it was saved by an injection of state capital, that rescue was itself part of a major reorganization of the film industry in 1934 which gave the state a much larger role. A General Directorate for Cinematography was created, with Luigi Freddi at its head and, while this did represent a dramatic increase in state intervention, it did not amount to the wholesale nationalization of film production – some 60 or so small producers continued to work, albeit invariably with state subsidy.[18] At the same time, responsibility for film censorship was moved to the Ministry of Press and Propaganda,[19] and in 1935, the National Agency for the Film Industry (ENIC) was established, giving the state a powerful new role in film exhibition.[20]

Two further initiatives finalized the state's new relationship with the film industry. In 1935, a new film school, the Experimental Centre of Cinema, was created and, following a fire at the Cines studio in 1935, Freddi agreed with the owner of the studio, Carlo Roncoroni, to build a vast new production facility on the outskirts of Rome. Cinecittà was inaugurated by Mussolini on 28 April 1937. It was owned and operated by Roncoroni until, on his death in September 1938, it was taken over by the state. As the best equipped production facility in Europe, Cinecittà quickly dominated Italian film production – between 1937 and 1939 two-thirds of all Italian films were made on its 10 sound-stages.[21] All these initiatives certainly achieved their economic objectives and, as we have already seen, production recovered, aided in no small part by the decision in 1938 to give ENIC monopoly rights over the distribution of foreign films. The four Hollywood majors immediately withdrew from Italy, and this dramatic reduction in the number of American imports prompted a huge increase in demand for Italian films.[22] In all of this, however, the original emphasis on cinema as entertainment was sustained. Freddi's programme of modernization and renewal was directed not towards the production of film propaganda, but rather towards enabling Italian studios to produce films that were capable of competing on equal terms with Hollywood product. Indeed, after a visit to Berlin in 1936, Freddi wrote a report that was highly critical of Nazi policy towards the film industry;[23] far from sending Italian film-makers to Germany, Freddi encouraged them to visit France and Hollywood.

Nevertheless, some propaganda feature films were made. In the years after 1930, four films focused on the Fascist revolution itself,[24] while 30 others were dominated by patriotic or military values (expressed in both historical and contemporary narratives). The ideology of these films was certainly compatible with Fascism, but whether they can all be accurately categorized as Fascist propaganda is at least open to question.[25] But even if they are seen in this way, 34 films represents less than 5 per cent of the total number of Italian films produced in the years 1930–1943; the vast majority of films conformed much more closely to the Hollywood model which Freddi strove so assiduously to follow. Film-makers worked within clearly defined genre categories, of which comedy was far and away the most popular, followed by melodrama and costume/historical dramas. The more rigorous scrutiny to which the surviving films have been subjected in recent years reveals that it is too crude to categorize them as simply 'escapist', for they did explore what Marcia Landy calls 'central aspects of everyday reality – the nature of sexual roles, the family, work, the physical environment, the conflict between rural and urban values'.[26] Yet it is nevertheless clear that, like the Hollywood films on which they were modelled, these films did serve to promote conformity and quiescence rather than criticism and dissent. As Landy herself emphasizes, time and again the films sought to 'reconcile class and sexual differences, to reaffirm the importance of family, and to exalt a sense of national identity couched in a progressive rhetoric'.[27] The films may not have constructed an explicitly Fascist ideology, but they did nothing to challenge the values on which that ideology was based.

Such then was the essentially conservative character of the Italian film industry at the end of the 1930s and yet, within precisely the same institutions, a set of ideas and practices was developed that would challenge that conservatism head on. At the heart of much of this was the new film school and two new film journals, *Cinema* (founded in July 1936) and *Bianco e Nero* (*Black and White*) established in 1937. Between them, they created the culture within which a rigorous and remarkably wide-ranging discussion about the nature and role of cinema could take place. The film school was run by the film-maker Luigi Chiarini and, while he was broadly supportive of the regime, he developed a curriculum that went far beyond the boundaries of Fascist orthodoxy, introducing students not just to the earlier achievements of Italian cinema, but to Soviet, French and American cinema as well. Indeed, Chiarini's most important colleague was the Marxist theoretician Umberto Barbaro and, not least because of his influence, there was a particular emphasis on the writings of Eisenstein and Pudovkin, as well as the Hungarian Marxist film-maker and theorist, Béla Balázs. The vibrant character of the academic culture of the Centre was increasingly mirrored in the pages of the two film journals, of which *Cinema* (with a circulation of over 10,000) was perhaps the more important.[28] In 1937, the editorship of *Cinema* passed to Mussolini's son Vittorio and, not only did this not lead to any softening of its stance, it became if anything even more open to novel ideas.[29]

As these debates developed, however, more and more attention was focused on the problem of realism. Students at the film school were encouraged to pay particular attention to those film-makers who had constructed realistic narratives, and while this led to an emphasis on the work of foreign directors,[30] they were also reminded that there was an important realist tradition within Italian cinema. Particular attention was focused on films like Nino Martoglio's *Lost in Darkness* (1914) in which, within the framework of a melodramatic narrative, great emphasis is placed on the detailed observation of the physical conditions of the Neapolitan slums.[31] Nor was this presented as an archaic tradition that had long since disappeared. Alessandro Blasetti, perhaps the most important director of the 1930s, had explored realist themes himself, notably in *Sun* (1929), a film about the draining of the Pontine marshes, and *1860* (1934) which explored

Garibaldi's invasion of Sicily through the lives of ordinary Sicilians. Both films were shot on location and, in *1860*, Blasetti had also made extensive use of non-professional actors. Not only were these films screened regularly, Blasetti himself also taught at the film school, always insisting on taking his students on 'field trips' to lunatic asylums, prisons and morgues, to give them an abiding sense of the 'real world'.[32]

This growing preoccupation with realism in film was reinforced and strengthened by comparable developments in literature. The translation into Italian in the early 1930s of American writers like Dos Passos, Hemingway and Steinbeck made a dramatic impact, representing, as Peter Bondanella accurately suggests, a kind of counter-culture, reinforcing yet again the growing sense of the profound limitations of Fascist culture.[33] Important as this was, however the young critics at *Cinema* were probably even more influenced by an earlier indigenous tradition of realist writing, exemplified most clearly in the work of the 19th-century Sicilian novelist Giovanni Verga. For Verga did not simply provide powerful examples of realist writing, he set out an approach that could serve equally well in the very different medium of cinema. Thus in the opening pages of *Gramigna's Lover* Verga told his readers that he would tell his story:

> ... more or less in the same simple and picturesque words of the people who told it me, and you, I am sure, will prefer to stand face to face with the naked honest fact rather than have to look for it between the lines of the book, or to see it through the author's lens.[34]

Thus, an understanding of earlier realist traditions in both literature and film, and of the contemporary realist films of American, French and some Italian film-makers, powerfully strengthened the growing conviction that Italian cinema could break away from what Barbaro (writing in 1943) defined as the dominant features of contemporary Italian film production, namely 'the historical pot-boiler, the Nineteenth Century rehashes, and the minor comedy of errors'.[35] The new cinema, he asserted, must reject the four dominant characteristics of contemporary Italian film production: 'naïve and mannered clichés', 'fantastic and grotesque fabrications which exclude human problems and the human point of view', historical set-pieces and adaptations from the novel and, finally, the rhetoric which showed Italians in general 'as inflamed by the same noble sentiments'.[36]

In the politics of the Liberation, the probity of neorealism was demonstrated in no small part by reference to its total rejection of Fascist cinema and yet, in reality, Fascist film culture constituted its essential precondition. Not only did the advocates of the new cinema owe an immense debt to the regime's own film school (and the journal edited by Mussolini's own son), the first clarion call for a new realist cinema came 10 years before Barbaro's, in an article written by the pro-Fascist journalist Leo Longanesi, who argued that 'realism is precisely what is lacking in our films'; it was necessary 'to take the movie camera into the streets, the courtyards, the barracks and the train stations'.[37] Moreover, even while the regime was still in power, a number of films were made which established the foundations on which the post-war neorealist cinema would be constructed. Thus, between 1940 and 1943 a number of directors, like Renato Castellani in *A Pistol Shot* (1942) or Luigi Chiarini (the director of the film school) in *Five Moons Street* (1941),[38] began to focus their cameras once more on the physical realities of the Italian landscape, rediscovering (at least in part) the world outside the studios that had been a feature of the work of the earlier Neapolitan film-makers.[39]

Even more remarkable, a quite different form of realist film-making was taking place at the very heart of the regime. Francesco De Robertis was in charge of a unit making documentary films within the Ministry of the Navy, and in 1941 he made *Men on the Bottom*. In a manner not unlike that being employed by wartime British documentary film-makers, he employed non-professionals in a film about the rescue of men trapped underwater during a naval exercise. De Robertis' approach made an enormous impact on the young Roberto Rossellini who made his first film, *The White Ship* (1941), under De Robertis' supervision. Rossellini drew his non-professional cast exclusively from the crew of the hospital ship and warship that were at the centre of the narrative, shot his film entirely on location, and skilfully combined his new footage with actuality footage of a naval battle. While Rossellini's two remaining wartime films, *A Pilot Returns* (1942) and *The Man of the Cross* (1943), returned to more traditional methods of film-making, other film-makers were also beginning to explore the possibilities of the new cinema.

Three films in particular, all made in 1942, demonstrated that a new realism was indeed possible. In two of them, Cesare Zavattini (one of the most well-known advocates of the new cinema), worked on scripts with established film-makers to inject a new realism into their films. Thus, he worked with Blasetti on *A Stroll in the Clouds* and, even more importantly, collaborated with Vittorio De Sica (the enormously successful light comedy actor) on the production of *The Children Are Watching Us*. That collaboration would ultimately prove immensely fruitful, resulting after the war in the production of three films that are at the very heart of neorealist cinema but, in 1942, it was the third film that was to make the largest impact. The film was *Obsession* (1942), its unlikely director, Luchino Visconti. For many years Visconti had lived the urbane and glamorous life of a rich young aristocrat and, after 1933, he spent most of his time in Paris. Those years in France changed his life, for it was in Paris that he encountered artists and left-wing intellectuals who challenged his apolitical conservatism. Moreover, in 1935 he was introduced to Jean Renoir, and the result was that Visconti gained his first small experience of film-making in 1936, working as third assistant director on two of Renoir's films – *A Day in the Country* and *The Lower Depths*. By the time he returned to Italy in 1938, he had been convinced that 'films could be a way to touch on truths we were very far away from ... When I went back to Italy I was really transformed.'[40] When Renoir was subsequently invited to Italy in 1939 to direct a film of Puccini's opera *Tosca*, he persuaded Visconti to go to Rome with him to work on the film, and that brought Visconti into contact for the first time with the group associated with *Cinema* and the film school; Visconti responded enthusiastically to their commitment to a new realism in Italian cinema.

At just the time that this new relationship was developing, the politics of the situation were transformed by the outbreak of war. Several members of the *Cinema* group were also members of the secret Communist Party in Rome, and increasingly the polemical radicalism of their articles about film would be paralleled by radical actions in support of the clandestine Resistance movement. Visconti himself did not join the Party, but he gave money to the Resistance and his palatial Roman villa became a safe house for its members – indeed, just before his death, he described this as 'the most interesting, most beautiful, most coherent period of my life ... The little I could give to the Resistance movement was the best thing I've ever done, and after that, my work ...'[41] However, it was at this time that his work in the Italian cinema began and, after flirting with a number of ideas, he developed a treatment for a film based on Verga's *Gramigna's Lover*. When that was rejected by the censor, he remembered that Renoir had given him a typed French translation of the American novel, *The Postman Always Rings Twice*, and it was this novel that would eventually become the film *Obsession*.

James M. Cain's tough, realist novel told the story of the intensely passionate relationship between Frank (an unemployed mechanic) and Cora, the wife of Nick, the owner of a roadside café and filling station. Frank and Cora murder Nick in a fake car accident and escape punishment; when Cora is subsequently killed in a real car accident, Frank is convicted of a crime that was never committed. In translating this novel into an Italian setting, Visconti worked closely with the *Cinema* group, very much as he had done on the articles which they had collaboratively written for the journal. In all, four of them worked on the screenplay,[42] and as a result the film came to stand as a kind of manifesto for the new cinema of realism. Not that Visconti's film embodied all, or even most, of the characteristics that were to become associated with neorealist cinema: he used the established actors Massimo Girotti and Clara Calamai in the two leading roles, the film was adapted from a novel, it did not focus attention on the realities of the contemporary wartime situation. But what Visconti did do was to take his cameras outside the studio, into the streets of Ancona and Ferrara, on the sandbanks of the river Po. And he told a story that broke right through the comfortable conventions of contemporary Fascist cinema, confronting head on the most intense and violent emotions of human desire.

Inevitably, the film provoked enormous controversy. At a private screening for Rome's social and intellectual elite, the response was mixed: shouts and insults were offset by intermittent applause; an ovation after the film was over, marred by Vittorio Mussolini storming out of the cinema, shouting 'That isn't Italy.'[43] But when the film was shown in public the response was more consistent. The film would last two or three evenings before it was either withdrawn altogether or so heavily cut as to be unrecognizable. On one occasion, it was withdrawn after the very first showing, the cinema itself being exorcised by an archbishop the following day. The Catholic Film Centre condemned the film, priests preached against it, and the Bologna paper *Avvenire d'Italia* articulated a dominant view in the press when it condemned the film as 'a concoction of repulsive passions, humiliation and decay' and 'an offence to the Italian people'.[44] In all, *Obsession* reached only a very small part of the Italian cinema audience and, because Visconti had failed to clear copyright for the novel, it could not be shown outside Italy.

For all its limited impact, *Obsession* provided the protagonists of the new cinema with the clearest possible evidence that such a cinema was indeed possible and yet, before much further work could be done, dramatic developments in the war made even the creation of a new cinema seem unimportant. The Allies landed in Sicily in July 1943 and by the time an armistice was signed in September, the Germans had occupied Rome and most of northern Italy. The radicalizing impact of these events is difficult to overstate, and the film-makers were certainly not immune to the dramatic changes that were taking place around them. Those, like Visconti, who had already been sympathetic, became more closely and more publicly associated with the anti-Fascist cause;[45] those, like Rossellini, who had worked with the regime, finally saw Fascism for what it was and refused to go north to work for Mussolini's puppet regime.[46] Rossellini quickly established links with the protagonists of the new cinema and began work on a project with De Santis, to be called *Freight Station*.[47] While some have argued that his decision was opportunistic, Peter Brunette insists that just like so many other Italians at this time, the harsh realities of life under German occupation led to a genuine conversion.[48]

Indeed, it was the cumulative experience of war, resistance and liberation that was the final, all-important catalyst in the birth of a neorealist cinema. Many important foundations were already in place, as some of the films made between 1941 and 1943 reveal, but in the end it was the experience of the war that was, in De Sica's words,

> ... decisive for us all. Each felt the mad desire to throw away all the old stories of the Italian cinema, to plant the camera in the midst of real life, in the midst of all that struck our astonished eyes. We sought to liberate ourselves from the weight of our sins, we wanted to look ourselves in the face and tell ourselves the truth, to discover what we really were, and to seek salvation.[49]

De Sica's words express the passionate moral imperative that was perhaps the single most important characteristic of neorealism. The bitter struggles of the last 18 months of the war had brutally exposed the compromises and the lies of the Fascist years, but they had also created an entirely new confidence that a new beginning could at last be made. Reality had to be confronted with honesty and truthfulness, and those who had argued so passionately for a new cinema of realism believed that they were ideally placed to do just that. Neorealism was therefore a cinema irredeemably tied to a particular moment in the Italian historical experience, and its first triumphant statement was seen in Italian cinemas just five months after the northern cities were liberated.

THE NEOREALIST FILMS AND THEIR AUDIENCE

The film was *Rome, Open City*; its director, Roberto Rossellini, the newest recruit to the group campaigning for a new cinema. The complex origins of the film go back to the weeks following the liberation of Rome in June 1944. The project started as a film about the life of a Catholic priest, Don Giuseppe Morosoni, who had been executed during the German occupation of Rome.[50] Rossellini wanted the former music hall comedian and character actor, Aldo Fabrizi, to play the part of the priest and thus asked Federico Fellini (who had worked as Fabrizi's gag writer in the past) to persuade Fabrizi to take the part – Fellini agreed, on the basis that he be allowed to write the part. The left-wing scriptwriter Sergio Amidei, who had written a script about the black market, agreed to incorporate this material into the emerging script, on the condition that an additional (fictitious) character, the Communist partisan Giorgio Manfredi, be included. Alberto Consiglio (a Neapolitan journalist) suggested the addition of a story about a partisan priest, Don Pappagallo, and the experiences of the two priests were eventually combined into the character of Don Pietro. Finally, Amidei had read an account of a pregnant woman who was gunned down while running after the truck in which her arrested husband was being taken away, and this incident developed into the character of Pina.

This mixture of factual and fictional strands was ultimately woven together into a dramatic narrative of the struggle in Rome in the winter of 1943–44, between the partisans and the occupying German forces and their Fascist allies. Giorgio Manfredi, a Resistance leader wanted by the Germans, has to deliver money to other members of the Resistance and plans to use a sympathetic Catholic priest, Don Pietro, to make the delivery. Manfredi is hiding in the apartment of his friend Francesco, who is to be married to Pina, already pregnant with his child. On the day of the wedding, the apartment block is raided; Manfredi escapes, but Francesco is arrested and taken away – as Pina chases after the truck in which he is held, she is gunned down and killed. Manfredi takes refuge in the apartment of his mistress, the nightclub entertainer, Marina, who (unknown to him) has been persuaded to become an informer by a Gestapo agent, Ingrid. Marina betrays Manfredi to the Gestapo and he is arrested, together with Don Pietro and an Austrian deserter. The deserter hangs himself in his cell; Manfredi is tortured to death; and Don Pietro is executed by firing squad.

Although shooting began in January 1945, the project was always short of money. What finance there was came from a variety of entrepreneurs and first time producers, and Rossellini himself had to sell almost everything that he and his estranged wife owned to finance the production. Where appropriate, shooting was on location, with the interiors shot in four sets constructed in a vacant basement of a building on Via degli Avignonesi, partly because its location enabled the crew to tap into the electricity supply that the Allied forces were providing for the newspaper *Il Messagero*.[51] The uncertain finances forced other economies on Rossellini: raw film stock, much of it from black market sources, was bought at different times in small quantities, with resulting differences in quality; the film was shot without sound or dialogue (because sound-synchronized film stock is much more expensive to process) and dubbed afterwards; Rossellini had to work without access to daily rushes (the processed film from the day's shooting). All of this has been used to characterize the film as the polar opposite of the polished, professional, studio-based productions of both Hollywood and Fascist cinema and, while there is some truth in such claims, it would be totally misleading to suggest that *Rome, Open City* was a work of improvisation, still less that its style was determined by the circumstances in which it was shot. As Brunette properly emphasizes, Rossellini knew exactly what he wanted and, difficult as some aspects of the production circumstances may have been, he made sure that the film realized those ambitions.[52]

Rossellini has always argued that the film was not well-received when it was first shown in Italy in September 1945, but in fact it enjoyed a number of favourable reviews and the lack of detailed discussion in the press was probably more a product of a severe lack of newsprint than any lack of enthusiasm for the film.[53] Moreover, the film (which had cost just 11 million lire to produce) quickly proved itself at the Italian box office, where it earned 61 million lire in its first four months, and went on to become the top-grossing Italian film of the 1945–46 season, with receipts of 162 million lire.[54] After winning the *Grand Prix* at the 1946 Cannes Film festival, it was quickly taken up by foreign distributors, enjoying its greatest successes in France and the United States. The film ran uninterrupted for over a year at a Manhattan cinema and ultimately grossed half-a-million dollars from its American release.[55]

Time and again contemporary reviews praised *Rome, Open City* for its new realism and, while there can be no doubt that contemporaries were startled by its newness, a more measured assessment reveals that the film was securely grounded in many of the well-established traditions of the narrative cinema. Thus, for example, while the film's central, sympathetic characters (Pina and Don Pietro above all else) are subtly drawn, their enemies are blacker than black caricatures. Major Bergmann, the Gestapo officer, is not just a sadist, he is an effeminate homosexual; his equally sadistic assistant, Ingrid, is a lesbian who seduces Marina by supplying her drug habit and giving her expensive presents. The melodramatic narrative is carefully structured to maximize audience sympathies with the central characters, most obviously by having Pina brutally shot down on the very morning of her wedding. The new realism of the film does not extend to the scenes in which Manfredi is tortured, where Rossellini follows the established tradition of providing just enough evidence of what is happening for the audience to be able to use its own imagination to understand the realities of Manfredi's off-screen screams. The music plays an entirely conventional role, reinforcing and underlining the audience's emotional response to each scene. The editing follows the conventions of the classical narrative film, achieving that seamless, almost invisible quality in which the audience's whole attention is focused on the characters and the unfolding events of the drama. Notwithstanding some of the *Cinema* critics' strictures about professional actors, all the important roles in the film are played by professionals.

Thus the film was firmly grounded in many of the conventions of the mainstream narrative film, and yet *Rome, Open City* is distinguished quite as much by the way in which Rossellini modified, subverted, or even abandoned those earlier traditions. To take the last point first. He may have used professional actors but, in almost every case, he cast them against type. Both Aldo Fabrizi (who played Don Pietro) and Anna Magnani (who played Pina) had made their reputations in the music hall and, more recently, in film comedies; neither had been seen in this kind of role before, and the shock of subverting an established screen *persona* played its part in enabling them to achieve such powerful performances. Within a broadly melodramatic structure, Rossellini enormously intensified the impact of certain key moments in the film by injecting moments of comedy in a manner that broke established genre conventions. Thus the killing of Pina would have been a powerful moment in any film; in Rossellini's film, it follows immediately after a scene in which Don Pietro has to create the illusion of ministering to a dying man in bed in order to prevent the Fascists from finding the weapons which have been concealed under his bed; in fact, the illusion of the sleeping man had been achieved by the priest knocking him out with a frying-pan. Rossellini cuts from this moment of slapstick comedy (scripted by Fellini) to the outside of the apartment block where the men who have been arrested are being driven away – Pina breaks loose from the soldiers who are holding her back; she runs screaming after the truck and is gunned down.

If these are two examples of the way in which Rossellini subverted existing conventions, the look of the film represents an even more complete departure from those conventions. In contrast to the carefully modulated placing of light and shade in a studio-based production, a combination of location shooting and the use of film stock of different quality and provenance gave the film a rough, raw, almost unfinished quality. In a different film culture that could have been seen as evidence of amateur incompetence but, because contemporary audiences associated those very characteristics with actuality, newsreel footage, it served to endow the film with a powerful sense of reality, even leading to speculation that Rossellini had shot some of the footage while the Germans still occupied Rome. If the film looked quite different from the films to which audiences were accustomed, the ideas that were at its heart broke just as decisively with the ideology of Fascist and Hollywood films. In a truly remarkable manner, the film faced up honestly to the terrible realities of war while, at the same time, communicating a unshakeable faith in the future: human beings who were true to their humanity could both defeat Fascism and build a better society thereafter. For example, the fact that Pina is shot on the morning of her wedding appears to be the very stuff of melodrama; the tragic pointlessness of that death, demonstrated by her fiancé Francesco being rescued almost immediately afterwards from the very same truck that had driven him away from her, clearly is not. Yet, in the meaning of the film, Pina's death, is not pointless. The night before, in a conversation with Pina on the stairs of their apartment block, Francesco had put into words a vision of the future made all the more memorable by her death:

> ... spring will come back, and it'll be more beautiful than ever, because we'll be free. We have to believe it, we have to want it! ... we shouldn't be afraid now or in the future. Because we're in the right, the right's on our side ... We're fighting for something that has to be, that can't help coming. Maybe the way is hard, it may take a long time, but we'll get there, and we'll see a better world![56]

Moreover, the manner of Pina's killing serves as a powerful reminder to the audience of the true character of Fascism and Nazism, a reminder that is underlined even more forcefully in the brutal torture of Manfredi and the execution of Don Pietro. Once again, Rossellini uses these events to underline the film's central affirmation of the strength of the human spirit. In the face of terrible torture, Manfredi does not betray his comrades; Don Pietro remains true to his faith to the end, commenting in his final words: 'Oh. It's not hard to die well. It's hard to live well.'[57] Remarkably, those words stand as a posthumous tribute to the Communist Manfredi as well. Rossellini had succeeded in constructing a convincing representation of the way in which the imperatives of the Resistance had cut right through the ideologies and beliefs that normally divided Italy so powerfully. Bergmann's attempts to exploit the priest's hostility to communism fall on deaf ears; priest and Communist stand together, united in their determination to defeat Fascism and in their commitment to build a better society after the war. While this was a message that attracted some clerical criticism even in 1945,[58] the optimism of the film's conclusion did not seem sentimental to a contemporary audience, not least because the spirit of the Resistance had created such high hopes for the future. Thus, Don Pietro's execution is watched by the same group of small boys who had earlier carried out their own act of Resistance sabotage, and the film ends with their walking back into a Rome dominated by the dome of St Peter's. The sacrifices have not been in vain; 'spring will come back'.

The new cinema could not have had a more successful inauguration than that achieved by *Rome, Open City*. Its commercial success (inside and outside Italy) created a climate in which producers became willing to finance low budget, 'realist' films with a contemporary focus and, more important, it appeared to vindicate the *Cinema* critics' faith in the potential of the medium to take honest and truthful images of the nation to the mass audience. Moreover, Rossellini's second post-war film, *Paisan*, which was an even more radical departure from the past, achieved considerable success as well, proving to be the ninth most popular Italian film in the 1946–47 season. The film was financed partly by the money *Open City* had made in America, partly by an Italian producer, Carlo Ponti.[59] Unlike, *Open City*, *Paisan* was not tightly scripted before shooting began. Rossellini's intention was to make a film that would encompass the wartime experience of the whole country and, as the crew travelled through Italy over the six months of production, scenes were modified as the film-makers responded to the conditions that they encountered. Indeed, Rossellini dispensed altogether with the conventional linear narrative of the mainstream feature film, constructing *Paisan* in six separate episodes, each located at different moments in the war. Each episode is introduced with newsreel footage and an explanatory voice-over (supplemented where necessary by maps), and when the actuality footage gives way to Rossellini's own footage, he maintains the grainy, realistically lit images that had been used in *Open City*.

Unlike *Rome, Open City*, Rossellini did not cast professional actors in all the major roles, and he claimed subsequently that *Paisan* was a film 'without actors in the true sense of the word', suggesting that he chose his actors by 'installing myself with my cameraman in the middle of the place where I hoped to shoot ... Passers-by gathered round me and I chose my actors in the crowd.'[60] While it was indeed the case that many important roles in the film were played by non-professionals, most notably perhaps by the boy who played the street urchin in the second episode, all the Americans in the film were professional actors, and Rossellini's claim that the actor who played the black GI in the second episode was not a professional[61] is simply untrue; the character was played by the black actor, Dots Johnson. In fact, Rossellini had been enthusiastic at the prospect of Rod Geiger (who had bought the American rights to *Rome, Open City*, and who partly financed *Paisan*) recruiting major Hollywood stars for the film and, while Geiger did not deliver the stars, he did deliver a group of experienced American actors, Dots Johnson among them.[62]

For all that, non-professional actors played a much more important role in *Paisan* than they had in *Rome, Open City* and the film certainly had an even stronger documentary feel than its predecessor. But that said, it is, of course, a work of imaginative fiction; Rossellini exploited the prevailing conventions of both the narrative and documentary film to create a powerful and persuasive illusion of reality. Many of the locations are real but, as Peter Bondanella emphasizes, many are not: when the tanks arrive to liberate Rome, for example, the scene was shot in Livorno; the Sicilian episode was shot, not near Catania (as the film suggests), but on the same coastline near Amalfi where the fifth episode was filmed, an episode which purported to be set in a monastery in northern Italy; many of the interior locations for the fourth episode were shot, not in Florence, but in Rome.[63] Much of the script was modified when Rossellini and his team arrived in a particular location, but such modifications were as much a product of the encounter between professional and non-professional actors, as they were of the encounter between the film-makers and the 'real' local people. In short, Rossellini's commitment to a new realism was never a commitment to the unthinking, mechanical observation of reality; neorealism was, as he himself put it, 'nothing other than the artistic form of truth'.[64] Indeed, on another occasion, he explicitly emphasized the importance of respecting both 'concreteness and imagination', complaining that an undue emphasis on 'the concrete' would destroy 'every feeling of humanity';[65] and in Rossellini's terms, that 'feeling of humanity' was at the very heart of neorealism.

Thus while *Paisan* was firmly rooted in the wartime experience, Rossellini was not concerned simply with recording the liberation of Italy from the first Allied landings in Sicily through to the bitterly contested encounters between the partisans and the Germans in the north. His film has a quite different focus, taking as its central theme the encounter between the American troops and the indigenous Italian population. The title, *Paisà* in Italian, is the colloquial form of the word *paisano*, which means countryman, neighbour, even friend; it was used by the American soldiers as a friendly greeting. Rossellini's film rigorously probes the character of the relationship that lay behind that apparent friendship. Thus, several of the episodes serve only to demonstrate the hopeless inability of individuals to transcend the huge linguistic and cultural divisions that separate them and, even where those divisions are overcome, the film's message is incomparably less optimistic than *Open City*. Nowhere is this more clear than in the extraordinary final episode, which focuses attention on the desperate struggles between the partisans and the Germans in the Po Valley. Here, Rossellini's ability to reconstruct a particular physical location is faultless, his mobile camera mounted low down at the level of the men as they crouch in their flat-bottomed boats, achieving an overwhelming sense of the desperate position in which they find themselves. Moreover, while at first glance the purpose of the cinematography is to pay attention to the 'concreteness', the precise physical characteristics of the situation, as the episode develops it becomes more and more clear that it is in fact focused on the 'imagination'. The very particular relationship between sky and water which, as André Bazin has emphasized, is sustained throughout the whole episode,[66] conveys an overwhelming sense of the hopeless struggle in which the men are engaged. For their battle is not in fact with the elements; it is with the Germans, whose resources and numerical superiority make them an insuperable enemy. In such a situation, even the American liaison officer (who speaks fluent Italian and is completely integrated into the partisan group) is powerless. The partisans are rounded up by the Germans and shot or drowned – when the American tries to protest, he too is shot.

Within the Christian ethic that is central to Rossellini's work, the American's willingness to lay down his life for his friends, reveals not only that he is indeed their *paisà*, but that his death, just like their deaths, reaffirms the triumph of the crucified Christ. But whether Rossellini's audience understood his theology is unclear – unlike the end of *Open City*, with its images of children and the holy city, *Paisan* ends with a shot of a dead partisan floating in the water, and it may well be that contemporary audiences simply saw the film as an adult and honest reconstruction of events that were still extraordinarily vivid in people's memory. But the important point is that they did see the film; *Paisan* may not have been the success that *Open City* had been, but it did attract a sizeable Italian audience and it also enjoyed a wide international distribution, being screened in many countries at much the same time as the earlier film. The new cinema of neorealism appeared to be on course, Rossellini's two films demonstrating both that the theoretical principles that had so animated the *Cinema* critics could be translated into practice, and that such films could reach that mass audience which was the precondition for their fulfilling their social objectives.

In the event, the success of these first two films could not have been more misleading for, looking at post-war Italian film production as a whole, only a very small number of neorealist films were ever made, and only very few of that small number were successful at the box office. Problems of definition have beset neorealism from the outset, and the absence of any agreed definition makes it impossible to define the extent of that failure precisely. There is broad agreement that, in the five years up to 1950 (when most neorealist films were made), neorealist films accounted for less than 10 per cent of all Italian film production;[67] the overwhelming majority of Italian film production in this period reverted to well-tried, popular genres – melodrama, historical epics and comedy. Equally, while precise figures depend once again on which films are regarded as 'truly' neorealist, most historians agree that only a very small proportion of neorealist films achieved that degree of box-office success which alone gives access to the truly mass audience; very many more proved to be complete disasters at the box office. Moreover, all agree that without the success that Rossellini's first two films enjoyed outside Italy, even fewer neorealist films would have been made. The small, international 'art house' audience that they reached brought the producers of Italian neorealist films all-important additional revenues; without this, even this very modest level of production would not have been achieved.

If we extend the analysis beyond Rossellini's first two films, and explore the history of those core neorealist films that are included in even the most narrowly defined lists of neorealist films, the extent of the failure of neorealism becomes clear. In addition to those first two films, such a core includes the third film in Rossellini's war trilogy, *Germany Year Zero* (1947), Visconti's *The Earth Trembles* (1948) and three films made by De Sica, *Shoeshine* (1946), *Bicycle Thieves* (1948) and *Umberto D.* (1951). For his final war film, Rossellini went to Germany to try to make sense of Nazism: the resulting film, *Germany Year Zero*, was shot partly on location in Berlin, partly in studios in Rome. It focused on Edmund Koeler, a deeply alienated 15-year-old boy living with his brother, sister and his bedridden father, in desperately impoverished conditions in a flat in post-war Berlin. Under the influence of his former teacher, a Nazi who preaches that the weak must die and only the strong will survive, Edmund poisons his sick father; in the aftermath of his father's death, he experiences some limited realization of what it is that he has done, and commits suicide by throwing himself off the top of an unfinished building.

In marked contrast to his two earlier films, *Germany Year Zero* was both 'very badly received' by the critics[68] and proved an even more spectacular failure at the box office, and, for all its remarkable qualities, that failure is not difficult to understand. While it retains some of the attributes of the earlier films, it lacks both the powerful dramatic narrative of *Open City*, and the immediate familiarity of the events of *Paisan*. Instead, *Germany Year Zero* presents a nightmarish vision of a world in which the moral bankruptcy of the people is precisely mirrored in the physical devastation of the city, photographed repeatedly in lengthy tracking shots which, in José Luis Guarner's words, acquire an 'obsessive ... hallucinatory feeling'[69] – a sharp contrast with the newsreel quality of *Open City*. An opening title asserts that the film reveals what happens when 'an ideology strays from the eternal laws of morality and of Christian charity',[70] but the fact that the film represented the legacy of Nazism so remorselessly, with not a hint of that 'Christian charity' that had been such a marked feature of Rossellini's earlier films, made it difficult, unpalatable viewing. In an Italy that was beginning to try to put the experience of the war behind it, the film could not find an audience.

Ever since the early 1940s, Visconti had been interested in making a film based on Verga's novel set in Aci Trezza in Sicily, *The House by the Medlar Tree*, but he was also deeply influenced by the Italian Marxist, Antonio Gramsci, who had argued that an alliance between southern peasants and northern industrial workers could provide the driving force for the Italian revolution.[71] Thus he developed the idea of a trilogy of films which would explore the revolutionary story of an alliance of fishermen, miners and peasants: defeated in the first film, they would ultimately achieve victory in the third and final film. *The Earth Trembles* was to be the first film in the trilogy – the other two were never made. It is built around one fishing family: the son, Antonio, indignant at the power of the middlemen who exploit the fishermen by buying their fish at artificially low prices, persuades the family to buy their own boat (by mortgaging their home) and thereby break free from the poverty in which they are trapped. The boat is destroyed in a storm and Antonio is forced to beg the middlemen for a job; the family's attempt to break free of the economic system, an abject failure.

With an initial three million lire provided by the Italian Communist Party, Visconti went to Sicily to start work. No sets were used; every scene was shot in its actual location, with additional lighting used only for the problematic night scenes at sea. While much had been prepared in advance, he recruited his actors exclusively from the fishermen and peasants with whom he lived and worked for the next six months, and they were actively involved in the construction of the dialogue: 'They put what I asked them to say into their own words. One of my assistants wrote down their suggestions. The phrases were polished up and then rehearsed and recorded.'[72] Thus, unlike every other Italian film of the time, the characters speak Sicilian, their dialogue captured on a synchronized soundtrack, recorded as the film was shot. In all these ways, Visconti's film represented perhaps the most whole-hearted attempt to realize the aspirations of the young *Cinema* critics, and yet it is perhaps the most formal of the neorealist films. In total contrast to the newsreel look of many of the other films, *The Earth Trembles* has a visual style all of its own. Every aspect of the *mise-en-scéne* is meticulously controlled, characters carefully located within a physical environment that is itself precisely framed by the camera. Everything is designed to reinforce the sense of a society in which people have been compelled to come to terms with the environment in which they live – they cannot control that environment, but the epic pattern of their lives, evolved over countless previous generations, enables them to survive. And in so doing, their lives acquire a dignity, a grandeur even, so vividly represented by the cinematography, whether in the slow panning movement of the camera, or in the length of the shots, which last for anything up to five minutes without a cut.

Notwithstanding these remarkable qualities, the two-and-a-half hours of Visconti's subtitled film did not make for easy viewing. Almost all the reviews were hostile, and Visconti was widely attacked by politicians for damaging the name of Italy, by exposing poverty and misery in this way.[73] The film was not given a general release and, although it was shown at the Venice Film Festival in the autumn of 1948, the reception was once again hostile. A cut version with the Sicilian dubbed into Italian was subsequently given a limited release but, even in this form, it failed to win an audience.[74] In the mounting Cold War hysteria that came to dominate Italy in the run-up to the 1948 election, Visconti's Communist affiliation alienated many, but Pierre Sorlin is probably right to suggest that it was above all else the style of the film that antagonized the audience.[75] Moreover, unlike some other neorealist films, it did not enjoy any greater success outside Italy – it was not released in France until 1952, and then only in a version cut to half the length of the original. *The Earth Trembles* was even considered too demanding for the international art house audience.

The same could not be said, however, about Vittorio De Sica's three neorealist films, *Shoeshine* (1946), *Bicycle Thieves* (1948) and *Umberto D.* (1952). All three were the product of a unique collaboration with the scriptwriter Cesare Zavattini, which took De Sica away from his established role as a matinee idol into the altogether less certain world of a neorealist director. Their first film together (*The Children Are Watching Us*) was made in 1942, but it was in the three post-war films that De Sica fully explored his own vision of neorealism. In many ways it was a curious alliance for, while Zavattini stood for the most austere model of neorealism (no studio sets, no professional actors, no plots), De Sica was steeped in the very different conventions of the mainstream cinema; their extraordinary collaboration somehow managed to draw on these very different traditions. Thus, while the leading roles in all three films were played by non-professionals, in stories that focused around ordinary, everyday events, with many scenes shot in real locations, De Sica never had any misgivings about shooting appropriate scenes in the studio, and all three films are characterized by an intricacy of plotting which was the very antithesis of the absence of plot which Zavattini had advocated – *Bicycle Thieves* even originated in a novel by Luigi Bartolini. In fact, the appearance of reality that was so powerfully constructed in these films was the product of the most careful preliminary preparation and planning, followed by a degree of control over everything that appeared in front of the camera of which even the most conventional, studio-bound director would have been proud.

Bicycle Thieves provides perhaps the clearest illustration of the way in which De Sica worked. Pre-production lasted six months, not simply because of the time and energy invested in the formulation of a highly developed screenplay, but also because De Sica's particular approach to using non-professional actors made casting enormously difficult. De Sica used non-professionals because they allowed him to exercise greater control over the performance than he could with professional actors – as he himself put it, 'the man in the street ... is raw material that can be moulded at will'.[76] Moreover, from very early on in the preparation of a script, he developed a quite definite conception of the kind of person he wanted to cast, and a great deal of time was taken up with looking for people to match these preconceptions.[77] Similarly, location shooting was not an opportunity to improvise a scene in its 'real' environment, but rather every aspect of the scene had to be meticulously planned and controlled to create for the audience the illusion that they were watching unstructured 'reality'. Thus, where the script called for the scene in the street market to be interrupted by a sudden thunderstorm, De Sica had 40 stall-holders and countless other extras on standby, days in advance, waiting for the first cloudy day; when that day came, the Rome fire brigade provided the torrential 'rain' which sends everyone scurrying for shelter. In the all-important scene where the central character's bicycle is stolen, the director's precisely formulated conception required not only that every element (cars, cyclists, pedestrians) be carefully choreographed, but also that the action be filmed by no less than six separate cameras, to give the director the variety of points-of-view on which he could draw in the finished sequence in the film.[78]

Not that any of this diminishes De Sica's achievement. Notwithstanding some of Zavattini's more extreme claims, neorealist cinema was never committed to the mechanical, unselfconscious recording of 'reality'. All of its directors, in their different ways, sought to expand the potential of the narrative film to create the illusion of reality, and De Sica's trilogy constitutes one of the most enduring achievements of the new cinema, not least in the remarkable performances which he elicited from his non-professional actors: the two boys in *Shoeshine*, the father and son in *Bicycle Thieves*, the elderly pensioner in *Umberto D*. Moreover, De Sica's ability to draw so powerfully on the traditions of the mainstream narrative film in constructing his own unique form of neorealism certainly resulted in films that Roy Armes has properly described as 'among the most accessible' in neorealist cinema.[79] All the more remarkable then, that De Sica found it just as difficult as Rossellini and Visconti to find an Italian audience for his films.[80] Cheap as *Shoeshine* was to make,[81] the extent of its failure at the Italian box-office was such that it failed to recover even its small production costs;[82] *Umberto D*. was such a box-office disaster that it destroyed any lingering hopes that any Italian producer would be willing to finance further neorealist films.[83] The only exception was *Bicycle Thieves* which achieved 11th place in the 1948–49 season, and a return of 252 million lire on its 100 million lire production costs,[84] although even this film failed on its initial release. When the film was premièred in Rome, De Sica deliberately waited outside until the film was over, but before he could ask the cinema manager what the response had been, a working-class man with his wife and family came out, angrily shouting at the manager: 'Give us our money back and put up a notice to tell families like us that the film's a b....y horror!'[85] The film was subsequently re-launched in all the major cities, with De Sica himself introducing the film, and this, according to the distributor, generated the interest out of which a successful release was eventually built.[86]

Thus, of the seven core neorealist films, four failed completely to reach the mass audience; of the remaining three, two (*Rome, Open City* and *Paisan*) were released at a time when Italy was still dominated by that extraordinary radical optimism which had developed out of resistance and liberation, and of which neorealism was itself a product – *Bicycle Thieves* represents the only example of a neorealist film that won its mass audience in what might be regarded as 'normal' times. Why then were neorealist films so unsuccessful? De Sica explained *Shoeshine*'s failure in terms of the fact that 'it was released when the first American films were reappearing',[87] and the tidal wave of Hollywood movies that engulfed Italian cinemas in the immediate post-war period was surely at the heart of the failure of the neorealist films. Nor was this an accidental development. Thomas Guback has shown just how assiduously the American government worked to support the interests of the post-war American film industry in overseas markets,[88] and post-Fascist Italy created an ideal opportunity for the simultaneous exploitation of political and commercial interests. From the outset, the Americans argued that 'the so-called Italian film was invented by the Fascists, therefore it has to be suppressed',[89] and accordingly Cinecittà was expropriated and turned into a refugee camp, only returning to film production in 1948. At precisely the same time, Hollywood films were imported in huge quantities – indeed, the United States had made it a condition of signing the peace treaty that all quotas on the import of foreign films be lifted.[90] At first, distribution was in the hands of the Psychological Warfare Branch of the Allied forces but, by the end of 1945, the Hollywood studios had reopened their Italian offices, setting up agencies and affiliates in all the major towns.

Hollywood films proved just as popular with Italian audiences as they did everywhere else and, as a result, exhibition boomed. The number of cinemas doubled between 1940 and 1954, and ticket sales also doubled from 400 million in 1945 to 800 million in 1954.[91] But, throughout the first five post-war years, the proportion of Italian films shown in Italian cinemas was always under 20 per cent,[92] and Italian films invariably took an even smaller proportion of box-office takings – just 13 per cent in 1946, for example.[93] Thus, as it became increasingly obvious that neorealist films could not compete with Hollywood products, a number of neorealist directors concluded that the only way forward was to try to incorporate the ideology of neorealism within established, popular film genres. Occasionally, as with Luigi Zampa's burlesque comedy, To Live in Peace (1946), that accommodation was with an established Italian genre, but more commonly it was with the major Hollywood genres. Thus both Alberto Lattuada's The Bandit (1946) and Without Pity (1948) were deeply indebted to film noir and the gangster film; Giuseppe De Santis' Bitter Rice (1948) was a social melodrama, with elements of the gangster film, the western and even the musical; Pietro Germi's The Path of Hope (1950) was strongly influenced again by the western.[94] Bitter Rice followed another Hollywood convention, establishing the actress Silvana Mangano as just that kind of sexy, glamorous film star whose idolization by cinema audiences the film had intended to subvert. As a way of reaching the mass audience, these strategies were often successful – The Bandit was fourth at the box office in the 1946–47 season, Bitter Rice fifth in the 1949–50 season[95] – but as one of neorealism's primary objectives had been precisely to turn its back on established genres, the production of these films was, in itself, a recognition of the extent of its failure. Indeed, these films provoked a vociferous and increasingly bitter debate about the nature of neorealism and nowhere was this more clear than in responses to Bitter Rice. The left-wing critic Guido Aristarco, for example, argued: that 'the workers cannot be educated with the bare legs of

Silvana',[96] and De Santis found himself pilloried in the leading Communist newspaper *L'Unità*.[97]

Such left-wing criticisms of neorealism were relatively uncommon but, almost from the outset, the neorealist films had been attacked by politicians from the centre and right. All this came to a head in 1949 when the new Christian Democrat government intervened to defend the film industry against the mounting Hollywood threat.[98] A number of measures were introduced to strengthen indigenous film production,[99] but such support was only available to those films which met with official approval and the government also took new powers to refuse export licences to any film that 'slandered Italy'. In effect, neorealist films would be starved of funding, and any that were made, would be cut off from access to that small but indispensable international art house market. Just in case anyone failed to understand the government's position, the release of *Umberto D.* prompted Giulio Andreotti (the minister responsible for the film industry), to write an open letter to De Sica in 1952, accusing him of making a film that had 'slander[ed] Italy abroad, presenting her as a country of social conflicts and flaunting her unemployed and underprivileged'.[100] While Andreotti's letter provoked a great deal of comment, the real battle had been lost long before, and a rather more important source of that failure was the sustained opposition of the Catholic Church. From the very beginning, the Church had found reason to criticise almost every neorealist film, and under its own system of film classification, most neorealist films were classified either as *adulti* (adults only), *adulti con riserve* (adults with reservations) or *esclusi* (forbidden).[101] Moreover, the Church was in a position to impose its views on a large part of the audience. Ever since the 1930s, it had owned its own cinemas and, as a result of an energetic post-war programme of expansion, by 1953 its 7000 cinemas accounted for a third of the national total. Thus not only was neorealism confronted by Hollywood and the state, it had to defend itself against the Church as well; it was clearly an overwhelming combination.

CONCLUSION

Neorealism was born out of an ambition to transform Italian cinema, to replace the well-established genres with an entirely new cinema of realism which, by reaching the mass audience, would transform the attitudes and aspirations of the Italian people as a whole. Not only did it fail to transform Italian cinema, with the vast majority of Italian film production continuing to pursue the well-worn genre formulas, only very few of the small number of neorealist films that were made ever reached the target audience. In practice, the forces ranged against neorealist cinema make that failure all too easy to understand. It was born in a very special set of circumstances that developed in Italy towards the end of the war, when the combination of the overthrow of Fascism and the ensuing struggle against German occupation created an unprecedented centre–left alliance, which appeared to hold out the prospect of a modern, progressive, secular Italian state. Within that context, the huge ambitions of neorealist cinema did not perhaps seem wildly optimistic, and the success of *Rome, Open City* appeared to be the triumphant vindication of those ambitions. In reality, almost as soon as the war was over, the unlikely wartime coalitions started to fall apart and the forces of the centre-right (backed wholeheartedly by the Catholic Church and the United States) re-asserted themselves, decisively defeating the left-wing parties in the 1948 election. In exactly the same way, the mass cinema audience turned its back on the neorealist films and turned instead to the glamour, the excitement and the high production values of Hollywood movies and, to a lesser extent, their Italian counterparts. Hollywood appeared to encapsulate all those aspirations that now came to dominate Italian society and, in such a culture, there was little or no place for difficult, uncompromising films that looked back to the immediate past or focused attention on the unsolved problems of the present.

The victory of the Italian centre-right, which led directly to the introduction of a film culture that was explicitly hostile to neorealism, might be seen as one of the causes of the failure of the new cinema, but in reality its victory represented the clearest possible evidence of the extent to which the new cinema had already failed. With only very few exceptions, neorealist films failed to win the box-office battle with Hollywood and, in this, the experience of these film-makers precisely mirrored the experience of their Soviet predecessors some 20 years earlier. Indeed, the parallel is even closer than this for, just like the Soviet films, neorealist films were enthusiastically received by film-makers and intellectuals outside Italy. Yet success with an art house audience abroad was no compensation for failure with the mass audience at home. The moral imperative at the heart of neorealism demanded that their films be seen by the mass audience, and the failure to reach that audience demonstrated once more just how difficult it was to use the cinema as an effective medium of mass communication and persuasion.

NOTES

1. Alberto Lattuada writing in June 1945, quoted in Pierre Leprohon, *The Italian Cinema*, translated from the French by Roger Greaves and Oliver Stallybrass, London, 1966, p. 98.

2. Martin Clark, *Modern Italy 1871–1995*, 2nd edition, London, 1996, p. 237. Much of this discussion of Fascist Italy is based on the same source.

3. Doug Thompson, *State Control in Fascist Italy: Culture and Conformity, 1925–1943*, Manchester, 1991, pp. 35–6.

4. Clark, *op. cit.*, p. 245.

5. Thompson, *op. cit.*, pp. 141–5.

6. Clark, *op. cit.*, pp. 312–14. The remainder of this discussion derives largely from the same source, pp. 314–25.

7. Clark, *op. cit.*, p. 317.

8. Pierre Sorlin, *Italian National Cinema 1896–1996*, London, 1996, p. 44.

9. They were reduced by 75 per cent between 1912 and 1914; David Forgacs, *Italian Culture in the Industrial Era 1880–1980: Cultural Industries, Politics and the Public*, Manchester, 1990, p. 51. Hereafter Forgacs (1990).

10. Sorlin, *op. cit.*, p. 52.

11. Mira Liehm, *Passion and Defiance: Film in Italy from 1942 to the Present*, Los Angeles, 1984, p. 7.

12. Morando Morandini, 'Italy from Fascism to neo-realism', in Geoffrey Nowell-Smith (ed.), *The Oxford History of World Cinema*, Oxford, 1996, p. 354.

13. Forgacs (1990), p. 69.

14. Sorlin, *op. cit.*, p. 72.

15. Forgacs (1990), p. 71.

16. Geoffrey Nowell-Smith, 'The Italian cinema under Fascism', in David Forgacs (ed.), *Rethinking Italian Fascism: Capitalism, Populism and Culture*, London, 1986, p. 146.

17. Law 918 (18 June 1931), quoted in Morandini, *op. cit.*, p. 353.

18. Sorlin, *op. cit.*, p. 76.

19. Marcia Landy, *Fascism in Film: The Italian Commercial Cinema, 1931–1943*, Princeton, 1986, p.10.

20. Liehm, *op. cit.*, p. 4.

21. *Ibid.*, p. 35.

22. There was never a complete ban on American films – *Stagecoach*, for example, was shown during the war (Forgacs, 1990, p. 91).

23. *Ibid.*, p. 72.

24. *Blackshirt* (1933), *Dawn over the Sea* (1935), *Old Guard* (1935) and *Redemption* (1942).

25. Morandini, *op. cit.*, p. 354. Morandini argues that Fascist propaganda is clearly evident in these films, while Pierre Sorlin, for example, suggests that films like *Scipio the African* should not be regarded in this way (Sorlin, *op. cit.*, pp. 78 ff).

26. Landy, *op. cit.*, p. 8.

27. *Ibid.*, p. 8.

28. *Bianco e Nero*, as the journal of the film school, adopted a rather more technical, specialized approach.

29. Antonio Vitti, *Giuseppe De Santis and Post-war Italian Cinema*, Toronto, 1996, p. 10.

30. American directors like Capra, Ford, Wyler and Vidor, or French directors like Carné, Duvivier and Renoir (Mira Liehm, *op. cit.*, p. 38). Some future film-makers gained first-hand experience working with French directors, notably Luchino Visconti, who worked with Renoir as third assistant director and costume designer on *A Day in the Country* (1936).

31. Ted Perry, 'Roots of neorealism', *Film Criticism*, Vol. 3, No. 2, Winter, 1979, p. 5.

32. Laurence Schifano, *Luchino Visconti: The Flames of Passion*, translated from the French by William S. Byron, London, 1990, p. 150.

33. Peter Bondanella, *Italian Cinema: From Neo-Realism to the Present*, New York, 1983, p. 25.

34. Quoted in Roy Armes, *Patterns of Realism*, London, 1971, p. 106.

35. Quoted in Armes, *op. cit.*, p. 388, n. 13. It was in this article that Barbaro revived the term neorealism, as a term used to describe French realist films of which he approved. The term itself had been used originally by Italian philosophers at the turn of the century and had reappeared in literary criticism at the end of the 1920s (Sorlin, *op. cit.*, p. 89).

36. Quoted in Eric Rhode, 'Why neorealism failed', *Sight and Sound*, Vol. 30, No. 1, Winter 1960/61, p. 27.

37. Peter Bondanella, *The Films of Roberto Rossellini*, Cambridge, 1993, p. 7. Hereafter, Bondanella (1993).

38. Other examples include Alberto Lattuada, *Giacomo the Idealist* (1943) and Mario Soldati, *The Little World of the Past* (1941). Because these films were based on late-nineteenth- or early-twentieth-century naturalistic novels, their directors were disparagingly categorized as 'calligraphers'.

39. In films like *Lost in Darkness* (1914), *Assunta Spina* (1915) and *Rustic Chivalry* (1915).

40. Visconti quoted by Schifano, *op. cit.*, p. 143.

41. *Ibid.*, p. 194.

42. De Santis, Puccini, Alicata and Pietrangeli. The novelist, Alberto Moravia, whose name did not appear on the credits because he was a Jew and a well-known opponent of the regime, also worked on the script (Gaia Servadio, *Luchino Visconti: A Biography*, London, 1981, p. 81).

43. Schifano, *op. cit.*, p. 179.

44. Quoted in Liehm, *op. cit.*, p. 58.

45. In April 1944 he was arrested and he was only released the day before the Allies reached Rome on 4 June (Servadio, *op. cit.*, pp. 85–95).

46. Unlike De Robertis who did and thereby effectively destroyed his post-war career.

47. Filming began at the Tiburtina Station in Rome until bombing forced the film-makers to stop (Vitti, *op. cit.*, p. 20).

48. Peter Brunette, *Roberto Rossellini*, Oxford, 1987, p. 38.

49. Millicent Marcus, *Italian Film in the Light of Neorealism*, Princeton, 1986, pp. xiii–xiv.

50. For a detailed discussion of the origins of the film see Bondanella (1993), pp. 46–53; and Peter Bondanella, *The Cinema of Federico Fellini*, Princeton, 1992, pp. 38–42, hereafter Bondanella (1992).

51. Brunette, *op. cit.*, p. 363, n. 4. Cinecittà was being used at the time as a refugee camp, although Rossellini's budget would probably have made it difficult to afford conventional studio facilities.

52. *Ibid.*, p. 42.

53. *Ibid.*, p. 52.

54. Vittorio Spinazzola, *Cinema e Pubblico: Lo Spettacolo Filmico in Italia 1945–*

1965, Rome, 1985, p. 18.

55. This represented a remarkable return for the American distributor who had persuaded Rossellini, during filming, to sell him the rights for $20,000. Fellini's colourful account of this aspect of the film is discussed in Bondanella (1993), p. 46.

56. This quotation is taken from the translation in the published edition of the film script: Roberto Rossellini, *The War Trilogy: Open City, Paisan, Germany – Year Zero*, edited and with an introduction by Stefano Roncoroni, translated from the Italian by Judith Green, London, 1973, pp. 69–70.

57. Quoted in Bondanella (1983), p. 38.

58. Thus the Church pronounced the film 'harmful to children' and objected to the way in which the priest was shown as acting on his own initiative, without reference to his bishop, and for becoming involved in politics (Sorlin, *op. cit.*, p. 90).

59. According to Fellini, it was Ponti who put up most of the money (Brunette, *op. cit.*, p. 61).

60. Armes, *op. cit.*, p. 76.

61. Rossellini claimed that 'the American Negro claimed to have played some supporting roles but I realised that in reality he had lied to me to get a job'; quoted in Armes, *op. cit.*, p. 76.

62. Bondanella (1993), p. 68.

63. *Ibid.*, p. 66.

64. Roberto Rossellini, 'Due parole sul neorealismo', *Retrospettive*, 4 April 1953, translated by and reproduced in David Overbey (ed. and trans.), *Springtime in Italy: A Reader on Neo-Realism*, London, 1978, pp. 89–90.

65. Quoted in Bondanella (1983), p. 33.

66. André Bazin, *What Is Cinema?* Volume 2, essays selected and translated by Hugh Gray, London, 1972, p. 36.

67. Two recent estimates put this even lower, however; Christopher Wagstaff suggesting a figure of 7.6 per cent (Christopher Wagstaff, 'The place of neorealism in Italian cinema from 1945 to 1954', in Nicholas Hewitt (ed.), *The Culture of Reconstruction, European Literature, Thought and Film, 1945–50*, Basingstoke, 1989, p. 87), while Pierre Sorlin argues that they represented less than 4 per cent (Sorlin, *op. cit.*, p. 93).

68. The phrase is Rossellini's own, quoted in Armes, *op. cit.*, p. 88.

69. José Luis Guarner, *Roberto Rossellini*, translated by Elisabeth Cameron, London, 1970, pp. 28–9.

70. Quoted in Brunette, *op. cit.*, p. 81.

71. Schifano, *op. cit.*, pp. 167–8, and Bondanella (1983), p. 67.

72. Visconti quoted in Leprohon, *op. cit.*, p. 111.

73. Servadio, *op. cit.*, p. 119.

74. Liehm, *op. cit.*, p. 84.

75. Sorlin, *op. cit.*, p. 101.

76. De Sica quoted in Bondanella (1983), p. 50.

77. Francis Koval, 'Interview with De Sica', *Sight and Sound*, Vol. 19 (New Series), No. 2, April 1950, p. 62.

78. Armes, *op. cit.*, p. 155.

79. *Ibid.*, p. 150.

80. The first two films were popular with the international art-house audience, although *Umberto D.* was not.

81. De Sica claimed it cost less than a million lire (Vittorio De Sica, 'The most wonderful years of my life', *Films and Filming*, Vol. 2, No. 3, December 1955, p. 6).

82. Sorlin, *op. cit.*, p. 94.

83. Geoffrey Nowell-Smith, with James Hay and Gianni Volpi, *The Companion to Italian Cinema,* London, 1996, p. 87.

84. Spinazzola, *op. cit.*, p. 18.

85. Vittorio De Sica, 'Money, the public and *Umberto D.*', *Films and Filming*, Vol. 2, No. 4, January 1956, pp. 28–9.

86. Wagstaff, *op. cit.*, p. 77.

87. De Sica, *op. cit.* (1955), p. 6.

88. Thomas H. Guback, *The International Film Industry: Western Europe and America Since 1945,* Bloomington, 1969.

89. The words are those of Rear Admiral Emery W. Stone, the American officer responsible for policy towards the film industry – quoted in Liehm, *op. cit.*, p. 61.

90. Legislation doing just that was enacted in October 1945 (Christopher Wagstaff, *op. cit.*, pp. 74–8).

91. *Ibid.*, p. 78.

92. Forgacs (1990), p. 120.

93. Wagstaff, *op. cit.*, p. 78.

94. The character of these strong generic influences is explored in Bondanella (1983), pp. 74–86.

95. Spinazzola, *op. cit.*, p. 18.

96. Vitti, *op. cit.*, p. 36.

97. Sorlin, *op. cit.*, p. 90.

98. The extent of Hollywood domination of the box-office was threatening indigenous film production, which declined from 69 in 1947 to 49 in 1948 (Forgacs, 1990, p. 120).

99. The dubbing of imported films was taxed; all Italian cinemas were required to show Italian films for at least 80 days a year; new state loans would be made available to fund film production. The results were dramatic: by 1950, Italian films accounted for nearly 30 per cent of domestic box-office takings and, by 1954, annual domestic film production exceeded 160 films (Wagstaff, *op. cit.*, p. 80).

100. Liehm, *op. cit.*, p. 91.

101. Wagstaff, *op. cit.*, p. 81.

Conclusion

This book began by setting out two very different views of the importance of cinema: Tsar Nicholas II suggesting that it was 'complete rubbish' and that 'no importance whatsoever should be attached to such stupidities'[1] while, in contrast, Anatoli Lunacharsky claimed that 'its effects reach where even the book cannot reach and it is, of course, more powerful than any kind of narrow propaganda.'[2] The five very different case studies that have been discussed here suggest that both Nicholas II and Lunacharsky were mistaken. Cinema certainly proved to be incomparably more important than the Tsar had anticipated, but Lunacharsky's optimistic view of the power of film as a medium of mass propaganda proved to be almost as misplaced. Indeed, almost every aspect of film propaganda presented formidable problems: it was difficult to ensure that appropriate films were made in the first place, it was more difficult to ensure that those films reached their target audience, and it was most difficult of all to ensure that those films that did reach their target audience made the impact on that audience that the propagandists had intended.

At first sight, the commissioning of appropriate films would appear to have been the easiest element in the implementation of successful film propaganda and yet all kinds of difficulties were encountered. The obstacles were various: in Britain, during the First World War, a commitment to factual war films required a degree of active co-operation from the service departments that proved extremely difficult to achieve; it even proved problematic in the Second World War where, once again, there was a considerable delay before effective films of this kind were produced. In Russia, the total dislocation of the film industry that was the product of war, revolution and civil war, combined with the hostility of most pre-revolutionary film-makers, required the complete reconstruction of the industry before any significant propaganda film production could take place. In post-war Italy, film-makers found it extremely difficult to persuade commercial film producers to back the kind of realist projects to which they were committed, and even that very small level of production would have been impossible had neorealist films not proved successful with an international art-house audience. Thus, in only two of the five case studies, Nazi Germany and Britain during the Second World War, did it prove easy to produce large numbers of appropriate films – and even here there was a critical delay of over a year before the British Ministry of Information's Films Division was in a position to exercise effective control over wartime film production.

Notwithstanding these many difficulties, however, one of the most striking features of the history of propaganda film production is the imaginative and creative way in which film-makers responded to the propagandists' commissions. That creativity is perhaps most immediately obvious in the documentary film, where the challenge of meeting the very particular demands of propaganda provoked almost constant experiment, innovation and achievement. Thus from *Battle of the Somme* in 1916, through the work of Vertov and Shub in the Soviet Union, the Riefenstahl documentaries in the 1930s, to the domestic and battlefront British documentaries of the Second World War, film-makers constantly developed new ways of shooting actuality footage, and new forms in which to present that footage to the audience. Impressive as all this was, however, the achievements of film-makers working in the propaganda fiction films were perhaps even more striking. Thus, in the case of both Soviet film-makers in the 1920s and Italian neorealist film-makers immediately after the Second World War, their work was characterized by such imagination and innovation that the greatest of their films represent some of the most enduring achievements of world cinema. Indeed, the quality of the most interesting films made in Britain during the Second World War has led many historians to see these years as a Golden Age in the history of British cinema.

Quite why so many films of quality were made as a result of propaganda commissions is far from clear, for the demands imposed by those who commissioned film propaganda could be quite as tough as any imposed in the commercial market-place. Yet, what many of these commissions had in common was an emphasis on the construction of persuasive representations of reality, and that requirement to concentrate on exploring and extending the limits of realism in film certainly provoked a rich response in the film-makers. Indeed, on more than one occasion, it led particular film-makers to abandon the traditional distinction between the documentary and fiction film, exploring instead the fertile ground in between. Thus, Eisenstein's *Battleship Potemkin*, or McAllister and Jennings' *Fires Were Started*, or Visconti's *The Earth Trembles*, all demonstrate in their very different ways just how limiting the conventions of studio-bound, fiction film-making can be, and just how rich, in contrast, the opportunities outside the star system, away from the studio back lot can be.

Yet, however distinguished individual propaganda films may have been, it proved to be extraordinarily difficult to ensure that such films reached their target audiences – indeed, in two of the case studies examined here (Soviet films in the 1920s and Italian neorealist films after the Second World War), the obstacles proved almost insurmountable. In both these examples, the propaganda films had to compete directly with Hollywood movies, and the fact that they lost that battle so comprehensively may have something to do with the prevailing economic and social conditions of the period. In times of great hardship, one of the most seductive aspects of cinema is its ability to offer a brief escape from the rigours of everyday life and, while that opportunity to escape is not necessarily dependent on the provision of escapist films, the particular pleasures of Hollywood movies may seem especially attractive in such circumstances; serious and demanding propaganda films certainly found it almost impossible to attract an audience.

In contrast, war creates a very special appetite for actuality battlefront footage and, with *Battle of the Somme*, Britain's First World War propagandists must have thought that all their optimism about cinema's unique ability to reach the mass audience had finally been vindicated. Yet, hugely popular as *Battle of the Somme* was, the public's appetite for such films proved extraordinarily short-lived, and a change in attitudes towards the war quickly undermined the appeal of the official films. Almost exactly the same happened in Nazi Germany. As long as the German forces were victorious, the public appetite for battlefront newsreels and documentary films seemed almost insatiable but, as soon as the fortunes of war changed, it declined just as quickly as in Britain 25 years earlier. British newsreels reporting unremittingly bad news in the first half of the Second World War proved almost as unpopular. In addition to the wartime documentary footage, a number of propaganda feature films also reached their target audience, predominantly in Nazi Germany and in Britain during the Second World War, and those that were successful invariably shared a number of important characteristics. Thus, audiences were kept unaware of the extent to which the production of these films was orchestrated by the state, and the films themselves demonstrated all the qualities that had traditionally proved so successful in the mainstream, popular cinema – strong narratives, high production values, popular stars.

There remains, however, the most important area of all, for even if the films did reach the target audience, they would only fulfil their brief as propaganda if the audiences took from those films the messages that the propagandists had set out to deliver. Indeed, in all the case studies we have examined, it was optimistic assumptions about cinema's ability to influence powerfully the attitudes and ideology of its audience that made it such an attractive medium in the first place. If the films failed to make that impact then, no matter how substantial their other achievements, as propaganda they would have failed. Here, the conclusions that emerge from the five case studies are remarkably consistent: access to the mass audience was the essential precondition for successful propaganda, but it was always only a precondition. Of the films that did reach that mass audience, those that were positively received were almost always films that confirmed and reinforced existing ideas and attitudes – films that set out to challenge and change those ideas and attitudes proved almost entirely unsuccessful. Indeed, it is even possible that the ability to reach the audience in the first place may have been prompted, at least in part, by the same considerations – *The Eternal Jew* provides one important example of a film whose very ideology may have kept most cinema-goers away.

Once again the two decisive examples are Nazi Germany and Britain during the Second World War, for it was here that significant numbers of propaganda films were seen by a large part of the target audience, and the reception that these films enjoyed is all too clear. For a variety of reasons, British wartime films presented a view of Britain's past and present that was both understood and accepted by the vast majority of the wartime cinema audience and, by and large, such films were well-received. In Nazi Germany, on the other hand, most propaganda films followed a much more radical agenda and, by and large, the ideas and attitudes of the target audience were not changed by the films that they saw. Even when Goebbels worked with the grain of existing attitudes, his achievements were much more mixed. He did have some success in constructing a very potent image of Adolf Hitler, in part by grounding the 'Hitler myth' in long-standing, traditional German attitudes towards leadership and the military, but his attempt to transform an existing, well-established anti-Semitism into a virulent racial hatred proved much less successful. In very different ways, therefore, the history of film propaganda in Nazi Germany and Britain during the Second World War serves to demonstrate not the power of film propaganda, but rather the powerful constraints within which such propaganda operates.

The history of Europe in that part of the twentieth century when cinema was the dominant medium in popular culture saw ordinary people come to occupy a more central role in the politics of their societies than at any time in their previous history. Because that change coincided with the invention and exploitation of the new mass media of communication, many political leaders (especially on the radical wings of European politics) made the assumption that these new media presented them with enormously powerful new tools with which to manipulate and control the people they governed. Indeed, they mistakenly believed that the new media like cinema created an entirely new opportunity to manipulate popular ideology at will, transforming (almost overnight) ideas and attitudes whose roots could be traced back deep into Europe's past. In practice, that power proved almost completely illusory. Cinema audiences exercised considerable discrimination, both in the films that they chose to see and in the meanings that they constructed in the films that they did see. They had grown up with the cinema, they understood its codes and conventions (at least as well as the propagandists who sought to exploit its power), and they were never merely the passive recipients of ideas handed down to them from the silver screen. Indeed, as we have seen again and again in this book, whenever the ideology of a film confronted or challenged the ideology of the audience, it was almost always the ideology of the film that was rejected. In sum, the aspirations, beliefs and ideologies of the ordinary men, women and children who made up the cinema audience proved to be very much more resistant to manipulation than so many of those who governed them had naïvely assumed; to that extent, the myth of the power of film propaganda was, in reality, incomparably more powerful than the film propaganda itself.

NOTES

1. Quoted in Richard Taylor, *Film Propaganda: Soviet Russia and Nazi Germany*, London, 1979, p. 35.
2. Anatoli Lunacharsky, 'Revolutionary Ideology and Cinema – Theses', 9 to 31 March 1924, in Richard Taylor and Ian Christie (eds), *The Film Factory: Russian and Soviet Cinema in Documents 1896–1939*, London, 1988, p. 109.

Further Reading

The notes at the end of each chapter indicate those sources which have proved most useful in the preparation of this book. In the following bibliography, I have identified sources in English that offer the opportunity for further reading on each of the five case studies.

* indicates works that include a full bibliography.

OFFICIAL FILM PROPAGANDA IN BRITAIN DURING THE FIRST WORLD WAR

S.D. Badsey, 'Battle of the Somme: British war-propaganda', *Historical Journal of Film, Radio and Television*, Vol. 3, No. 2, 1983, pp. 99–115.

* Cate Haste, *Keep the Home Fires Burning*, London, 1977.

Nicholas Hiley, 'Hilton DeWitt Girdwood and the origins of British official filming', *Historical Journal of Film, Radio and Television*, Vol. 13, No. 2, 1993, pp. 129–48.

Nicholas Hiley, 'The British cinema auditorium', in K. Dibbets and B. Hogenakamp (eds), *Film and the First World War*, Amsterdam, 1995.

Geoffrey H. Malins, *How I Filmed the War*, London, 1920; reprinted with an introduction by Nicholas Hiley, London, 1993.

Luke McKernan, *Topical Budget: The Great British News Film*, London, 1992.

* Nicholas Reeves, *Official British Film Propaganda During the First World War*, London, 1986.

Nicholas Reeves, 'Film propaganda and its audience', *Journal of Contemporary History*, Vol. 13, 1993, pp. 463–94.

Nicholas Reeves, 'The power of film propaganda: myth or reality?', *Historical Journal of Film, Radio and Television*, Vol. 13, No. 2, 1993, pp. 181–201.

Nicholas Reeves, 'Cinema, spectatorship and propaganda: *Battle of the Somme* (1916) and its contemporary audience', *Historical Journal of Film, Radio and Television*, Vol. 17, No. 1, 1997, pp. 5–28.

M.L. Sanders, 'Wellington House and British propaganda during the First World War', *Historical Journal*, Vol. 18, No. 1, 1975, pp. 119–46.

M.L. Sanders, 'British film propaganda in Russia 1916–1918', *Historical Journal of Film, Radio and Television*, Vol. 3, No. 2, 1983, pp. 117–29.

* M.L. Sanders and Philip M. Taylor, *British Propaganda During the First World War*, London, 1982.

R. Smither, ' "A wonderful idea of the fighting": the question of fakes in *The Battle of the Somme*', *Historical Journal of Film, Radio and Television*, Vol. 13, No. 2, 1993, pp. 149–68.

FILM PROPAGANDA IN THE SOVIET UNION, 1917–1928

Ian Christie and Richard Taylor (eds), *Eisenstein Rediscovered*, London, 1993.

* Peter Kenez, *The Birth of the Propaganda State*, Cambridge, 1985.

* Peter Kenez, *Cinema and Soviet Society 1917–1953*, Cambridge, 1992.

Vance Kepley, Jr, 'The origins of the Soviet cinema', *Quarterly Review of Film Studies*, Vol. 10, No. 1, Winter 1985; reprinted in Richard Taylor and Ian Christie, *Inside the Film Factory*, London, 1991.

Vance Kepley, Jr, and Betty Kepley, 'Foreign films on Soviet screens, 1922–1931', *Quarterly Review of Film Studies*, Vol. 4, No. 4, Fall 1979.

Jay Leyda, *Kino*, London, 1973.

Richard Stites, *Russian Popular Culture: Entertainment and Society since 1900*, Cambridge, 1992.

Richard Taylor, 'A medium for the masses: agitation in the Soviet Civil War', *Soviet Studies*, Vol. 22, 1971.

* Richard Taylor, *The Politics of the Soviet Cinema 1917–1929*, Cambridge, 1979.

* Richard Taylor, *Film Propaganda: Soviet Russia and Nazi Germany*, London, 1979; revised edition, London, 1998.

Richard Taylor and Ian Christie, *The Film Factory: Russian and Soviet Cinema in Documents 1896–1939*, London, 1988.

Richard Taylor and Ian Christie, *Inside the Film Factory*, London, 1991.

Kristin Thompson, 'Government policies and practical necessities in the Soviet cinema of the 1920s', in Anna Lawton, *The Red Screen: Politics, Society, Art in Soviet Cinema*, London, 1992.

Denise Youngblood, *Soviet Cinema in the Silent Era, 1918–1935*, Ann Arbor, 1985.

* Denise Youngblood, *Movies for the Masses: Popular Cinema and Soviet Society in the 1920s*, Cambridge, 1992.

NATIONAL SOCIALIST FILM PROPAGANDA IN GERMANY, 1933–1945

Michael Burleigh, 'Euthanasia and the Third Reich', *History Today*, Vol. 40, February 1990, pp. 11–16.

Michael Burleigh, *Death and Deliverance: 'Euthanasia' in Germany 1900–1945*, Cambridge, 1994.

David Culbert, 'Leni Riefenstahl and the diaries of Joseph Goebbels', *Historical Journal of Film, Radio and Television*, Vol. 13, No. 1, 1993, pp. 85–93.

David Culbert, '*Kolberg*: film, filmscript and Kolobrzeg today', *Historical Journal of Film, Radio and Television*, Vol. 14, No. 4, 1994, pp. 449–66.

David Culbert and Martin Loiperdinger, 'Leni Riefenstahl's *Tag der Freiheit*: the 1935 Nazi Party Rally film', *Historical Journal of Film, Radio and Television*, Vol. 12, No. 1, 1992, pp. 3–40.

Stig Hornshøj-Møller and David Culbert, '*Der Ewige Jude* (1940): Joseph Goebbels' unequalled monument to anti-Semitism', *Historical Journal of Film, Radio and Television*, Vol. 12, No. 1, 1992, pp. 41–68.

David Stuart Hull, *Film in the Third Reich: A Study of the German Cinema 1933–1945*, Berkeley, 1969.

Ian Kershaw, *Popular Opinion and Political Dissent in the Third Reich: Bavaria 1933–1945*, Oxford, 1988.

Erwin Leiser, *Nazi Cinema*, London, 1974.

Martin Loiperdinger and David Culbert, 'Leni Riefenstahl, the SA, and the Nazi Party Rally films, Nuremberg 1933–1934: *Sieg des Glaubens* and *Triumph des Willens*', *Historical Journal of Film, Radio and Television*, Vol. 8, No. 1, 1988, pp. 3–38.

P. Paret, '*Kolberg* (1945) as a historical film and historical document', *Historical Journal of Film, Radio and Television*, Vol. 14, No. 4, 1994, pp. 467–74.

Julian Petley, *Capital and Culture: German Cinema 1933–45*, London, 1979.

* Richard Taylor, *Film Propaganda: Soviet Russia and Nazi Germany*, London, 1979; second edition, London, 1998.

Susan Tegel, 'Veit Harlan and the origins of "Jud Süss", 1938–1939: opportunism in the creation of anti-Semitic film propaganda', *Historical Journal of Film Radio and Television*, Vol. 16, No. 4, 1996, pp. 515–19.

Susan Tegel, *Jew Süss/Jud Süss*, Trowbridge, 1996.

David Welch (ed.), *Nazi Propaganda: The Power and the Limitations*, London, 1983.

* David Welch, *Propaganda and the German Cinema 1933–1945*, Oxford, 1983.

David Welch, 'Nazi wartime newsreel propaganda', in K.R.M. Short (ed.), *Film and Radio Propaganda in World War II*, London, 1983.

* David Welch, *The Third Reich: Politics and Propaganda*, London, 1993.

Brian Winston, 'Reconsidering "Triumph of the Will": was Hitler there?', *Sight and Sound*, Vol. 50, No. 2, Spring 1981, pp. 102–7.

OFFICIAL FILM PROPAGANDA IN BRITAIN DURING THE SECOND WORLD WAR

Anthony Aldgate and Jeffrey Richards, *Britain Can Take It: The British Cinema in the Second World War*, Oxford, 1986.

Charles Barr, 'War record', *Sight and Sound*, Vol. 58, No. 4, Autumn 1989, pp. 260–5.

James Chapman, '*The Life and Death of Colonel Blimp* (1943) reconsidered', *Historical Journal of Film, Radio and Television*, Vol. 15, No. 1, 1995, pp. 19–54.

* James Chapman, *The British at War: Cinema, State and Propaganda 1939–1945*, London, 1998.

Clive Coultass, *Images for Battle*, London, 1989.

Margaret Dickinson and Sarah Street, *Cinema and State: The Film Industry and the Government 1927–84*, London, 1985.

John Ellis, 'Victory of the voice', *Screen*, Vol. 22, No. 2, 1981, pp. 69–72.

Helen Forman, 'The non-theatrical distribution of films by the Ministry of Information', in Nicholas Pronay and D.W. Spring (eds), *Propaganda, Politics and Film 1918–1945*, London, 1982.

Toby Haggith, 'Post-war reconstruction as depicted in official British films of the Second World War', *Imperial War Museum Review*, No 7.

Tom Harrison, 'Films and the Home Front: the evaluation of their effectiveness by Mass-Observation', in Nicholas Pronay and D.W. Spring (eds), *Propaganda, Politics and Film 1918–1945*, London, 1982.

Geoff Hurd (ed.), *National Fictions: World War Two in British Films and Television*, London, 1984.

Annette Kuhn, '*Desert Victory* and the People's War', *Screen*, Vol. 22, No. 2, 1981, pp. 45–68.

* Ian McLain, *Ministry of Morale: Home Front Morale and the Ministry of Information in World War II*, London, 1979.

Robert Murphy, *Realism and Tinsel*, London, 1989.

* Siân Nicholas, *The Echo of War: Home Front Propaganda and the Wartime BBC, 1939–45*, Manchester, 1996.

Julian Poole, 'British cinema attendance in wartime: audience preference at the Majestic, Macclesfield, 1939–1946', *Historical Journal of Film, Radio and Television*, Vol. 7, No. 1, 1987, pp. 15–34.

Vincent Porter and Chaim Litewski, '*The Way Ahead*: case history of a propaganda film', *Sight and Sound*, 50, Spring 1981.

Nicholas Pronay, 'The news media at war', in Nicholas Pronay and D.W. Spring (eds), *Propaganda, Politics and Film, 1918–45*, London, 1982.

Nicholas Pronay, ' "The Land of Promise": the projection of peace aims in Britain', in K.R.M. Short (ed.), *Film and Radio Propaganda in World War II*, London, 1983.

Jeffrey Richards, 'Wartime British cinema audiences and the class system: the case of *Ships with Wings* (1941)', *Historical Journal of Film, Radio and Television*, Vol. 7, No. 2, June 1987.

Jeffrey Richards and Anthony Aldgate, *Best of British*, Oxford, 1983.

Jeffrey Richards and D. Sheridan, *Mass Observation at the Movies*, London, 1987.

Elizabeth Sussex, *The Rise and Fall of the British Documentary*, Berkeley, 1975.

Paul Swann, *The British Documentary Film Movement*, Cambridge, 1984.

Philip M. Taylor (ed.), *Britain and the Cinema in the Second World War*, London, 1988.

Frances Thorpe and Nicholas Pronay, *British Official Films in the Second World War*, Oxford, 1980.

Dai Vaughan, *Portrait of an Invisible Man. The Working Life of Stewart McAllister, Film Editor*, London, 1983.

ITALIAN NEOREALIST FILMS

Roy Armes, *Patterns of Realism*, London, 1971.

* Peter Bondanella, *Italian Cinema: From Neorealism to the Present*, New York, 1983; revised edition, New York, 1991.

Peter Bondanella, *The Films of Roberto Rossellini*, Cambridge, 1993.

Peter Brunette, *Roberto Rossellini*, Oxford, 1987.

* David Forgacs, *Italian Culture in the Industrial Era 1880–1980: Cultural Industries, Politics and the Public,* Manchester, 1990.

James Hay, *Popular Film Culture in Fascist Italy: The Passing of the Rex*, Bloomington, 1987.

George Huaco, *The Sociology of Film Art*, London, 1965.

Marcia Landy, *Fascism in Film: The Italian Commercial Cinema, 1931–1943*, Princeton, 1986.

Pierre Leprohon, *The Italian Cinema*, London, 1972.

Mira Liehm, *Passion and Defiance: Film in Italy from 1942 to the Present*, London, 1984.

Elaine Mancini, *Struggles of the Italian Film Industry during Fascism 1930–1935*, Epping, 1985.

Millicent Marcus, *Italian Film in the Light of Neorealism,* Princeton, 1986.

Morando Morandini, 'Italy from Fascism to neo-realism', in Geoffrey Nowell-Smith (ed.), *The Oxford History of World Cinema*, Oxford, 1996.

Geoffrey Nowell-Smith, with James Hay and Gianni Volpi, *The Companion to Italian Cinema*, London, 1996.

David Overbey, *Springtime in Italy: A Reader on Neo-Realism*, London, 1978.

Laurence Schifano, *Luchino Visconti: The Flames of Passion*, translated from the French by William S. Byron, London, 1990.

Gaia Servadio, *Luchino Visconti: A Biography*, London, 1981.

* Pierre Sorlin, *Italian National Cinema 1896–1996*, London, 1996.

Doug Thompson, *State Control in Fascist Italy: Culture and Conformity, 1925–1943*, Manchester, 1991.

Antonio Vitti, *Giuseppe De Santis and Post-war Italian Cinema*, Toronto, 1996.

Christopher Wagstaff, 'The place of neorealism in Italian cinema from 1945 to 1954', in Nicholas Hewitt (ed.), *The Culture of Reconstruction: European Literature, Thought and Film, 1945–50*, Basingstoke, 1989.

General Index

Index of Film Titles